Lecture Notes in Computer Science 16101

Founding Editors

Gerhard Goos
Juris Hartmanis

AF173220

The series Lecture Notes in Computer Science (LNCS), including its subseries Lecture Notes in Artificial Intelligence (LNAI) and Lecture Notes in Bioinformatics (LNBI), has established itself as a medium for the publication of new developments in computer science and information technology research, teaching, and education.

LNCS enjoys close cooperation with the computer science R & D community, the series counts many renowned academics among its volume editors and paper authors, and collaborates with prestigious societies. Its mission is to serve this international community by providing an invaluable service, mainly focused on the publication of conference and workshop proceedings and postproceedings. LNCS commenced publication in 1973.

Despina Michael-Grigoriou · Gabriel Zachmann ·
Regis Kopper · Sang Ho Yoon ·
Stefanie Zollmann · Patrick Bourdot
Editors

Virtual Reality
and Mixed Reality

22nd EuroXR International Conference, EuroXR 2025
Winterthur, Switzerland, September 3–5, 2025
Proceedings

 Springer

Editors

Despina Michael-Grigoriou (ID)
GET Lab, Cyprus University of Technology
Limassol, Cyprus

Gabriel Zachmann (ID)
University of Bremen
Bremen, Germany

Regis Kopper (ID)
Iowa State University
Ames, IA, USA

Sang Ho Yoon (ID)
Korea Advanced Institute of Science
and Technology (KAIST)
Daejeon, Korea (Republic of)

Stefanie Zollmann (ID)
Aarhus University
Aarhus, Denmark

Patrick Bourdot
CNRS, University Paris-Saclay
Orsay, France

ISSN 0302-9743   ISSN 1611-3349 (electronic)
Lecture Notes in Computer Science
ISBN 978-3-032-03804-3   ISBN 978-3-032-03805-0 (eBook)
https://doi.org/10.1007/978-3-032-03805-0

This Springer imprint is published by the registered company Springer Nature Switzerland AG
The registered company address is: Gewerbestrasse 11, 6330 Cham, Switzerland

If disposing of this product, please recycle the paper.

Preface

In this LNCS volume, we are pleased to present the scientific proceedings of the 22nd EuroXR International Conference (EuroXR 2025), co-organized with the ZHAW Zurich University of Applied Sciences, Switzerland, held during September 3–5, 2025.

This conference followed a series of successful international conferences initiated in 2004 by the INTUITION Network of Excellence on Virtual and Augmented Reality, which was supported by the European Commission until 2008. From 2009 through 2013, it was embedded in the Joint Virtual Reality Conferences (JVRC). After that, it was known as EuroVR, and then EuroXR International Conference, in line with the renaming of the umbrella association.

The focus and aim of the EuroXR conferences is to present, each year, novel results and insights in Virtual Reality (VR), Augmented Reality (AR), and Mixed Reality (MR), together referred to under the term eXtended Reality (XR), including software systems, immersive rendering technologies, 3D user interfaces, and applications.

EuroXR also aims to foster engagement between European industries, academia, and the public sector, to promote the development and deployment of XR techniques in all fields. To this end, all EuroXR conferences include not only a scientific track, but also an application-oriented track, demos and posters sessions, and a lab tour.

Since 2017, the EuroXR Association has collaborated with Springer to publish the proceedings of the scientific track of its annual conference in their LNCS series. In order to maintain the scientific standards to be expected from such a conference, we established a number of committees overseeing the process of creating a scientific program: the scientific program chairs, leading an International Program Committee (IPC) made up of international experts in the field, and the EuroXR academic task force.

The proceedings of the applications track were kindly published by VTT, Finland. The selection process for those submissions was overseen by a committee working separately from the scientific committee, with their own selection criteria.

For the 2025 issue of the LNCS proceedings, a total of 51 papers were submitted to the scientific track, out of which 17 long papers were accepted. This amounts to an acceptance rate of 33%.

The selection process involved at least 3 double-blind peer-reviews by members of the IPC (in many cases even 4), followed by a rebuttal phase, and a final discussion and scoring phase amongst the reviewers. Based on the review reports, the scores, and the reviewers' discussions, the scientific program chairs took the final decision and wrote a meta-review for each paper.

This year, the scientific program of EuroXR 2025 and, hence, this LNCS volume, was organized into four sections: Rendering and Streaming, Content Synthesis and Creation, Human Factors and Perception, Interaction Techniques.

In addition to the regular conference tracks—including the Scientific track reported in these proceedings, as well as the Application, Poster, and Demo tracks—EuroXR has this year specially invited Prof. Nadia Magnenat-Thalmann, Founder and Director of MIRALab at the University of Geneva, Switzerland, and Prof. Daniel Thalmann, Honorary Professor at EPFL and Director of Research Development at MIRALab Sàrl, Switzerland, for a Tribute Session in their honor. This session celebrates their outstanding careers and pioneering contributions to the field of XR research.

Complementing this exceptional event, three keynote speakers have also been invited: Ms. Anne Bajart, Deputy Head of Unit at DG CONNECT of the European Commission; Mr. Matthieu Worm, from Siemens Digital Industries Software and Director of the European Virtual Worlds Partnership; and Mr. David Nahon, Immersive Experience Innovation Director at Dassault Systèmes.

Finally, several dedicated sessions were held for European HORIZON projects, including full two-day afternoon joint final events for the CORTEX2 and SPIRIT projects, workshop sessions organized by the OPENVERSE, THEIA-XR, and LUMI-NOUS projects, as well as a project session for SUN-XR. Additionally, we welcomed an internal meeting of the non-profit international association GraphicsVision.ai.

We would like to thank all the IPC members and external reviewers for their insightful reviews, which helped ensure the high quality of papers selected for the scientific track. Furthermore, we would like to extend our gratitude to all the applications track chairs, demos and posters chairs, and, last but not least, the local organizers of EuroXR 2025.

We are also grateful to Springer for their support and advice during the preparation of this LNCS volume.

July 2025

Despina Michael-Grigoriou
Gabriel Zachmann
Regis Kopper
Sang Ho Yoon
Stefanie Zollmann
Patrick Bourdot

Organization

General Chairs

Wolfgang Schäfer   ZHAW, Winterthur, Switzerland
Wolfgang Stuerzlinger   Simon Fraser University, Canada
Luciana Nedel   Federal University of Rio Grande do Sul, Brazil

Scientific Program Chairs

Despina Michael-Grigoriou   Cyprus University of Technology, Cyprus
Gabriel Zachmann   University of Bremen, Germany
Regis Kopper   Iowa State University, USA
Sang Ho Yoon   Korea Advanced Institute of Science & Technology, South Korea
Stefanie Zollmann   Aarhus University, Denmark
Patrick Bourdot   CNRS & Université Paris-Saclay, France

Application Program Chairs

Barbara Schiavi   France
Jérôme Perret   Haption, Germany
Kaj Helin   VTT, Finland
Frédéric Nöel   INP Grenoble, France
Thomas Hulin   German Aerospace Center (DLR), Germany
Bhuvaneswari Sarupuri   TOPdesk, Hungary
Alina Kadlubsky   Hochschule Mittweida, Germany
Fabio Mosca   Another Reality, Italy

Posters and Demos Chairs

Electra Tsaknaki   University of Cyprus, Cyprus
Mario Lorenz   TU Chemnitz, Germany
Armin Grasnick   IU International University of Applied Sciences, Germany
Kayvan Mirza   Optinvent, France

Vladimir Kuts   Taltech, Estonia

Organization Team

Patrick Bourdot   CNRS & Université Paris-Saclay
Mónica González   EuroXR, France
Jérôme Perret   Haption, Germany
Gabriel Zachmann   University of Bremen, Germany
Wolfgang Schäfer   ZHAW, Switzerland

International Program Committee

Ackermann, Philipp   ZHAW, Switzerland
Agarwal, Soumya   Indian Institute of Technology Bombay, India
Alcañiz, Mariano   Universitat Politècnica de València, Spain
Allison, Robert   York University, Canada
Amano, Toshiyuki   Wakayama University, Japan
Anastasovitis, Eleftherios   Information Technologies Institute, Greece
Anjos, Rafael   University of Leeds, UK
Arlati, Sara   STIIMA, CNR, Italy
Banakou, Domna   NYU Abu Dhabi, UAE
Bareth, Marlo   University of Bremen, Germany
Barone, Nunzio   Politecnico di Bari, Italy
Bauer, Valentin   IRCAM, France
Boulanger, Pierre   University of Alberta, Canada
Brument, Hugo   TU Wien, Austria
C. Torres, Sergio   Universitat Oberta de Catalunya, Spain
Capobianco, Antonio   Université de Strasbourg, France
Castet, Julien   Immersion, France
Cattin, Philippe   University of Basel, Switzerland
Chakravarthula, Praneeth   UNC Chapel Hill, USA
Chen, Weiya   Huazhong University of Science and Technology,
                                       China
Chen, Kenneth   New York University, USA
Cho, Hyunsung   Carnegie Mellon University, USA
Cho, Isaac   Utah State University, USA
Choi, Seungmoon   Pohang University of Science and Technology,
                                       South Korea
Cisternino, Ivan   Politecnico di Bari, Italy
Daiber, Florian   DFKI; Saarland Informatics Campus, Germany

De Antonio, Angelica	Universidad Politécnica de Madrid, Spain
Edgar, Drew	University of Glasgow, UK
Férey, Nicolas	Université Paris-Saclay, France
Fernandez, Jorge	Purdue University, USA
Ferrer Hernandez, Manuel	Universitat Politècnica de València, Spain
Ferrise, Francesco	Politecnico di Milano, Italy
Fiorentino, Michele	Politecnico di Bari, Italy
Fluri, Luca	FHNW, Switzerland
Fuhrmann, Arnulph	TH Köln, Germany
Fujita, Kazuyuki	Tohoku University, Japan
Galvez, Akemi	Universidad de Cantabria, Spain
Gattullo, Michele	Politecnico di Bari, Italy
Gelder, Beatrice	Maastricht University, Netherlands
Gonzalez, Pascual	Universidad de Castilla-La Mancha
Gorbunov, Andrey	AVIAREAL, Russia
Górski, Filip	Poznań University of Technology, Poland
Grasnick, Armin	IU International University of Applied Sciences, Germany
Hadjpanayi, Christos	Cyprus University of Technology, Cyprus
Häfner, Polina	KIT, Germany
Han, Hyunyoung	KAIST, South Korea
Hasanzadeh, Sogand	Purdue University, USA
Hecquard, Jeanne	Inria, France
Hoek, Krista	Leiden University Medical Center, Netherlands
Hudcovic, Thomas	University of Bremen, Germany
Hulin, Thomas	DLR, Germany
Hynes, Eoghan	Technological University of the Shannon, Ireland
Iglesias, Andres	Universidad de Cantabria, Spain
Interrante, Victoria	University of Minnesota, USA
Jalan, Priyansh	Trinity College Dublin, Ireland
Jörg, Sophie	University of Bamberg, Germany
Johnsen, Kyle	University of Georgia, USA
Jorge, Joaquim	University of Lisbon, Portugal
Kaber, David	University of Florida, USA
Karagiannis, Ioannis	ICCS, Greece
Kastner, Kevin	HS Mannheim, Germany
Kaufmann, Hannes	Vienna University of Technology, Austria
Kim, Kangsoo	University of Calgary, Canada
Kitamura, Yoshifumi	Tohoku University, Japan
Krüger, Björn	University of Bonn, Germany
Kruijff, Ernst	Vertigo Systems, Germany
Kuhlen, Torsten	RWTH Aachen University, Germany

Kuts, Vladimir	Tallinn University of Technology, Estonia
Kwak, Dongkyu	KAIST, South Korea
Ladevèze, Nicolas	CNRS, Université Paris-Saclay, France
Lamberti, Fabrizio	Politecnico di Torino, Italy
Lammert, Anton	Bauhaus-Universität Weimar, Germany
Latoschik, Marc	University of Würzburg, Germany
Laviola, Enricoandrea	Politecnico di Bari, Italy
Lavoue, Guillaume	LIRIS, CNRS, France
Lee, Hojeong	KAIST, South Korea
Lindlbauer, David	Carnegie Mellon University, USA
Lorenz, Mario	TU Chemnitz, Germany
Malpica, Sandra	Universidad de Zaragoza, Spain
Manzke, Michael	Trinity College Dublin, Ireland
Mayer, Anjela	KIT, Germany
McKendrick, Zachary	University of Waterloo, Canada
Mesarosova, Alena	Universitat Politècnica de València, Spain
Mestre, Daniel	Aix-Marseille Université, France
Miao, Haichao	Lawrence Livermore National Laboratory, USA
Michael-Grigoriou, Despina	Cyprus University of Technology, Cyprus
Molina Massó, José Pascual	Universidad de Castilla-La Mancha, Spain
Moustakas, Konstantinos	University of Patras, Greece
Mühlenbrock, Andre	University of Bremen, Germany
Mühlhaus, Sebastian	Bauhaus-Universität Weimar, Germany
Nie, Tongyu	University of Minnesota, USA
Niknam, Sahar	University of Luxembourg, Luxemburg
Noah, Naheem	University of Denver, USA
Nóbrega, Rui	NOVA LINCS, Portugal
Olivier, Anne-Hélène	Inria, France
Oncins, Estella	Universitat Autònoma de Barcelona, Spain
Pittarello, Fabio	Università Ca' Foscari Venezia, Italy
Plexousaki, Alexandra	FORTH, Greece
Plopski, Alexander	Graz University of Technology, Austria
Pons, Olivier	.
Poyade, Matthieu	Glasgow School of Art, UK
Reiners, Dirk	University of Florida, USA
Ricci, Marina	Politecnico di Bari, Italy
Ritchie, James	Heriot-Watt University, UK
Riva, Giuseppe	Università Cattolica del Sacro Cuore, Italy
Roddy, Mark	XR Ireland, Ireland
Romano, Sara	Politecnico di Bari, Italy
Roth, Daniel	TU München, Germany
Rücker, Fabian	Fraunhofer IGD, Germany

Sacco, Marco   STIIMA, CNR, Italy
Santhosh, Sandhya   Collins Aerospace, USA
Sato, Kosuke   Osaka University, Japan
Schott, Ephraim   Bauhaus-Universität Weimar, Germany
Settgast, Volker   Fraunhofer Austria Research Gmbh, Austria
Shehu, Visar   South East European University,
                                    North Macedonia
Si-Mohammed, Hakim   University de Lille, France
Soccini, Agata Marta   Università di Torino, Italy
Sprenger, Janis   DFKI, Germany
Sziebig, Gabor   SINTEF, Norway
Tan, Toni   University of Bremen, Germany
Thalmann, Daniel   EPFL, Switzerland
Torneiro, Andre   Polytechnic Institute of Cávado and Ave, Portugal
Tsaknaki, Electra   Independent Researcher, Greece
Uva, Antonio Emmanuele   Politecnico di Bari, Italy
Vazquez, Jorge   Purdue University, USA
Vignais, Nicolas   University of Rennes, France
Walczak, Krzysztof   Poznań University of Economics and Business,
                                    Poland
Waldow, Kristoffer   TH Köln, Germany
Wang, Yu   TU Wien, Austria
Wang, Lili   Beihang University, China
Wang, Xiaokun   University of Science and Technology Beijing,
                                    China
Weissker, Tim   RWTH Aachen University, Germany
Welch, Greg   University of Central Florida, USA
Xylomenos, George   Athens University of Economics and Business,
                                    Greece
Zachmann, Gabriel   University of Bremen, Germany
Zahabi, Maryam   Texas A&M University, USA
Zender, Raphael   Zeppelin University, Germany
Zhang, Huadong   Rochester Institute of Technology, USA
Zhao, Lizhi   Beihang University, China
Zioulis, Nikalaos   Moverse, Greece

Contents

Human Factors and Perception

Interaction Techniques

Rendering and Streaming

Seeing Through the Robot's Eyes: Adaptive Point Cloud Streaming for Immersive Teleoperation

Nunzio Barone[✉], Walter Brescia, Gabriele Santangelo, Antonio Pio Maggio, Ivan Cisternino, Luca De Cicco, and Saverio Mascolo

Dipartimento di Ingegneria Elettrica e dell'Informazione, Politecnico di Bari, Via Orabona n.4, Bari, Italy
{nunzio.barone,walter.brescia,g.santangelo,a.maggio4,i.cisternino, luca.decicco,saverio.mascolo}@poliba.it

Abstract. Autonomous Mobile Robots (AMRs) are increasingly deployed in diverse scenarios to automate tedious and hazardous tasks. Nonetheless, challenges such as complex environments, sensor occlusions, and limitations of autonomous navigation systems often require human intervention. Teleoperation offers a viable solution, allowing operators to remotely control AMRs when autonomy fails, without requiring physical presence. A key requirement for effective teleoperation is the real-time delivery of rich sensory information to the operator. Head-Mounted Displays (HMDs), combined with volumetric videos, provide an immersive visualization of the robot's surroundings, enabling natural viewpoint changes and improved spatial awareness compared to traditional 2D video streams. In this paper, we present a teleoperation framework to stream in real-time volumetric videos in the form of point clouds to an operator wearing a HMD. The system includes a distance-based sampling strategy that dynamically adapts the point cloud bitrate to the estimated time-varying network bandwidth, addressing constraints imposed by limited computational resources on both the robot and the HMD. The framework is implemented on a real mobile robot and evaluated under various network conditions, including a 5G connection, demonstrating its effectiveness and robustness in supporting immersive remote teleoperation. Code is available at our GitHub repository (https://github.com/ Diane-Spirit).

Keywords: Point cloud real-time streaming · Immersive teleoperation · mobile robots

1 Introduction

Autonomous Mobile Robots (AMRs) are increasingly adopted across several domains due to their ability to perform tasks without direct human intervention. AMRs use a range of sensors – such as LiDARs, RGB cameras, and stereo

© The Author(s), under exclusive license to Springer Nature Switzerland AG 2026
D. Michael-Grigoriou et al. (Eds.): EuroXR 2025, LNCS 16101, pp. 3–21, 2026.
https://doi.org/10.1007/978-3-032-03805-0_1

cameras – to perceive their surroundings and build environment models to support autonomous decisions and task execution.

Despite these capabilities, AMRs may fail to complete tasks autonomously in scenarios involving sensor occlusions, complex or cluttered environments, narrow passages, or hard-to-detect obstacles. In such cases, human intervention is required to resolve issues beyond the robot's autonomous capabilities.

In this context, teleoperation is a viable solution for remotely assisting AMRs when autonomy is compromised. It allows human operators to intervene in real-time, navigating the robot past obstacles or correcting localization and planning errors without the need to be physically present. This approach helps increasing operational efficiency and allows centralized operators to manage multiple robots deployed across different locations.

To make teleoperation effective, the human operator should be provided with accurate and real-time information about the robot's environment, allowing safe and efficient robot control.

Head Mounted Displays (HMDs), together with *volumetric videos*, can improve operator's *spatial awareness*, since they provide an immersive experience and allow natural viewpoint changes that are not possible with conventional 2D displays and videos.

The volumetric content is generated on the remote robot and must be streamed to the HMD in real-time, requiring a dedicated *streaming pipeline* suitable for handling the high data rates and low-latency constraints of immersive content delivery.

Volumetric video is typically represented in the form of meshes or point clouds (PCs), both of which are characterized by very high bandwidth requirements [17]. In the context of robot teleoperation, the need for *real-time* data transmission is critical. In fact, latency may hinder the operator's ability to respond promptly, resulting in degraded performance and a less effective control experience. These challenges are further exacerbated by the limited computational resources typically available on ARMs, which constrain the selection of software frameworks to those with low processing requirements, excluding many solutions designed for high-performance workstation and laptop systems.

In this scenario, the rapid deployment of the Fifth Generation (5G) networks represents a key enabler, particularly for the real-time transmission of high-volume data [15]. Compared to previous generations, 5G provides a significantly increased bandwidth [12], enabling higher data rates and reduced latency – both critical for immersive teleoperation applications.

This work addresses the challenge of real-time point cloud transmission for volumetric video streaming in the teleoperation of AMRs. The main contributions of this paper are as follows:

- we design a transmission pipeline for streaming volumetric video, telemetry data, and control commands from remote AMRs to an HMD;
- we introduce a sampling strategy that dynamically adapts the size of the transmitted point cloud to the available network bandwidth, reducing latency while preserving the operator's ability to safely control the robot;

– we build a framework for HMDs that supports rendering of point clouds under real-time constraints.

The proposed system is evaluated through experiments on a real mobile robot, including deployment over a 5G testbed. The sampling strategy is evaluated in different bandwidth conditions, highlighting how it reacts to prevent congestion and latencies. Moreover, we evaluate the *Motion-to-Photon* (MtP) latency of the framework with teleoperation tests across two countries, validating the proposed teleoperation pipeline in real use-cases.

2   Related Work

Teleoperation of remote mobile robots navigating an environment poses several challenges. In order to properly control a robot, the delay between the control input, its actuation, and the visual feedback must remain below 150 ms [1,13]. This constraint is further exacerbated by the limited computational capabilities of the on-board computing unit. Bandwidth limitations require careful consideration of data transmission volumes, as point cloud data impose impractical bandwidth demands, especially in mobile networks [2,3,15]. Consequently, compression and filtering algorithms are required to achieve feasible data volumes.

Although point cloud compression schemes, such as G-PCC [8] and V-PCC [9], provide high compression efficiency and support for both lossy and loss-less compression, they exhibit with high encoding/decoding latency [16]. Google Draco [7] achieves 4× compression rate, but proves to be unsuitable for real-time applications, particularly when executed on embedded devices [3,11].

In [11], the authors introduce GROOT, an end-to-end volumetric video streaming pipeline addressing efficient decoding for embedded devices. A key difference in our work stems from the main application: teleoperating a robot, which also involves streaming control commands. In this work, we propose a framework that takes advantage of WebRTC's *media track* and *data channel* for the streaming pipeline. The former is designed for real-time audio/video transmission over the Real-time Transport Protocol (RTP), while the latter serves as a bidirectional channel for sending any other type of data over the Stream Control Transmission Protocol (SCTP).

A volumetric video streaming framework using WebRTC to address low latency in videoconferencing is introduced in [6]. However, this approach assumes a static background and a distance-based filter to filter points farther than a given distance, a condition generally encountered in videoconferencing applications but incompatible with teleoperation scenarios. Moreover, their compression relies on Google Draco, which only works well with smaller point clouds [3,11].

In [16], the authors propose a learning-based compression scheme for adaptive bitrate point cloud streaming. While their system provides efficient compression and adaptive bitrate streaming capabilities, the number of frames in the segments directly impact compression efficiency. Nevertheless, the overall latency prevents the framework from being deployed in teleoperation use-cases.

Notice that it is possible to employ background removal strategies for video-conferencing, significantly reducing the number of points. However, such strategies are inapplicable to the teleoperation of mobile robots. In fact, during navigation, receiving a more detailed 3D environment allows operators to follow safer trajectories and anticipate dynamic obstacles.

3 Teleoperation Framework

Figure 1 shows the proposed system, which consists of two main components: a mobile robot equipped with an *Nvidia Jetson Xavier NX* and a commercial HMD, the *Meta Quest 3*, connected to the Internet via a 5G network.

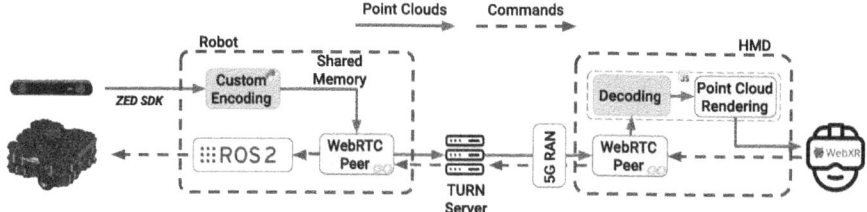

Fig. 1. The proposed immersive teleoperation system

The robot's software stack is based on three main components:

– **Robot point cloud producer**: implemented in Python language, this module acquires point clouds from the ZedSDK[1] and applies a filtering and custom encoding strategy to adapt the point cloud bitrate to the measured available bandwidth (see Sect. 3.2);
– **WebRTC robot peer**: implemented in Golang [10] using the *Pion* WebRTC library [14], this component is responsible for transmitting the encoded point clouds and receiving commands from the remote peer. It interacts with other software onboard using shared memory;
– **ROS2 relay node**: bridges shared memory and ROS2 topics to allow the communication of telemetry and commands to and from ROS2[2] topics;
– **ROS2 navigation nodes**: manage robot locomotion using its navigation stack[3] and handle incoming control commands.

The HMD's software stack consists of two main components:

– **WebRTC HMD peer (Pion Bridge)**: developed in Golang and compiled as a standalone application, it maintains the connection with the WebRTC robot peer, receiving the point cloud stream and transmitting control commands to the robot. It is also referred to as Pion Bridge since it acts as a communication bridge between the peer connection and the UI.

---

[1] https://www.stereolabs.com/en-it/developers/release.
[2] https://github.com/ros2.
[3] https://docs.nav2.org/index.html.

– **WebXR User Interface**: implemented in Javascript as a single script to maximize performance, this module performs point cloud decoding and rendering in real-time.

In the following, a detailed description of each component is provided. In particular, Sect. 3.1 describes the WebRTC pipeline, including details about the *Signaling server*. Section 3.2 describes the components onboard the robot that enable the point cloud streaming and the actuation of the received control commands. Finally, Sect. 3.3 presents the framework running on the HMD which implements the reception, reconstruction, and rendering of point clouds, as well as sending control commands.

3.1   WebRTC Pipeline

Signaling. This phase is managed by the *signaling server*, the main component of the WebRTC infrastructure that allows the exchange of connection metadata between the Robot Peer and the Pion Bridge. The signaling server has been implemented in `Node.js` and relies on the WebSocket protocol to support continuous, bidirectional communication between peers. Two WebSockets endpoints are exposed on separate ports: port 3001 for the Robot and port 3002 for the Pion Bridge.

Internally, the server maintains an in-memory data structure that represents its current state. This structure includes the list of registered robots, the Session Description Protocol (SDP) offers sent by the robots, the corresponding answers generated by the clients, and the ICE Candidates exchanged by both parties during the connection negotiation process.

This architecture allows *decoupled and asynchronous* peer management: either the robot or the Pion Bridge may connect first, without compromising the consistency or reliability of the signaling process.

Communication. A WebSocket connection is used to allow communication with the signaling server based on JSON messages. Two main interaction categories are defined: those originating from the robots and those from the client (Pion Bridge).

In particular, the following messages define the interaction between a robot and the signaling server during WebRTC session management:

– *Register*: The robot sends its identifier and the SDP Offer to register with the signaling server.
– *Offer*: The robot updates its SDP offer, typically following a disconnection or renegotiation event.
– *Candidate*: The robot transmits newly discovered ICE candidates to the signaling server for connection establishment.
– *Deregister*: The robot requests its cancellation from the list of active robots to avoid inconsistent states with the Pion Bridge.

The interaction between the Pion Bridge and the signaling server is managed through a defined set of WebSocket messages:

- *getRobots*: The client queries the signaling server for the current list of registered robots and their associated SDP offers.
- *Answer*: The client sends the SDP answer for a specific robot.
- *Candidate*: The client transmits the ICE candidates it has collected for a specific robot.

Connection Lifecycle. The connection process begins with the *robot registration* phase. The robot initiates a WebSocket connection to the signaling server on port 3001 and transmits a `register` message specifying its name and `sdpOffer`. In response, the server assigns a unique identifier (*robotId*) to the robot and returns it.

Next, during the *client connection* phase, the client establishes a WebSocket connection on the port 3002 and retrieves the list of registered robots by sending a `getRobots` message.

Once the list of available robots is obtained, the *SDP negotiation* begins. The client generates an *sdpAnswer* for each robot and sends it to the server, which forwards it to the corresponding robot to complete the WebRTC handshake.

This is followed by the *ICE candidate exchange*. Both the robot and the client communicate their locally discovered ICE candidates to the signaling server using `candidate` messages. These are then relayed to the respective peer to support the establishment of a direct peer-to-peer connection.

In case of a network change or peer disconnection, the robot can update its `sdpOffer` on the signaling server, ensuring consistency and allowing the client to retrieve updated information via a new `getRobots` request to reestablish the connection.

Finally, the *deregistration* phase occurs either explicitly, when the robot sends a `deregister` message, or implicitly, when the WebSocket connection is closed. In both cases, the signaling server removes the robot from the list of active peer.

3.2   The Robot's Framework

Volumetric Content Capture. Volumetric content is captured onboard the robot in the form of point clouds using the ZED SDK [18], accessed through a custom Python script. The stereo camera is configured to acquire images in HD1080 resolution at a frame rate of 30 FPS. These image frames are processed internally by the ZED SDK to generate point clouds, which are extracted at an arbitrary frequency (in our case 18 FPS). Due to the unified memory architecture of the Nvidia Jetson Xavier NX, each point cloud frame is stored in a $(480 \cdot 480) \times 4$ `Float32` tensor using PyTorch. The first three `Float32` encode 3D spatial coordinates (x, y, z) of each point, while the fourth `Float32` value encodes the RGBA color information. This representation allows for efficient memory usage and compatibility with subsequent processing stages. The resulting point cloud is thus represented by a matrix $\mathbf{P} \in \mathbb{R}^{(480 \cdot 480) \times 4}$, where each row corresponds to a single point, as shown below:

$$\mathbf{P} = \begin{bmatrix} \mathbf{x} & \mathbf{y} & \mathbf{z} & \mathbf{c} \end{bmatrix} = \begin{bmatrix} x_1 & y_1 & z_1 & c_1 \\ x_2 & y_2 & z_2 & c_2 \\ \vdots & \vdots & \vdots & \vdots \\ x_n & y_n & z_n & c_n \end{bmatrix} \tag{1}$$

This volume of data cannot be streamed directly, as it would require a bandwidth of $480 \cdot 480 \cdot 4 \cdot 32 \cdot 18 = 530 \, \text{Mbps}$, which exceeds the practical limits of current mobile networks [2,3,15]. Therefore, a bandwidth reduction strategy should be designed to enable real-time streaming over mobile connections.

Quantization and Filtering. To reduce the bandwidth required for point cloud transmission to practical levels, two complementary strategies are adopted: *quantization* and *filtering*.

Quantization: The coordinates of each points' position are quantized to 16 bits. Color information is quantized into a total of 16 bits, distributed across channels as follows: 6 bits for red, 6 bits for green, and 4 bits for blue. With this quantization approach, each point occupies 64 bits, thus reducing the data volume by 50% compared to the original 128-bit representation.

Filtering: Despite quantization, the bandwidth requirements for transmitting full point clouds remain excessive. To further reduce the data rate and adapt it to the time-varying network bandwidth while preserving task-relevant information, a filtering strategy is introduced.

Due to real-time constraints and the limited resources available on typical AMR platforms, traditional compression schemes are often impractical. Therefore, we propose a lightweight distance-based filtering approach, which prioritizes points based on their proximity to the robot.

The following formalizes known parameters. Next, the sampling strategy is introduced.

Known Parameters: The filtering algorithm operates under the following known parameters:

- $n = 480 \cdot 480$ number of points in the raw point cloud $\mathbf{P}$;
- Target frame rate (FPS), specified by the application;
- λ: a tunable parameter that controls the steepness of the distance-based prioritization;
- D: a threshold distance below which all points are prioritized;
- Point size after quantization: 64 bits;
- The *Maximum Frame Size* (MFS), in bits, that can be computed as:

$$MFS = \frac{BW}{FPS} \tag{2}$$

where BW is the estimated available bandwidth.

– The *Maximum Number of Transmittable Points per Frame*, $N_{\max}$:

$$N_{\max} = 150 \cdot \left\lfloor \frac{1}{150} \cdot \max\left(\min\left(\frac{MFS}{64}, n\right), \frac{0.10 \cdot n}{FPS}\right) \right\rfloor \qquad (3)$$

This expression ensures: 1) that the total number of transmitted points does not exceed the available bandwidth; 2) packet alignment, as the number of points per frame must be a multiple of 150 (matching the packet structure described in Sect. 3.2) and guaranteeing the transmission of at least 10% of the raw point cloud.

WebRTC, which employs the Google Congestion Control (GCC) algorithm [4], provides feedback on the target bitrate BW in bits per second, reflecting the current network conditions. This target bitrate acts as a system constraint: exceeding it leads to queuing delays and degraded performance [5].
Sampling Strategy: To satisfy these constraints, we apply an importance-based sampling scheme that prioritizes points based on their depth (z-coordinate). This importance value, referred to as *validity*, is defined in Eq. 4. The underlying assumption is that points closer to the robot (with smaller z-values) are more relevant for navigation and collision avoidance purposes, while points farther away (with larger z-values) do not represent immediate obstacles.

$$\mathbf{v} = \frac{1}{\left(\frac{\mathbf{z}}{\max(\mathbf{z})}\right)^{\lambda} + \varepsilon}, \quad \mathbf{v} \in \mathbb{R}^{n \times 1} \qquad (4)$$

where ε is a small positive constant to avoid division by zero.
The validity values of all points below the guaranteed distance D are then brought to the maximum value of v for all points (Eq. 5) to associate them with the highest priority.

$$v_i = \begin{cases} \max(\mathbf{v}) & \text{if } z_i < D \\ v_i & \text{otherwise} \end{cases} \quad \text{for } i = 1, \ldots, n \qquad (5)$$

The resulting *validity* is then employed as a priority vector to sample a number $N_{\max}$ of points from the original point cloud using a weighted random sampling implemented in Pythorch using *Pythorch.multinomial*.

Shared Memory. To ensure effective, low-latency, and thread-safe communication among these components, a shared memory and semaphore system has been implemented, based on memory-mapped files in /dev/shm/, a portion of shared RAM accessible as a filesystem. A total of four memory portions have been instantiated: two for data and two for their corresponding semaphores, to enable synchronization between reading and writing operations.

– shared_pc: Transfers the processed point cloud from the Python component to the GoLang component. This is done via a binary buffer with a 3-byte header, which will contain the data size, and a payload of 1,843,200 bytes

($480 \times 480 \times 8$ bytes, the maximum PointCloud size allowed by the Codec). An header file (`shared_pc_head`) is then used to hold the following information:

- an access flag, which is set to 1 when a new frame is available in the `shared_pc` memory, while the reading process resets its value to 0 after reading, in order to allow a new writing operation. Notice that this does not act as a semaphore, but rather as a notification flag to enable synchronization between the writing and reading processes.
- a second flag that indicates the user's intention to perform latency tests on the Codec.
- the bandwidth obtained from Pion GoLang, as feedback for the Point-Cloud Codec.
– `shared_control`: Used for sending commands to be executed on the Robot from the GoLang component to ROS2. These commands are represented by a standard `geometry_msgs/Twist` message, which includes two three-dimensional vectors (linear and angular, of type Vector3) and an incremental counter to track the command sequence, for a total of 52 bytes.

A second synchronization flag, `shared_control_read`, that synchronizes access to the `shared_control` file.

WebRTC Robot Peer. The GoLang component of the Robot's software stack is responsible for establishing the bidirectional connection with the Pion Bridge Peer, through the signaling Server, and for sending and receiving data.

Since point clouds are an unconventional data type and are not natively supported by Pion (the main WebRTC library for Go), a Custom Media Track has been implemented to extend `webrtc.TrackLocal` to transport 3D data via the RTP protocol.

– *Codec and metadata*: To enable Pion to send data without employing any codec, a 90 kHz video/pcm payload type is registered. Each point cloud frame is then divided into RTP packets, to which the following header is attached:
  - `FrameNr` (`uint32`): Sequential frame number;
  - `FrameLen` (`uint32`): Total frame length in Bytes;
  - `SeqOffset` (`uint32`): Offset in Bytes of the current portion;
  - `SeqLen` (`uint32`): Size of the current portion in Bytes;
  - `Data`: Data buffer, up to 1200 Bytes.

  Each packet contains 150 points, each represented by 8 bytes: 6 bytes for the spatial position (X Y Z coordinates) and 2 bytes for the color. The final packet size is 1200 Bytes, where the first 900 Bytes correspond to the spatial components (X Y Z ... X Y Z) of each point, and the remaining 300 Bytes represent the color data for each point (C C C ... C). This *packetization* process is shown in Fig. 2.
– *Congestion control and feedback*: Pion's interceptors (send-side GCC, TWCC, NACK, and PLI) are instantiated and added to the Custom Media Track to allow the Python codec to obtain a bandwidth estimate, and to prevent congestion or increased latency;

– *Media Track Flow*: On track startup, a dedicated *goroutine* monitors the shared memory. As soon as a new point cloud buffer becomes available, the data is packetized into 1200-byte segments; the header defined above is added to each segment, and then every packet is dispatched. At the end of this process, a current bandwidth estimate is requested from GCC and then relayed to the Python component using Shared Memory.

At startup, along with the Custom Media Track, the following DataChannels are created:

– *Control*: Instantiated by the robot, it is responsible for receiving movement commands to be executed via ROS2. These commands are encoded in JSON (linear and angular fields) and written to shared memory. It is also used to receive the user's intention to perform a latency test;
– *Bandwidth*: Instantiated by the Pion Bridge Peer, it is responsible for receiving 4 Bytes that indicate the bandwidth estimate produced by the other Peer. Although the estimate provided by Pion's GCC implementation is currently used, it may prove useful for future implementations;
– *ControlTrack*: Instantiated by the Pion Bridge Peer, it handles the remote management of RTP transmission (start/stop), via "start" and "stop" text messages.

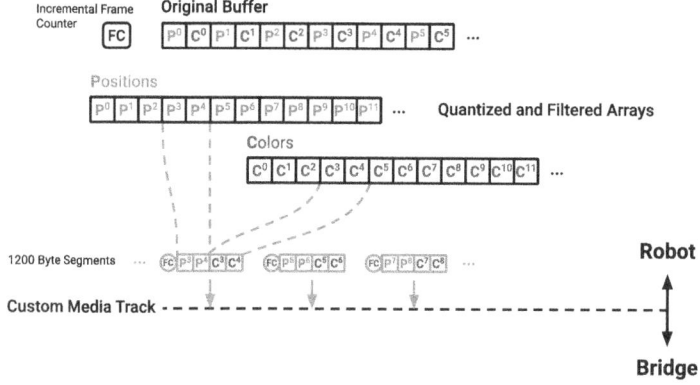

Fig. 2. Point Cloud Frame Packetization

3.3   HMD's Software Stack

WebRTC HMD's Peer. After the *Web-UI* initialization, a connection is established with three distinct WebSocket endpoints by the WebRTC Peer: the *Control Socket*, the *Telemetry Socket* and the *Streaming Socket*. In this way, the WebRTC peer acts as a local *bridge* between the WebRTC streams and the HMD's User Interface.

Concerning the WebSockets, the *Control Socket* (`controlSocket`) manages the control messages between the Web-UI and the HMD's WebRTC Peer. It also handles the operator's choice of which robot to teleoperate, which in turn defines the source of the point cloud stream.

A key function of the `controlSocket` is the transmission of an initialization command to the local Pion Bridge. This command includes the `signalingURL`, which contains the address of the signaling server. Providing this URL enables the Pion Bridge to establish WebRTC connections. Additionally, this socket requests updates on the list of available robots and updates the UI accordingly. Then, the Pion Bridge routes only the RTP track of the selected robot, temporarily suspending all other connections by sending a *stop command* on the *ControlTrack DataChannel*, effectively reducing bandwidth consumption. Thus, the Pion Bridge practically behaves like a *multiplexer*, switching views and controls between different robots.

The *Telemetry Socket* (`telemetrySocket`) is tasked with sending teleoperation commands from the *Web-UI* to the local Pion Bridge. These commands, generated from user inputs on the HMD, are then relayed by the Pion Bridge to the selected remote robot.

The *Streaming Socket* (`streamingSocket`) receives the point cloud packets. To prevent the degradation of one connection from affecting all others, the Pion Bridge allows the establishment of multiple concurrent WebRTC connections in distinct processes. After receiving the point cloud packets, the Pion Bridge reconstructs the coordinates and colors buffers (see Sect. 3.2) and sends it to the point cloud rendering pipeline (Sect. 3.3). *Point cloud frame reconstruction*: To optimize the aggregation process, two separate buffers are pre-allocated: one for coordinates, whose size is 900 Bytes, and one for colors, occupying 300 Bytes. As each packet arrives, its coordinates and color data are appended to the corresponding buffers, as shown in Fig. 3. This process is presented in Fig. 3.

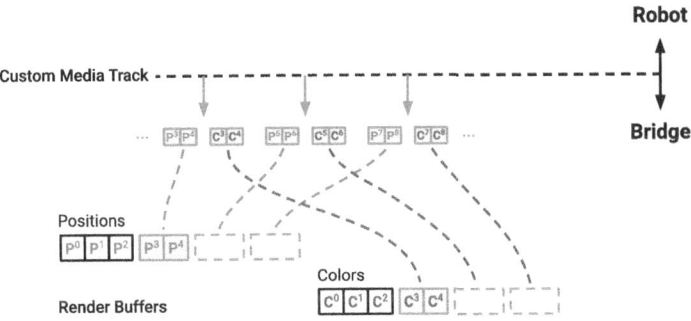

Fig. 3. Point Cloud Frame Depacketization

After the full point cloud frame is received, these buffers are combined and resized proportionally to the number of points received in the frame.

The final structure is a buffer consisting of the coordinates for the first 75% and the colors for the remaining 25%. The buffer is then sent to the *point cloud rendering pipeline* to be rendered on the *Web-UI*.

Point Cloud Rendering Pipeline. The HMD's WebRTC peer calculates the number of points using the buffer size. Then, using the byte offset, the data type and the data size, it translates and casts the point cloud frame into a *typed array*. This approach minimizes the access to memory, as typed arrays always refer to the same memory address, and avoids unnecessary computation.

Then, leveraging *ThreeJS*, a library that enables the use of typed arrays, three-dimensional geometries are defined through the use of the *Buffer Geometry* class[4]. This kind of 3D objects have their own attributes that are then used by the rendering pipeline, implemented using WebGL[5], to draw the geometry onto the canvas. In this step, the position and color attributes are updated to match the ones received. This forces a geometry update and allows for the rendering of incoming frames. The main advantage of using WebGL is represented by the wide range of data types supported by the shader programs involved in the rendering step. This allows for a seamless implementation of encoding strategies based on quantization.

To efficiently render the point cloud, a custom `ShaderMaterial` is employed to avoid any unnecessary calculation and ensuring the best visual quality. The custom ShaderMaterial is done through a vertex and a fragment shader in OpenGL Shading Language (GLSL), responsible of reading the attributes from the buffers and using them to render each individual point with the right position, color and dimension on the screen.

The vertex shader is employed to calculate the final screen position of each point and implementing an *adaptive sizing mechanism*. In particular, it dynamically adjusts the rendered size of each point, `gl_PointSize`, to enhance depth perception and visual clarity specifically for dense point clouds. The adaptive sizing logic is designed to offer nuanced visual control. In particular, let p_{base} be the size of points; s_{obj} the scale of the point cloud in the scene; and z_{local} the z coordinate of the point with respect to the origin of the point cloud; then, each point's size `gl_PointSize` is calculated as follows:

$$\text{gl\_PointSize} = p_{base} \cdot \frac{s_{obj}}{w_{clip}} \cdot (1 + |z_{local} \cdot f_{scaleZ}|)$$

where w_{clip} estimates the distance between the user's point of view and each point; f_{scaleZ} is a sensitivity parameter to control how significantly the point's Z-position affects its final rendered size;

Note that the term $\frac{s_{obj}}{w_{clip}}$ applies perspective scaling, making points further from the camera appear smaller, and accounts for the scale of the object in the WebGL

---

[4] https://threejs.org/docs/#api/en/core/BufferGeometry.
[5] https://developer.mozilla.org/en-US/docs/Web/API/WebGL_API.

scene, ensuring the final screen size of the point scales properly when manipulating the point cloud object. The term $(1 + |z_{local} \cdot f_{scaleZ}|)$ refines the size of each point, ensuring that p_{base} is the minimum point size.

The proposed scaling technique provides valuable depth cues related to the object's internal structure, supplementing the standard perspective projection. For optimal performance, this computation is executed within the vertex shader, leveraging the parallel processing capabilities of the GPU. Moreover, points are rendered as circles instead of squares to enhance the visual quality.

At runtime, the parameters for adaptive point sizing are determined by empirical functions. These functions were initially proposed and later qualitatively assessed to strike an optimal balance between simplicity and the visual quality of the experience.

Notice that the point cloud elaborations are executed inside a `WebWorker`, while the rendering process is handled by the main thread of the browser. The two components communicate through messages handled by callbacks and support zero-copy buffer transmission, vital to satisfy the latency requirements. This separation ensures a fluid user experience, reducing motion sickness that could otherwise be caused by dropped frames.

Teleoperation Commands. XR controllers are used to send commands to the remote AMR. The teleoperation commands are represented in linear and angular velocity values derived from the controller's thumbstick: the linear command is set based on the y-axis value, while the angular command is derived from the x-axis value.

Once a teleoperation command is generated, a throttling check is performed to ensure that commands are sent at a fixed rate. Then, commands are sent to the Pion Bridge via the `telemetrySocket`.

4   Results and Discussions

In this section we evaluate the key components and provide insights on the proposed framework. In particular, Sect. 4.1 presents the tests conducted on the sampling strategy under different network conditions and λ values; in Sect. 4.2, in order to provide insights on the performance of the framework as a whole, we evaluate the Motion-to-Photon (MtP) latency of the framework, defined as the sum of the latency for sending the user command and the latency to receive the new point cloud from the robot; Sect. 4.3 provides key insights on the framework's performance with respect to industrial contexts and VR comfort requirements.

4.1   Sampling Results

In this section, we evaluate the performance of the sampling strategy in different bandwidth conditions and λ values. For the purpose, we fix $D = 3.85$ m and FPS $= 10$ Hz.

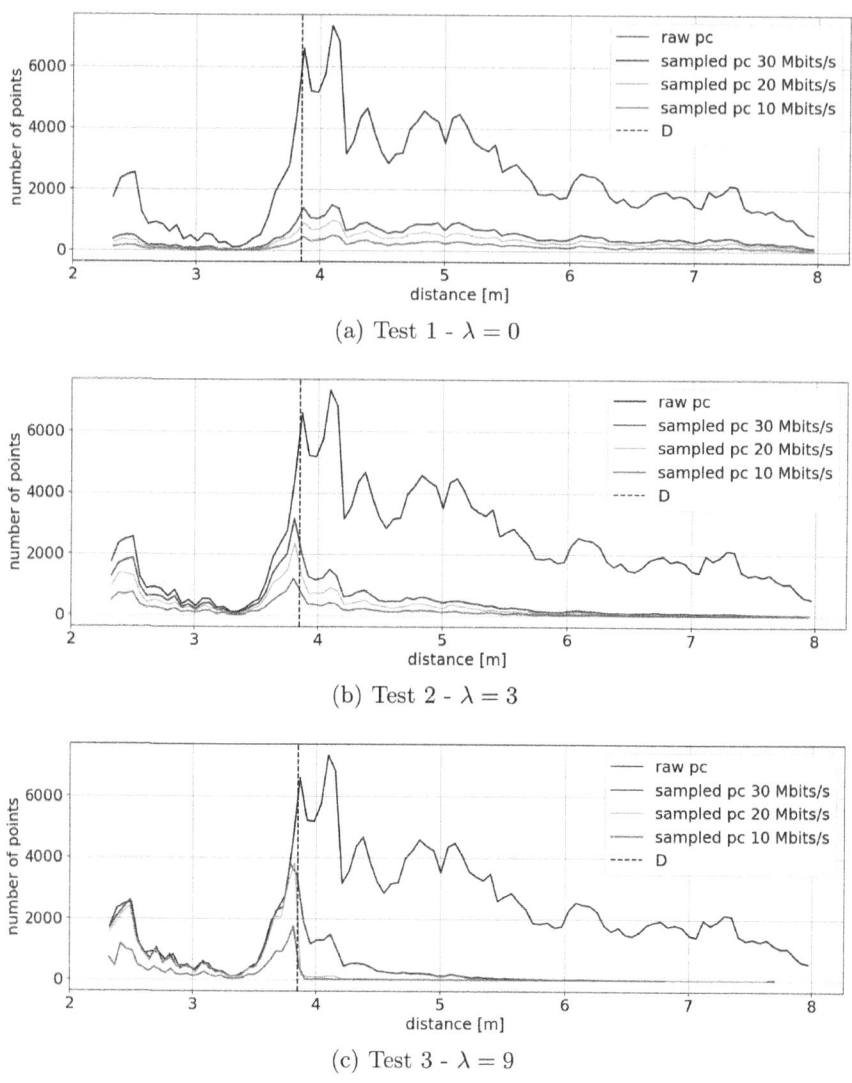

(a) Test 1 - $\lambda = 0$

(b) Test 2 - $\lambda = 3$

(c) Test 3 - $\lambda = 9$

Fig. 4. Sampling Strategy with different λ values

Sampling with Different λ Values. Figure 4 presents the effects of different bandwidth conditions on the sampling strategy when fixing different λ values. It is shown how lower λ values lead towards a uniform sampling strategy, which hinders the prioritization during sampling of all points closer than D (see Fig. 4(a)). Higher λ values, instead, benefit the prioritization of those points, effectively matching the original distribution for distances below D at the expenses of further points (see Fig. 4(c)).

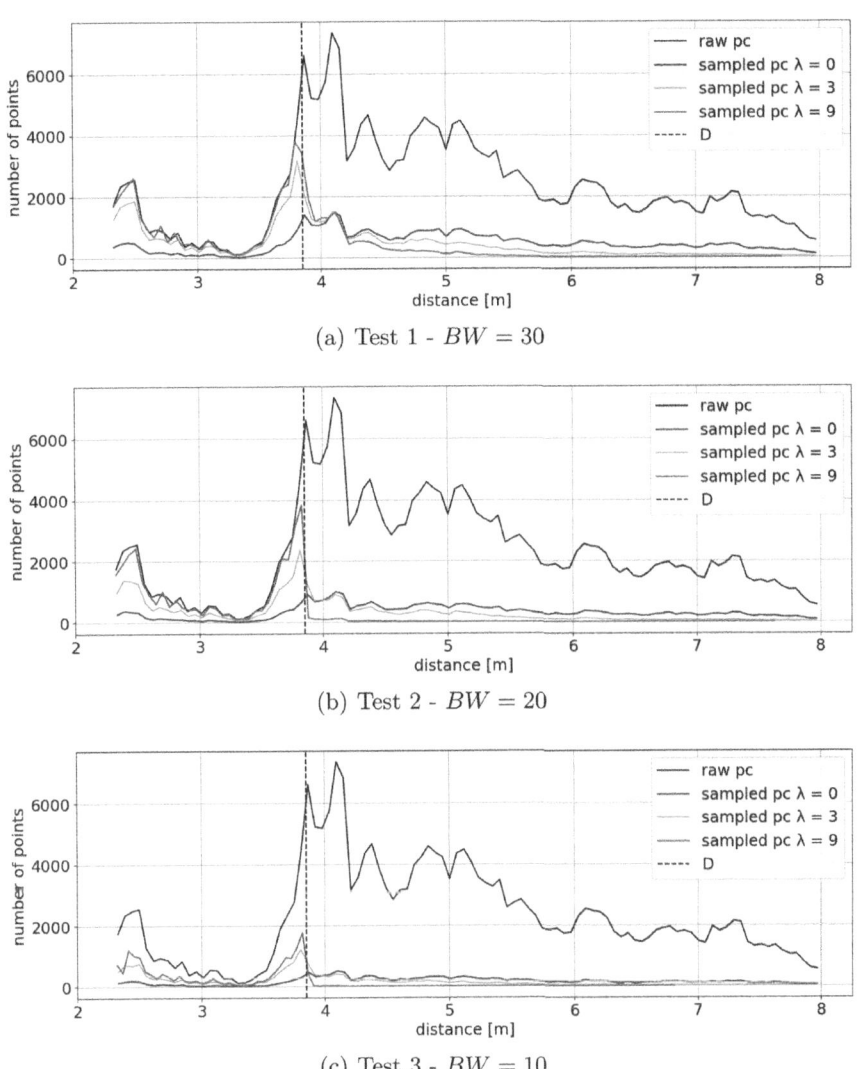

(a) Test 1 - $BW = 30$

(b) Test 2 - $BW = 20$

(c) Test 3 - $BW = 10$

Fig. 5. Sampling Strategy in different bandwidth conditions

Sampling in Different Bandwidth Conditions. Then, we test different λ values under three different bandwidth conditions.

When the bandwidth prevents the streaming of points closer than D, then the distribution of retained points will be scaled down to prevent congestion (i.e. critical delays). In these conditions, when λ assumes higher values, the retained points after D are dramatically reduced.

It is important to note that, since we are using a weighted probability distribution to sample the point cloud, the distribution of sampled points still depends on the distribution of the original point cloud. In particular, the lower λ, the higher this dependency is accentuated. This effect can be seen in Fig. 5, where setting $\lambda = 0$ results in having a uniform *validity* for all distances. When applied to the raw point cloud distribution, it follows the same trend, but scaled down to satisfy the constraint on the N_{max} points to be sent. On the contrary, as Fig. 5(c) shows, higher λ values retain the (scaled down, due to lower bandwidth) original distribution for all distances lower than D, effectively prioritizing those points with respect to those at a distance higher than the threshold.

4.2   Results on the Testbed

Latency Test. In order to measure the *Motion-to-Photon* (MtP) delay between the moment the user applies a control input and the moment the new point cloud frame is received, we embed a flag in the command message and store its timestamp. Once the robot receives the control command with the flag, it will turn the next point cloud frame color green. Then, on the HMD's side, once a frame of green points is received, its timestamp is saved and compared with the control command's one. Moreover, for testing purposes, the green point cloud will still be rendered. This provides the user with a visual hint of the actual MtP delay.

In order to simulate real use cases, for this test the human operator (with an HMD) and the robot, are deployed 1748.5 kilometers apart in straight-line distance. In particular, the user is located at the University of Surrey (UK) and the Robot at Politecnico di Bari (Italy). The average available link bandwidth, measured with *iperf3*[6], is 41.44 Mbit/s, while the average RTT is 42.4 ms.

Figure 6 shows two experiments with different bandwidths conditions. The figure shows the measured latency as well as the number of points transmitted. The latter is used to provide information on both the reaction of the adaptation system to bandwidth changes and the quality of the received point cloud (where a higher number of points is associated with better quality).
Throughout the tests, the latency remains under 400 ms, with spikes associated to sudden drops in bandwidth. Note that such result is to be expected, since the framework modulates the number of points to be sent proportionally to the measured bandwidth. This effectively prevents high latencies at the expenses of the point cloud density, enabling the operator to timely stop the robot if the bandwidth hinders the streaming of a satisfying number of points.

4.3   Discussions

A key feature of the rendering pipeline is the decoupled point cloud elaboration - rendering process. Using different threads for handling and rendering point clouds received enables the viewport to always be reactive and responsive to the user inputs (i.e. head movements and viewport manipulation). This separates the point cloud capture and reception FPS from the viewport FPS, alleviating

---

[6] https://iperf.fr/iperf-download.php.

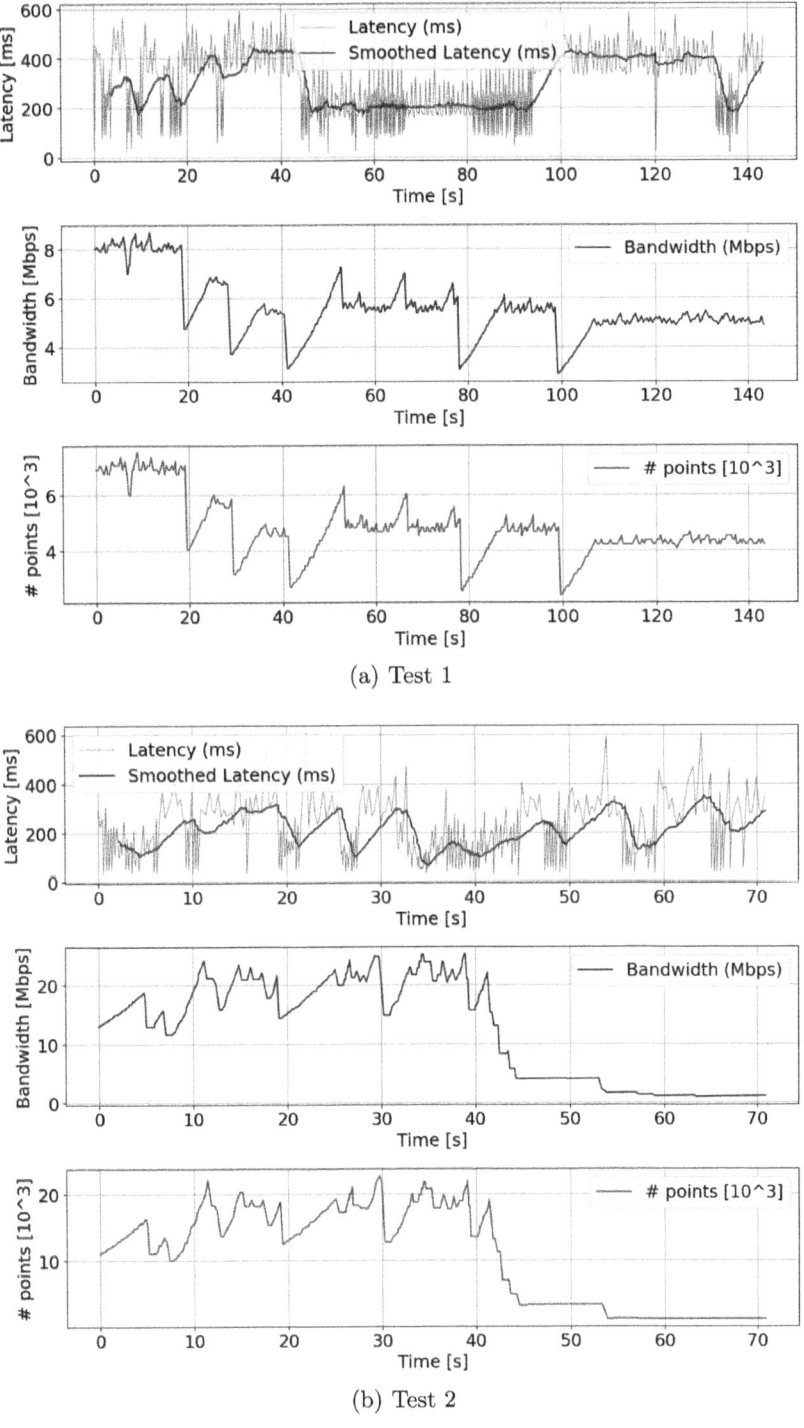

(a) Test 1

(b) Test 2

Fig. 6. Network tests

well-known VR issues of motion sickness and improving overall operator comfort. In fact, the viewport FPS is only related to the TreeJS performance on the HMD. Moreover, in the worst case where point clouds are not received at all, the user head movement will still produce a movement in the viewport. In order to thoroughly assess such aspects, we plan to extend this work with user experience evaluations through, e.g., motion sickness assessments (Simulator Sickness Questionnaire) and operator workloads (NASA Task Load Index). These evaluations will serve as starting point for further improvements on the proposed framework.

5   Conclusions

In this paper, we proposed a framework for immersive teleoperation of AMRs, introducing a real-time volumetric video streaming pipeline. Leveraging both quantization and an adaptive sampling strategy, the framework is able to adapt to different bandwidth conditions, ensuring low latencies even in low bandwidth conditions.

Tests conducted show that the proposed distance-based sampling strategy effectively prioritizes relevant information for navigation purposes. Furthermore, employing the WebRTC for transmission allowed for real-time interaction with the robot, keeping averages latencies compatible with the practical teleoperation requirements, especially in 5G enabled networks.

Further tests could be conducted to study how the proposed framework affects the Quality of Experience (QoE) during operations. Moreover, the sampling strategy could be further optimized to better react to bandwidth oscillations.

Acknowledgments. This work has been funded by the European Union through the DIANE project winner of the Open Call n.1 of the SPIRIT project (101070672).

References

1. 5GAA: Tele-operated driving (ToD): system requirements, analysis and architecture (2020). https://5gaa.org/tele-operated-driving-tod-system-requirements-analysis-and-architecture/. Accessed 18 Jan 2025
2. Barone, N., Brescia, W., Mascolo, S., De Cicco, L.: Apeiron: a multimodal drone dataset bridging perception and network data in outdoor environments. In: Proceedings of the 15th ACM Multimedia Systems Conference. MMSys '24, pp. 401–407, New York, NY, USA. Association for Computing Machinery (2024). https://doi.org/10.1145/3625468.3652186
3. Barone, N., et al.: Real-time point cloud transmission for immersive teleoperation of autonomous mobile robots. In: Proceedings of the 16th ACM Multimedia Systems Conference. MMSys '25, New York, NY, USA, pp. 311–316. Association for Computing Machinery (2025). https://doi.org/10.1145/3712676.3719263

4. Carlucci, G., De Cicco, L., Holmer, S., Mascolo, S.: Congestion control for web real-time communication. IEEE/ACM Trans. Networking **25**(5), 2629–2642 (2017). https://doi.org/10.1109/TNET.2017.2703615

5. De Cicco, L., Carlucci, G., Mascolo, S.: Congestion control for webrtc: Standardization status and open issues. IEEE Communications Standards Magazine **1**(2), 22–27 (2017). https://doi.org/10.1109/MCOMSTD.2017.1700014

6. De Fré, M., van der Hooft, J., Wauters, T., De Turck, F.: Scalable mdc-based volumetric video delivery for real-time one-to-many webrtc conferencing. In: Proceedings of the 15th ACM Multimedia Systems Conference. pp. 121–131, New York, NY, USA. Association for Computing Machinery (2024)

7. Google: Google draco. https://github.com/google/draco

8. Group, M.P.E.: Information technology - coded representation of immersive media - part 9: Geometry-based point cloud compression (g-pcc) (2023). https://www.iso.org/standard/78990.html, published March 2023

9. Group, M.P.E.: Information technology - coded representation of immersive media - part 5: Visual volumetric video-based coding (v3c) and video-based point cloud compression (v-pcc) (2025). https://www.iso.org/standard/89030.html, published March 2025

10. Inc., G.: The go programming language. https://go.dev/

11. Lee, K., Yi, J., Lee, Y., Choi, S., Kim, Y.M.: Groot: a real-time streaming system of high-fidelity volumetric videos. In: Proceedings of the 26th Annual International Conference on Mobile Computing and Networking. MobiCom '20, New York, NY, USA. Association for Computing Machinery (2020). https://doi.org/10.1145/3372224.3419214

12. Lv, J., Lin, Y., Hou, M., Li, Y., Gao, Y., Dong, W.: Accurate bandwidth and delay prediction for 5g cellular networks. ACM Trans. Internet Technol. **25**(2) (2025). https://doi.org/10.1145/3703629

13. Musicant, O., Botzer, A., Shoval, S.: Effects of simulated time delay on teleoperators' performance in inter-urban conditions. Transp. Res. Part F Traffic Psychol. Beh. **92**, 220–237 (2023). https://doi.org/10.1016/j.trf.2022.11.007, https://www.sciencedirect.com/science/article/pii/S1369847822002753

14. Pion: Pion webrtc. https://github.com/pion/webrtc

15. Raca, D., Leahy, D., Sreenan, C.J., Quinlan, J.J.: Beyond throughput, the next generation: a 5g dataset with channel and context metrics. In: Proceedings of the 11th ACM Multimedia Systems Conference. MMSys '20, New York, NY, USA, pp. 303–308. Association for Computing Machinery (2020). https://doi.org/10.1145/3339825.3394938

16. Rudolph, M., Rizk, A.: Learned compression in adaptive point cloud streaming: Opportunities, challenges and limitations. In: Proceedings of the 16th ACM Multimedia Systems Conference. MMSys '25, pp. 328–334, New York, NY, USA. Association for Computing Machinery (2025). https://doi.org/10.1145/3712676.3719266, https://doi.org/10.1145/3712676.3719266

17. Schwarz, S., et al.: Emerging mpeg standards for point cloud compression. IEEE J. Emerg. Sel. Top. Circuits Syst. **9**(1), 133–148 (2018)

18. Stereolabs: Stereolab zed sdk - using the depth sensing API. https://www.stereolabs.com/docs/depth-sensing/using-depth#getting-point-cloud-data

Ultra-low Latency Point Cloud Streaming in 5G

Y. Thomas⊙ and G. Xylomenos$^{(✉)}$⊙

Mobile Multimedia Laboratory, Department of Informatics, Athens University of Economics and Business, Athens 10434, Greece
{thomasi,xgeorge}@aueb.gr

Abstract. Point cloud streaming is a key component of 5G (and beyond) networks, serving as a foundation for holographic communication. While it enables immersive experiences, it also poses significant challenges to network infrastructure. Uncompressed point cloud streams produce Gbps traffic volumes, while compressed streams often suffer from multi-second latencies. Therefore, the feasibility of real-time applications that require ultra-low motion-to-eye latency, such as Network Music Performance and Remote Driving, remains unclear. In this work, we design and implement a novel point cloud streaming tool, based on the Draco encoder, Intel's RealSense SDK, and OpenGL. We deploy our prototype implementation in a private 5G stand alone network and provide an in-depth analysis of the latency and throughput of point cloud streaming. Our results show that deploying volumetric streaming services over 5G networks is still a challenging task. However, a combination of simple cost-reduction strategies can bring it significantly closer to feasibility.

Keywords: Ultra-low latency · Volumetric · Streaming · Draco

1 Introduction

A *Point Cloud* (PC) in the context of volumetric video is a collection of 3D points that represent the shape and structure of objects or scenes in space [14]. Each point typically includes spatial coordinates (x, y, z) and may also carry additional attributes like color or reflectance. PC streaming is used to transmit dynamic volumetric content, such as people, environments, or objects, captured by one or more depth cameras, for real-time rendering in AR/VR/XR applications. Unlike stereoscopic 3D video, which offers a sense of depth from a single point of view, volumetric video can be rendered from different points of view.

PC streaming is gaining popularity as 5G and Beyond 5G networks become increasingly available [6–8]. These networks promise throughput and latency that can support previously infeasible services, such as holographic communication for human-to-human or human-to-robot interactions. Notable examples include Network Music Performance [13] and Remote Driving [4]; these require ultra-low latency communication, typically less than 100 ms of motion-to-eye latency, as well as high throughput, often up to hundreds of MBps.

D. Michael-Grigoriou et al. (Eds.): EuroXR 2025, LNCS 16101, pp. 22–39, 2026.
https://doi.org/10.1007/978-3-032-03805-0_2

While many studies have explored PC streaming performance, to the best of our knowledge, there are no detailed performance evaluations of volumetric streaming for ultra-low latency applications. Most published works exploit TCP [9,10,17], which offers recovery from packet losses, but due to its retransmissions, is unsuitable for ultra-low latency applications. Some works do employ UDP [15,16,18], but they convert the PC to a planar (2D) format, thus losing the ability to render it in 3D from different points of view. Of course, latency is not just due to network transmission: PC compression and decompression are computationally demanding tasks. Since the level of compression affects the bandwidth required for the PC stream, understanding the performance of PC streaming requires understanding the effects of the compression settings.

In this work, we design and implement a PC streaming tool and analyze in depth its performance in terms of latency, bitrate, and transmission resiliency. Our tool is built upon the Intel RealSense SDK for PC capture, the Draco encoder library for compression and decompression, a custom lightweight transport protocol, and OpenGL for rendering the 3D data. Most importantly, the tool allows individual analysis of the latency introduced by each stage in the PC processing pipeline, on both the producer and consumer sides. Our goal is to reveal performance bottlenecks and set directions for future research towards achieving ultra-low latency PC streaming.

We evaluate our tool in a private 5G *Stand Alone* (SA) network. We explore different strategies to adjust latency and bitrate, such as selecting the Draco compression level, lowering PC resolution, omitting color attributes and parallelizing compression. Our results offer a preliminary characterization of the conditions under which PC streaming becomes practical under real 5G conditions.

The remainder of the paper is organized as follows. In Sect. 2, we discuss related work on PC streaming. In Sect. 3, we introduce our novel streaming tool and present our evaluation setup, while in Sect. 4 we present our evaluation results and discuss future research directions. Finally, in Sect. 5, we summarize our conclusions.

2   Background Work

The literature on PC streaming is extensive, including several surveys. In [14], the authors deliver a comprehensive survey of volumetric streaming, providing a qualitative categorization of the approaches into Dynamic Meshes versus Time Varying Meshes, and Volumetric Mesh versus PC streaming. Emphasis is put on the computational cost of compression to reduce bitrate and its impact on latency, underscoring the benefits of exploiting *Mobile Edge Computing* (MEC).

Another survey covers latency and bitrate reduction methods [2]. The authors categorize designs into network-based and user-based. The network-based designs analyze network conditions, such as error-rate, to adapt the streaming setup. The user-based designs analyze user behavior, such as field of view transitions, and proactively adapt the streaming setup. A survey specific to PC streaming is presented in [6]. The study covers work on encoding techniques, encompassing recent advancements in user-centric PC streaming, AI-driven PC streaming, and low-latency-focused PC streaming. It also points out some "transformative metaverse enablers", such as MEC, VLC, and network coding.

It is worth mentioning individually some papers that address PC encoding. In [5], the authors compare 4 codecs: Google's Draco, Corto, MPEG's Open 3D Graphics Compression (O3dgc) and OpenCTM, investigating the compression of vertex normals and attributes. The paper discusses live streaming, providing a simple model of the transmission pipeline to calculate an expected frame rate, as well as lower and upper bounds for end-to-end latency. The model suggests that Draco can deliver the lowest end-to-end latency (50–120 ms) for RTTs larger than 20 ms. In [19], the authors introduce an encoding scheme that reduces bitrate 55–99% with no quality loss, by transforming 3D PCs to 2D depth images, consisting of a color image and a depth map, and then compressing them using 2D encoders. However, they do not discuss the latency of this method. In [12], the authors deliver a QoE analysis of different encoding mechanisms, reporting that Draco requires higher data footprint to achieve the same mean opinion score as learning-based RS-DLPCC, while solutions that render PC to 2D video perform the best. Latency is also not discussed in this study.

Other papers focus on the design of protocols and services for streaming PCs in 5G networks. In [8], the authors discuss exploiting 5G edge computing in a function-as-a-service manner, where end-users upload the volumetric stream to a broker located in the 5G MEC, which transcodes media in a personalized and adaptive fashion. In [3] the authors investigate the addition of an MCU for the real-time delivery optimization of multiple PC streams. This design presents reduced computation and network requirements, at the cost of extra latency. ViVo [7] is a PC streaming platform for mobile end-users, covering the entire pipeline from capturing to rendering. It considers visibility limitations to determine which video content to fetch. It also considers parallel processing during decoding, which can increase the FPS on smartphone devices up to 400%.

The 3D streaming protocols tend to prioritize bandwidth economy, at the expense of latency, thereafter TCP is often used, despite its ill fit to real-time media transmission. In [10], the authors introduce a novel MPEG DASH-inspired technique for PC transmission which adapts streaming quality to connection quality. GROOT [9] is a streaming framework that enables real-time transmission and decoding on mobile devices. It introduces a novel tree data structure that enables parallelizing and, in turn, accelerating the PC decoding process. The authors report less than 100 ms motion-to-eye latency in a LAN. Yuzu [17] is similar to GROOT, using coding to reduce the bandwidth cost of 3D streaming by exploiting AI and perception-driven methods. Its evaluation shows that processing latency, without any transmission delays, can be less than 50 ms.

Other studies exploit UDP for transmission, to keep network latency below one RTT. To handle the large bitstream, those studies tend to convert PCs to a 2D format and incorporate reliability mechanisms, such as *Forward Error Correction* (FEC), to handle lost or late packets, especially in wireless networks. In

[15], the authors introduce a network coding module for unequal error protection and FEC for 3D streams, which are encoded in 2D format. In [16], the authors introduce a FEC mechanism for stereoscopic 3D video, which consists of two 2D streams. In [18], the authors combine FEC with *Scalable Video Coding* (SVC) to transmit panoramic video, which is 3D spherical video converted into 2D. SVC is considered in [1], where the authors propose a multicast PC streaming protocol. The PC is encoded in different complementary layers that can be combined to achieve different levels of QoS, thus adapting to end-user needs and capabilities.

While UDP minimizes latency, it lacks the efficient control mechanisms for high-bandwidth transmission that TCP offers. Therefore researchers in [11] propose a best-of-both-worlds solution which exploits QUIC.

3   Experiment Setup

We developed and evaluated our PC streaming tool on a simple setup that consists of two applications, a producer and a consumer, running on different network nodes.[1] The producer captures, encodes, and transmits volumetric video to the consumer, which receives, decodes, and renders the stream. The nodes are connected in a peer-to-peer fashion using a 5G SA network; there is no *Selective Forwarding Unit* (SFU) between them, to keep communication latency as low as possible. In the following, we discuss individually the networking, streaming and software setup, and present the performance metrics explored in this study.

3.1   Networking Setup

The experiments took place at a private 5G testbed. The site offers an area of around 500 m^2 outdoor space which is covered by a private 5G SA network configured in the 3.7–3.8 GHz industrial spectrum. Band N78 has been exploited, a mid-band 5G band that is one of the most widely deployed for 5G due to its balance between coverage and capacity. Experimenting in a private 5G SA testbed means that the measurements are not affected by competing traffic, therefore presenting more accurate and clear results which, in turn, offer more trustworthy observations and conclusions.

The producer and consumer nodes were off-the-shelf Asus TUF A15 Ryzen 9 laptops running Ubuntu 24.04. The two nodes accessed the 5G network via the Gigabit Ethernet port of two Teltonika RUTX50 modems. DHCP was enabled to the modems, thus providing a private IPv4 address to the connected nodes. In the 5G network, the modems were using SIM cards that were assigned IPv4 addresses in a VLAN, that rendered the two modems visible to each other. To enable peer-to-peer connection at the producer and consumer nodes, port forwarding was enabled in the modems to push all traffic from the modem's VLAN address to the private node's address. Thereafter, the two nodes were able to exchange packets using the VLAN addresses of their dedicated modems, without requiring NAT traversal.

---

[1] Source Code is available at https://github.com/mmlab-aueb/nmp/tree/master/ volumetric_streaming_app.

Table 1. Connection characteristics in peer-to-peer mode.

Link	5G band	Throughput (MBps)	One-way latency (ms)
5G (SA)	N78	20.1	12.2 (st.dev. 1)

The nodes had excellent signal quality, performing close to the theoretical optimal, as presented in Table 1, which shows the characteristics of the peer-to-peer connection. The connection measurements were made via the `ping` and `iperf` Linux tools (using UDP), respectively.

It is worth noting that bandwidth measurements with `iperf` yielded quite different results for different transport protocols. Throughput using TCP was less than 8 MBps, while UDP delivered 20.1 MBps (or, more than 160 Mbps). After experimenting with our application, we discovered that excessively bursty transmissions led to significant losses at bitrates that were a fraction of the 5G link capacity; our video encoder was very bursty, as it emitted a very large number of packets after encoding each frame. We solved this problem by adding a 1 μs latency between successive packets, thus shaping our traffic. We assume that the buffers of the RUTX50 modems were not large enough to handle the burstiness of our sender, or even common TCP connections that send packets in groups, especially in the slow-start phase.

3.2   Streaming Setup

The producer application (sender) was equipped with an Intel RealSense D435i depth camera connected via a USB type-C port. The consumer application (receiver) rendered the video in the laptop display, rather than AR glasses, as measuring latency when using glasses and headsets is very challenging. Further details on the streaming parameters are presented in the following subsection.

3.3   Software Setup

Producer App. The Producer application is implemented as a two-threaded C++ program, as shown in Fig. 1 (left side); one thread handles frame capturing, PC conversion and compression and the other thread handles PC transmission. During initialization, the capturing thread connects to the depth camera which is controlled via Intel's librealsense SDK,[2] and enters its main loop, which includes the following stages: capture a frame, encode it into a PC with the librealsense SDK, convert it to a Draco PC, compress it with the Draco library and push it to the other thread via shared memory. The sequential execution of the main loop stages means that the FPS rate is not fixed: it is determined by the processing latency at the main loop. However, this design facilitates measuring the latency of each individual stage.

---

[2] https://github.com/IntelRealSense/librealsense.

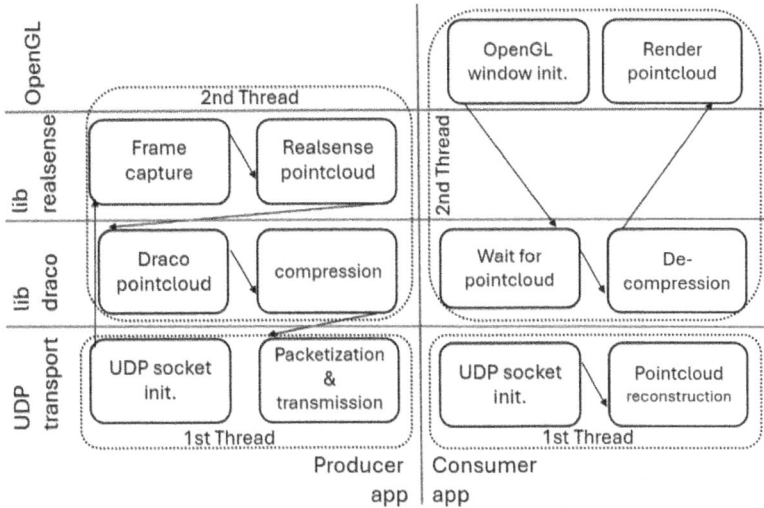

Fig. 1. Processing pipeline at the Producer (left) and Consumer (right) apps; each horizontal plane represents a technological layer.

During initialization, the transmission thread establishes a UDP socket for sending. Then, upon receiving a compressed PC from the capturing thread, it fragments it into 1400-byte chunks that fit in network packets and sends them to the receiver app. Transmission is achieved via UDP, exploiting a custom lightweight transport protocol to enable PC reconstruction. The protocol defines two header fields, a 4-byte frame sequence ID and a 4-byte chunk sequence ID, with a fixed 1400 byte payload. The receiver reconstructs the PC based on the chunk ID, which is multiplied by the chunk size to estimate the chunk's position within the frame. The receiver infers that a PC is "fully" transmitted when the first chunk for the next frame ID arrives.

Note that the transmission of PCs in narrowband links, like older Wi-Fi, can be significantly slower than the PC capture. The communication of the two threads is based on a circular buffer with a First-In-First-Out processing policy, which can lead to latency build-up due to extensive buffering. Therefore, our buffer size is limited to 10 PCs, dropping the oldest PC when the buffer is saturated. This restricts the buffering latency to 10 times the frame rate, which is roughly 0.33 s in case of 30 FPS.

Multithreaded Compression. A PC can be broken into independent sub-PCs that can be (de)compressed individually, enabling parallelization and thus reducing overall compression latency. The producer implementation supports parallel compression of sub-PCs using multithreading, where each thread executes the "Draco pointcloud" and "compression" tasks of Fig. 1 for a different sub-PC. The use of multithreading is optional and the number of threads is configurable; when enabled, the Realsense PC is divided into N equally sized sub-PCs, each assigned to one of the N threads, which then generate N compressed Draco PCs. These are subsequently reconstructed into a logically single PC and transmitted as one PC. The structure of the logically single PC consists of two fields per sub-PC: a 4-byte flag for sub-PC length and a byte-array for the sub-PC. This operation is transparent to all tasks but the compression and decompression, allowing seamless adaptation to different thread counts.[3]

Consumer App. The consumer is implemented as a two-threaded C++ program, as shown in Fig. 1 (right side); one thread handles reception and the other thread handles PC decoding and rendering. During initialization, the reception thread opens a UDP socket for chunk reception and enters its main loop, where it receives the chunks and reconstructs the compressed Draco PCs. The PCs are pushed to the decoding thread via shared memory. Reconstruction does not impose any buffering latency, as each PC is pushed when the first chunk of the next frame is received.

During initialization, the decoding thread creates a window for rendering the PCs and enters its main loop, where it waits for compressed PCs from the reception thread. When a PC is pushed, it is decoded using the Draco library and rendered using OpenGL. Currently, decoding and rendering (at the consumer) are conducted sequentially by the same thread, as these are faster than encoding (at the producer); this could change to improve performance, if needed.

Rendering is based on OpenGL using the GLFW library[4] in a 1280×720 window. For each point in the PC frame, the consumer draws the coordinates and the color using functions *glVertex3fv* and *glTexCoord2fv*, respectively. In addition, call-back functions for mouse and keyboard events are implemented, allowing the user to customize the PC projection in real-time.

Currently, the consumer does not leverage multithreading for decompression. When the producer uses multithreaded compression, the consumer processes the individual sub-PCs sequentially. While a multithreaded consumer could reduce decompression latency, it would increase implementation complexity. Our preliminary evaluation suggests that the potential performance gain is limited in our setup; multithreaded decompression may be more beneficial in resource-constrained devices, such as smartphones.

3.4   Scene and Encoding Setups

The PC frame in these experiments is captured at the default resolution of the Intel D435i (848×480), which is roughly 0.4 M points. Each point is represented by its coordinates (3×32-bit floats, quantized by Draco to 3×11-bit integers) and its RGBA color (4×8-bit integers). Compression uses the Kd-Tree Encoder with 16-bit quantization analysis of the Draco library.

---

[3] To enhance resilience to lost chunks, it is advised to list the sub-PC lengths in the first chunk of the PC, akin to an indexing table.

[4] https://www.glfw.org/.

The efficiency of Draco compression depends on the properties of the scene. Under the same compression level, the size of a compressed PC of a simple scene, e.g., a white wall 30 cm from the camera, is a fraction of the size of a complex scene, e.g., an overview of our $50\,m^2$ lab. Therefore, to provide a fair comparison of different encoding setups, all experiments were conducted using the same camera angle. The scene is close to what would be the case for music teaching, that is, a relatively complex scene with 1–2 m depth, which produced around 70% of the maximum PC size.

In the experiments, we test different encoding setups by controlling four parameters. First, we test the Draco compression levels, ranging from 1–10, with 1 being the fastest and 10 the most compact. Second, we modify the size of the PC stream, by dropping 25 or 50% of the points. Third, we experiment with different numbers of compression threads to reduce compression latency. Finally, we test performance with and without color information; the latter is denoted as a *color-less* PC.

3.5   Performance Metrics

We analyze performance via the following metrics:

- Processing Latency (ms): The total time to process a PC. At the producer, it shows the time from frame capture until the PC is put in the network. At the consumer, it shows the time from the receipt of the first chunk of the PC until the OpenGL window renders the PC.
- Compression Latency (ms): The time required to compress a frame using the Draco library.
- PC Size (Bytes): The size of a (compressed) frame.
- Transmission latency (ms): At the producer, it shows the total time to fragment a compressed PC into UDP chunks and put in network. At the consumer, it shows the time for receiving all the chunks of a PC and reconstructing them into a PC; due to the consumer's design, this metric shows the inter-PC arrival time.
- End-to-end latency (ms): The time from the frame capture at the producer until the end of the rendering at the consumer.
- Reliability (%): The percentage of *entire* PCs delivered to the consumer without errors.

Measurement Method: End-to-end latency and reliability metrics are estimated post-experiment by jointly analyzing the logs of the consumer and producer applications.[5] The clocks of the producer and consumer nodes are synchronized at the millisecond level using the NTP protocol over a secondary LAN connection specifically used for synchronization. The producer logs the time of capturing a frame and the consumer logs the time after a PC is rendered, thus allowing us to

---

[5] The logs of the experiments presented in this paper are available at https://zenodo.org/records/15736910.

estimate the "end-to-end" latency. To assess transmission reliability, the producer and consumer log the hashes of the PC transmitted and received, respectively. Although partial PCs can be (partially) rendered, only flawless PC transmissions are considered successful.

The other measurements are straight-forward. The C++ applications log the system time between the execution of the different tasks to infer the individual latencies. Similarly, the PC size is determined by measuring the number of bytes pushed in the network.

Frame Rate Estimation: The FPS rate is not adjustable at the producer app; it depends on the processing latency, e.g., a processing latency of 33 ms leads to roughly 30 FPS. To allow bitrate comparisons, we define the bitrate for 30 FPS ($bitrate_{30}$) as the product of the compressed frame size (including transport overhead) with 30.

Deployability Limits: We define latency and bitrate limits to assess the setup's deployability over real networks. In particular, the processing latency at both applications should be less than 33 ms (for 30 FPS), the bitrate should be at most 20 MBps (the uplink of our 5G SA links) and the end-to-end latency should be below 100 ms. Although these limits are not absolute, e.g., the FPS rate can be increased by parallel processing [7], they serve as a rough performance baseline.

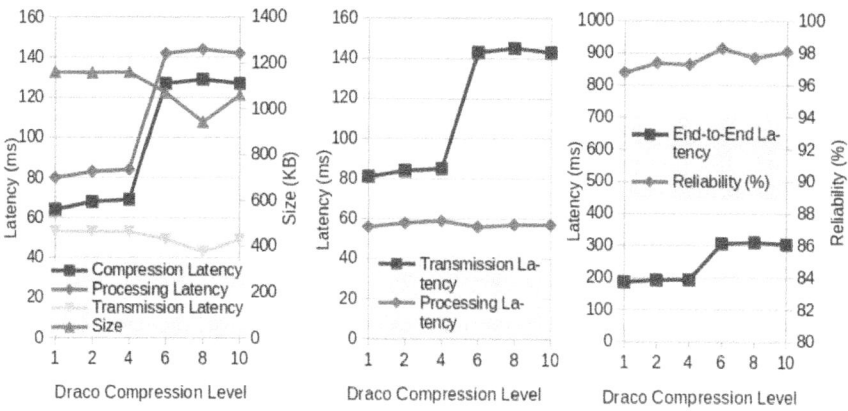

Fig. 2. Producer (left), consumer (center), and shared metrics (right) against Draco compression level (1–10).

4   Evaluation Results

4.1   Draco Compression

First, we explore the effect of Draco compression levels on system performance. Figure 2 includes three sub-figures that show the producer, consumer and shared metrics (from left to right), respectively, for 10 compression levels. The producer figure shows the PC frame size (right y-axis) and the transmission, processing and compression latencies (left y-axis) for different Draco compression levels in the producer app. The results verify that lower levels of compression deliver lower latencies and higher PC sizes, although the relation is not linear; the performance difference is most evident between levels 4 and 6. The results also reveal that the compression latency is roughly 80% of the overall processing latency, thus highlighting the importance of optimizing compression. Regarding compression efficiency, the difference between the fastest and slowest compression modes is 50% and 23% for compression latency and PC size, respectively. The transmission latency is affected by the PC size, since larger PCs require the emission of more UDP chunks. Due to the size of the processing latency (80–144 ms), frames are skipped, leading to a low FPS rate, which translates into a low bitrate (7.5–14.1 MBps), that can be transferred effectively from the 5G network. However, the (theoretical) bitrate$_{30}$ of these setups is 31–34 MBps, which is far beyond the capacity of the 5G link.

The consumer figure shows that the impact of the Draco compression level on the performance of the consumer application is minor. Processing latency, which comprises decompression and rendering latency, is almost indistinguishable for all levels. We do not show the rendering and decompression latencies separately, but they are roughly equal, each around 50% of the processing latency, or 25–30 ms. The transmission latency at the consumer, which shows the inter-PC arrival time, is identical to the processing latency at the producer, showing that the latter controls the rate of transmission.

Finally, the shared metrics show that reliability ranges between 96.8 and 98.3%, while end-to-end latency is 186–310 ms. The former verifies that the network can handle the low bitrate (7.5–14.1 MBps), required by our low effective

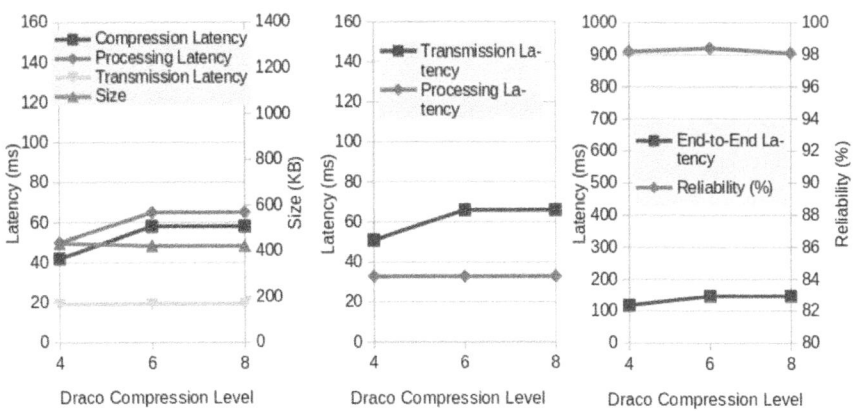

Fig. 3. Producer (left), consumer (center), and shared metrics (right) against Draco compression level (4–8) for color-less PCs.

FPS rate. The latter suggests that achieving low-latency volumetric streaming is feasible when sufficient network capacity is available, indicating that bandwidth remains the most critical challenge.

Overall, our measurements indicate that this basic setup is not capable of delivering good quality ultra-low latency volumetric streaming in the 5G testbed. The lowest bitrate$_{30}$ that Draco can offer is roughly twice the available capacity, the fastest processing latency at the producer is 2–3 times higher than what is required for 30 FPS, and the lowest end-to-end latency is twice the 100 ms deployability target.

4.2   Removing Color Information

To assess the impact of color, we repeated the previous experiments, but discarding all color information before compressing the PC at the producer. Figure 3 includes three sub-figures that show the producer, consumer and shared metrics (from left to right), respectively, for compression levels 4, 6 and 8. The producer figure shows the color-less PC frame size (right y-axis) and the transmission, processing and compression latencies (left y-axis). Comparing these results against the results when color is included (Fig. 2), we can see that color accounts for roughly 50% of the processing latency and 66% of the resulting PC frame size and transmission latency, suggesting that color-less PCs are fairly inexpensive to compress and transfer. Regarding compression efficiency, when color is omitted, the difference between compression levels 4 and 6 is 28% and 3% for compression latency and PC frame size, respectively, suggesting that compression levels have a lower impact without color information. The bitrate$_{30}$ of the color-less modes is roughly 12.5 MBps.

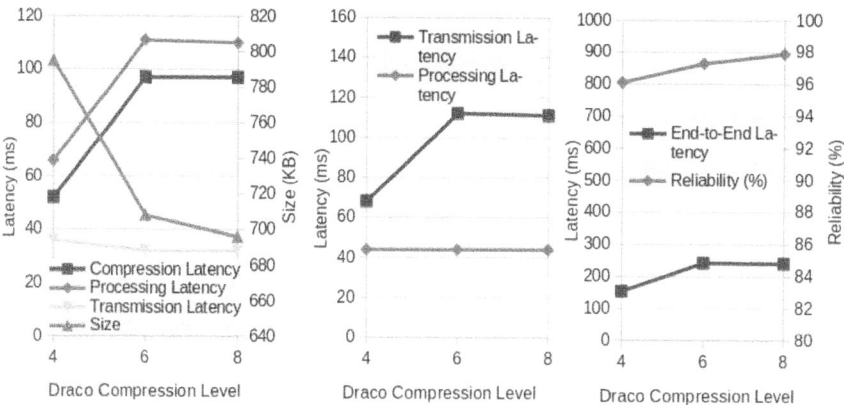

Fig. 4. Producer (left), consumer (center), and shared metrics (right) against Draco compression level (4–8) for 75% PC resolution.

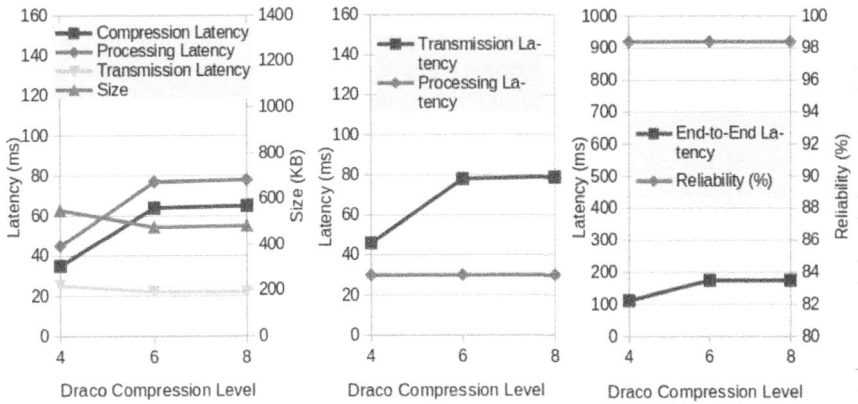

Fig. 5. Producer (left), consumer (center), and shared metrics (right) against Draco compression level (4–8) for 50% PC resolution.

The consumer and shared metrics offers a similar image, indicating that transferring color-less information is closer to being deployable. In color-less PCs, the consumer processing latency is 33 ms, supporting the 30 FPS goal, and the consumer transmission latency is equal to the producer processing latency, showing that the latter is the performance bottleneck. Finally, the 5G link is not saturated, offering 98.4% reliability, and 118–147 ms of end-to-end latency.

Overall, operating in color-less mode significantly enhances the setup's deployability over real 5G networks, underscoring the importance of developing more efficient color compression methods for PCs.

4.3 Reducing PC Resolution

A different method to reduce latency and throughput requirements is to reduce the detail of the PC, therefore we decrease the PC resolution by dropping 25% and 50% of the points in each PC frame. The points are discarded before creating the uncompressed Draco PC at the producer; discarded points are uniformly distributed in the PC. We repeated the previous experiment with color information for compression levels 4–8, plotting the results in Fig. 4 and Fig. 5, respectively.

Compared to the basic setup (Fig. 2), the data indicate that reducing resolution leads to an almost linear decrease in compression latency and PC size. Therefore, if an X% reduction in the bitrate or latency is required, it can be accomplished via a roughly X% reduction in the resolution of the PC that is compressed and transmitted. The reduction is evident in the producer, consumer and shared metrics; reliability remains above 96% in all cases, showing that the induced bitrate fits within the 5G link. Additionally, the $bitrate_{30}$ is within the deployability bandwidth limit for all setups, except when compression level is 4 and resolution is 75% where the $bitrate_{30}$ is 23.2 MBps.

By reducing the resolution of the PC, the bandwidth requirement is satisfied by the 5G network capacity. However, the producer processing latency, which is higher than the 30 FPS limit, remains a significant performance bottleneck. End-to-end latency is close to the 100 ms limit, dropping to 112 ms in the best case. Overall, the 50% resolution reduction helps in rendering volumetric streaming realistic in 5G networks and may be considered a justified trade-off. Of course, the impact of this quality drop on QoE should also be investigated.

4.4   Multithreaded Encoding

To reduce the processing latency and increase the effective FPS, multi-threaded (de)compression is a promising mechanism. In this section, we experiment with different numbers of compression thread, namely, 2 and 3. For simplicity, we keep decompression single-threaded, since the consumer node is not the latency bottleneck in our setup. The results are depicted in Fig. 6 and Fig. 7 for 2 and 3 compression threads, respectively.

The most evident differences compared to the single-threaded setup are found in the producer metrics. Specifically, compression latency is linearly reduced, dropping by roughly 50% and 66% when 2 and 3 threads are exploited, respectively. This result verifies that multithreading can effectively reduce compression latency and, in turn, increase FPS. However, multithreaded compression penalizes compression efficiency, thus delivering larger PCs. In particular, the PC size is increased by up to 14% and 23% for 2 and 3 threads, respectively, resulting in a bitrate$_{30}$ of 31-38MBps. We hypothesize that the compression of multiple smaller sub-PCs is less effective than compressing a single large PC, since redundant or similar points that span across the PC could be isolated into separate sub-PCs. Altogether, by reducing the processing latency and increasing the PC size, the producer transmission latency has now become the performance bottleneck, requiring 49–60 ms.

Regarding the consumer metrics, the processing latency is not affected, since decompression and rendering remain single-threaded. We assume that equivalent reduction could be achieved through multithreading in the decompression latency, which accounts for roughly 50% of processing latency, that is 25 ms. On the other hand, the transmission latency (or inter-PC time) is significantly reduced, led by the new performance bottleneck, producer transmission latency.

Finally, the shared metrics provide interesting observations in both end-to-end latency and reliability. First, end-to-end latency is reduced by roughly 50% compared to single-threaded performance, verifying that reducing the producer's processing latency can have a significant impact on overall system performance. Second, in the case of compression level 4, the combination of low FPS and increased PC size produces a bitrate of 21.2 MBps that exceeds the available bandwidth. Consequently, severe packets loss is introduced, compromising reliability by roughly 10% and raising end-to-end latency in the order of seconds.

Overall, the use of multithreading in our setup is both a gift and a curse. It significantly reduces the producer processing latency, which is the performance

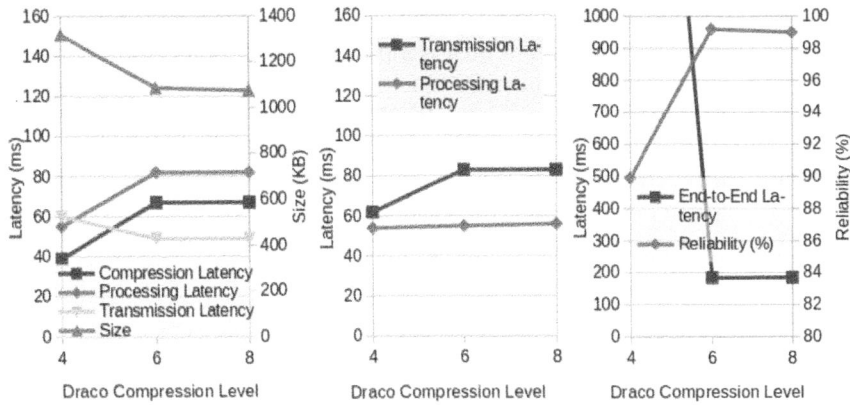

Fig. 6. Producer (left), consumer (center), and shared metrics (right) against Draco compression level (4–8) for 2 compression threads.

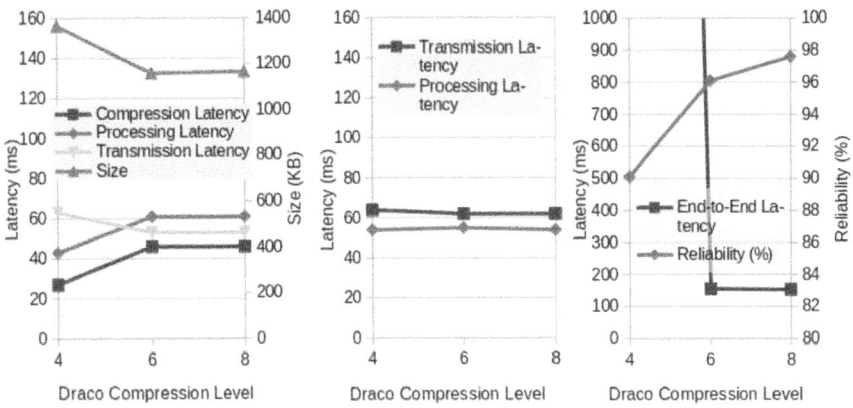

Fig. 7. Producer (left), consumer (center), and shared metrics (right) against Draco compression level (4–8) for 3 compression threads.

and latency bottleneck, but it also increases the PC size, thus requiring more bandwidth resources than what the network can offer.

4.5   Combining Methods

Each of the previous methods present apparent trade-offs that limit their effectiveness. Combining different methods may offer a more balanced solution, hence we experiment with multithreaded encoding using 2 threads, and a 50% resolution reduction. The results are presented in Fig. 8.

The results suggest that performance can be greatly improved by combining multithreaded compression, to reduce processing latency, and resolution reduction, to control the traffic overhead caused by multithreaded compression. Specifically, the setup for compression level 4 is a promising solution towards ultra-low latency volumetric streaming in real 5G networks. The producer and consumer achieve a 30 FPS streaming rate and the 5G network supports the produced 18.7 MBps bitrate (and $bitrate_{30}$). Due to the deployable bitrate, reliability is 97.2% but end-to-end latency is 128 ms, near, yet above, the 100-ms deployability limit. It is worth noticing that, even though decompression is single-threaded, the multithreaded producer is still the performance bottleneck.

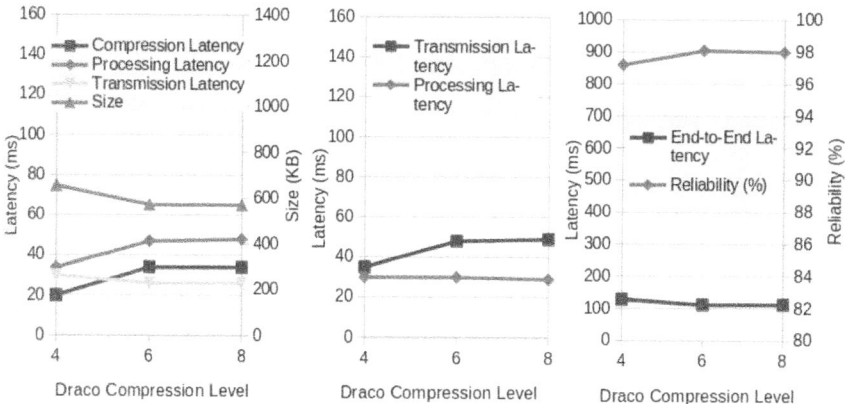

Fig. 8. Producer (left), consumer (center), and shared metrics (right) against Draco compression level (4–8) for 2 compression threads and 50% PC resolution.

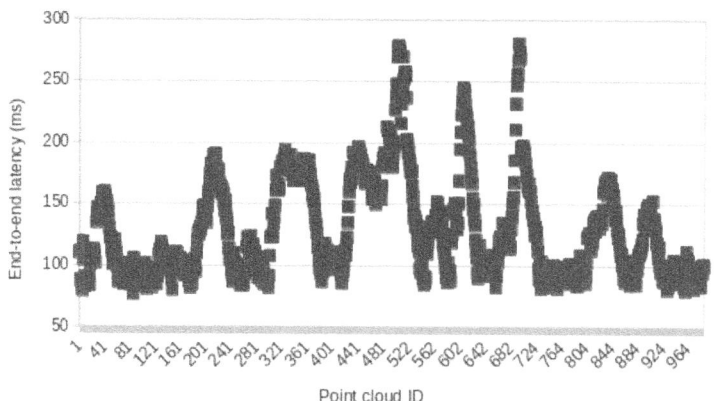

Fig. 9. Variance of end-to-end latency of PCs.

4.6   End-to-End Delay Variance

Finally, we delve deeper in end-to-end delay in order to analyze and identify the key factors contributing to latency exceeding the deployability limit. Figure 9 depicts the end-to-end latency of the 1000 PCs for the setup that combines multi-threaded compression and 50% resolution reduction (Fig. 8). The results suggest that the minimum possible end-to-end latency is roughly 80 ms. This coincides with the lowest individual processing and transmission latency measurements at the producer and consumer, which together sum to 80 ms as well. However, end-to-end latency exhibits significant variance in time (st.dev. is 40 ms), much larger than the variance of producer and consumer processing latency. Thereafter, it can be assumed that the network is not fast enough to steadily deliver low-latency packet tranmissions. The induced bitrate (18.7 MBps) approaches the maximum measured capacity of the 5G network, indicating that the network is operating near its highest theoretical performance.

5   Conclusions

We conducted a performance analysis of PC streaming for real-time applications that require ultra-low latency in a private 5G SA network. Even though we only scratch the surface of a multi-disciplinary topic which touches upon information theory, multimedia, computer graphics and networking, we provide some data points and future research directions for making volumetric streaming practical in 5G networks. In the following, we list the most notable outcomes of our work:

- Decompression performance is not significantly affected by the Draco coder's compression level.
- Assuming symmetric processing capabilities, the producer (encoder) is the performance bottleneck.
- Color is a significant part of the traffic footprint and the processing latency. Combining a color-less PC with inexpensive color compression, such as JPEG, could be a promising solution.
- Reducing PC resolution is effective in reducing communication cost. Techniques that identify and drop the most "insignificant" points within the PC are expected to have a positive impact.
- Multithreading can greatly reduce compression time, but at the cost of inflating the bitrate.
- Scene complexity has a significant impact on performance. If possible, simplifying the scene can a strong effect in reducing bandwidth requirements.
- A combination of the previous methods can make volumetric streaming achieve sub-100 ms latencies in 5G SA networks.
- Unregulated UDP and TCP can lead to underutilization of the 5G resources.

Acknowledgment. The work reported in this paper has been partly funded by the EU through the subgrant Telepresence-Enhanced Network Music Performance (TEN-eMP, SPIRIT OC1) of project SPIRIT (grant agreement No. 101070672). The SPIRIT project has also received funding from the Swiss State Secretariat for Education, Research and Innovation (SERI). The work has also been partly funded by the EU through the cascading action Adaptive Video Delivery for Network Music Performance (AViD-NMP, 6G-XR OC3) of project 6G-XR (grant agreement No. 101096838). The 6G-XR project has received funding from the Smart Networks and Services Joint Undertaking (SNS JU).

References

1. Akhtar, A., et al.: Low latency scalable point cloud communication in VANETs using V2I communication. In: IEEE International Conference on Communications (ICC), pp. 1–7 (2019)
2. Alkhalili, Y., Meuser, T., Steinmetz, R.: A survey of volumetric content streaming approaches. In: IEEE International Conference on Multimedia Big Data (BigMM), pp. 191–199 (2020)
3. Cernigliaro, G., Martos, M., Montagud, M., Ansari, A., Fernandez, S.: PC-MCU: point cloud multipoint control unit for multi-user holoconferencing systems. In: 30th ACM Workshop on Network and Operating Systems Support for Digital Audio and Video, pp. 47–53 (2020)
4. Chen, C., Lu, Z., Xu, Y., Pang, S., Ma, Y.: Research on real-time video transmission in intelligent vehicle outdoor remote driving system based on 5G network. In: International Seminar on Artificial Intelligence, Networking and Information Technology (AINIT), pp. 16–21 (2024)
5. Doumanoglou, A., Drakoulis, P., Zioulis, N., Zarpalas, D., Daras, P.: Benchmarking open-source static 3D mesh codecs for immersive media interactive live streaming. IEEE J. Emerg. Sel. Top. Circ. Syst. $9(1)$, 190–203 (2019)
6. Enenche, P., Kim, D.H., You, D.: On the road to the metaverse: point cloud video streaming: perspectives and enablers. ICT Express $11(1)$, 93–104 (2024)
7. Han, B., Liu, Y., Qian, F.: Vivo: visibility-aware mobile volumetric video streaming. In: 26th Annual International Conference on Mobile Computing and Networking, pp. 1–13 (2020)
8. Konstantoudakis, K., et al.: Serverless streaming for emerging media: towards 5G network-driven cost optimization: a real-time adaptive streaming FaaS service for small-session-oriented immersive media. Multimedia Tools Appl. **81**, 12211–12250 (2022)
9. Lee, K., Yi, J., Lee, Y., Choi, S., Kim, Y.M.: Groot: a real-time streaming system of high-fidelity volumetric videos. In: 26th Annual International Conference on Mobile Computing and Networking, pp. 1–14 (2020)
10. Liu, Z., et al.: Point cloud video streaming: challenges and solutions. IEEE Netw. **35**(5), 202–209 (2021)
11. Palmer, M., Krüger, T., Chandrasekaran, B., Feldmann, A.: The QUIC fix for optimal video streaming. In: Workshop on the Evolution, Performance, and Interoperability of QUIC, pp. 43–49 (2018)
12. Prazeres, J., Pereira, M., Pinheiro, A.: Quality analysis of point cloud coding solutions. Electron. Imag. **34**, 1–6 (2022)
13. Turchet, L., Rinaldi, C., Centofanti, C., Vignati, L., Rottondi, C.: 5G-enabled internet of musical things architectures for remote immersive musical practices. IEEE Open J. Commun. Soc. (2024)

14. Viola, I., Cesar, P.: Volumetric video streaming: current approaches and implementations. In: Immersive Video Technologies, pp. 425–443 (2023)
15. Yang, H., et al.: A 3D-DCT and convolutional FEC approach to agile video streaming. In: IEEE International Conference on Mobile Ad Hoc and Smart Systems (MASS), pp. 636–644 (2022)
16. You, D., Kim, D.H.: Combined inter-layer FEC and hierarchical QAM for stereoscopic 3D video transmission. Wirel. Pers. Commun. **110**(3), 1619–1636 (2020)
17. Zhang, A., Wang, C., Han, B., Qian, F.: YuZu: neural-enhanced volumetric video streaming. In: 19th USENIX Symposium on Networked Systems Design and Implementation (NSDI 22), pp. 137–154 (2022)
18. Zhang, Y., Zhang, J., Huo, Y., Xu, C., El-Hajjar, M., Hanzo, L.: Scalable panoramic wireless video streaming relying on optimal-rate FEC-coded adaptive QAM. IEEE Trans. Veh. Technol. **69**(10), 11206–11219 (2020)
19. Zhong, J., et al.: Low-bitrate volumetric video streaming with depth image. In: SIGCOMM Workshop on Emerging Multimedia Systems, pp. 39–44 (2024)

Evaluating Pose Forecasting
for Compensating Network Latency in Full
Body Movements

Jan Bohnerth[1,2(✉)], Janis Sprenger[1,2], Selvakumar Panneer[3],
Björn Browatzki[4], Anindita Ghosh[1,2], and Philipp Slusallek[1,2]

[1] Deutsches Forschungszentrum für Künstliche Intelligenz GmbH (DFKI),
Trippstadter Str. 122, 67663 Kaiserslautern, Germany
[2] Saarland Informatics Campus, 66123 Saarbrücken, Germany
Jan.Bohnerth@dfki.de
[3] Intel Corporation, Santa Clara, 2200 Mission College Blvd, California, USA
[4] Intel Deutschland GmbH, Am Campeon 10, 85579 Neubiberg, Germany

Abstract. Network latency presents a critical challenge for interactive
multi-user virtual reality (VR) applications, particularly when transmitting the users' full-body motion data to remote collaborators. Such
latency can significantly degrade the quality of interaction, leading to
a less immersive and less effective user experience. Pose forecasting,
which involves predicting future motion sequences based on observed
past motions, offers a potential solution. However, it has not yet been
widely adopted for compensating latency for full-body motion transmission. In this work, we extend and evaluate two state-of-the-art neural network architectures for predicting future animation sequences, enabling
client-side compensation of network latency. To support our methods, we
construct a custom motion capture dataset with VR-specific full-body
movements, along with an animation-specific data encoding that integrates both joint position and rotation data. Our experimental results
show that predictive latency compensation can reduce the positional
error of the reconstructed motion by a factor of up to 2.5 and is robust
to noisy network connections containing jitter and packet loss. Despite
these promising results, we identify several open challenges and outline
directions for future work necessary for successful deployment of predictive compensation in real-world VR systems.

Keywords: Virtual Reality · Latency · Motion Forecasting · Motion
Capture · Animation

1 Introduction

Latency is a primary source for user dissatisfaction in multi-user applications,
such as multiplayer games, virtual teaching, and collaborative tasks in the Metaverse [33]. Due to the inherent limitations of data transmission over networks,

D. Michael-Grigoriou et al. (Eds.): EuroXR 2025, LNCS 16101, pp. 40–61, 2026.
https://doi.org/10.1007/978-3-032-03805-0_3

latency fundamentally increases with increasing physical distance between multiple devices. While regional connections can achieve relatively low-latency values ranging from 3 to 21 ms, intra-European connections typically experience latencies between 15 and 60 ms, and trans-continental connections suffer from delays between 100 and 500 ms [38]. Although emerging technologies such as 5G networks and long-distance satellite constellations will reduce these delays, instantaneous data transmission will remain physically unattainable. Traditional applications compensate latency by reducing the volume of transmitted data, and leveraging mathematical functions to predict the most likely future state of a component before the required data is received. With classical animations, the animation sequences are pre-shared during installation time or the application start, and only low-dimensional information of the high-level user input is used for synchronization during runtime (e.g., velocity, direction, animation time, etc.). This information can be predicted by assuming simple heuristics (e.g., linear interpolation of direction and velocity) [33].

However, with the rise of metaverses and interactive virtual reality (iVR) applications in particular, users do not want to play pre-defined animations, but move the bodies of their avatars themselves, corresponding to their actual movements in reality. In highly interactive applications like collaborative medicine, teaching, or gaming, minimizing the lag between the physically performed motion and the displayed motion on the remote client is crucial to make them work at all. However, transmitting the performance of a real person comes with two major challenges. First, virtual reality headsets operate at 90 to 120 Hz (8 to 11 ms) and thus require a very fast transmission of data. Second, the full-body movement has a higher dimensionality, which can result in 1 MBit/s of data transfer with two users and no data compression (24 joints, three translation and four rotation channels, 90 Hz). Traditional methods of networking, like snapshot synchronization and interpolation [3], deterministic lock-step networking [27], and rollback netcode [3], are suboptimal for the application, as the overhead increases the transmission time beyond the acceptable rate.

Pose forecasting methods can predict future postures based on a past observed sequence of poses. Traditionally, pose forecasting methods have been applied in human-robot collaboration, visual surveillance, and autonomous driving [36]. As such, these methods focus on the prediction of postures relative to the camera (of the robot or autonomous vehicle) and are rarely used for the actual animation of virtual characters in game-like environments [1].

We present investigations into the usage of posture forecasting to compensate for the data transmission lag on the client. Poses of the remote users are annotated with time stamps on the source client, and on the target client. Pose forecasting networks are utilized to predict the most likely future animation sequence of the remote user based on the past received poses. Our main contributions are as follows.

- Adaptation and evaluation of two state-of-the-art pose forecasting architectures for latency compensation using graph convolutions and the discrete cosine transform

- A blending framework to reduce discontinuities upon conflicting predictions
- Integration into the Unreal Engine to allow a direct transfer to actual VR applications
- Simulated network transfer within the Unreal Engine to allow tick-accurate control of the latency parameters and, thus, fine-grained evaluations

Our results suggest that adapting pose forecasting architectures for latency compensation reduces the errors and effects caused by latency. Especially in noisy network scenarios with low base latency but high packet loss, the models significantly reduce the positional error and jerk caused by the lag, jitter, and loss. The evaluation of our blending integration shows that it can reduce the jerk further when combined with the base latency compensation, even though the impact of the blending is limited. Thus, new predictive latency models need to be developed, that focus on further reducing the adverse effects of delayed data transmission.

2   Related Work

2.1   Latency Compensation:

Latency compensation spans over a multitude of different areas. Architectures are already in place for multi-user applications that help minimize latency by how and what data is transferred. Most applications utilize a central game server that maintains authority over the application's state. It uses the incoming client data to update its internal state and then synchronizes the clients based on that new state. Some network architectures, such as deterministic lock-step networking, focus more on fast data exchange.

In deterministic *lock-step networking* [27], instead of sending the state of the game or system, the client will only send the inputs done by the user. This reduces the needed bandwidth tremendously, since it only scales with the size of the input rather than the amount, fidelity, or complexity of game objects or kinematic structures. However, as the server and client need to execute the same commands, the result of a command execution must be deterministic to avoid deviations. Additionally, the server is required to wait for all player inputs before updating the game state. This makes it unfeasible to be used in applications with a lot of players and especially in the context of sending full-body motion data.

In comparison, a *snapshot interpolation* architecture focuses more on accurate synchronization, requiring more bandwidth usage [3]. Every client captures a snapshot of their current state. The server then creates a synchronized simulation based on all the snapshots it has received. To reduce the effects of jitter and packet loss, an interpolation buffer is used to extrapolate information in the case of slightly delayed or dropped snapshots, at the cost of potential inconsistency. Since this method mostly fits our use case, our approach will be partially based on this network architecture.

Specifically in the competitive video game genres requiring minimal latency (e.g. multi-player shooters), a lot of research was conducted to reduce the latency experienced by players [33]. In these applications, reduced latency increases immersion, competitive integrity, and thus, improves the overall user experience [10]. Most work in that specific area focuses on forecasting the player inputs or movements, while simulating the game state on a (dedicated) server [6,19,20,28]. However, the user input in these applications is low-dimensional and high-level control of the player character, like the movement direction and velocity. This process becomes more difficult as more complex data is exchanged between players, such as full-body pose data, which includes joint position and rotation data.

Recently, a novel network architecture (DanceGraph) specifically targeting multi-player dance applications in VR was proposed, which reduces latency by circumventing the game-tick and reducing the number of steps between the perception system (camera) and the remote display system (VR headset) [31]. The framework was extended with a telemetry system to measure end-to-end latency within the DanceGraph framework [18]. Corresponding to their use case, a DCT-based forecasting method for pair dancing was presented, that predicts the joint movements of two characters with a dual-window approach and limited performance [1].

A combination of both latency compensation and motion forecasting is shown in the work of Schwind et al. [30]. They conducted two studies of the effects that motion forecasting and compensating for latency have on users in a VR setting. Their work also simulates a set delay in the application, that is then compensated with a forecasting model. However, it does not include other latency parameters, such as packet loss or jitter, but focuses on the perception of and the impact on the user.

2.2   Motion Forecasting:

The most recent successful approaches to motion forecasting and motion prediction have been utilizing deep neural networks. Especially for challenges using 3D motion capture data, Recurrent Neural Networks (RNNs) are good candidates in the area of predicting motion sequences for short time periods. Building upon this idea, more approaches also started incorporating encoders and decoders to interpret high-dimensional motion data more accurately and efficiently. Fragki-adaki et al. [7] utilized this combination of RNN and the encoder-decoder architecture to create a first model, to predict human poses from videos. To create an architecture that is more robust for real-world applications, Chiu et al. [4] created an action-agnostic RNN model for both short and long-term pose forecasting. They show that even without the utilization of action labels in training and testing, the model is capable of producing similar or better results then models trained in an action labeled context. Similar improvements in accuracy can also be found in models that were trained to forecast human action or future images, while respecting both short and long-term dynamics for spatiotemporal sequences. Both Jain et al. [14] and Wang et al. [37] show, that combining spatiotemporal sequences or graphs, with the capabilities of RNNs, leads further improvements in both action labeled and action agnostic context.

To reduce the loss of information on the original input, Tian et al. [35] built upon the encoder-decoder architecture and combine it with ParallelSRU units, instead of Long Short-Term Memory (LSTM) or Gate Recurrent Unit (GRU) architectures. Their results show, that this can reduce the computational cost while also retaining high-dimensional information in complex tasks such as human behavior prediction.

Besides this, Lin et al. [23] show that using RNNs to only generate initial forecasts, that are then used by a different model, a Convolutional Neural Network (CNN) in this case, can lead to better results. Li et al. [21] show the capabilities of utilizing CNN in combination with an encoder-decoder structure, creating a convolutional encoding module to capture both short and long-term dependencies better than chain structured RNNs. CNNs themselves can also be used in Generative Adversarial Networks (GANs) usually utilized as discriminator for feature extraction [11] or the task of generating motion itself [23].

With the intention of generating more natural looking human motion, Cui et al. [5] incorporated the adversarial learning in their deep generative graph convolution network. Another approach, by Li et al. [22] also shows the advantage of utilizing graph neural networks in combination with RNNs and an encoder-decoder structure to generate more accurate 3D human motion. More recent work has also shown the potential of transformer and diffusion-based models, some of which are able to generate human motion with only minimal input data (e.g. prompt, starting and end frame) [2,15,25,40]. However, while the results of these models are at the state-of-the-art level, there are a multitude of challenges that they are not designed around. The first one is latency and real time application. Especially diffusion models take some time to generate usable results in the area of motion forecasting. This makes it so their time to generate motion sequences exceeds the requirements of predicting in real time (applications where a sequence needs to be generated every 8.33 ms to 16.6 ms). And this is a challenge most approaches did not try to solve in the past.

The work by Guo et al. [9] (siMLPe) is one example that shows state-of-the-art results, while reducing the amount of parameters in the network to about one tenth of what other RNNs and GCNs require. Their approach focuses on creating a light-weight network that utilizes discrete cosine transform, while predicting the residual displacement of the joints with Multi-Layer Perceptrons (MLPs). This allows their model to work in real time while generating accurate human motion sequences and is ideal for our approach.

Compared to this, Sofianos et al. [32] propose a Space-Time-Separable Graph Convolutional Network (STS-GCN). Similar to other work, their model is given encoded body joint coordinates, which are observed for each given input frame. The forecasts of the model are the predicted future values leveraging the space-time representation. Different to other GCNs, their STS-GCN is modeled with three different types of relations within one spatio-temporal encoding GCN. The three types are joint to joint, time to time and joint to time relations. This allows their approach to generate state-of-the-art results for the task of human motion forecasting, on datasets such as Human3.6M [13] and AMASS [26].

2.3   Source of Latency in VR

In VR applications, there are different sources of latency between the performed motion of one user to the generated image in the headset of another user (motion-to-photon latency) [18,31]. We can group the sources of latency with network latency being the most important for this work:

- Motion perception latency: Duration of the perception of the pose of user A on client A
- Network sender latency: Duration of the client A to send the perceived pose to the network
- Network latency: Duration of the data package from the socket of client A to client B
- Network receiver latency: Duration of the client B to receive, decode and incorporate the remote pose
- Display latency: Duration of the client B to visualize the pose of user A to user B.

3   Approach

3.1   Environment Setup

We consider an environment in which multiple clients exchange full-body motion with each other. For our implementation, we assume direct synchronization between clients without a central server. Thus, a source Client A sends data packages (poses of User 1) to the remote Client B, and each data package requires time to reach the remote client. Both clients share a synchronized clock; thus, the latency of each data package is known but not constant, as jitter affects the average latency (lag) and packet loss can occur. While we analyze only a unidirectional setting for simplicity, actual applications usually have a bidirectional setting, in which Client B would send the data of its own User 2 back to Client A in parallel, resulting in delayed information in Client A as well. In Client B, the received poses are sorted in a sequence of actually performed poses (GT Buffer). Based on this buffer containing outdated information, future pose sequences can be predicted with pose forecasting neural networks. The corresponding pose for the current time step is then displayed to User 2. A concept of this architecture is shown in Fig. 1.

For this work, we assume that the motion perception and network sending tasks are performed on a single tick, and thus, their latency is constant. Similarly, the display latency is considered constant with the same tick latency. The network transfer latency depends on the clients' location and physical distance. In addition, jitter can influence the latency and package can get lost.

Motion capture data and, thus, neural networks for motion forecasting operate on a constant update time. While motion data can be captured at 120 fps, the motion forecasting algorithms operate on lower framerates [9,32]. However, motion forecasting does not only predict a single next posture but the most likely

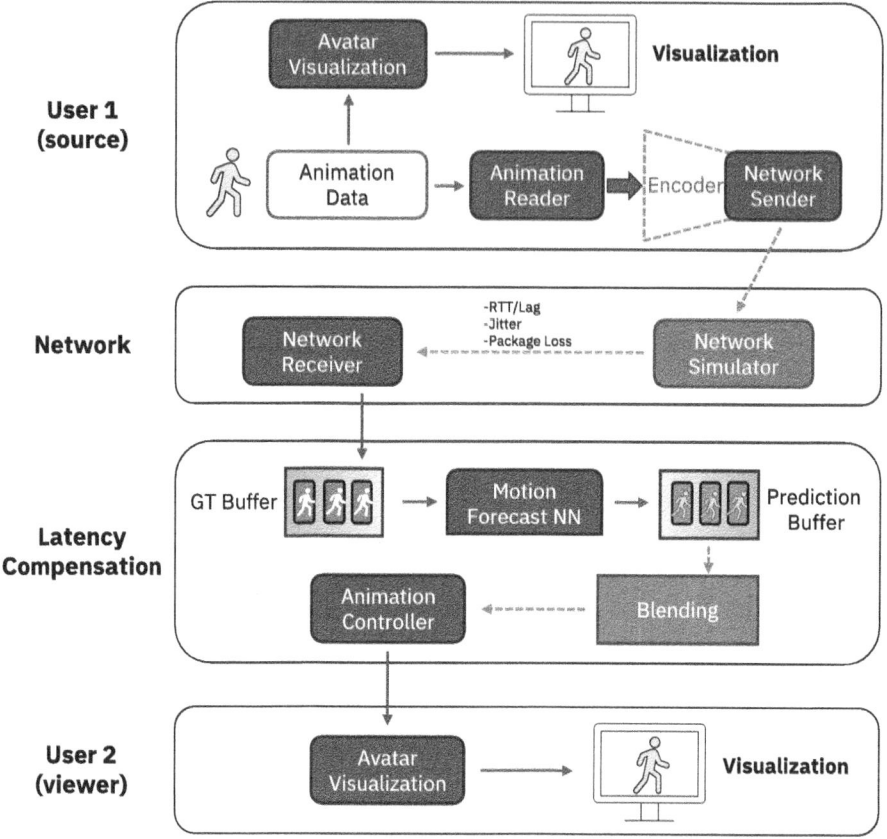

Fig. 1. Conceptual architecture of the environment. From the top: The user movements are recorded, visualized on the ego-headset, and sent to the network interface. An optional network simulator can simulate lag, jitter, and packet loss before the data packages are received. Based on the ground truth (GT) buffer of past poses, possible future poses are predicted with a neural network. After blending with the past state, poses are handed to the animation controller and displayed in the second user's VR headset. Gray arrows denote optional steps that can be skipped.

future sequence of poses. Thus, if the motion forecasting operates at 30 fps, the in-between frames can be interpolated (or subsampled) to smooth the animation to 90 fps, similar to regular keyframe animations.

To enable an accurate comparison of different latency compensation algorithms, we implemented a simulated network transfer within the Unreal Engine. Unlike actual network interfaces or simulated network layers within the operating system, the simulated transfer within the game engine allows for a direct comparison of the displayed motion to the perceived motion on a per-tick basis and, thus, is more accurate.

3.2   Latency Compensation Networks

Forecasting algorithms can predict the most likely sequence of future poses based on a sequence of past poses. Hence, when latency delays the incoming data, the forecasted poses can be used to display the poses of the remote user. Thus, whenever a new pose is received on the client, it can be added to the "Ground Truth Motion Buffer" (GT Buffer), which in turn is used as a basis to perform a prediction that is stored in the "Prediction Motion Buffer" (Prediction Buffer). Each pose is annotated with the timestamp corresponding to the shared clock between both clients. In case of packet loss and missing data, the keyframes are interpolated in the GT Buffer. At each game update, the corresponding frame for the current timestamp is selected: either the last received frame (latency of 0 ms), a predicted frame (e.g., latency of 60 ms), or a subsampled frame (e.g., latency of 55 ms), which is an interpolation of the surrounding keyframes.

Based on this design, pose forecasting methods are required to predict future animation significantly faster than the elapsed time of a single frame. In case of a fixed time step of $33.\overline{3}$ ms, the motion prediction must be executed in less than 30 ms. We selected two state-of-the-art architectures for motion forecasting: Space-Time-Seperable Graph Convolutional Networks (STS-GCN) [32] and siMLPe [9]. To train the approaches, we captured motion data for movements typically performed in virtual reality applications and derived a new motion encoding specific for the visualization of meshed characters in game engines.

3.3   Motion Dataset

For the training of the neural networks, 25 min of motion data was captured containing VR-specific motions using the full-body motion capture system MVN Awinda [29]. The motion capture system uses 17 inertia measurement units (IMUs) that are strapped to the human body to record animations and the corresponding software enables an export to common motion transfer formats (e.g., *.fbx, *.bvh). The recorded motions contain various VR-related actions comprised of short distance locomotion, standing, sitting (ground), sitting (chair), swinging, stretching, reaching and pointing while moving/sitting. Figure 2 shows screenshots of different poses within the dataset. After encoding the training data, the individual sequences were randomly split into 90% training and 10% testing samples. Since all training, testing and initial validation data was recorded by the same subject, this split was done with a time-level strategy. For the validation of latency within Unreal Engine, another 8.3-minute recording containing all actions in a single sequence was conducted. The validation sequence was not utilized during training. Additionally, a cross validation file was recorded after the initial evaluation. This new file was recorded by a different subject and contains "moving while boxing", a motion type different from the ones used in the training and testing.

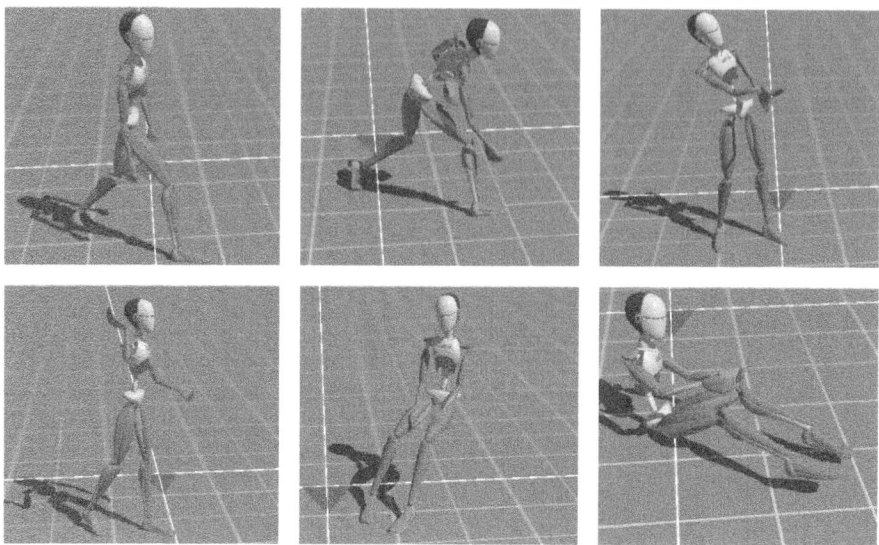

Fig. 2. Motion capture examples from our dataset - Left to right, top to bottom: stretching, reaching, swinging (baseball), throwing, sitting (chair), sitting (ground).

3.4   Motion Encoding

Pose forecasting is usually performed on 3D cartesian joint coordinates or joint-local rotation values. However, recent approaches for interactive character animation [12,34,39] have demonstrated the benefit of combining joint position and joint rotation predictions in a root-local coordinate system. To reduce the computation and implementation effort within the game engine, we propose a simplified neural network input consisting of the global joint transformation matrices (unscaled) in combination with the root-transformation matrix and its inverse for every frame. During inference, the neural network first performs the transformation of the whole animation sequence to a coordinate system local to the last root transformation. Each transformation matrix can be expressed as

$$T = \begin{bmatrix} | & | & | & | \\ \mathbf{b}_1 & \mathbf{b}_2 & \mathbf{b}_3 & \mathbf{p} \\ | & | & | & | \\ 0 & 0 & 0 & 1 \end{bmatrix} \tag{1}$$

and naturally contains redundancy. In particular, $\mathbf{b}_1$, $\mathbf{b}_2$ and $\mathbf{b}_3$ form an orthonormal basis. We leverage this aspect further, by only utilizing the vectors $\mathbf{b}_1$, $\mathbf{b}_2$, and $\mathbf{p}$ and thus encode the information of a single joint with nine floating values.

After the network prediction, we can first recreate the transformation matrices, by normalizing the basis vectors and recomputing the orthonormal basis with

$$\mathbf{b}_3 = \mathbf{b}_1 \times \mathbf{b}_2 \tag{2}$$
$$\mathbf{b}_1 = \mathbf{b}_2 \times \mathbf{b}_3 \tag{3}$$

Afterward, the neural network transforms the root-local prediction back into the global coordinate system and returns the predicted sequence to the game engine. As this process does not contain any trainable parameters, the transformation is performed in a preprocessing step during training. Thus, the users benefit from a simple motion encoding, while the network training benefits from a consistent root-local motion representation and a reduced latent space of nine floating values per joint. We conducted initial tests with joint-local rotations but they failed to provide a smooth reconstruction of the overall global animation and therefore, were not further considered.

3.5 Pose Forecasting Networks

STS-GCN [32] combines a spatio-temporal encoding in a graph convolutional network GCN in combination with temporal convolutions. The adjacency matrix of a single GCN layer is separated into its spatial and temporal component $A^{st} = A^s A^t$ such that a single layer is formulated as follows

$$H^{l+1} = \sigma A^{s-(l)} A^{t-(l)} H^{(l)} W^{(l)} \tag{4}$$

where $A^{s-(l)} \in \mathbb{R}^{C^V \times V}$ is the adjacency matrix of layer l modeling the full joint-joint relations for each time step, $A^{t-(l)} \in \mathbb{R}^{T \times T}$ modeling the time-time relations for each joint, $W^{(l)} \in \mathbb{R}^{C^{(l)} \times C^{(l+1)}}$ are the trainable graph convolutional weights of layer l, σ is the activation function (PReLU), V is the number of observed joints (24) and T the number of frames (30). The network utilizes a total of four GCN layers. A four-layer temporal convolution decoder (TCN) is utilized to estimate the future joint coordinates. Unlike the original implementation of STS-GCN, we added residual connections to the last frame of the input sequence to let the network train the residual displacement rather than the actual joint transforms.

siMLPe [9] uses a discrete cosine transform (DCT) to encode temporal information before applying a multi-layer perceptron model to predict future temporal information. The DCT matrix $D \in \mathbb{R}^{T \times T}$ for a sequence length T is given as:

$$D_{i,j} = \sqrt{\frac{2}{T}} \frac{1}{\sqrt{1 + \delta_{i,0}}} \cos\left(\frac{\pi}{2T}(2j+1)_i\right) \tag{5}$$

where $\delta_{i,j}$ denotes the Kronecker delta

$$\delta_{i,j} = \begin{cases} 1, & \text{if } i = j \\ 0, & \text{if } i \neq j \end{cases} \tag{6}$$

The full network can be described as

$$x_{t+1:t+n} = (D^{-1}S^{-1})F(SD(x_{1:t}))) \tag{7}$$

where D and D^{-1} are the DCT and inverse DCT (iDCT) and S and S^{-1} are spatial encoders using a single fully connected layer over the spatial domain defined w.l.g. as

$$S = z_0 W_0 + b_0 \tag{8}$$

with z_0 being the output of the DCT, $W_0 \in \mathbb{R}^{C \times C}$ and $b_0 \in \mathbb{R}^C$ the learnable parameters and C the dimensionality of a single pose information in linearized form. The core part of the network F consists of $m = 42$ fully connected layers operating across the temporal domain defined as

$$z_i = z_{i-1} + LN(W_i z_{i-i} + b_i) \tag{9}$$

where z_i is the output of the previous layer, $W_i \in \mathbb{R}^{T \times T}$ and $b_0 \in \mathbb{R}^T$ are the learnable parameters of the layer, and LN denotes a layer normalization operation. Unlike the original implementation, our implementation computes the DCT and iDCT directly in the PyTorch model, thus can be exported to ONNX and computed using the corresponding acceleration frameworks in any game engine.

3.6 Training Parameters

Both networks are trained for 310 epochs on the same motion data using a batch size of 256 using stochastic gradient descent (ADAM algorithm [17]) with a weight decay of 1e-4. The learning rate is adjusted using cosine annealing with warm restarts [24] reducing the learning rate to 5e-8 over an initial duration of 10 epochs, which is doubled after every restart. The training data is randomly selected into 90% training and 10% testing data (consistent for both models).

Both models are trained with the same loss function, which is composed of different features. All losses are computed in the root-local space during training. Deviation of the predicted joint positions is penalized with the mean per joint position error (MPJPE) calculating the average L2-norm across different joints. The prediction of the two basis vectors of the joint rotation matrix is penalized mean per joint angle (MPJR) between the ground-truth and predicted basis vectors. A deviation of a unit length (1) of the basis vectors is penalized using the L2-norm (UNIT) and a deviation from the orthogonality between both basis vectors is penalized by computing the squared dot product (ORTH). The total loss is computed as follows. The MPJR is scaled by a factor of 10, to boost the quality of the final reconstruction. Similar factors for UNIT and ORTH were not necessary.

$$\text{Loss} = \text{MPJPE} + \text{UNIT} + \text{ORTH} + 10 \times \text{MPJR} \tag{10}$$

While Guo et al. [9] report significant differences between siMLPe and STS-GCN, we observed a very similar training loss between both methods, once trained with the same optimizer and learning rate scheduler settings (see Fig. 3).

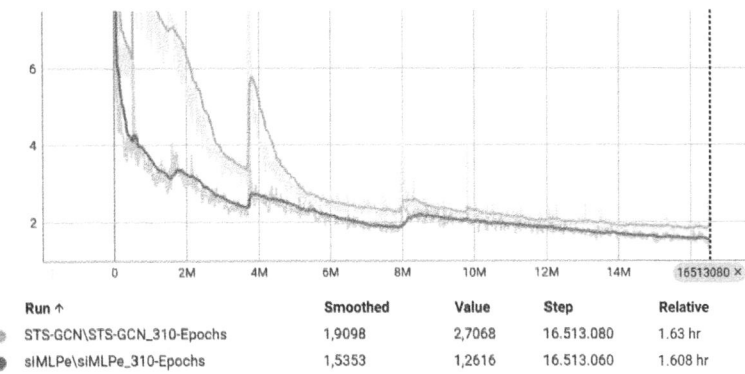

Run ↑	Smoothed	Value	Step	Relative
◉ STS-GCN\STS-GCN_310-Epochs	1,9098	2,7068	16.513.080	1.63 hr
● siMLPe\siMLPe_310-Epochs	1,5353	1,2616	16.513.060	1.608 hr

Fig. 3. Development of the training loss for both models overall training iterations. The bold graphs are smoothed with a factor of 0.93.

3.7   Post-processing with Motion Blending

To reduce the aforementioned effects of jitter and jerk in the visualization, the additional option for motion blending is used. Whenever a new prediction is performed, the old and new prediction are linearly blended to reduce sudden jumps between individual frames. Every predicted frame, that would have a timestamp smaller than the current displayed frame will be overwritten by the previous prediction, while every frame beyond the current one will be blended from the old predictions to the new ones. The main effect of this blending is to smooth out the motion that is visualized, causing a reduction in jitter and jerk. The effect of additional motion blending is evaluated separately.

4   Evaluation

4.1   Prediction Performance

Both neural networks were trained on an NVIDIA RTX 3080 (Desktop) GPU for around 1.6 h. The predictive performance of the individual networks was tested on the testing set of our training data. Until a prediction horizon of 366 ms, STS-GCN performs more accurate predictions w.r.t. the MPJPE. Overall, siMLPe produces the most accurate predictions. Table 1 shows an excerpt of the prediction errors and Fig. 4 the average prediction error for all time steps.

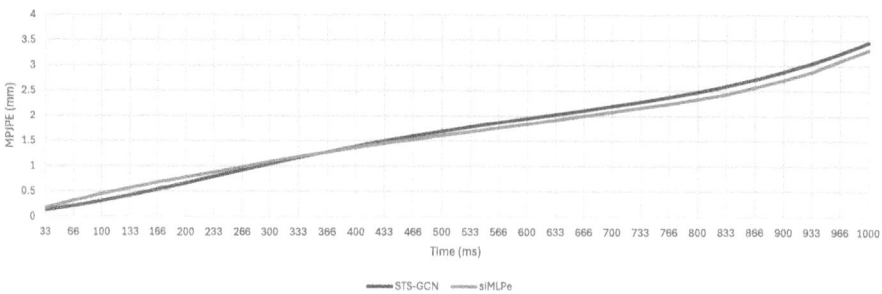

Fig. 4. Prediction error measured as the MPJPE (in mm) for all time steps (ms). Lower is better.

Table 1. Prediction results on our testing dataset for a subset of different prediction time steps (ms). We report the MPJPE in *mm*. Lower is better.

Time (ms)	33	66	200	367	433	600	766	900	1000	Mean
STS-GCN [32]	**0.13**	**0.21**	**0.66**	1.28	1.5	1.95	2.38	2.88	3.47	1.69
siMLPe [9]	0.18	0.32	0.78	**1.28**	**1.45**	**1.84**	**2.25**	**2.72**	**3.32**	**1.65**

4.2   Latency Compensation Performance

Both neural networks were integrated into Unreal Engine 5 using ONNX and Unreal's Neural Network Engine (NNE) running the network on the CPU. The latency compensation performance was evaluated with a motion capture sequence containing various VR-related movements with a duration of 8.3 min that was not used during training. The median prediction time of a future animation sequence (one second of motion) is 3.377 ms for STS-GCn and 2.953 ms for siMLPe. The evaluation was performed with an Intel Core i9-14900HX (Mobile). The reconstruction performance was evaluated under different combinations of network settings. Each combination has a **transmission lag** between 0 and 600ms in 60ms steps, a **jitter** of either 0ms or 60ms and a **packet loss** of 0%, 20% or 40%. For each of them, the aforementioned evaluation file of 8.3 min was utilized to evaluate the models. For each frame, the MPJPE of the generated frame by the latency compensation is computed with respect to the pose of the animation source (without latency). In addition, a no-latency-compensation model is utilized as a baseline, which displays only the last received posture without any predictive or interpolative capability. To evaluate the smoothness of the displayed animation, the mean squared jerk or average third derivative (acceleration) of joint movements is measured.

Using pose forecasting methods compared to no forecasting methods improves the MPJPE on average by a factor of 2.2 (STS-GCN) and 2.5 (siMLPe), calculated from all combinations of lag, jitter and packet loss. Figure 5 displays the average prediction error for the different lags for scenarios without packet loss or jitter. The MPJPE of the forecasting methods is below 2 mm during the first 180 ms for these scenarios. The effects of jitter and packet loss on position error were marginal when using latency compensation approaches. In the case of a 40% change of packet loss and jitter up to 60 ms, the MPJPE increased by 0.58 (STS-GCN) and 0.72 (siMLPe), respectively. As shown in Fig. 6, this error was evenly distributed over all lag durations.

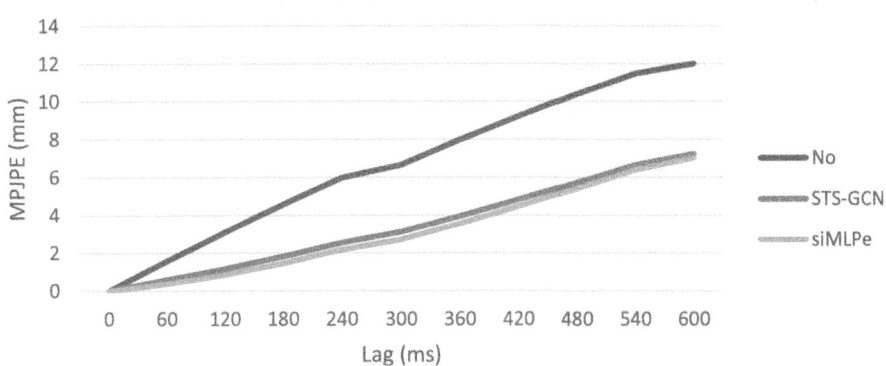

Fig. 5. Compensation error measured as the MPJPE (mm) in the different lag settings for both latency compensation methods and the baseline (no latency compensation). Both packet loss and jitter are 0 for these values. Lower is better.

Although the predicted motion is mostly smooth when the signal is delayed moderately (up to 180 ms), sudden jumps due to higher mispredictions and corrections of mispredictions are more common on a higher delay. While motion blending could improve the performance (mean squared jerk) for STS-GCN under the jitter condition (see Fig. 7), there was no meaningful improvement under any other condition or with the siMLPe approach. While the mean squared jerk under stable network conditions is significantly better when no latency compensation is performed, as the motion is only displayed delayed, the benefit of predictive latency compensation methods becomes apparent under noisy network conditions (see Fig. 8). In case of a mean lag below 180 ms, both latency compensation methods significantly outperform no latency compensation in both accuracy and jerk.

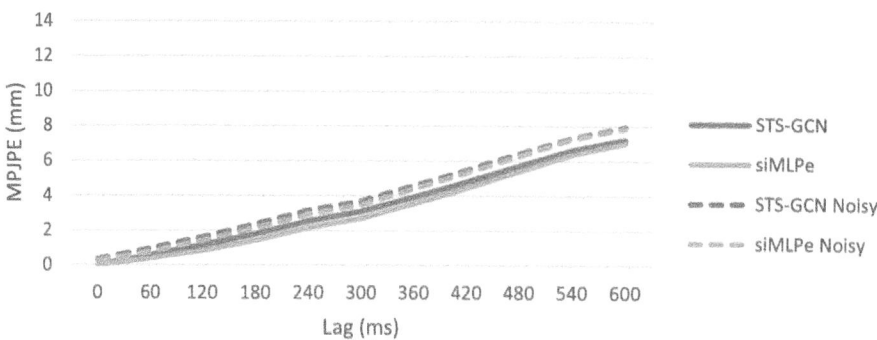

Fig. 6. Compensation error measured as the MPJPE (mm) in the different lag settings for both latency compensation methods with a noisy network connection (40% packet loss, 60 ms jitter) and with a stable connection. Lower is better.

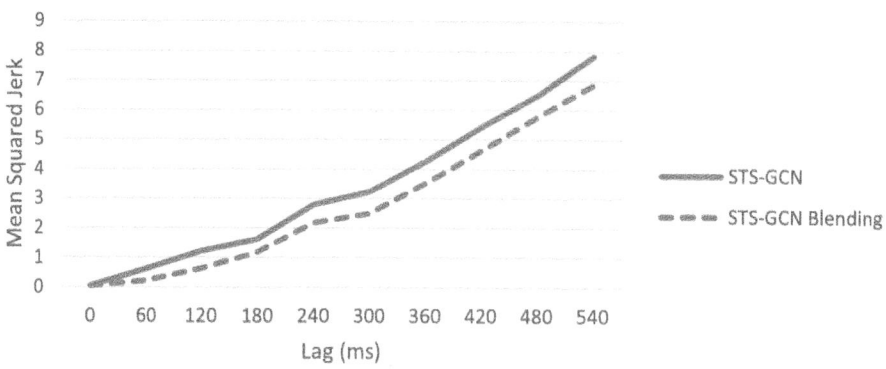

Fig. 7. Mean squared jerk for the STS-GCN and STS-GCN using blending with a noisy network connection (60 ms jitter). The mean squared jerk of the source animation is 0.05. Lower is better.

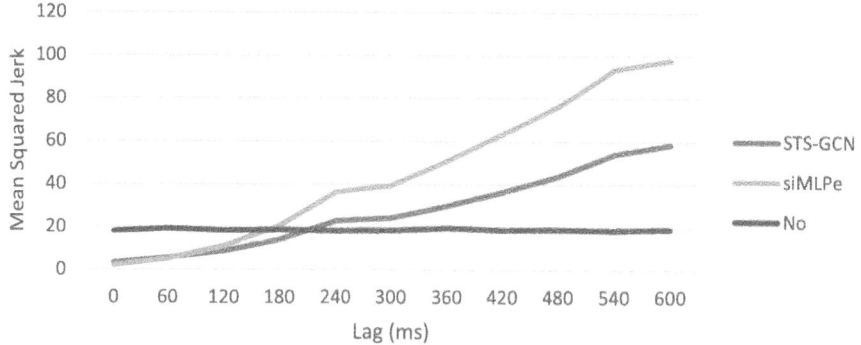

Fig. 8. Mean squared jerk for both latency compensation methods and the baseline (no latency compensation) with a noisy network connection (40% packet loss, 60 ms jitter). Lower is better.

4.3   Subjective Evaluation

Already at 33 ms lag, the delay becomes noticeable when no latency compensation is utilized, especially for fast movements. While latency compensation with the siMLPe model appears more accurate and fluent on lower lag rates (33 - 133 ms), latency compensation with STS-GCN appears better on medium range lag rates (133 - 267 ms). The visual quality of both models degrades with larger lag rates (above 333 ms). This includes network conditions with noisy transmissions (jitter, packet loss). Figure 9 displays frames from two sample sequences in a low lag rate with jitter and packet loss and shows a comparison between the two methods and no compensation. The strong mismatches highlighted in the first row are drastically reduced by STS-GCN and siMLPe, shown in the second and third row.

Particularly under noisy transmission conditions, both latency compensation approaches outperform no latency compensation. When packages are lost, the

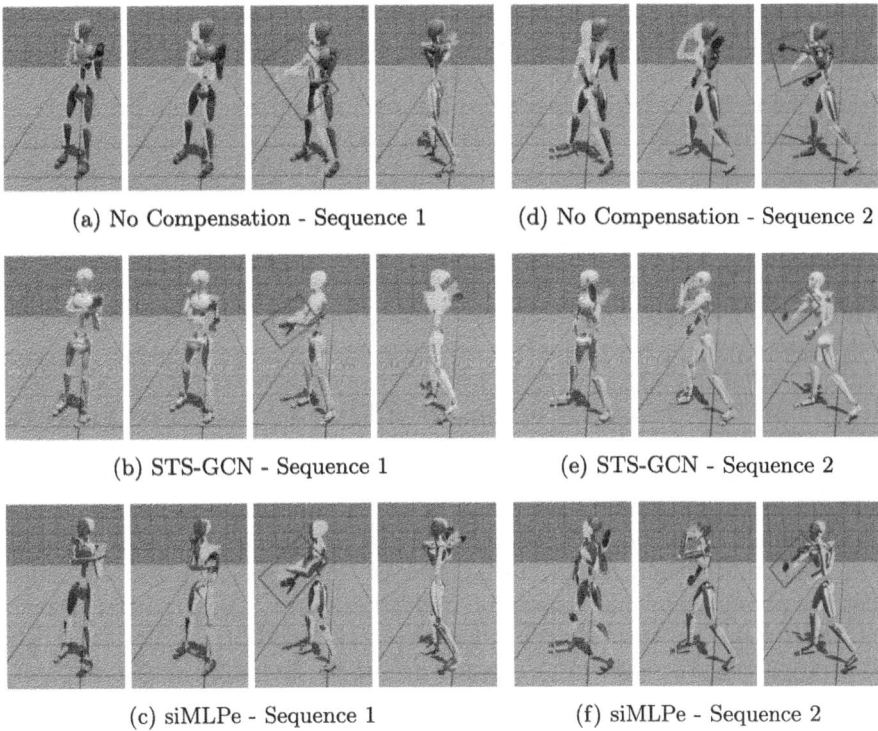

   (a) No Compensation - Sequence 1   (d) No Compensation - Sequence 2

       (b) STS-GCN - Sequence 1   (e) STS-GCN - Sequence 2

       (c) siMLPe - Sequence 1   (f) siMLPe - Sequence 2

Fig. 9. Individual frames of two exemplary sequences for No latency compensation, and latency compensation with STS-GCN and siMLPe rendered on top of the ground-truth pose (without latency, transparent). The network was configured with a smaller lag of 120 ms, up to 60 ms jitter, and 20% packet loss. For every method (row), a red rectangle highlights the most apparent differences, which can be seen for the third frame of each sequence. (Color figure online)

animation appears jerky and missing movements without a latency compensation up to the point where the semantics of the motion are not understandable anymore. While MPJPE and mean jerk indicate, that both models significantly improve the accuracy and smoothness, there is still a notable jitter present. Specifically for lower lag rates, this jitter can be higher than no latency compensation for certain fast motion types (e.g. swinging). This is most apparent in the STS-GCN model, which introduces a very apparent jitter. The siMLPe model generates more smooth and natural motion in comparison. Because of this, there is an argument to be made, to evaluate the models on additional metrics besides MPJPE and jerk, to get a better representation.

Additionally, a cross validation file was recorded by a different subject, to compare against the aforementioned evaluation. It contains "moving while boxing", a motion type different from the ones used in training, testing and evaluating. The result of this comparison was, that the models performed worse in this cross validation, compared to the previous evaluation. While the siMLPe model was able to yield slightly better accuracy than the baseline (no latency compensation), the STS-GCN performed worse. Both models also showed a significantly higher jerk in the cross validation. While the measured jerk of our siMLPe model indicated a better performance over the whole validation file, there were multiple instances where its outputs seemed less smooth and less natural than the no latency compensation.

5   Discussion and Outlook

In this work, we adapted and evaluated two state-of-the-art pose forecasting architectures to address the challenge of network latency in transmitting full-body motion data. To facilitate this, we developed a controlled simulation environment within Unreal Engine to accurately simulate network transfer with complete control over the latency parameters of lag, jitter, and packet loss. Both aforementioned architectures were used to create latency compensation models. We decided to capture 25 mins of VR-specific motion data, which was utilized to create training and testing data. To improve the prediction results and reduce the inference time, we adjusted the motion encoding used by the neural networks to an animation friendly format. As a result the global transform data of a single joint is represented by nine instead of 16 floating values. Due to the reconstruction process of the transformation matrices, this encoding will not cause any information loss. We also saw that transforming the global transformation data into a root-local space and using residual connections yield better prediction results. By computing the root-local transformation within the network graph, the usability within the game engine and the computation time during inference was reduced.

To ensure accurate evaluation results, we captured a separate 9.5 mins of motion capture data, which included a validation set of all the important, previously determined VR motion types and a cross validation file only containing motion data not previously seen by the models.

Our results demonstrate, that the created latency compensation models can reduce the effects of lag, jitter and packet loss in real time. To measure this, we created a scene in Unreal Engine, that incorporated all different latency compensation methods, as well as no latency compensation. The extracted data, comprised of positional difference to the source transform data, was then used to calculate mean per joint positional error (MPJPE) and mean squared jerk. These measurements were done for a multitude of combinations on lag, jitter and packet loss. Specifically, in the cases of low to medium base lag (below 333 ms), the latency compensation shows robustness towards high noise, caused by jitter and packet loss. With higher lag, the MPJPE will still be a lot lower compared to the no latency, but at the cost of causing an increase in mean squared jerk, possibly due to jumps between predicted frames.

To reduce the measured jerk, we also incorporated a blending method, with the goal of reducing potential jumps between frames. The blending was realized, with our implementation of utilizing a buffer for the sequence of predictions. This allowed us to linearly blend from the previous prediction sequence to the new prediction values. The impact of this blending approach on the reduction of the jerk was limited, but proves to be promising. This should also lead to a reduction in the jitter and unnatural appearance of the generated motion from the models. To further evaluate this in the future, additional metrics will be included and the model training will be adjusted as well.

5.1   Future Work

Our results suggest, that the compensation of short and consistent lag is feasible with existing methods. However, the smoothness of the predicted animation and a smooth recovery from mispredictions are the most detrimental factors for further adoption in actual applications. Future models are required to combine the ability for plausible and smooth animations [8] with the prediction of future time series. In particular, the usage of input data masking during training to simulate missing or auto-regressively generated past frames, as well as an integration of the previous future prediction seems a promising direction to maintain temporal consistency and reduce the requirements for further blending.

While our models were able to learn from the position and rotation matrices that we chose, a continuous representation could improve the training and overall results of the models, as shown by Zhou et al. [41]. Since our initial results indicated that joint-local representations can cause more propagating errors and were less suitable for reconstructing a global animation, we will conduct more tests on this in the future.

Pose-forecasting itself has excellent benchmarks using the datasets Human 3.6 m [13] or AMASS [26]. However, we realized neither the dataset nor the evaluation paradigms are ideal to evaluate the performance for latency compensation or latency affected evaluation. Although our approaches yield excellent MPJPE results, having a smooth and coherent motion sequence and avoiding unrealistic jerks are critical to achieve a plausible visualization in a VR game. Koniaris et al. [18] have already shown some of the requirements for benchmarks and telemetry. However, we think that a simplified version, that neural network researchers can use with ease is required to allow the efficient development and fair comparison of future models.

Another important aspect of multi-client VR applications is bandwidth usage. The amount of data transferred can lead to major restrictions. Especially in applications with more than 50 players, as our current implementation would require over 10 mbit/s (up and downstream) to synchronize the animations with all other clients. Therefore, future work should incorporate data compression before sending the data. A distributed neural network approach, in which an encoder reduces the dimensionality before sending and a decoder, which forecasts the future animation sequence directly based on the latent code could reduce bandwidth, while requiring minimal computational overhead. In addition, using temporal relations by encoding not single temporal poses but utilizing tokenization, including spatio-temporal information [16].

Lastly, to gather information on the impact of these approaches as well as the perception of the users, we aim to create multiple user studies in the future. While the initial one will focus on gathering input on video results and giving the user an option to rate quality (smoothness) and accuracy, a more thorough user study will be conducted in VR further into the project.

Acknowledgements. This work has been funded by the German State of Saarland and Intel in the IntelSaar-Animations, Future of Graphics and Media: Avatar Latency Compensation project (GRA 5032 - 05039).

References

1. Ademola, A., Sinclair, D., Koniaris, B., Hannah, S., Mitchell, K.: DeFT-Net: dual-window extended frequency transformer for rhythmic motion prediction. In: Hunter, D., Slingsby, A. (eds.) Computer Graphics and Visual Computing (CGVC). The Eurographics Association (2024). https://doi.org/10.2312/cgvc.20241220

2. Bringer, L., Wilson, J., Barton, K., Ghaffari, M.: MDMP: multi-modal diffusion for supervised motion predictions with uncertainty. arXiv preprint arXiv:2410.03860 (2024)

3. Bryant, B., Saiedian, H.: An evaluation of videogame network architecture performance and security. Comput. Netw. **192**, 108128 (2021). https://doi.org/10.1016/j.comnet.2021.108128

4. Chiu, H.k., Adeli, E., Wang, B., Huang, D.A., Niebles, J.C.: Action-agnostic human pose forecasting. In: 2019 IEEE Winter Conference on Applications of Computer Vision (WACV), pp. 1423–1432. IEEE (2019). https://doi.org/10.1109/WACV.2019.00156

5. Cui, Q., Sun, H., Yang, F.: Learning dynamic relationships for 3D human motion prediction. In: Proceedings of the IEEE/CVF Conference on Computer Vision and Pattern Recognition, pp. 6519–6527 (2020)

6. Duarte, E.P., Jr., Pozo, A.T., Beltrani, P.: Smart reckoning: reducing the traffic of online multiplayer games using machine learning for movement prediction.

Entertainment Comput. **33**, 100336 (2020). https://doi.org/10.1016/j.entcom.2019.100336

7. Fragkiadaki, K., Levine, S., Felsen, P., Malik, J.: Recurrent network models for human dynamics. In: 2015 IEEE International Conference on Computer Vision (ICCV), pp. 4346–4354 (2015). https://doi.org/10.1109/ICCV.2015.494

8. Ghosh, A., Dabral, R., Golyanik, V., Theobalt, C., Slusallek, P.: ReMoS: 3D motion-conditioned reaction synthesis for two-person interactions. In: Leonardis, A., Ricci, E., Roth, S., Russakovsky, O., Sattler, T., Varol, G. (eds.) Computer Vision - Eccv 2024, pp. 418–437. Springer, Cham (2025)

9. Guo, W., Du, Y., Shen, X., Lepetit, V., Alameda-Pineda, X., Moreno-Noguer, F.: Back to MLP: a simple baseline for human motion prediction. In: Proceedings of the IEEE/CVF Winter Conference on Applications of Computer Vision, pp. 4809–4819 (2023)

10. Halbhuber, D., Schlenczek, M., Bogon, J., Henze, N.: Better be quiet about it! The effects of phantom latency on experienced first-person shooter players. In: Proceedings of the 21st International Conference on Mobile and Ubiquitous Multimedia, pp. 172–181 (2022). https://doi.org/10.1145/3568444.3568448

11. Hernandez, A., Gall, J., Moreno-Noguer, F.: Human motion prediction via spatio-temporal inpainting. In: Proceedings of the IEEE/CVF International Conference on Computer Vision, pp. 7134–7143 (2019)

12. Holden, D., Komura, T., Saito, J.: Phase-functioned neural networks for character control. ACM Trans. Graph. **36**(4) (2017). https://doi.org/10.1145/3072959.3073663

13. Ionescu, C., Papava, D., Olaru, V., Sminchisescu, C.: Human3.6M: large scale datasets and predictive methods for 3D human sensing in natural environments. IEEE Trans. Pattern Anal. Mach. Intell. **36**(7), 1325–1339 (2014). https://doi.org/10.1109/TPAMI.2013.248

14. Jain, A., Zamir, A.R., Savarese, S., Saxena, A.: Structural-RNN: deep learning on spatio-temporal graphs. In: Proceedings of the IEEE Conference on Computer Vision and Pattern Recognition, pp. 5308–5317 (2016)

15. Jiang, B., Chen, X., Liu, W., Yu, J., Yu, G., Chen, T.: MotionGPT: human motion as a foreign language. Adv. Neural. Inf. Process. Syst. **36**, 20067–20079 (2023)

16. Jiang, B., Chen, X., Liu, W., Yu, J., Yu, G., Chen, T.: MotionGPT: human motion as a foreign language. Adv. Neural Inf. Process. Syst. **36** (2024)

17. Kingma, D.P., Ba, J.: Adam: a method for stochastic optimization. arXiv preprint arXiv:1412.6980 (2017)

18. Koniaris, B., Sinclair, D., Mitchell, K.: Dancemark: an open telemetry framework for latency-sensitive real-time networked immersive experiences. In: 2024 IEEE Conference on Virtual Reality and 3D User Interfaces Abstracts and Workshops (VRW), pp. 462–463 (2024). https://doi.org/10.1109/VRW62533.2024.00091

19. Lee, S.W., Chang, R.K.: On shot around a corner in first-person shooter games. In: 2017 15th Annual Workshop on Network and Systems Support for Games (NetGames), pp. 1–6. IEEE (2017). https://doi.org/10.1109/NetGames.2017.7991545

20. Lee, S.W., Chang, R.K.: Enhancing the experience of multiplayer shooter games via advanced lag compensation. In: Proceedings of the 9th ACM Multimedia Systems Conference, pp. 284–293 (2018). https://doi.org/10.1145/3204949.3204971

21. Li, C., Zhang, Z., Lee, W.S., Lee, G.H.: Convolutional sequence to sequence model for human dynamics. In: Proceedings of the IEEE Conference on Computer Vision and Pattern Recognition, pp. 5226–5234 (2018)

22. Li, M., Chen, S., Zhao, Y., Zhang, Y., Wang, Y., Tian, Q.: Dynamic multiscale graph neural networks for 3D skeleton based human motion prediction. In: Proceedings of the IEEE/CVF Conference on Computer Vision and Pattern Recognition, pp. 214–223 (2020)

23. Lin, X., Amer, M.R.: Human motion modeling using DVGANs. arXiv preprint arXiv:1804.10652 (2018)

24. Loshchilov, I., Hutter, F.: SGDR: stochastic gradient descent with warm restarts. arXiv preprint arXiv:1608.03983 (2017)

25. Lucas, T., Baradel, F., Weinzaepfel, P., Rogez, G.: PoseGPT: quantization-based 3D human motion generation and forecasting. In: European Conference on Computer Vision, pp. 417–435. Springer (2022). https://doi.org/10.1007/978-3-031-20068-7_24

26. Mahmood, N., Ghorbani, N., Troje, N.F., Pons-Moll, G., Black, M.: Amass: archive of motion capture as surface shapes. In: 2019 IEEE/CVF International Conference on Computer Vision (ICCV), pp. 5441–5450 (2019). https://doi.org/10.1109/ICCV.2019.00554

27. Mieschke, P.: Deterministic lockstep in networked games (2024)

28. Motoo, T., Kawasaki, J., Fujihashi, T., Saruwatari, S., Watanabe, T.: Client-side network delay compensation for online shooting games. IEEE Access 9, 125678–125690 (2021). https://doi.org/10.1109/ACCESS.2021.3111180

29. Movella: Xsens MVN Awinda (2025). https://www.movella.com/products/motion-capture/xsens-mvn-awinda

30. Schwind, V., et al.: The effects of full-body avatar movement predictions in virtual reality using neural networks. In: Proceedings of the 26th ACM Symposium on Virtual Reality Software and Technology, pp. 1–11 (2020). https://doi.org/10.1145/3385956.3418941

31. Sinclair, D., Ademola, A.V., Koniaris, B., Mitchell, K.: DanceGraph: a complementary architecture for synchronous dancing online. In: Proceedings of the 36th International Conference on Computer Animation and Social Agents (CASA), presented at CASA 2023. Limassol, Cyprus (2023)

32. Sofianos, T., Sampieri, A., Franco, L., Galasso, F.: Space-time-separable graph convolutional network for pose forecasting. In: Proceedings of the IEEE/CVF International Conference on Computer Vision (ICCV), pp. 11209–11218 (2021)

33. Soorya, V., Bhat, S.S., Shaik, S., Rajagopal, S.M., Bhaskaran, S.: Advanced latency compensation techniques for seamless online gaming experiences. In: 2024 IEEE 9th International Conference for Convergence in Technology (I2CT), pp. 1–7 (2024). https://doi.org/10.1109/I2CT61223.2024.10543857

34. Starke, S., Zhao, Y., Zinno, F., Komura, T.: Neural animation layering for synthesizing martial arts movements. ACM Trans. Graph. 40(4) (2021). https://doi.org/10.1145/3450626.3459881

35. Tian, W., Luo, F., Shen, K.: PSRUNet: a recurrent neural network for spatiotemporal sequence forecasting based on parallel simple recurrent unit. Mach. Vis. Appl. 35(3), 1–15 (2024)

36. Toyer, S., Cherian, A., Han, T., Gould, S.: Human pose forecasting via deep Markov models. In: 2017 International Conference on Digital Image Computing: Techniques and Applications (DICTA), pp. 1–8 (2017). https://doi.org/10.1109/DICTA.2017.8227441

37. Wang, Y., et al.: PredRNN: a recurrent neural network for spatiotemporal predictive learning. IEEE Trans. Pattern Anal. Mach. Intell. 45(2), 2208–2225 (2022). https://doi.org/10.1109/TPAMI.2022.3165153

38. WonderNetwork: Global ping statistics (2025). https://wondernetwork.com/pings
39. Zhang, H., Starke, S., Komura, T., Saito, J.: Mode-adaptive neural networks for quadruped motion control. ACM Trans. Graph. **37**(4) (2018). https://doi.org/10.1145/3197517.3201366
40. Zhang, M., et al.: MotionDiffuse: text-driven human motion generation with diffusion model. arXiv preprint arXiv:2208.15001 (2022)
41. Zhou, Y., Barnes, C., Lu, J., Yang, J., Li, H.: On the continuity of rotation representations in neural networks. In: Proceedings of the IEEE/CVF Conference on Computer Vision and Pattern Recognition, pp. 5745–5753 (2019). https://doi.org/10.1109/CVPR.2019.00589

Exploring the Virtualization of Real-World Objects Through Spatial Augmented Reality

Toshiyuki Amano$^{(\boxtimes)}$ and Eiki Kawashima

Graduate School of Systems Engineering, Wakayama University, Wakayama, Japan
amano@wakayama-u.ac.jp

Abstract. This paper investigates the problem of appearance-based virtualization of physical objects in spatial augmented reality, where projected imagery should simultaneously preserve object recognizability, integrate artistic style, and maintain color harmony with a virtual background. We implemented two baseline methods—*Average Color, Texture Overlay*—and a transformer-based style transfer approach ($StyTr^2$) and conducted a user study evaluating them across three perceptual criteria: contour clarity (Q1), painterly touch integration (Q2), and color harmony (Q3). The results show that while *Average Color* excels at contour preservation, and *Texture Overlay* is superior for stylistic and chromatic integration, only $StyTr^2$ achieves a perceptual balance across all criteria. Quantitative analysis confirms that $StyTr^2$ yields the most stable performance with the lowest overall variance. Notably, it received particularly high ratings for painterly touch in scenarios featuring fine-grained texture, such as pointillist styles, suggesting its effectiveness in reproducing style-specific surface qualities.

Keywords: Spatial Augmented Reality · Appearance Manipulation · Style Transfer · Object Virtualization

1 Introduction

The concept of the Metaverse has evolved from speculative fiction to an increasingly tangible technological paradigm. While immersive virtual environments provide significant opportunities for creativity and social interaction, they also raise concerns regarding user detachment from the physical world. As noted by John Hanke, CEO of Niantic, dystopian visions of the metaverse where people are fully immersed in artificial realities, isolated from their physical environments, are not only undesirable, but potentially harmful [1].

In response to such concerns, the notion of a Real-World Metaverse has gained traction. This paradigm emphasizes the seamless integration of virtual content with the physical environment, aiming to enhance rather than replace real-world experiences. In this vision, the physical and digital objects are interconnected, allowing users to engage with both simultaneously, thereby enriching their interactions with the world around them.

To realize this Real-World Metaverse, it is not enough to simply augment physical objects with virtual content. It is essential to virtualize the physical

© The Author(s), under exclusive license to Springer Nature Switzerland AG 2026
D. Michael-Grigoriou et al. (Eds.): EuroXR 2025, LNCS 16101, pp. 62–78, 2026.
https://doi.org/10.1007/978-3-032-03805-0_4

objects themselves. By "virtualization of real-world objects," we refer to the perceptual transformation of physical entities, making them appear as though they belong to a virtual or non-physical domain. Unlike conventional augmentation, which overlays virtual information onto objects while maintaining their original materiality, virtualization shifts the perceived identity of an object—its texture, material, or visual form—toward that of a digital entity. This enables physical objects to function as an integrated virtual experience without losing their physical presence. In this paper, we define *object virtualization* as the perceptual transformation of a real-world object's appearance to visually harmonize it with a stylized virtual environment, achieved through spatial augmented reality.

In this study, we define the process of virtualization within the context of Spatial Augmented Reality (SAR) [2]. Specifically, when a real-world object is projected upon by a SAR system, it should exhibit the following characteristics:

- The real-world object retains its physical presence and remains visible.
- The textures and details of the virtual space are seamlessly reproduced onto the physical object.
- The color palette of the virtual space is reflected on the object, giving it a "virtual" appearance.

These characteristics define how a real-world object can be visually transformed and integrated into the virtual environment through SAR, laying the foundation for our exploration of object virtualization in the Real-World Metaverse.

Among the various technologies for achieving such virtualization, SAR, particularly projection-based methods, presents a compelling solution. Unlike head-mounted displays, SAR allows for the manipulation of object appearance through projection, enabling multiple users to experience shared augmented content within the physical space.

One of the most compelling capabilities of SAR is appearance manipulation—the modification of an object's perceived visual properties through projection [3–5]. Unlike conventional projection mapping, appearance manipulation aims not only to overlay images, but to perceptually enhance or alter the appearance of material [6–10]. These techniques suggest the potential of SAR to virtualize real-world objects by manipulating how they are perceived. However, it remains unclear what forms of appearance transformation most effectively for the virtualization.

In this study, we investigate the potential of SAR for real-world object virtualization from a user-centered perspective. Specifically, we examine how different types of appearance manipulation affect user perception when a physical object is transformed into a virtual entity. We implement a system that leverages Style-Transformer to project stylized imagery onto real objects, thereby simulating a transformation into a painterly (artwork-inspired) virtual space. In addition, we compare this stylized projection with two baseline methods: *Average Color* projection and *Texture Overlay* projection. Through a controlled user study, we analyze participants' subjective impressions of these different appearance manipulation methods, aiming to explore the feasibility and design considerations of SAR-based object virtualization in the context of the Real-World Metaverse.

Recent research in Augmented Reality (AR) has increasingly focused on achieving higher levels of spatial and optical consistency, exploring not only geometric alignment but also perceptual integration through realistic rendering and material-aware augmentation. Within this landscape, SAR has re-emerged as a promising platform for shared, display-free augmentation. In particular, appearance manipulation techniques in SAR have shown the potential to alter an object's perceived material or stylistic attributes using projection-based feedback systems.

However, while many prior studies have focused either on photorealistic enhancement or stylistic transformation in isolation, little attention has been paid to the challenge of *balancing multiple perceptual goals*—such as recognizability, texture integration, and color harmony—required to fully virtualize physical objects in a perceptually convincing way.

Our study addresses this gap by systematically evaluating different projection strategies with respect to these perceptual dimensions, and by demonstrating how a transformer-based style transfer model ($StyTr^2$) can achieve a desirable trade-off across them. This approach advances the current state of AR research by moving beyond functional augmentation toward a more expressive and perceptually grounded form of object virtualization.

Our contributions are summarized as follows:

- We define the problem of appearance-based virtualization in SAR as the perceptual integration of object contours, painterly texture, and color harmony.
- We implement and compare three representative projection methods— *Average Color, Texture Overlay*, and $StyTr^2$—using a coaxial projection-feedback system.
- We conducted a structured user study across five artworks and three perceptual questions, quantitatively analyzing user preferences with score averages, variances, and 2D scatter plots.
- We show that while no method dominates all criteria, $StyTr^2$ offers the best perceptual balance, making it the most suitable candidate for satisfying the combined virtualization requirements.

2   Related Work

2.1   Appearance Manipulation

Since the early days of SAR research, efforts have focused on addressing three key requirements for augmented reality: geometric alignment, optical consistency, and temporal alignment. Additionally, substantial work has been conducted on related topics such as projection blur compensation and dynamic projection onto moving or deforming objects [3,4].

While projection mapping is widely recognized as a primary application of SAR, its potential extends beyond this domain. SAR has demonstrated the ability to compensate for issues such as projection on textured surface, or recover degradation, thus enabling the enhancement or transformation of object appearances. Notable examples include the optical restoration of deteriorated artworks [12], dynamic range extension for low-contrast objects fabricated using 3D printing techniques [11], and reality enhancement through the projection of wrinkles onto avatars [13]. These applications fall under the category of appearance manipulation, which differs from traditional projection mapping in that they not only enhance, but also effectively replace the real-world appearances as perceived by the viewer.

One of the challenges in appearance manipulation is real-time application, which requires continuously estimating the reflectance properties and projecting images to alter the object's appearance while maintaining projection integrity. A prior study addressed this challenge by proposing a technique for real-time gloss manipulation using a coaxial optical system combined with a projector-camera setup [7]. This approach was later extended to enable viewpoint-dependent appearance manipulation, utilizing structural color objects and silk materials that exhibit color changes depending on the viewing angle [14]. Additional research has explored analytical methods using multi-projector-camera systems to achieve viewpoint-dependent color manipulation based on reflection analysis, enabling color adaptation according to the observer's perspective [15].

These techniques collectively enable the manipulation of physical objects' appearances through projection, providing a powerful foundation for the virtualization of real-world objects. Building on these advancements, this study employs the projector-camera framework to explore virtualization of physical objects.

2.2   Style Transformer

Image style transfer is a technique that renders an image with artistic features guided by a reference style image while preserving its original content structure. Neural Style Transfer (NST), first introduced by Gatys et al. [16], demonstrated that content and style representations could be effectively replaced using deep convolutional neural networks. Since then, NST has evolved into a powerful tool for altering visual appearance while maintaining semantic integrity.

Recent studies such as LAPIG (Language-Guided Projector Image Generation) have explored the use of text-guided style transfer for projection-based appearance manipulation. LAPIG combines a projector-camera system with surface adaptation and stylization mechanisms to project generated images onto textured physical surfaces. Its use of text-guided neural style transfer demonstrates the potential of abstract prompts to virtualize real-world appearances [17].

However, in our study, where the goal is to seamlessly connect physical and virtual spaces, stylization must be directly guided by reference images that represent the visual space scene materiality or rendering techniques. Consequently, non-text-guided style transfer approaches, such as [16], are more suitable. These techniques allow fine-grained stylization based on image-to-image mappings and are better aligned with the demands of SAR, where the appearance of the projection must be tightly registered to the geometry of the physical object. A crucial

Fig. 1. Experimental setup for evaluating real-world object virtualization: (a) Physical objects (both 3D and planar) are placed in front of a display showing a stylized painterly virtual scene. (b) Stylized imagery is projected onto the physical objects using a projector-camera system, enabling them to appear visually integrated into the virtual environment from the participant's viewpoint.

consideration in SAR-based virtualization is that stylized output must maintain spatial consistency with the surface of the real-world object to avoid misalignment during projection. To address this, positional encoding mechanisms, commonly used in transformer-based image generation models, are essential. These encodings embed spatial location information into the model, allowing it to maintain geometric coherence between the input and output images. There are two primary types of positional encoding: functional and parametric, both of which offer different trade-offs in flexibility and generalization.

For SAR applications, scale-invariant positional encoding is particularly desirable, as it enables content-aware stylization that adapts across different spatial scales while preserving surface alignment. To meet these requirements, we adopt $StyTr^2$ (Image Style Transfer with Transformers) [18], a transformer-based style transfer framework that integrates scale-invariant positional encoding and effectively separates content and style representations. This framework enables us to generate stylized projection images that retain structural consistency with the physical object while altering its perceived material properties.

3   Methods

3.1   Experimental Setup

To evaluate the effectiveness of virtualization, we constructed an experimental setup in which physical objects appear perceptually integrated into a stylized virtual environment. The scene simulates a painterly virtual world displayed on a 27-inch LCD monitor (iMac Retina 5K, 27-inch, 5120×2880 resolution) placed at the rear of the setup. Physical objects, both three-dimensional and planar, are placed in front of the display, and illuminated with stylized projections using a calibrated projector-camera system.

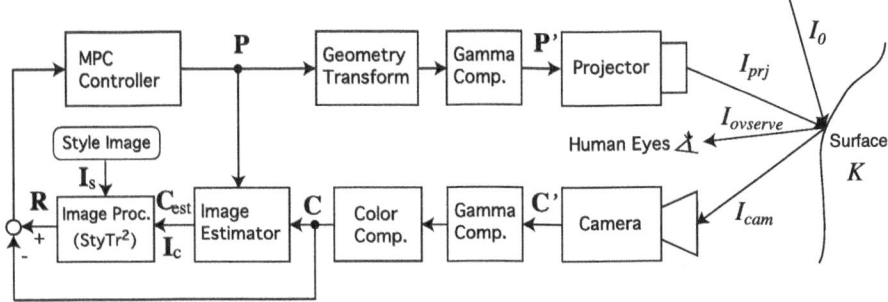

Fig. 2. Example of a stylized process: From left to right, each image shows the content image (the object's estimated original appearance), the style image (the background painting), and the stylized result, which is used as the target image in the projector-camera feedback system.

The projection system consists of a full HD projector (EPSON EH-TW6600, 1920×1080 resolution, 2500 lumens) and a color camera (Point Grey Grasshopper2, 1600×1000 resolution ROI) aligned in a coaxial optical configuration with a beam-splitting mirror. The geometry is calibrated using gray code projection to ensure pixel mapping for the projector camera feedback. All projections are performed at a distance of approximately 90 cm from the object surface. The participant viewpoint is fixed approximately 70 cm in front of the scene, providing an optimal perspective to evaluate the appearance transformation (see Fig. 1). This setup enables controlled evaluation of appearance manipulation techniques for object virtualization in the context of a Real-World Metaverse.

To assess the generalizability across different object geometries, we employed both three-dimensional and planar physical objects. The 3D object is a painted figurine with varied colors, while the planar object is a full-color print on matte paper using an inkjet printer. These objects were selected because their materials exhibit diffuse reflectance, making them well-suited for effective appearance manipulation. Moreover, both objects feature chromatic surfaces, ensuring that color changes and stylistic transformations are perceptually salient. We consider them representative of everyday physical items commonly encountered in real-world scenarios, striking a balance between material realism and projection compatibility.

3.2 Projector and Camera System

In the appearance control process [7], we employ a coaxial projector-camera feedback system to estimate the surface reflectance characteristics of the target object. Given the projected color image $\mathbf{P}(x,y) \in \mathbb{R}^3$, where $x \in [0, W-1]$ and $y \in [0, H-1]$ denote the image coordinates, and the captured color image $\mathbf{C}(x,y) \in \mathbb{R}^3$, the appearance control computes the object's appearance under a white-light illumination, denoted as the estimated appearance $\mathbf{C}_{\text{est}}(x,y) \in \mathbb{R}^3$, as illustrated in Fig. 3.

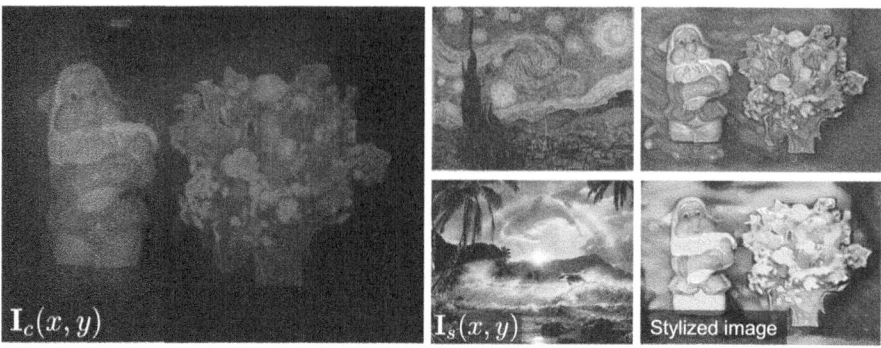

Fig. 3. Diagram of appearance control employing $StyTr^2$: The system estimates the object's appearance under white-light illumination and applies transformer-based style transfer. The stylized result is then projected back onto the object with geometric alignment.

Subsequently, user-defined image processing is applied to $\mathbf{C}_{est}$ to generate the desired target image $\mathbf{R}(x, y) \in \mathbb{R}^3$. The projector-camera system then adjusts the projected image $\mathbf{P}(x, y)$ so that the resulting captured image $\mathbf{C}(x, y)$ visually matches the target image $\mathbf{R}(x, y)$. Although the resolutions of $\mathbf{P}$ and $\mathbf{C}$ may differ in general, our implementation uses a pixel mapping process to geometrically align both images. Therefore, in the following description, $\mathbf{P}$ and $\mathbf{C}$ are assumed to share the same spatial resolution with one-to-one pixel correspondence.

In our study, we utilize the estimated appearance $\mathbf{C}_{est}$ as the *content image* $\mathbf{I}_c(x, y)$ and a painterly artwork as the *style image* $\mathbf{I}_s(x, y)$ for stylization. To achieve this, we employ $StyTr^2$ [18], a transformer-based style transfer framework that serves as the core method in our appearance control pipeline, as shown in Fig. 2.

Unlike traditional CNN-based methods, $StyTr^2$ is designed to better capture long-range dependencies and preserve fine structural details, both of which are essential for transferring painterly style onto physical surfaces. It features separate transformer encoders for the content and style images, along with a transformer-based decoder that synthesizes the stylized output by integrating domain-specific representations.

In particular, $StyTr^2$ introduces a content-aware positional encoding (CAPE), which ensures scale-invariant and spatially coherent transformations. This makes the method especially effective for generating stylized projections that align with the underlying geometry of real-world objects while conveying the visual richness of the artwork [18].

The resulting stylized image, produced by the style transfer model, is used as the target image $\mathbf{R}$ in the appearance control feedback loop. This allows the system to project a stylized version of the object's natural appearance, effectively virtualizing it into a painterly aesthetic while maintaining geometric consistency.

To evaluate the effectiveness of style-based virtualization, we implemented two baseline projection methods for comparison: *Average Color* projection and *Texture Overlay* projection. Let Ω denote the set of all pixel coordinates in the style image. In the *Average Color* projection, the mean color is computed as

$$\bar{\mathbf{I}}_s = \frac{1}{|\Omega|} \sum_{(x,y)\in\Omega} \mathbf{I}_s(x,y) \in \mathbb{R}^3,$$

and is uniformly assigned to all pixels in the projected image, i.e.,

$$\mathbf{P}(x,y) = \bar{\mathbf{I}}_s.$$

In the *Texture Overlay* projection, the style image itself is directly used as the projection, i.e., $\mathbf{P}(x,y) = \mathbf{I}_s(x,y)$. To ensure that the projection does not interfere with the content displayed on the background LCD display, a binary mask is applied to the projected image $\mathbf{P}(x,y)$, restricting projection only to the region corresponding to the physical object.

3.3 Virtual Spaces and Virtualization Results

To simulate diverse painterly virtual environments, we selected five iconic artworks by Vincent Van Gogh, Claude Monet, Georges Seurat, Christian Lassen, and Edvard Munch. These paintings represent varied visual styles—ranging from impressionistic and pointillist to surreal and expressionistic—allowing us to evaluate how different projection methods interact with distinct artistic aesthetics.

Figure 4 illustrates the results of applying the three projection methods (*Average Color*, *Texture Overlay*, and *StyTr²*) to physical objects within each virtual space.

Average Color: This method maintains the clearest visibility of the physical object by projecting a uniform illumination derived from the average color of the style image. While it does not alter the texture or surface details of the object, this simplicity enables strong perceptual separation between the object and the background. Interestingly, in some cases, such as with Lassen, the global color harmony between the object and the background contributes to a visually coherent and immersive scene, despite the absence of texture manipulation.

Texture Overlay: By directly projecting the style image onto the object, this method effectively conveys painterly richness and stylistic continuity, particularly in cases like Munch. However, this high degree of stylistic fidelity comes at the cost of object recognizability. In several instances, such as Gogh and Lassen, the overlay completely rewrites the physical appearance, resulting in an overly immersive scene in which the object's physical boundaries nearly vanish—raising questions about perceptual integration versus occlusion in the context of virtualization.

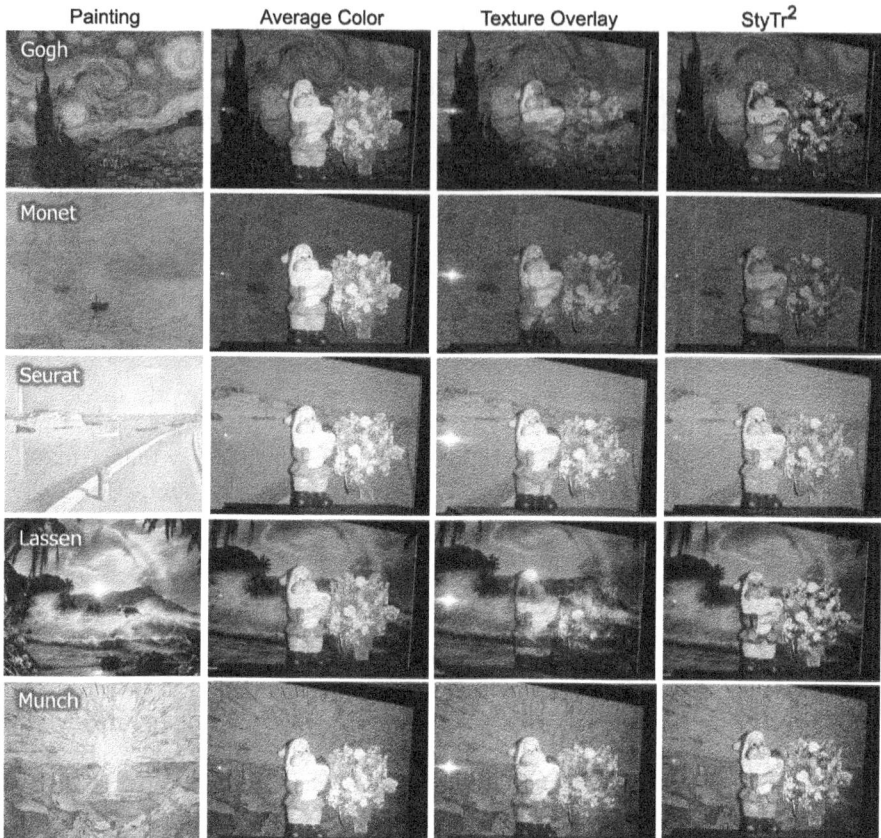

Fig. 4. Virtual spaces and corresponding virtualization results: Each row shows (from left to right) the original painting representing the virtual environment, followed by three virtualized scenes of physical objects placed in front of the display. The objects are augmented using three different virtualization methods.

StyTr²: *StyTr²* adaptively synthesizes stylized projections that integrate the object's original appearance with the visual characteristics of the source painting. This often results in perceptually convincing transformations, as seen in results like Gogh and Lassen, where the object appears naturally embedded within the painterly environment. Notably, even when the overall appearance change is subtle—as in Seurat—the projection introduces fine-grained stylistic cues (e.g., pointillist textures) that align with the aesthetic of the style image. This suggests that *StyTr²* can balance stylistic immersion with structural clarity.

3.4   Evaluation Procedure

We conducted a pairwise comparison experiment to evaluate the visual virtualization quality of stylized object appearances. Participants were asked to observe the scene and evaluate the degree to which the physical objects appeared to belong to the painterly virtual space.

Following Thurstone's method of pairwise comparison, participants sequentially viewed two stylized projections selected from three methods (*Average Color*, *Texture Overlay*, and *StyTr²*), and were asked to choose the one that better satisfied specific criteria. This method allows for relative evaluation with high consistency and low cognitive load.

Three questions were asked for each pair:

- **Q1**: Which projection provides a clearer object contour?
- **Q2**: Which projection shows more consistent touch (painterly texture) between the object and the background?
- **Q3**: Which projection better reflects the color harmony of the background?

These three questions are grounded in perceptual elements commonly used to evaluate visual coherence in painted artworks. *Contour clarity* refers to the visual distinctness of object boundaries, which is crucial for perceiving object structure. *Painterly touch* captures the consistency of surface textures or brushwork between the object and the background, contributing to stylistic integration. *Color harmony* assesses how well the object's coloration aligns with the color palette of the background painting, affecting the overall visual coherence.

Five artworks shown in previous section were used as style images. In each trial, a selected painting was shown on an LCD display behind the physical object. A white occlusion board was placed between the display and the viewing aperture to control visibility and eliminate afterimages.

Each comparison trial followed this procedure:

1. Display the selected painting with the occlusion board in place.
2. Project version *a* onto the physical object.
3. Remove the board and allow the participant to observe the scene for 15 s.
4. Reapply the board to occlude the scene.
5. Project version *b* onto the object.
6. Repeat the 15-second observation.
7. Collect participant responses to Q1–Q3.

All combinations of three projections were evaluated. The occlusion steps were based on the method proposed by Zhong et al. [19], where a neutral luminance plane was used between observations to reduce visual aftereffects.

4 Results of Perceptual Evaluation

4.1 Participant Demographics

We recruited 15 participants (1 female, 14 male; age range: 21–25 years, mean = 22.1, SD = 1.33) for the user study. All participants reported normal or corrected-to-normal vision and no known visual impairments, including color blindness. Participants were naïve to the purpose of the experiment and had no prior exposure to the projection system used in the study.

Table 1. Z-scores of projection methods (*Average Color*, *Texture Overlay*, and $StyTr^2$) for each painting and question.

	Average Color			Texture Overlay			$StyTr^2$		
	Q1	Q2	Q3	Q1	Q2	Q3	Q1	Q2	Q3
Gogh	1.97	−1.31	−1.17	−2.30	1.31	1.31	0.33	0.000	−0.135
Monet	1.97	−1.86	−1.06	−1.59	1.76	0.97	−0.38	0.096	0.096
Seurat	1.50	−3.09	−3.09	−0.97	1.50	1.59	−0.54	1.59	0.71
Lassen	0.87	−1.31	−1.17	−2.10	0.97	0.55	0.11	0.34	0.62
Munch	1.31	−1.17	−1.17	−0.88	0.97	1.06	−0.43	0.21	0.11
Average	1.52	−1.75	−1.53	−1.57	1.30	1.09	−0.18	0.45	0.28
Variance	0.22	0.63	0.76	0.41	0.12	0.15	0.14	0.42	0.13

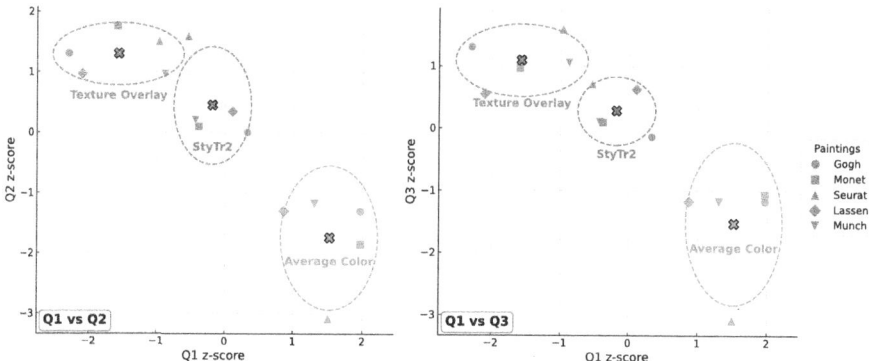

Fig. 5. Comparison of projection methods (*Average Color*, *Texture Overlay*, and $StyTr^2$) in terms of Q1 (object contour clarity) vs. Q2 (touch consistency) and Q1 vs. Q3 (color harmony): Each X-mark represents the average z-score of the method across all paintings, with 3σ ellipses indicating the variance. Colored points denote individual painting scores, using different marker shapes for each painting.

4.2 Overall Method Comparison

To quantitatively assess how each projection method contributes to the perceptual criteria required for appearance-based virtualization, we first computed the mean selection scores and standard deviations for each method across five paintings and three evaluation questions (Q1: contour clarity, Q2: painterly touch integration, Q3: color harmony). The aggregated results are summarized in Table 1.

This table reveals distinct performance profiles for the three projection methods. *Average Color* achieved the highest scores in Q1 (mean = 1.52), but received the lowest ratings in Q2 and Q3 (means = 0.19 and 0.24, respectively). *Texture Overlay*, on the other hand, excelled in Q2 and Q3 (means = 1.61 and 1.60), but performed poorly in Q1 (mean = 0.35), likely due to texture interference with edge clarity. $StyTr^2$ exhibited moderate scores across all questions (Q1 = 0.28, Q2 = 0.93, Q3 = 1.16), suggesting a balanced perceptual profile.

To further visualize the overall performance distribution, we plotted the Q1–Q2 and Q1–Q3 score pairs for each projection method in a 2D scatter plot (Fig. 5). The ellipses in the plot represent 3σ confidence regions based on the per-painting score distributions. This visualization enables comparison of both *central tendency* and *variability* among the methods.

As shown in Fig. 5, *Average Color* clusters in the upper-left region, indicating strength in Q1 but very low performance in Q2 and Q3. In contrast, *Texture Overlay* appears in the lower-right, highlighting its superiority in stylistic and color integration but weakness in contour preservation. $StyTr^2$ is positioned centrally with the smallest spread, indicating consistent moderate performance across all dimensions.

From these distributions, it becomes evident that $StyTr^2$ is the only method that avoids major compromises in any of the three dimensions. While it does not achieve the highest score in any single category, it consistently meets a reasonable threshold across all criteria. This is further supported by its lowest cumulative variance (0.05) compared to *Average Color* (1.61) and *Texture Overlay* (0.11), emphasizing $StyTr^2$'s stability and balance.

Given that this study defines virtualization as the simultaneous fulfillment of Q1–Q3, $StyTr^2$ emerges as the most effective method in approximating this ideal. Its ability to maintain structural clarity, stylistic coherence, and perceptual harmony across diverse artworks makes it a compelling candidate for future adaptive or unified projection strategies.

4.3   Consistency Across Different Paintings

To determine whether the optimal projection method depends on the style, we compared the selection scores for each method across five paintings and three evaluation criteria (Q1âÄŞQ3). As shown in Fig. 6, the overall ranking of methods remained consistent regardless of painting. For Q1 (object contour clarity), *Average Color* achieved the highest average score across all paintings (mean = 1.74, variance = 0.02), while *Texture Overlay* consistently scored the lowest (mean = 0.35, variance = 0.06). This confirms its robustness for preserving contours across visual styles. For Q2 (touch integration) and Q3 (color harmony), *Texture Overlay* was the top performer (Q2: mean = 1.61, variance = 0.03; Q3: mean = 1.60, variance = 0.02), outperforming both $StyTr^2$ and *Average Color* with low variability. *Average Color* showed the lowest scores in both cases, indicating its inability to convey painterly qualities. These results demonstrate that the perceptual advantages and disadvantages of each projection method are stable across different paintings, supporting the use of method-specific strategies depending on the visual goal (e.g., contour fidelity vs. stylistic integration).

While the overall difference was not statistically significant, the $StyTr^2$ received relatively high ratings for Q2 in the case of Seurat. This suggests that $StyTr^2$ may effectively reproduce painterly touches resembling pointillist textures on physical objects.

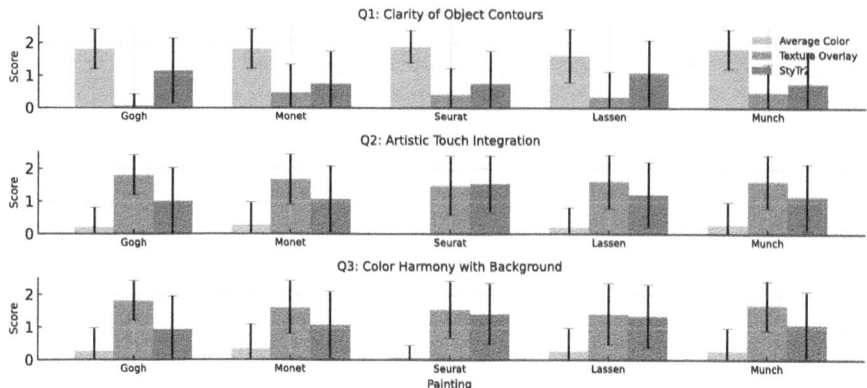

Fig. 6. User evaluation scores for each projection method across five paintings and three perceptual questions. *Average Color* consistently performed best for Q1, while *Texture Overlay* was most preferred for Q2 and Q3. These trends were consistent across all artworks, indicating method-specific perceptual advantages that are robust to painting style.

4.4   Summary of Findings

While this study includes clear comparisons across projection methods, we did not perform statistical significance testing (e.g., ANOVA or Wilcoxon signed-rank test) due to the limited sample size (N = 15). Instead, we report z-scores and variances to characterize the trends and perceptual consistency observed in participant responses.

Overall, *Average Color* achieved the highest scores in Q1 (mean = 1.52), and the lowest in Q2 and Q3. *Texture Overlay* performed best in Q2 and Q3, but poorly in Q1. $StyTr^2$, while not leading in any single metric, maintained moderate performance across all three questions with the lowest overall variance, suggesting it is the most balanced method for fulfilling the perceptual criteria of virtualization.

These results support our hypothesis that different projection strategies offer different strengths, but only $StyTr^2$ consistently meets the combined requirements of object virtualization across various artworks. Notably, in the case of *Seurat*, $StyTr^2$ received relatively high ratings for Q2, suggesting its potential to effectively reproduce painterly touches resembling pointillist textures. This indicates that $StyTr^2$ not only provides balance, but may also offer style-specific advantages depending on the characteristics of the artwork.

5   Discussion

5.1   Occlusion and Projection Shadows

While the coaxial projector-camera system allows precise appearance control from the frontal viewpoint, it inherently suffers from occlusion artifacts when viewed from off-axis positions. As illustrated in Fig. 4, side parts of the object surface that are not directly visible from the projector may receive little to no illumination. Although participants did not report any perceptually disruptive projection shadows during the evaluation, this remains a limitation of the current system. Future extensions may include multi-projector setups to address view-dependent occlusions and improve immersion under multi-user or dynamic viewing conditions.

5.2 Material Properties and Directional Reflectance

We acknowledge that the 3D physical object (dwarf) used in our study exhibits some degree of specular reflection, which is visible in the projection results. As with this object, many real-world materials—such as metal or glass—exhibit non-Lambertian, view-dependent reflectance. Such optical properties pose challenges for achieving perceptually consistent virtualization, especially when the target appearance assumes a matte materiality.

Our current implementation does not explicitly address these directional reflectance effects and therefore assumes that the material reflectance remains approximately Lambertian under the projection-viewing geometry. To extend virtualization techniques to such complex materials, future research should explore light-field projection methods that enable viewpoint-dependent BRDF control via multi-angle projection [20]. These systems can overlay multiple directional projections to suppress undesired specular highlights according to the observer's perspective, enabling a more faithful integration of real-world materials into immersive virtual environments. In addition, future work should explore dynamic scenes involving object motion or user interaction to evaluate the temporal and interactive robustness of the proposed virtualization methods.

5.3 Geometric Alignment and Shape Abstraction

In our study, the goal of virtualization is to alter the surface appearance of real-world objects while preserving their original geometry. The appearance control system projects stylized imagery using a coaxial projector-camera setup. This configuration ensures that the projected imagery is geometrically aligned with the object's surface texture, even when applied to curved surfaces independently viewing position. Therefore, our method provides accurate geometry for multiple users simultaneously. However, our system does not support geometric deformation of the object itself, such as cartoon-style exaggeration or structural abstraction. This is a fundamental limitation of the current virtualization framework.

5.4 Potential Applications and Generalization

While our study focused on painterly virtual environments as an illustrative test case, the proposed approach to object virtualization via spatial augmented reality is broadly applicable across various domains. For instance, this method can be extended to product design visualization, where physical prototypes are dynamically styled with different surface appearances (e.g., materials, finishes, branding) that are adapted to specific spatial or aesthetic contexts. In cultural heritage or museum settings, objects can be visually restored or recontextualized without requiring any physical alteration. Furthermore, in mixed reality training environments, physical tools or objects could be dynamically re-styled to simulate wear, degradation, or domain-specific visual cues, enhancing immersion and situational realism.

6   Conclusion

In this study, we investigated the visual virtualization of real-world objects through projection-based appearance control. We introduced an evaluation framework grounded in three perceptual criteria—object contour clarity, consistency of painterly texture, and color harmony with the background—and conducted a user study comparing a transformer-based style transfer projection technique with two baseline methods: *Average Color, Texture Overlay*.

Our findings demonstrate that each method has distinct strengths and weaknesses: *Average Color* preserves structure but lacks stylistic richness; *Texture Overlay* conveys artistic texture and color harmony effectively but compromises contour clarity; and $StyTr^2$ achieves moderate yet stable performance across all criteria. Importantly, $StyTr^2$ exhibited the lowest overall variance, indicating perceptual consistency and robustness.

Although $StyTr^2$ does not always outperform in individual criteria, its balanced performance makes it the most promising candidate for achieving the complex perceptual requirements of virtualization. Furthermore, in the case of *Seurat*, it notably received high ratings for painterly touch (Q2), suggesting that $StyTr^2$ is also capable of reproducing style-specific features such as pointillist textures. This finding underscores not only its general versatility, but also its potential to adapt to the visual characteristics of diverse virtual environments.

Acknowledgements. This work was supported by JSPS KAKENHI Grant Numbers JP24K02979, JP25H01886.

References

1. The metaverse is a Dystopian nightmare. https://nianticlabs.com/news/real-world-metaverse. Accessed 26 March 2025
2. Raskar, R., Welch, G., Low, K., Bandyopadhyay, D.: Shader lamps: animating real objects with image-based illumination. In: Proceedings of the 12th Eurographics Workshop on Rendering Techniques, pp. 89–102 (2001)
3. Bimber, O., Iwai, D., Wetzstein, G., Grundhöfer, A.: The visual computing of projector-camera systems. Comput. Graph. Forum **27**(8), 2219–2245 (2008). https://doi.org/10.1111/j.1467-8659.2008.01175.x

4. Grundhöfer, A., Iwai, D.: Recent advances in projection mapping algorithms, hardware and applications. Comput. Graph. Forum **37**(2), 654–675 (2018). https://doi.org/10.1111/cgf.13387.1
5. Iwai, D.: Projection mapping technologies: a review of current trends and future directions. Proc. Jpn. Acad. Ser. B Phys. Biol. Sci. **100**(3), 234–251 (2024)
6. Okazaki, T., Okatani, T., Deguchi, K.: A projector-camera system for high-quality synthesis of virtual reflectance on real object surfaces. IPSJ Trans. Comput. Vis. Appl. **2**, 71–83 (2010)
7. Amano, T.: Projection based real-time material appearance manipulation. In: 2013 IEEE Conference on Computer Vision and Pattern Recognition Workshops, pp. 918–923 (2013). https://doi.org/10.1109/CVPRW.2013.135
8. Siegl, C., et al.: Real-time pixel luminance optimization for dynamic multi-projection mapping. ACM Trans. Graph. **34**(6), 237:1-237:11 (2015)
9. Murakami, K., Amano, T.: Materiality manipulation by light-field projection from reflectance analysis. In: Bruder, G., Yoshimoto, S., Cobb, S. (eds.) ICAT-EGVE 2018 - International Conference on Artificial Reality and Telexistence and Eurographics Symposium on Virtual Environments, The Eurographics Association (2018)
10. Nomoto, T. , Koishihara, R., Watanabe, Y.: Realistic dynamic projection mapping using real-time ray tracing. ACM SIGGRAPH 2020 Emerging Technologies SIGGRAPH 2020 (2020)
11. Shimazu, S., Iwai, D., Sato, K.: 3D high dynamic range display system. In: 10th IEEE International Symposium on Mixed and Augmented Reality, pp. 235–236 (2011)
12. Aliaga, D.G., Law, A.J., Yeung, Y.H.: A virtual restoration stage for real-world objects. ACM Trans. Graph. **27**, 1 (2008)
13. Bermano, A., Brüschweiler, P., Grundhöfer, A., Iwai, D., Bickel, B., Gross, M.: Augmenting physical avatars using projector-based illumination. ACM Trans. Graph. **32**(6), 189:1-189:10 (2013)
14. Amano, T., Ushida, S., Miyabayashi, Y.: Viewpoint-dependent appearance-manipulation with multiple projector-camera systems. In: International Conference on Artificial Reality and Telexistence and Eurographics Symposium on Virtual Environments, pp. 101–107 (2017)
15. Amano, T., Yoshioka, H.: Viewing-direction dependent appearance manipulation based on light-field feedback. In: Bourdot, P., Interrante, V., Kopper, R., Olivier, A. H., Saito, H., Zachmann, G. (eds.) Virtual Reality and Augmented Reality. EuroVR 2020. LNCS, vol. 12499, Springer (2020)
16. Gatys, L.A., Ecker, A.S., Bethge, M.: Image style transfer using convolutional neural networks. In: 2016 IEEE Conference on Computer Vision and Pattern Recognition, pp. 2414–2423 (2016). https://doi.org/10.1109/CVPR.2016.265
17. Deng, Y., Ling, H., Huang, B.: LAPIG: language guided projector image generation with surface adaptation and stylization. IEEE Trans. Vis. Comput. Graph. (2025). https://doi.org/10.1109/TVCG.2025.3549859
18. Deng, Y., et al.: StyTr^2: image style transfer with transformers. In: Proceedings of the IEEE/CVF Conference on Computer Vision and Pattern Recognition, pp. 11326–11335 (2022). https://doi.org/10.1109/CVPR52688.2022.01105

19. Zhong, F., Jindal, A., Yöntem, A.Ö., Hanji, P., Watt, S.J., Mantiuk, R.K.: Reproducing reality with a high-dynamic-range multi-focal stereo display. ACM Trans. Graph. Proc. SIGGRAPH Asia **40**(6), 241 (2021). https://doi.org/10.1145/3478513.3480513
20. Amano, T., Nishida, S.: Enhancing materiality in adaptive BRDF display with light ray diffusion. In: Reyes-Lecuona, A., et al. Virtual Reality and Mixed Reality. EuroXR 2024. LNCS, vol. 15445. Springer, Cham (2025). https://doi.org/10.1007/978-3-031-78593-1_9

Content Synthesis and Creation

A Modular Hybrid Telepresence System Integrating Immersive 360-Degree Video with On-Demand High-Resolution Imaging

Jiapeng Chi[✉][iD], Carsten Neumann, Carolina Cruz-Neira,
and Dirk Reiners[✉]

University of Central Florida, Orlando, FL 32816, USA
{Jiapeng.Chi,dirk.reiners}@ucf.edu

Abstract. Telepresence technologies are increasingly essential for effective remote collaboration and interaction across various sectors, including industry, healthcare, and education. Traditional telepresence systems predominantly rely on conventional video capture, offering limited immersion despite adequate resolution for detailed visual tasks. Although 360-degree video provides enhanced immersion through panoramic views, practical constraints such as insufficient resolution and streaming bitrate significantly degrade detailed visual inspection capabilities. To overcome these limitations, we propose a modular hybrid telepresence system that integrates immersive 360-degree video with targeted high-resolution imagery captured by standard cameras. Implemented on a mobile telepresence robot (Double 3) and displayed within a portable Cave Automatic Virtual Environment (CAVE)-like system named VDen, our solution features a modular image registration framework capable of switching between multiple feature-matching algorithms (SIFT, LoFTR, Light-Glue+DISK). Experimental results validate our system's capability to effectively balance immersive panoramic perception and detailed visual inspection, outperforming traditional telepresence and purely super-resolution-based approaches.

Keywords: Telepresence · 360-degree video · Feature matching

1 Introduction

Telepresence enables remote users to perceive and interact with distant environments via advanced communication and sensory interfaces [15,33]. It is widely used across industries, healthcare, and education to support seamless remote collaboration. The COVID-19 pandemic further accelerated demand for such systems [54].

Despite its broad adoption, most telepresence systems still rely on conventional video, offering only limited immersion. Users increasingly seek deeper presence—feeling physically on-site. A promising solution is 360-degree video,

© The Author(s), under exclusive license to Springer Nature Switzerland AG 2026
D. Michael-Grigoriou et al. (Eds.): EuroXR 2025, LNCS 16101, pp. 81–103, 2026.
https://doi.org/10.1007/978-3-032-03805-0_5

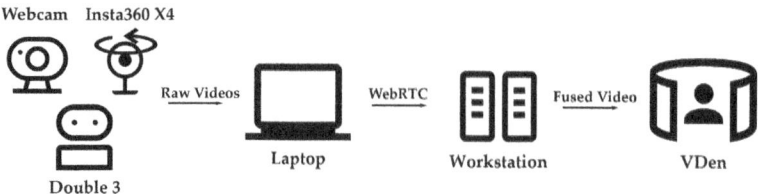

Fig. 1. System Overview. Overall pipeline of our proposed hybrid telepresence system. A 360-degree camera and a 1080p webcam are mounted on the Double 3 robot to capture panoramic and detailed video streams, respectively. An encoder system, in our case just a laptop, encodes and simultaneously transmits both video streams via WebRTC to a remote workstation. Upon receiving the streams, the workstation performs image fusion to integrate the panoramic and high-resolution videos into one view. The fused video stream is then delivered to the immersive VDen environment, providing users with an immersive panoramic experience while enabling detailed inspection of specific areas in high clarity. Icons used in this figure are from Google Material Icons (licensed under Apache License 2.0).

which provides fully panoramic views [34,48], enhancing realism and collaboration [49].

However, adopting 360-degree video introduces resolution challenges. Consumer-grade cameras (e.g., Insta360 X4 [19]) can stream 4K/30 fps, but perceived resolution drops sharply in immersive settings, where only a small portion of the spherical view is visible at a time. Wireless streaming often uses low bitrates to maintain smoothness, further degrading image quality. Professional systems like the Insta360 Pro 2 support 8K/30 fps [18] and improve fidelity but remain bulky and insufficient for high-detail telepresence. As detailed in Sect. 2.3, even 8K panoramas cannot match desktop display clarity in large immersive systems.

Techniques like tile-based adaptive streaming and super-resolution [7,11,13, 16,23] help manage bandwidth and resolution but cannot restore fine details that were never captured [5]. Previously, we proposed RA360SR [9], a real-time dual-camera super-resolution system using Unity3D-based post-processing and acceleration-adaptive upscaling guided by user head movement. While effective, super-resolution alone cannot recover missing visual information when source resolution is fundamentally limited.

To address these limitations, we propose a novel hybrid telepresence system that integrates 360-degree video with high-resolution images captured by standard cameras. Figure 1 illustrates an overview of the proposed system. Specifically, we use Double Robotics' Double 3 telepresence robot as a mobile platform, and present the combined video streams within a Cave Automatic Virtual Environment (CAVE)-like system called VDen. By allowing users to experience panoramic immersion while also viewing clear, high-definition details in specific areas, our approach better balances immersion and clarity. In scenarios requiring close inspection—such as remote collaboration or detailed visual analysis—our

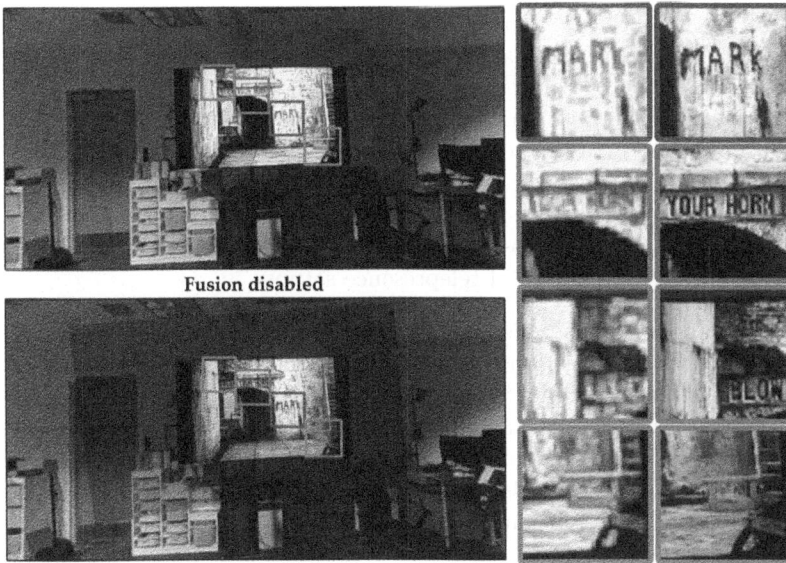

Fig. 2. Visual Output with Fusion Disabled vs. Enabled. This figure illustrates the differences between fused and unfused views in our hybrid telepresence system. Along with the full-scene comparison, two columns present magnified local regions: the left column corresponds to fusion disabled, and the right column corresponds to fusion enabled. The fusion method improves local detail fidelity while maintaining global context. The test image used in this scene is sourced from the DIV2K dataset [1].

system displays a high-resolution image on demand. To seamlessly fuse these two video streams, we adopt a modular image registration design capable of dynamically switching between multiple feature matching methods, including SIFT (Scale-Invariant Feature Transform) [24], LoFTR (Local Feature TRansformer) [46], and LightGlue [25] combined with DISK (DIScrete Keypoints) [50]. Our preliminary evaluations indicate that the latter two approaches achieve a higher frame rate than traditional methods such as SIFT. The modularity allows the fusion module to adaptively switch between these techniques, and we anticipate integrating more efficient feature matching methods in future developments. Meanwhile, the 360-degree stream preserves situational awareness and immersion. Figure 2 illustrates the visual difference between fused and unfused outputs of our system using the same scene. The fused view clearly demonstrates enhanced clarity in the high-resolution regions, highlighting the benefits of our hybrid approach in maintaining both immersion and detail.

Our main contributions are summarized as follows:

– We present a hybrid telepresence framework that fuses a 360-degree video feed with targeted high-resolution capture, enabling both panoramic immersion and crisp detail.

- We detail the hardware and software integration using a Double 3 robot and a VDen system to create a portable, cost-effective CAVE-like telepresence experience.
- We provide theoretical analysis of resolution requirements for 360-degree telepresence in CAVE-like environments, highlighting the gap between ideal resolutions and current hardware limitations.
- We experimentally demonstrate the feasibility and advantages of our approach in real-time scenarios, comparing performance with super-resolution-based solutions and standard telepresence setups.

The remainder of this paper is organized as follows: Sect. 2 presents related work on telepresence platforms and CAVE systems, and explores the resolution requirements for 360-degree telepresence. Section 3 discusses the proposed hybrid system architecture, including hardware details and software integration. Section 4 provides experimental results, evaluating the performance of various feature matching methods and presenting visual quality comparisons with super-resolution-based solutions. Finally, Sect. 5 summarizes the conclusions and outlines future research directions.

2   Related Work

2.1   Cave Automatic Virtual Environment (CAVE) and VDen

The Cave Automatic Virtual Environment (CAVE), introduced at SIGGRAPH 1992, is an immersive VR system that projects synchronized images onto multiple surrounding screens, enabling users wearing 3D glasses and position-tracking devices to freely explore virtual environments [10,31]. Unlike head-mounted displays (HMDs), CAVE offers a large-scale, very wide field of view immersive experience, finding applications in education [51], art [22], and simulation training [29].

Traditional CAVE systems, however, suffer from limited portability and high costs. To address these issues, a more portable, cost-effective version called VDen was proposed [20]. Our study employs a VDen for enhanced flexibility while maintaining key properties of traditional CAVEs, such as large screen distance and high resolution demands [32,35,36,44]. The VDen uses panels measuring approximately 2 m × 2 m.

Currently, we are developing a next-generation high-resolution CAVE using 360 Hz 4K laser projectors, each screen measuring approximately 5.8 m × 3 m. This new system significantly expands the display area, necessitating higher-quality video inputs and thus motivating our hybrid telepresence approach for clearer visuals without relying solely on high-resolution panoramic capture.

Given VDen's resolution limitations, detailed visuals in 360-degree video can appear unclear. Therefore, to anticipate the needs of the new CAVE, we include a desktop version of our system to benchmark visual fidelity, allowing us to evaluate the trade-offs between immersive projection and high-resolution detail.

2.2 Telepresence Platforms and Robotic Systems

Telepresence, first proposed by Marvin Minsky in 1980, enables users to remotely perceive, interact with, and influence physical environments [33]. Its applications span healthcare, education, corporate meetings, and industrial control, evolving from basic video conferencing to sophisticated robotic platforms [54]. Notable telepresence robots include Double 3 [12], Gobe Robots [14], and Ava Robotics [2]. These systems typically combine a display screen, camera, and a wheeled mobile base.

In this project, we utilize the Double 3 robot, designed for remote work and learning. Double 3 autonomously navigates using 3D sensors for obstacle avoidance, simplifying operation [12]. However, our practical tests revealed instability and distortion in Double 3's built-in video feed, alongside reduced image quality due to latency considerations. Therefore, we opted for a Logitech BRIO webcam to achieve stable, high-resolution video streaming.

2.3 Resolution Challenges and Requirements for 360-Degree Telepresence

360-degree video significantly enhances telepresence by offering continuous, immersive panoramic views that improve situational awareness [34]. However, this broad visual coverage inherently reduces spatial resolution, as limited pixels are stretched over a wide field of view. As a result, fine-grained details such as text or facial expressions become harder to perceive [47]. Network bandwidth constraints can further degrade visual fidelity by triggering dynamic resolution scaling [53].

These challenges primarily stem from the high bandwidth and computational requirements of high-resolution panoramic streaming. For instance, 4K 360-degree video may demand over 400 Mb/s—far exceeding conventional video rates [56]. Real-time encoding and decoding increase this burden, often requiring resolution downgrades to maintain smooth playback. To mitigate these issues, software-based strategies have emerged. Compression with codecs like H.265/HEVC and AV1, combined with adaptive protocols (e.g., DASH), prioritize bandwidth for user-visible regions [53]. AI-driven super-resolution techniques enhance clarity without increasing bandwidth [11], while adaptive systems adjust video quality based on network and scene complexity [47].

Yet hardware limitations continue to constrain resolution. Thus, determining theoretical resolution thresholds for immersive displays (e.g., CAVEs or VDens) is essential for benchmarking and guiding future telepresence systems.

Resolving this requires understanding resolution across projection formats. Equirectangular projection (2:1) introduces polar distortions, reducing effective resolution, while cubemap conversion offers more uniform spatial quality. Ultimately, delivering consistent visual fidelity on large immersive displays depends on resolution, field of view, and viewing distance.

To quantify these relationships, we analyze the geometric dependencies between screen size, viewing position, and angular resolution. Figure 3 illustrates

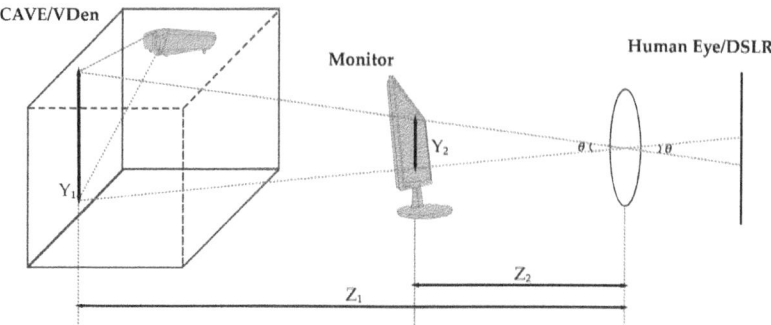

Fig. 3. Schematic illustration of variables for FOV and PPD calculation. This figure depicts the geometric relationships and variables involved in calculating the Field of View (FOV) and Pixels Per Degree (PPD) for both the CAVE projection screen and a standard desktop display. The variables include screen sizes (Y_1, Y_2), viewing distances (Z_1, Z_2), and the FOV in radians (θ).

the relationships among screen dimensions, viewing distances, and the field of view (FOV). Compared to HMDs or standard desktop displays, a CAVE/VDen typically involves a greater viewing distance Z from a much larger screen size Y. Shen et al. [42] modeled the human eye as a digital single-lens reflex (DSLR) camera, noting that the perceived size (retinal image) depends on the field of view θ and distance. Specifically, the viewing angle is computed as

$$\theta_i = 2\arctan\left(\frac{Y_i}{2\,Z_i}\right), \quad i = 1 \text{ (CAVE)}, \ 2 \text{ (Reference)}. \tag{1}$$

Here, Y_1 and Y_2 represent the screen widths of the CAVE/VDen system and the reference desktop display, respectively, while Z_1 and Z_2 are the corresponding viewing distances.

To maintain an equivalent visual experience—i.e., the same pixels per degree (PPD)—the ratio of the display resolutions must match the ratio of the field-of-view angles:

$$\frac{R_1}{R_2} = \frac{\theta_1}{\theta_2}. \tag{2}$$

Substituting (1) into (2), one obtains:

$$\frac{R_1}{R_2} = \frac{\arctan\left(\frac{Y_1}{2\,Z_1}\right)}{\arctan\left(\frac{Y_2}{2\,Z_2}\right)}. \tag{3}$$

For example: assume the user stands 1 m from a 2 m × 2 m VDen screen, aiming to replicate the same PPD as standing 0.6 m from a 27-in. 1080p monitor ($R_2 = 1920$). By applying the above equations, the VDen screen would require a resolution of approximately 3248 × 3248. If replacing the 1080p reference with a 4K display, the required resolution increases to approximately 6496 × 6496.

Converting Cubemap Faces to Equirectangular. When dealing with 360-degree content, many systems employ a cubemap representation of six faces (each of size $l \times l$). To avoid pixel loss when converting to an equirectangular format with a 2:1 aspect ratio ($W : H = 2 : 1$), one typically equates the total pixel count of the cubemap $(6\,l^2)$ with that of the equirectangular image $(W \times H)$. Thus,

$$W \times H = 6\,l^2, \quad \text{where} \quad \frac{W}{H} = 2. \tag{4}$$

Solving (4) yields

$$H = \sqrt{3}\,l, \quad W = 2\sqrt{3}\,l. \tag{5}$$

Hence, if a single cubemap face requires 3248×3248 pixels to achieve the desired clarity for one VDen screen $(l = 3248)$, the corresponding equirectangular resolution would be approximately $W \approx 11252$ and $H \approx 5626$ $(\approx 2 : 1)$. Similarly, increasing the resolution of each cubemap face proportionally raises the required equirectangular resolution, reaching 22504×11252 for 4K-equivalence.

However, theoretical resolution estimates do not account for the architectural complexities of CAVE and VDen systems, which rely on multiple side-by-side 3D projectors to create a seamless immersive environment. To ensure proper blending and geometric correction, adjacent projectors must overlap, resulting in significant pixel loss. Consequently, both the projector resolution and the 360-degree video input must exceed theoretical thresholds to compensate for this redundancy. Achieving such high resolutions poses a substantial challenge: reproducing the visual fidelity of a standard 1080p or 4K desktop monitor is difficult on both the capture and display sides given current hardware limitations. Most commercial 360-degree cameras fall short of these requirements, and even advanced projection systems struggle to maintain sufficient pixel density with real-time performance. These constraints expose the inherent limitations of current telepresence technologies and motivate our proposed approach, which seeks to improve immersion and visual clarity within practical hardware constraints.

2.4   WebRTC and Streaming Technologies

Web Real-Time Communication (WebRTC) is a protocol standardized by W3C and IETF for real-time peer-to-peer audio, video, and data exchange without plug-ins [26,45]. It offers the low latency essential for telepresence and conferencing by enabling direct UDP connections, typically achieving peer-to-peer paths in about 92% of sessions [45]. Unlike traditional TCP-based streaming, WebRTC employs dynamic congestion control tailored for fluctuating network conditions, ensuring high throughput and minimal delay [21].

Shen et al. [40] demonstrated WebRTC's latency advantage over RTSP and commercial video streaming, with average packet delays as low as 5.112 ms compared to RTSP's 37.807 ms. These results confirm WebRTC's superiority for real-time interactive applications. Given the critical need for low-latency video and responsive control in telepresence robots, we adopted WebRTC to deliver a seamless remote operation experience.

2.5 Image Registration and Feature Matching Techniques

Image registration and feature matching are fundamental tasks in computer vision, aiming to align images captured from different viewpoints, times, or sensors [57]. Registration aligns images into a unified framework and is critical in fields such as medical imaging [30], remote sensing [28], and 3D reconstruction [41]. Feature matching, essential for registration, identifies and matches keypoints to estimate geometric transformations [27]. Traditional approaches use handcrafted features like SIFT [27] and SURF [3], robust to scale, rotation, and illumination changes. Recent methods leverage deep learning to learn local descriptors [25,50], apply Transformer architectures [46], and use reinforcement learning to optimize keypoint selection [50]. Given our need to align images from varied conditions, we employ a combination of traditional and modern techniques.

Traditional methods like SIFT [27] and SURF [3] detect local extrema or approximate Hessian matrices for keypoint identification, ensuring invariance to scale and rotation. However, they often struggle under extreme viewpoint changes or in low-texture areas, motivating more robust alternatives.

LoFTR, proposed by Sun et al. [46], introduces a detector-free Transformer-based approach, directly computing dense correspondences via attention mechanisms. Its global receptive field enables effective matching in low-texture and repetitive pattern regions, outperforming traditional keypoint-based methods. However, LoFTR lacks multi-scale fusion and struggles with complex visual structures, limiting its localization accuracy and robustness [37].

DISK, by Tyszkiewicz et al. [50], applies reinforcement learning to optimize keypoint selection, maximizing correct matches and improving performance under challenging conditions. It excels in dense, discriminative keypoint extraction but degrades when limited by computational resources [55]. LightGlue, introduced by Lindenberger et al. [25], refines matches through an adaptive Transformer-based attention mechanism, balancing speed and accuracy. Its dynamic stopping strategy accelerates easier matching tasks but may slow down for low-overlap or complex scenes.

By combining DISK's robust keypoint detection with LightGlue's efficient matching refinement, we achieve both high accuracy and real-time performance, meeting the stringent demands of telepresence and immersive system applications.

3   Methodology

In this section, we describe the design and implementation of our proposed modular hybrid telepresence system. Our approach integrates immersive panoramic experiences provided by a 360-degree camera with targeted high-resolution imagery captured by complementary standard cameras. Figure 4 presents the System Pipeline Diagram, providing a comprehensive visualization of the data flow and processing steps within our system.

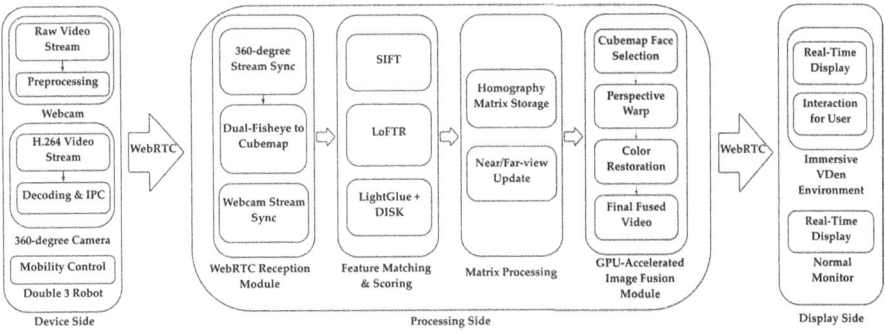

Fig. 4. System Pipeline Diagram. This diagram illustrates the complete data flow and processing pipeline of our proposed modular hybrid telepresence system. The system is divided into three main sections: the device side (Double 3 robot equipped with a 360-degree camera and a 1080p webcam), the processing side (laptop and workstation performing video stream management, homography estimation, and GPU-accelerated image fusion), and the display side (VDen immersive visualization environment). Video streams captured from the cameras are transmitted via WebRTC, processed for adaptive alignment based on near and far viewing scenarios, and fused into a unified immersive view. The final fused video is then rendered in the VDen environment for user interaction.

3.1   Hardware Design

Our telepresence system is built on the Double Robotics Double 3 platform, equipped with an Insta360 X4 panoramic camera and a Logitech Brio webcam for high-resolution image capture. Since the robot provides limited built-in mounting options, we developed a custom hardware solution to integrate both cameras in a compact and stable manner.

As shown in Fig. 5, a custom-made aluminum mounting frame was designed to securely hold the two cameras while maintaining horizontal alignment. To further enhance stability during movement, a vibration damper was incorporated into the frame. This configuration ensures a consistent viewpoint between the two cameras, which is critical for accurate image fusion.

A notable hardware constraint arose from system compatibility: the initial goal was to run the 360-video processing on the Double Robot's built-in system, to simplify the setup as much as possible. That turned out to be impossible, as the Insta360 X4 SDK is only supported on x86-based systems, rendering it incompatible with the Double 3's ARM-based Linux operating system. To address this, we used two 40-foot USB cables to connect both cameras to an external Windows laptop. This setup, while introducing cabling and additional hardware complexity, allows for reliable SDK operation and high-resolution video capture. Wireless alternatives were not adopted due to bandwidth limitations and the need for low-latency streaming.

The Windows laptop serves as an intermediate processing node, capturing both video streams and transmitting them via WebRTC to a remote workstation.

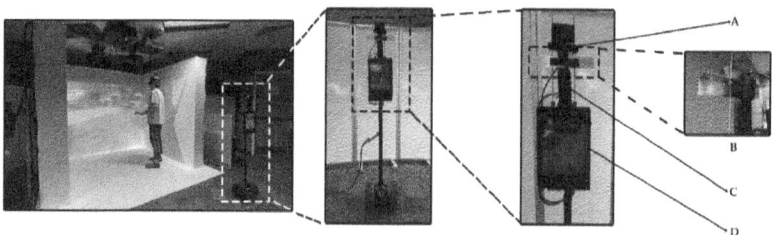

Fig. 5. System Hardware and Immersive Setup. The combined diagram illustrates both the immersive display and robot hardware configuration. (A) Logitech Brio webcam. (B) Custom aluminum mounting frame with vibration damper. (C) Insta360 X4 panoramic camera. (D) Double 3 telepresence robot. The system integrates high-resolution and panoramic video capture with immersive real-time visualization in the VDen environment.

On the receiving side, a Unity3D-based visualization system renders the fused video in real time. This completes the interactive telepresence loop within an immersive VDen environment.

3.2   Software Design

Video Capture and Transmission. On the laptop connected to the telepresence robot, panoramic video from the Insta360 X4 is managed through a C++ application leveraging FFmpeg and OpenCV libraries. Specifically, the incoming H.264-encoded stream is decoded and converted from YUV to BGR format, ensuring compatibility with subsequent processing stages. Each frame is encapsulated into a structured message containing metadata such as timestamps and resolution details, preparing it for inter-process communication.

In parallel, the Logitech Brio Webcam, attached to a Windows-based laptop, captures high-resolution frames directly via standard camera interfaces. These frames undergo similar processing, including RGB conversion and precise timestamping. Both video feeds are independently transmitted through dedicated WebRTC streams, managed by Python-based modules utilizing asynchronous WebRTC libraries.

To minimize latency critical for responsive teleoperation, our WebRTC implementation carefully selects codecs and disables certain retransmission mechanisms. This enables simultaneous transmission of panoramic video (2880×1440, 30 fps) and high-resolution video (1080p, 30 fps) at approximately 8 Mbps each, satisfying stringent real-time performance requirements and ensuring immersive and responsive visualization within the VDen system.

Video Stream Reception, Distribution, and Processing. On the receiving workstation, a Python-based orchestration module establishes parallel WebRTC connections for both the panoramic and high-resolution video streams. After exchanging signaling parameters, each stream independently transmits encoded video data in real time. We leverage the `aiortc` library for WebRTC implementation, tuning codec preferences to minimize latency by disabling retransmission codecs. Internally, incoming frames are buffered, timestamped, and distributed via a ZeroMQ pipeline, decoupling decoding and processing stages. This modular design ensures stable real-time responsiveness and mitigates computational bottlenecks. Frames from the panoramic stream are decoded and converted from a dual-fisheye format into a cubemap representation using a GPU-accelerated transformation pipeline based on bilinear interpolation. Simultaneously, frames from the high-resolution camera are captured and transmitted through a separate WebRTC channel after RGB conversion.

To better preserve scene details during cubemap generation, we match the effective pixel density of the dual-fisheye input to that of the cubemap output. Since a dual-fisheye frame only contains two valid circular regions, its effective pixel area can be approximated by:

$$\text{Effective Pixels} = 2\pi \left(\frac{H}{2}\right)^2 = \frac{\pi H^2}{2} \quad \text{or equivalently} \quad \frac{\pi W^2}{8}. \tag{6}$$

where W and H are the width and height of the input dual-fisheye frame, respectively. Balancing this effective pixel count with the cubemap pixel count $(6l^2)$ yields the required cubemap face size:

$$l \approx \sqrt{\frac{\text{Effective Pixels}}{6}}. \tag{7}$$

For example, targeting a cubemap face size of $l = 1024$ requires the original fisheye frame to have an effective resolution of approximately 4000×2000 pixels. In our system, although the input resolution (2880×1440) slightly undersamples this target, bilinear interpolation during sampling mitigates aliasing artifacts while preserving sufficient scene detail for immersive telepresence applications.

This cubemap representation substantially mitigates geometric distortions inherent in dual-fisheye or equirectangular formats by approximating each cubemap face as a perspective projection. It also simplifies selective region fusion by enabling efficient extraction of cubemap faces overlapping with the high-resolution camera's field of view, thereby optimizing subsequent image registration and fusion tasks.

Feature Matching and Image Fusion. Our image fusion pipeline employs GPU-accelerated operations to ensure real-time performance, utilizing PyTorch alongside Kornia [39] for optimized real-time image processing. Images from both camera streams are first converted into GPU-compatible tensor formats and resized for consistent scale matching. Synchronization between streams is dynamically managed using adjustable frame-offset parameters, ensuring precise temporal alignment during fusion.

To robustly align the panoramic cubemap and high-resolution webcam images, we implemented a modular approach supporting multiple feature matching techniques:

SIFT: SIFT extracts robust, scale-invariant features ideal for precise matching between the panoramic cubemap and webcam images.

LoFTR: LoFTR leverages transformer-based architecture to generate dense feature correspondences directly from grayscale image pairs, eliminating explicit keypoint detection.

LightGlue and DISK: The combination of LightGlue and DISK provides efficient and robust learned keypoint detection and matching. LightGlue's lightweight architecture facilitates rapid matching computations, while DISK delivers depth-invariant sparse keypoints robust to viewing angle variations and illumination changes.

Only one of the three methods is used at runtime; users can flexibly switch between SIFT, LoFTR, or LightGlue+DISK depending on their specific performance or accuracy requirements. This modularity is motivated by our earlier analysis in Sect. 2.5, which highlights the strengths and limitations of each technique under varying conditions.

All three methods utilize GPU-accelerated RANSAC for homography estimation due to its superior robustness, even when feature matching accuracy is high. In typical operation, the relative positions of both cameras remain fixed, theoretically suggesting a constant homography matrix. However, practical use requires distinct homography matrices for near-field and far-field scenarios. If the user does not frequently switch viewing distances or move the robot extensively, real-time model or algorithm execution becomes unnecessary, allowing for the use of a single, stored homography matrix.

In our implementation, unless manually reconfigured by the user, the system automatically executes the feature matching algorithms and RANSAC for each of the initial 30 frames upon startup. Each generated homography matrix is evaluated based on the number of inlier matches identified by RANSAC. The matrix yielding the highest score among these initial frames is selected and stored for subsequent use, eliminating the need for continuous real-time computation. Users retain the option to manually activate feature matching algorithms if the automatic selection does not meet their expectations.

3.3   Adaptive Color Restoration Module

Due to inherent differences between 360-degree cameras and standard webcams, noticeable color discrepancies frequently arise during image fusion, impacting visual coherence and realism, particularly within immersive environments such as VDen.

To resolve this issue, we adopt the adaptive color restoration method proposed by Reinhard et al. [38], integrated into our image fusion pipeline. Specifically, after performing homography-based fusion of high-resolution webcam images onto corresponding cubemap faces, we utilize a mean-standard deviation based color transfer in the LAB color space. The source and reference images are first converted from RGB to LAB color space, capturing luminance and chromaticity independently. We compute or cache channel-wise means and standard

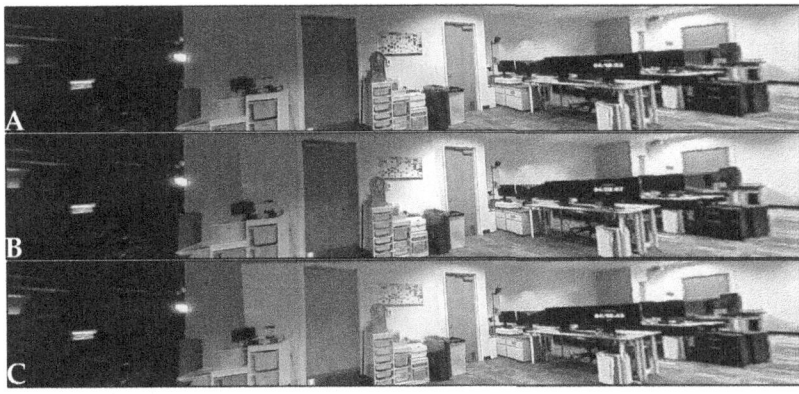

Fig. 6. Adaptive Color Restoration Example. (A) Original images from the 360-degree and high-resolution cameras. (B) Direct fusion result without color correction, showing noticeable chromatic inconsistencies. (C) Final result after applying adaptive LAB-based color restoration, achieving consistent color appearance and improved visual coherence.

deviations for both source and reference images, enabling efficient adaptive color adjustments. A mean-standard deviation matching procedure is then applied to harmonize the color characteristics of fused images with those of the original cubemap images. Additionally, to maintain visual fidelity in low-luminance regions, we implement a masking step that selectively preserves original colors in dark areas. This prevents unnatural color shifts in poorly lit regions, further enhancing overall image coherence.

The resulting fused images thus maintain precise color alignment and spatial detail consistency, significantly improving the immersive telepresence experience. Figure 6 visually demonstrates the effectiveness of this adaptive color restoration process by comparing original images, direct fusion results, and the final outputs after applying the LAB-based adaptive color restoration method.

3.4   Adaptive Homography Selection for Near and Far Views

Since the relative position between the 360-degree camera and the standard webcam mounted on the robot remains constant, theoretically, only a single homography matrix is necessary to align their images. In practice, however, we observed notable disparities arising from the physical offset between the two camera lenses. This offset becomes particularly significant when aligning images of near-field objects compared to far-field objects. Consequently, distinct homography matrices are needed for accurately aligning images depending on whether the user's focus is near or far. Figure 7 illustrates the alignment discrepancies caused by lens offset in both near-field and far-field scenarios. These visual comparisons clearly demonstrate the need for adaptive homography selection based on the user's viewing depth.

Given the dynamic requirements of telepresence scenarios, where users may alternately focus on near and far objects, our solution incorporates an adaptive homography selection strategy. Upon system startup, all three feature matching algorithms (SIFT, LoFTR, and LightGlue+DISK) are executed fully across the initial frames, each generating candidate homography matrices. These matrices are evaluated using a scoring algorithm based on the robustness of feature correspondences.

Specifically, our scoring algorithm evaluates the number and quality of matched keypoints determined by RANSAC inlier counts. The homography producing the highest consistent match score across the initial frames is automatically selected and stored as the optimal transformation. During subsequent operations, if users wish to switch between focusing on near-field and far-field scenes, they can manually trigger an update. The homography selection module then recomputes and evaluates candidate matrices to determine the most suitable transformation for the user's current viewing requirement. This adaptive strategy ensures continuously accurate image fusion, significantly enhancing the visual coherence and realism of the telepresence experience.

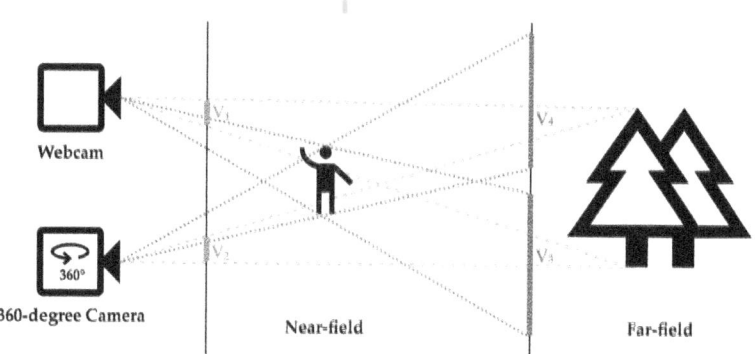

Fig. 7. Lens Offset Effects in Near and Far Focus Scenarios. V_1 and V_2 show the near-field views captured by the 1080p webcam and the 360-degree camera, respectively. V_3 and V_4 illustrate the distant-field views from the same camera pair. These examples highlight the visual misalignment caused by lens offset under different viewing conditions. Icons used are from Google Material Icons (licensed under Apache License 2.0).

4 Experiments and Evaluation

4.1 Experimental Setup

Our experimental evaluation was conducted using a telepresence robot platform, Double Robotics' Double 3, which provides stable mobility and remote control capability, enabling seamless navigation within test environments.

The panoramic camera (Insta360 X4) and the Logitech Brio webcam are mounted securely on the Double 3 robot. A Windows-based laptop equipped with an AMD Ryzen 9 5900HS CPU, 32 GB RAM, and an NVIDIA RTX 3080 GPU handles video capture, pre-processing, and initial video streaming tasks. The 360-degree video stream from the Insta360 X4 is captured at a resolution of 2880 × 1440, which is currently the highest supported livestream resolution in wired mode for this device, with a bitrate of approximately 8 Mbps. The Logitech Brio webcam simultaneously delivers a high-definition video stream at 1920 × 1080 resolution.

On the receiving side, a dedicated workstation equipped with an Intel Core i7-14700KF processor, 64 GB RAM, and an NVIDIA RTX 4090 GPU is responsible for real-time video reception, decoding, cubemap projection, image fusion, and rendering. The original 2880 × 1440 fisheye video is projected into a cubemap format with six 1024 × 1024 faces, enabling spatially consistent alignment with the perspective high-resolution webcam stream.

Although our telepresence system is designed to be viewed in the immersive VDen environment, capturing live visual data directly from this setup posed practical limitations. Therefore, we conducted evaluations and visual demonstrations using an ultrawide display connected to the workstation. This display setup approximates a 180-degree field of view, facilitating both accurate visual analysis and consistent screenshot acquisition.

All screenshots and visual examples included in this paper were captured in fullscreen play mode using the Unity development system (version 2023.2.20f1). Experiments were carried out in controlled indoor environments specifically designed to reflect realistic telepresence scenarios. To evaluate the robustness and adaptability of our system, we tested under two distinct lighting conditions: a bright setting simulating a well-lit office and a challenging low-light scenario with reduced visibility. Furthermore, both near-field and far-field viewing scenarios were included to validate performance under varying depth conditions and camera-object distances.

Table 1. Performance comparison of feature matching methods (in milliseconds).

Stage	SIFT	LightGlue+DISK	LoFTR	Fusion Only
Pre-processing	14.34	13.86	14.27	15.09
Run Model/Algorithm	145.78	28.53	20.35	—
Homography Estimation	13.08	14.77	13.35	—
Final Processing	8.54	9.23	8.44	9.06
Total Time	**181.74**	**66.39**	**56.88**	**24.15**
Theoretical FPS	**5.50**	**15.06**	**17.58**	**41.41**
Actual FPS	**3.90**	**11.25**	**12.60**	**30.00**

4.2   Performance Evaluation of Feature Matching Methods

We conducted extensive performance evaluations to compare three different feature matching methods—SIFT, LightGlue+DISK, and LoFTR—in terms of processing time and computational efficiency. Experiments were performed across four distinct scenarios, comprising bright-light and low-light conditions, as well as near-field and far-field views. Each scenario involved capturing and processing over 600 frames while the telepresence robot executed random forward, backward, and rotational movements to simulate realistic operational dynamics. To ensure the accuracy of our statistical analysis, we excluded the first 30 frames from each scenario to avoid initialization artifacts. Occasionally, some frames exhibited insufficient matched features and were omitted from the calculations to avoid skewing the results.

The average processing times for each method are summarized in Table 1. Additionally, we evaluated a scenario labeled "Fusion Only", in which the homography matrix was precomputed. Specifically, for each of the three methods, we initially processed approximately 30 frames and assessed the generated homography matrices using the previously described scoring method. The highest-scoring matrix from each method was stored and subsequently employed to fuse the video streams. The "Fusion Only" performance reported in the table is the averaged time obtained after running fusion with the saved matrices from all three methods.

The "Pre-processing" stage shown in Table 1 includes operations such as image copying, tensor conversion, cubemap generation, and image resizing. The "Final Processing" stage involves warping images according to the homography matrix and blending them into the final fused output.

Analyzing the results, we observe that SIFT exhibits significantly slower performance, primarily due to the computationally intensive feature extraction and matching stages. LoFTR and LightGlue+DISK demonstrate considerably faster performance, with LoFTR slightly outperforming LightGlue+DISK, although the difference is minimal. The "Fusion Only" scenario shows the highest efficiency, highlighting the advantage of using a precomputed homography matrix in real-time applications.

It is important to note that the actual frames per second (FPS) achieved during practical operation were lower than the theoretical FPS calculated directly from the timing data, due to additional overheads introduced by network transmission, encoding, decoding, and other processing tasks involved in the overall telepresence system workflow. Moreover, the final operational FPS naturally cannot exceed the original video source rate of 30 fps. Additionally, due to potential frame loss during network transmission, the actual operational FPS may fluctuate and fall below these theoretical measurements.

4.3   Visual Quality Comparison with Super-Resolution

To further assess the effectiveness of our hybrid image fusion approach, we conducted a comparative analysis against representative super-resolution (SR)

Fig. 8. Qualitative comparison between our fused output and real-time SR methods (Bicubic++ and ESPCN). Although SR methods run faster, the resulting detail quality is significantly lower due to limited input resolution and generalized model design.

upscaling methods, including both real-time and state-of-the-art (SOTA) techniques. The goal of this comparison is not to claim superiority over SR methods in general, but rather to demonstrate their current limitations in addressing the specific needs of real-time telepresence scenarios.

Since our high-resolution imagery originates from an actual 1080p webcam rather than being generated, we do not compare full-resolution frames directly. Instead, for fairer and more illustrative visual comparisons, we focus on the boundary region of the fused image—where the high-resolution webcam data is integrated with the 360-degree panoramic feed. This region most clearly reflects the distinct advantages and potential limitations of our fusion strategy compared to SR-based enhancement.

Comparison with Real-Time Super-Resolution Methods. We selected two lightweight, real-time SR methods for comparison: Bicubic++ [4] and ESPCN [43]. These models are designed for speed and low computational cost, making them appropriate baselines for real-time telepresence. Each SR model was tested using the official pre-trained versions, configured with a scale factor of ×3.

To ensure consistency, we replayed a fixed sequence of robot actions (including forward movement and turns) and recorded the corresponding video streams after applying each of our three feature matching algorithms (SIFT, LoFTR, and LightGlue+DISK). From this captured content, we extracted the relevant 1024×1024 cubemap face for use as input to the SR models. Notably, we did not apply SR to the entire 360-degree video, as our fusion pipeline also operates on localized cubemap faces.

It is important to note that the SR models were only evaluated on their core inference performance (i.e., the time required to execute the model itself). Pre- and post-processing steps differ significantly between SR pipelines and our own system, making direct end-to-end timing comparisons inappropriate. Table 2 summarizes the runtime of each real-time SR method's core module. Figure 8 illustrates the visual output for a typical test frame.

Table 2. Comparison of core module runtime across real-time SR methods and feature matching methods. All values represent average per-frame runtime in milliseconds (ms).

Method Type	SIFT	LoFTR	LightGlue+DISK	Bicubic++	ESPCN
Runtime (ms)	145.78	20.35	28.53	0.37	33.46

From the results, we observe that Bicubic++ achieves excellent speed, significantly outperforming our feature-based fusion pipeline in terms of runtime. However, the upscaled frames exhibit poor detail fidelity—likely due to the limited resolution of the original 360-degree input. Visual textures and small-scale features remain indistinct and often appear blurred or washed out.

Comparison with State-of-the-Art Super-Resolution Methods. We also tested several SOTA SR models known for their high-fidelity results: DRCT [17], HAT [8], RealBasicVSR [6], and Real-ESRGAN [52]. All models were evaluated using their official pre-trained weights and a fixed scale factor of ×4. As with the real-time methods, we extracted 1024×1024 cubemap face regions from our recorded test sequences for input.

While these models produce visually sharper results compared to the real-time methods, they also exhibit notable artifacts—especially in dynamic or texture-rich regions. Some fine details are smoothed over, and certain areas show hallucinated textures or incorrect structures. These effects are particularly pronounced in Real-ESRGAN and RealBasicVSR outputs, where pre-trained weights may not generalize well to 360-degree telepresence content. Figure 9 provides visual comparisons with our fused outputs.

In addition to visual limitations, these models are also computationally intensive and thus unsuitable for real-time telepresence applications. On our evaluation workstation equipped with an RTX 4090 GPU, the average per-frame processing time was approximately 189989.10 ms for DRCT, 61359.64 ms for HAT, and 1339.26 ms for Real-ESRGAN. RealBasicVSR, which operates on a sequence of frames rather than individual ones, required an average of 568.80 ms

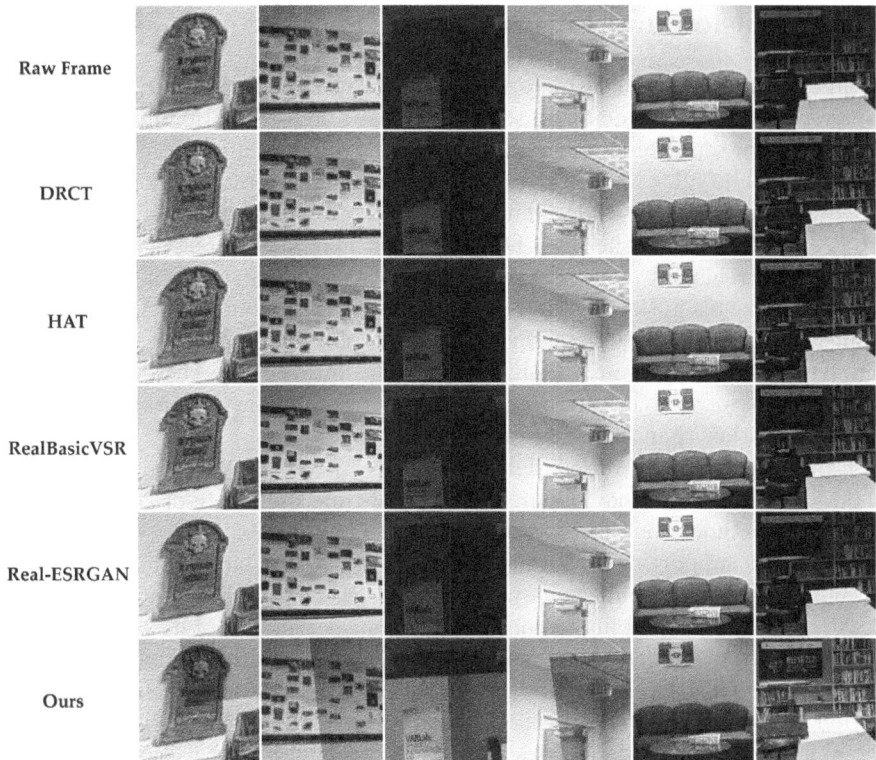

Fig. 9. Visual comparison between our fusion-based method and several state-of-the-art super-resolution techniques (DRCT, HAT, RealBasicVSR, Real-ESRGAN). SOTA methods provide higher perceptual sharpness than real-time SR, but suffer from over-smoothing and incorrect detail generation in areas where domain mismatch occurs.

per output frame. These timings exclude any additional preprocessing or post-processing overhead. Despite producing visually sharper outputs in certain cases, these models still fall short of the low-latency and robustness requirements necessary for immersive, interactive 360-degree telepresence.

Summary. Overall, these comparisons highlight that current SR methods—while effective for general image enhancement tasks—face substantial limitations when applied to immersive, detail-critical telepresence scenarios. Real-time methods are fast but insufficient in detail reconstruction, while SOTA methods introduce perceptual artifacts and lack real-time capability. Moreover, SR models require extensive domain-specific fine-tuning to achieve satisfactory results, which is impractical in many telepresence deployments. In contrast, our hybrid fusion approach leverages real high-resolution content without hallucination, offering a balanced and scalable solution that aligns with both the performance and clarity demands of immersive telepresence.

5   Conclusion and Future Work

In this paper, we present a modular hybrid telepresence system that combines immersive 360-degree video with selectively fused high-resolution imagery. Using a dual-camera setup on a Double 3 robot, our system maintains full situational awareness while allowing selective inspection of fine details via overlaid high-res views. We introduce a modular, GPU-accelerated fusion pipeline supporting SIFT, LoFTR, and LightGlue+DISK feature matchers, along with a flexible homography scheme to optimize performance across diverse viewing conditions.

We analyze resolution demands for immersive telepresence in CAVE-like environments, showing that matching desktop display quality often requires over 11K equirectangular input—highlighting the limitations of current hardware. This motivates our hybrid strategy, augmenting immersive content with high-res inserts rather than full-scene super-resolution.

Experiments under varied lighting and perspectives confirm our system's adaptability and efficiency. Compared to real-time and state-of-the-art super-resolution methods, our fusion approach delivers superior clarity in regions of interest while supporting real-time streaming. We also demonstrate that reusing precomputed homographies cuts processing overhead in stable-view settings.

Nevertheless, several limitations and challenges remain. First, as display resolutions continue to rise—toward 4K and beyond—our current real-time fusion pipeline may not scale effectively without further optimization or hardware acceleration. Second, our current method for selecting near-field or far-field homography matrices relies on manual triggering, which could hinder user experience in dynamic scenes. Third, our fusion strategy is frame-based and does not yet leverage temporal redundancy. Additionally, although we incorporated an Adaptive Color Restoration Module to mitigate color and brightness differences between the 360-degree and high-resolution camera streams, noticeable inconsistencies remain, especially under low-light conditions. Future work will aim to further improve color consistency through enhanced correction models or learning-based approaches.

In future work, we plan to investigate using the high-resolution camera stream to selectively update unchanged regions of the 360-degree video, thereby improving perceptual continuity and enhancing immersion. We also aim to explore automatic, scene-aware homography adaptation and learning-based correspondence models fine-tuned on hybrid telepresence data. More efficient cubemap projection and image blending strategies are under consideration to reduce latency. Finally, we envision extending our system toward multi-user and multi-camera collaborative environments, enabling richer, more interactive remote presence experiences.

References

1. Agustsson, E., Timofte, R.: NTIRE 2017 challenge on single image super-resolution: dataset and study. In: The IEEE Conference on Computer Vision and Pattern Recognition (CVPR) Workshops (2017)

2. AVA Robotics: AVA robotics (2024). https://www.avarobotics.com/. Accessed Mar 2025
3. Bay, H., Ess, A., Tuytelaars, T., Van Gool, L.: Speeded-up robust features (SURF). Comput. Vis. Image Underst. **110**(3), 346–359 (2008)
4. Bilecen, B.B., Ayazoglu, M.: Bicubic++: slim, slimmer, slimmest-designing an industry-grade super-resolution network. In: Proceedings of the IEEE/CVF Conference on Computer Vision and Pattern Recognition, pp. 1623–1632 (2023)
5. Cao, M., et al.: NTIRE 2023 challenge on 360deg omnidirectional image and video super-resolution: datasets, methods and results. In: Proceedings of the IEEE/CVF conference on computer vision and pattern recognition, pp. 1731–1745 (2023)
6. Chan, K.C., Zhou, S., Xu, X., Loy, C.C.: Investigating tradeoffs in real-world video super-resolution. In: Proceedings of the IEEE/CVF Conference on Computer Vision and Pattern Recognition, pp. 5962–5971 (2022)
7. Chen, J., Hu, M., Luo, Z., Wang, Z., Wu, D.: SR360: boosting 360-degree video streaming with super-resolution. In: Proceedings of the 30th ACM Workshop on Network and Operating Systems Support for Digital Audio and Video, pp. 1–6 (2020)
8. Chen, X., et al.: HAT: hybrid attention transformer for image restoration. arXiv preprint arXiv:2309.05239 (2023)
9. Chi, J., Reiners, D., Cruz-Neira, C.: RA360SR: a real-time acceleration-adaptive 360-degree video super-resolution system. In: 2022 IEEE International Symposium on Mixed and Augmented Reality Adjunct (ISMAR-Adjunct), pp. 202–206. IEEE (2022)
10. Cruz-Neira, C., Sandin, D.J., DeFanti, T.A., Kenyon, R.V., Hart, J.C.: The cave: audio visual experience automatic virtual environment. Commun. ACM **35**(6), 64–73 (1992)
11. Dasari, M., Bhattacharya, A., Vargas, S., Sahu, P., Balasubramanian, A., Das, S.R.: Streaming 360-degree videos using super-resolution. In: IEEE INFOCOM 2020-IEEE Conference on Computer Communications, pp. 1977–1986. IEEE (2020)
12. Double Robotics: Double robotics (2024) https://www.doublerobotics.com/. Accessed Mar 2025
13. Gaddam, V.R., Riegler, M., Eg, R., Griwodz, C., Halvorsen, P.: Tiling in interactive panoramic video: approaches and evaluation. IEEE Trans. Multimedia **18**(9), 1819–1831 (2016)
14. GoBe Robotics: GoBe robotics (2024). https://gobe.blue-ocean-robotics.com/. Accessed Mar 2025
15. Hilty, D.M., et al.: A review of telepresence, virtual reality, and augmented reality applied to clinical care. J. Technol. Behav. Sci. **5**(2), 178–205 (2020). https://doi.org/10.1007/s41347-020-00126-x
16. Hosseini, M.: View-aware tile-based adaptations in 360 virtual reality video streaming. In: 2017 IEEE Virtual Reality (VR), pp. 423–424. IEEE (2017)
17. Hsu, C.C., Lee, C.M., Chou, Y.S.: DRCT: saving image super-resolution away from information bottleneck. In: Proceedings of the IEEE/CVF Conference on Computer Vision and Pattern Recognition, pp. 6133–6142 (2024)
18. Insta360: Insta360 pro 2 (2024). https://www.insta360.com/product/insta360-pro2. Accessed Mar 2025
19. Insta360: Insta360 x4 (2024). https://www.insta360.com/product/insta360-x4. Accessed Mar 2025
20. Jaeger, A.: The VDen: An IPT Designed for Usability. University of Arkansas at Little Rock (2019)

21. Jansen, B., Goodwin, T., Gupta, V., Kuipers, F., Zussman, G.: Performance evaluation of webRTC-based video conferencing. ACM SIGMETRICS Perform. Eval. Rev. **45**(3), 56–68 (2018)
22. Keefe, D.F., Feliz, D.A., Moscovich, T., Laidlaw, D.H., LaViola Jr, J.J.: Cave-Painting: a fully immersive 3D artistic medium and interactive experience. In: Proceedings of the 2001 Symposium on Interactive 3D Graphics, pp. 85–93 (2001)
23. Le Feuvre, J., Concolato, C.: Tiled-based adaptive streaming using MPEG-DASH. In: Proceedings of the 7th International Conference on Multimedia Systems, pp. 1–3 (2016)
24. Lindeberg, T.: Scale invariant feature transform (2012)
25. Lindenberger, P., Sarlin, P.E., Pollefeys, M.: LightGlue: local feature matching at light speed. In: Proceedings of the IEEE/CVF International Conference on Computer Vision, pp. 17627–17638 (2023)
26. Loreto, S., Romano, S.P.: Real-Time Communication with WebRTC: Peer-to-Peer in the Browser. O'Reilly Media, Inc. (2014)
27. Lowe, D.G.: Distinctive image features from scale-invariant keypoints. Int. J. Comput. Vision **60**, 91–110 (2004)
28. Ma, J., Jiang, X., Fan, A., Jiang, J., Yan, J.: Image matching from handcrafted to deep features: a survey. Int. J. Comput. Vision **129**(1), 23–79 (2021)
29. Maciejewski, P., Gawlik-Kobylińska, M., Lebiedź, J., Ostant, W., Aydın, D.: To survive in a CBRN hostile environment: application of cave automatic virtual environments in first responder training. In: Proceedings of the 3rd International Conference on Applications of Intelligent Systems, pp. 1–5 (2020)
30. Maes, F., Collignon, A., Vandermeulen, D., Marchal, G., Suetens, P.: Multimodality image registration by maximization of mutual information. IEEE Trans. Med. Imaging **16**(2), 187–198 (1997)
31. Manjrekar, S., Sandilya, S., Bhosale, D., Kanchi, S., Pitkar, A., Gondhalekar, M.: Cave: an emerging immersive technology–a review. In: 2014 UKSIM-AMSS 16th International Conference on Computer Modelling and Simulation, pp. 131–136. IEEE (2014)
32. Michopoulos, J., Paredis, C.J., Rosen, D.W., Vance, J.M.: Advances in Computers and Information in Engineering Research. American Society of Mechanical Engineers, New York (2014)
33. Minsky, M.: Telepresence (1980)
34. Narciso, D., Bessa, M., Melo, M., Coelho, A., Vasconcelos-Raposo, J.: Immersive 360ÃĆÂž video user experience - impact of different variables in the sense of presence and cybersickness. Univ. Access Inf. Soc. **18**, 77–87 (2019)
35. Neira, C.C., Reiners, D.: Portable cave automatic virtual environment system (2019). US Patent 10,412,380
36. Neira, C.C., Reiners, D.: Portable cave automatic virtual environment system (2021). US Patent 10,911,744
37. Qu, H., Hu, Z., Wu, J.: Multi-scale parallel gated local feature transformer. Sci. Rep. **15**(1), 7684 (2025)
38. Reinhard, E., Adhikhmin, M., Gooch, B., Shirley, P.: Color transfer between images. IEEE Comput. Graphics Appl. **21**(5), 34–41 (2002)
39. Riba, E., Mishkin, D., Ponsa, D., Rublee, E., Bradski, G.: Kornia: an open source differentiable computer vision library for PyTorch. In: Proceedings of the IEEE/CVF Winter Conference on Applications of Computer Vision, pp. 3674–3683 (2020)
40. Santos-González, I., Rivero-García, A., Molina-Gil, J., Caballero-Gil, P.: Implementation and analysis of real-time streaming protocols. Sensors **17**(4), 846 (2017)

41. Schonberger, J.L., Radenovic, F., Chum, O., Frahm, J.M.: From single image query to detailed 3D reconstruction. In: Proceedings of the IEEE Conference on Computer Vision and Pattern Recognition, pp. 5126–5134 (2015)
42. Shen, C.T., Liu, H.H., Yang, M.H., Hung, Y.P., Pei, S.C.: Viewing-distance aware super-resolution for high-definition display. IEEE Trans. Image Process. **24**(1), 403–418 (2014)
43. Shi, W., et al.: Real-time single image and video super-resolution using an efficient sub-pixel convolutional neural network. In: Proceedings of the IEEE Conference on Computer Vision and Pattern Recognition, pp. 1874–1883 (2016)
44. Springer, J.P., Neumann, C.P., Reiners, D., Cruz-Neira, C.: Create and experience compelling scenarios in VR: a hardware and software system architecture. In: Advances in Computers and Information in Engineering Research, vol. 1, pp. 557–595. ASME Press (2014)
45. Sredojev, B., Samardzija, D., Posarac, D.: WebRTC technology overview and signaling solution design and implementation. In: 2015 38th International Convention on Information and Communication Technology, Electronics and Microelectronics (MIPRO), pp. 1006–1009. IEEE (2015)
46. Sun, J., Shen, Z., Wang, Y., Bao, H., Zhou, X.: LoFTR: aetector-free local feature matching with transformers. In: Proceedings of the IEEE/CVF Conference on Computer Vision and Pattern Recognition, pp. 8922–8931 (2021)
47. Talisainen, A., Leoste, J., Virkus, S.: Comparative analysis of telepresence robots' video performance: evaluating camera capabilities for remote teaching and learning. Appl. Sci. **14**(1), 233 (2023)
48. Tam, W.J., Stelmach, L.B., Corriveau, P.J.: Psychovisual aspects of viewing stereoscopic video sequences. In: Stereoscopic Displays and Virtual Reality Systems V, vol. 3295, pp. 226–235. SPIE (1998)
49. Tang, A., Fakourfar, O., Neustaedter, C., Bateman, S.: Collaboration in 360 videochat: Challenges and opportunities (2017)
50. Tyszkiewicz, M., Fua, P., Trulls, E.: Disk: learning local features with policy gradient. Adv. Neural. Inf. Process. Syst. **33**, 14254–14265 (2020)
51. Wang, X., et al.: Examining the effects of an immersive learning environment in tertiary AEC education: Cave-VR system for students' perception and technology acceptance. J. Civ. Eng. Educ. **150**(2), 05023012 (2024)
52. Wang, X., Xie, L., Dong, C., Shan, Y.: Real-ESRGAN: training real-world blind super-resolution with pure synthetic data. In: Proceedings of the IEEE/CVF International Conference on Computer Vision, pp. 1905–1914 (2021)
53. Wong, E.S., Wahab, N.H.A., Saeed, F., Alharbi, N.: 360-degree video bandwidth reduction: technique and approaches comprehensive review. Appl. Sci. **12**(15), 7581 (2022)
54. Youssef, K., Said, S., Al Kork, S., Beyrouthy, T.: Telepresence in the recent literature with a focus on robotic platforms, applications and challenges. Robotics **12**(4), 111 (2023)
55. Zhao, X., Wu, X., Miao, J., Chen, W., Chen, P.C., Li, Z.: Alike: accurate and lightweight keypoint detection and descriptor extraction. IEEE Trans. Multimedia **25**, 3101–3112 (2022)
56. Zink, M., Sitaraman, R., Nahrstedt, K.: Scalable 360 video stream delivery: challenges, solutions, and opportunities. Proc. IEEE **107**(4), 639–650 (2019)
57. Zitova, B., Flusser, J.: Image registration methods: a survey. Image Vis. Comput. **21**(11), 977–1000 (2003)

XRSynthesizer: Synthesizing Modular XR UI Components for Adaptive, Multi-Context Spatial Interaction

Alexandra Plexousaki[1]([📧]) [iD], Asterios Leonidis[1,2] [iD], Maria Korozi[1] [iD],
Spyridon Tzagkarakis[1], and Constantine Stephanidis[1,2] [iD]

[1] Institute of Computer Science (ICS), Foundation for Research
and Technology - Hellas (FORTH), Heraklion, Greece
{aplex,leonidis,korozi,stzagkarak,cs}@ics.forth.gr
[2] Department of Computer Science, University of Crete, Heraklion, Greece

Abstract. Extended Reality (XR) technologies are reshaping digital interaction by shifting from traditional 2D interfaces to immersive, always-on, and context-aware 3D User Interfaces (3D UIs) that surround users and dynamically adapt to environmental changes. However, current XR development practices typically require XR UIs to be hardcoded as single, monolithic instances within individual applications. This approach limits adaptability, hinders cross-project reuse, and constrains the support for multiple, modular UI components that can coexist and dynamically adapt within a shared XR environment. We introduce XRSynthesizer, a framework that enables the dynamic assembly and adaptation of independent XR UIs in a spatial UI conglomerate at runtime. Leveraging cloud-based storage and an orchestrator-driven retrieval process, XRSynthesizer decouples UI creation from the host application, allowing developers to register, distribute, and update XR UIs independently of the application's build cycle. Through a structured four-stage workflow—starting from the creation of a single XR UI to real-time synthesis of multiple independent XR UIs into a unified, context-aware interactive experience— the framework promotes modularity, reduces development overhead, and supports flexible, context-driven XR experiences.

Keywords: User Interface Toolkits · Extended Reality ·
Context-Aware Systems

1 Introduction

Extended Reality (XR)—encompassing Virtual Reality (VR), Augmented Reality (AR), and Mixed Reality (MR)—is reshaping human-computer interaction by merging digital content with the physical world. XR applications are rapidly expanding across domains such as entertainment, healthcare, education, and industry, enabling spatially aware and intuitive interactions beyond conventional 2D Graphical User Interfaces (GUIs).

© The Author(s), under exclusive license to Springer Nature Switzerland AG 2026
D. Michael-Grigoriou et al. (Eds.): EuroXR 2025, LNCS 16101, pp. 104–123, 2026.
https://doi.org/10.1007/978-3-032-03805-0_6

As XR systems evolve, the transition from static 2D layouts to immersive 3D User Interfaces (3D UIs) has introduced new design challenges. 3D UIs leverage spatial depth, motion, and perspective to enhance User Experience (UX) [1], yet their development remains complex, particularly when interfaces must adapt dynamically to changing contexts and user behavior. In many emerging XR scenarios, multiple applications contribute distinct user interface components to a shared immersive environment. For example, an XR workspace may feature simultaneously real-time dashboards from an analytics platform, communication controls from a messaging service, and interactive tools from a design application—each operating as a discrete isolated module. Managing these interfaces in a unified and responsive manner requires dynamic composition of XR UIs at runtime.

A key challenge in such environments is the need for runtime adaptability. Adaptive UIs—capable of adjusting layout, visibility, and behavior—are essential for reducing cognitive load and maintaining user safety [2], while Pervasive Augmented Reality systems aim to enable continuous, context-aware digital augmentation [3]. In this paper, we adopt a practical definition of *context* as any application-specific state or developer-defined trigger that informs when and how XR UIs should appear, transform, or disappear during execution. This includes real-time events such as user proximity, gaze direction, or task progression, which can prompt interface transformations—for instance, shrinking a detailed UI into a compact visual indicator when a user steps away from its focal area. In fact, we distinguish this from software-driven updates, where newer UI versions are fetched and integrated during runtime without user-driven context; while both modes enhance flexibility, only the former constitutes context-aware adaptation.

Addressing this challenge, this paper presents *XRSynthesizer*—a framework for modular XR UI development that decouples interface design from application logic. XRSynthesizer enables developers to design, register, and distribute XR UIs independently, supporting dynamic retrieval and integration at runtime based on contextual factors. The framework introduces a four-stage workflow: (1) *XR UI Creation*, (2) *XR UI Distribution*, (3) *XR Consolidation*, and (4) *XR Synthesis*. This pipeline facilitates real-time assembly of modular XR components, cross-project reusability, and responsive UI adaptation. By supporting the dynamic synthesis of interface components, XRSynthesizer enhances both the flexibility and scalability of XR application development.

The remainder of the paper first reviews related work on adaptive and modular XR UIs, then outlines key challenges and design goals. It then describes the architecture and key components of the XRSynthesizer framework, detailing its four-stage pipeline for XR UI synthesis and integration. The system's functionality is illustrated through a series of implementation examples highlighting modularity and extensibility. To assess the framework's utility, a demonstration-based expert evaluation using heuristic claims tailored for developer toolkits is presented. The paper concludes with a discussion of the results, limitations, implications, and directions for future work.

2   Related Work

Designing adaptive and reusable user interfaces (UIs) remains a central challenge in the development of XR systems. A number of frameworks have addressed this by proposing modular design patterns, dynamic interface adaptation techniques, and improved workflows for UI management.

The complexity and steep learning curve of native XR development environments often impede novice developers from efficiently creating adaptive UIs [6]. Approaches advocating for no-code authoring tools and adaptive user interfaces that adjust to developer expertise levels [5] highlight the need for frameworks that streamline UI creation workflows [4]. XRSynthesizer addresses these challenges by providing a cloud-based platform for modular, context-driven synthesis of XR UIs, effectively lowering the barrier to entry and enabling developers to compose, distribute, and integrate interactive widgets dynamically without deep expertise in underlying XR systems.

One major strand of research focuses on dynamic adaptation and context-awareness in user interfaces. The Adaptive User Interfaces Toolkit (AUIT) [7] enables developers to define adaptation objectives that are automatically optimized at runtime, such as visibility, reachability, and consistency. This approach reduces the need for manual scripting of UI adaptations and ensures fluid transitions as user and environmental conditions evolve.

Todi et al. [2] propose a structured framework for the computational design and adaptation of XR user interfaces, where adaptation decisions are driven by answering five core questions: what, how much, where, how, and when to present interface elements. Their model emphasizes the importance of timing and presentation as key elements in minimizing user distraction and maintaining usability in complex 3D environments.

Beyond adaptation, the modularity and reusability of UI components have been addressed in systems such as the Widget Framework Toolkit (WF Toolkit) [8]. While closely aligned with our goals, the WF Toolkit operates at a lower level of abstraction, focusing on individual widget components. This framework proposes a component-based approach for widget construction and integration within Unity applications, allowing developers to design reusable XR UIs that can be deployed across projects without extensive re-engineering. Similarly, Ubi-Interact [9] facilitates distributed interaction handling in XR environments through a modular, publish-subscribe communication model that allows UI components to be instantiated, synchronized, and adapted across multiple devices and application instances in real time.

Despite the progress made by these frameworks, most existing solutions rely on statically embedded widget architectures or predefined runtime configurations, which limits their flexibility in scenarios requiring on-the-fly interface composition or cross-project reuse of interactive components. In contrast, *XRSynthesizer* introduces a cloud-based model for XR UI distribution and runtime synthesis. By decoupling UI creation from the application build process and enabling real-time context-driven instantiation, the framework promotes scalability, modularity, and adaptability for XR applications.

3   Motivation

Many XR applications today require interface elements that adapt dynamically to system state, user behavior, and environmental context. From the user's perspective, wearing an XR head-mounted display (HMD) means their physical space is augmented with interactive digital content tailored to immediate needs and surroundings. For example, a user working alone at their office desk might see an arrangement of XR UIs—such as a to-do list and a weather summary—positioned for personal productivity. The to-do list UI is configured to respond to user presence and productivity-related triggers. The weather UI is connected to a remote API, enabling it to reflect environmental conditions and user scheduling data.

When the same user enters a meeting room, the system could present those same applications with altered configurations, alongside additional collaborative tools like a video call application designed to activate automatically when remote participants are detected, all adjusted to support group interaction (see Fig. 1). Such scenarios illustrate a broader paradigm shift: XR is evolving beyond the traditional model of launching apps on demand, toward an environment where digital experiences appear and adapt seamlessly—more like accessing a website than opening an application. The user does not explicitly launch software; instead, interface components manifest automatically in response to contextual triggers such as location, proximity, or task state.

An inevitable development challenge arises when such applications are built by multiple contributors. Considering the above scenario, one developer may be responsible for designing the to-do list widget that appears near the user when relevant metrics are available and changes accordingly when in a group setting, for example, in a meeting. Another developer may create a video call XR UI that activates in the presence of remote participants, and similarly, a third developer is responsible for creating a weather app XR UI. Consequently, a separate developer —serving as the integrator— is tasked with overseeing the main application and defines the rules that govern when and how these XR UIs are presented, based on runtime events and contextual information. Under traditional workflows, this setup requires tight coordination across development teams, with every UI element statically compiled into the application. Even small modifications can necessitate a full rebuild of the application, limiting flexibility and slowing iteration (see Fig. 4.a).

XRSynthesizer is introduced as a solution to this modularity and integration bottleneck. It provides a structured pipeline that decouples the creation, distribution, and integration of XR UIs. Each one is developed independently using the XRSynthesizer Creator plugin, where its behavior, visual characteristics, and interaction logic are defined. These XR UIs are then uploaded to a shared cloud repository. Separately, the main application is developed using the XRSynthesizer Builder plugin, which allows it to retrieve and instantiate XR UIs dynamically at runtime. This design greatly reduces the need to modify or rebuild the core application when introducing or adjusting individual UI elements. Particularly for small interaction-related updates, the ability to push changes solely to the relevant XR UI components streamlines maintenance and allows the main application to remain stable and lightweight (see Fig. 4.b). Lastly, a centralized orchestration server coordinates the behavior of the active widget set based on high-level application logic and developer-defined triggers, such as user proximity, input patterns, or environmental cues. These triggers reflect the contextual conditions under which XR UIs are presented, updated, or removed at runtime, enabling context-aware adaptation.

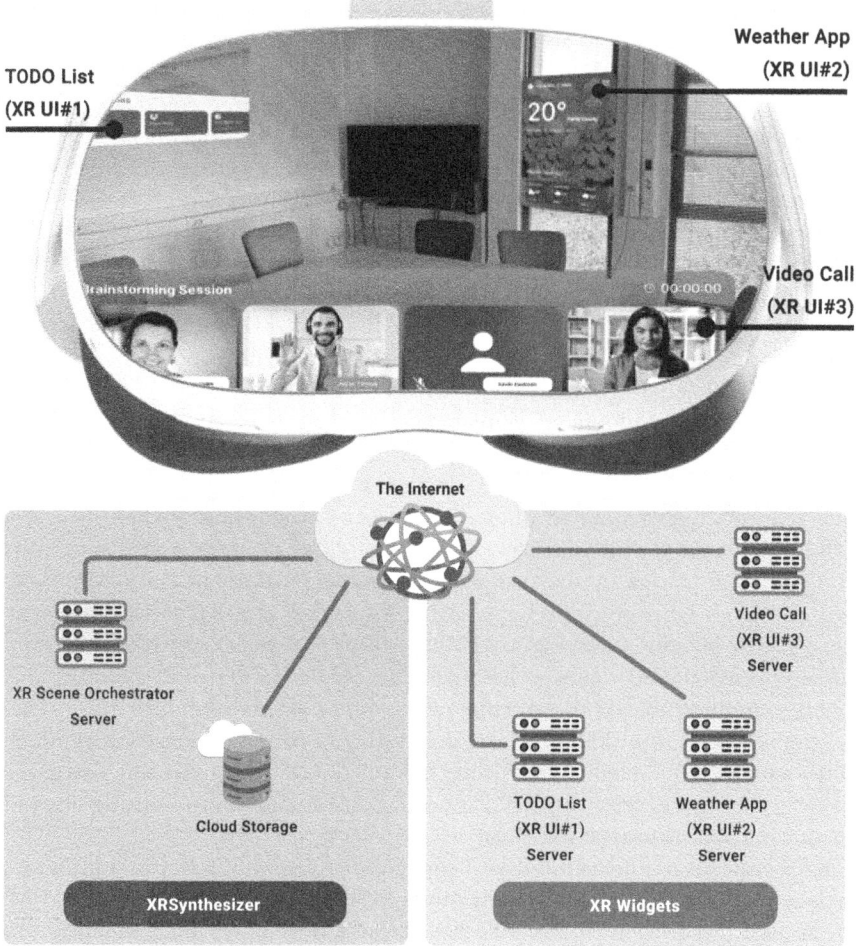

Fig. 1. The orchestration of XR UIs within a meeting room scenario using XRSynthesizer to accommodate group interaction

By separating UI development from application integration, XRSynthesizer enables parallel development, reduces redundant effort, and supports the reuse of interface components across distinct XR scenarios.

This paradigm shift from static to dynamic XR UI integration facilitates more scalable, collaborative, and adaptable development workflows.

4   The XRSynthesizer Framework

Building upon established methodologies in XR development, the proposed framework is designed to enable the dynamic instantiation and modular management of XR UIs. The core principle of XRSynthesizer is the decoupling of XR UI creation and deployment from the XR environment. This design allows XR applications to dynamically retrieve, instantiate, and update UIs at runtime, significantly reducing development time and enhancing resource reusability. Unlike traditional approaches, where UI elements and interactive components must be precompiled into the application build, XRSynthesizer enables on-demand XR UI retrieval and integration, eliminating the need for frequent application updates when modifying or introducing new UI elements. This is especially advantageous for small, interaction-specific updates, which can be deployed independently without affecting the broader application lifecycle.

The framework operates as a distributed system, integrating both local execution on the head-mounted display (HMD) and cloud services to manage XR UI storage, retrieval, and contextual deployment. As illustrated in Fig. 1, the XR application runs on the HMD, orchestrating the loading and rendering of dynamically retrieved XR UIs. These elements are stored externally within a cloud repository, enabling applications to remain lightweight while still supporting a broad range of interactive XR UIs. The XR Scene Orchestrator Server plays a pivotal role in this architecture by managing the synthesis and deployment of XR UIs based on application state, user interactions, external system inputs and contextual information. By acting as an intermediary commander between the XR application and the cloud storage, the server enables context-sensitive UI instantiation, adaptation or even removal.

Each XR UI maintains independent connections with external communication sources, allowing it to exchange real-time data with remote servers, RESTful APIs, or other external services. These connections enable each XR UI to realize its business-specific objectives by dynamically adapting to changing conditions within the application environment. Consequently, XRSynthesizer supports highly flexible and adaptable XR experiences. The framework's cloud repository further enhances scalability, ensuring that developers can register, update, and deploy XR UIs without requiring manual asset management within the main application (see Fig. 4.c).

XRSynthesizer operates above the level of traditional GUI composition. Rather than providing primitive widgets like buttons or text elements, it assumes that XR UIs are already implemented as complete, interactive modules. Customization, in this context, refers to how developers configure, deploy, and orchestrate these self-contained interfaces —such as a to-do list or HVAC controller— within the broader context of use, rather than constructing them from scratch.

By leveraging a modular approach to UI management, XRSynthesizer enhances the scalability of XR applications, making it particularly suitable for large-scale deployments and collaborative development environments. The ability to dynamically load and modify XR UIs without modifying the primary application's source code significantly reduces maintenance efforts while ensuring long-term sustainability. Additionally, the separation of interface logic from the application's core functionalities allows for incremental improvements and feature additions, ensuring that applications remain adaptable to future technological advancements and user demands.

4.1   XRSynthesizer Workflow - The Four-Stage Process

As illustrated in Fig. 2, the XRSynthesizer framework follows a structured four-stage workflow to enable the modular, scalable creation and integration of XR UIs. This design fosters collaborative development by clearly separating XR UI creation from application integration and runtime synthesis, allowing developers to build reusable, interactive components that can be dynamically managed without modifying the core application.

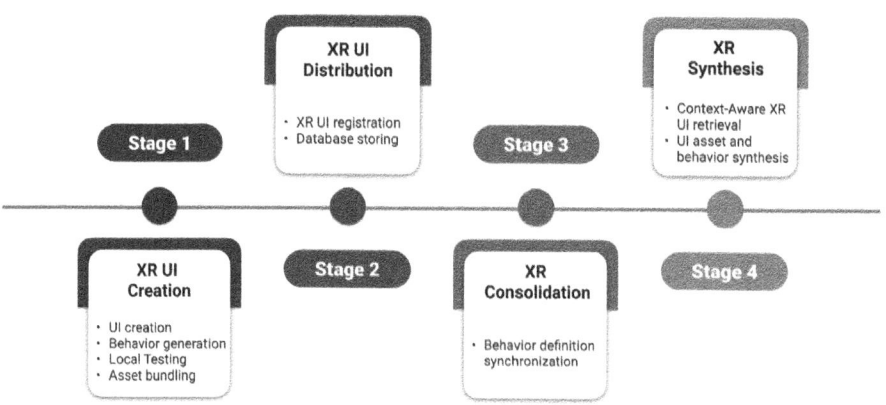

Fig. 2. The four-stage process of the XRSynthesizer framework

Stage 1: XR UI Creation. The initial stage includes the conceptualization, design, and creation of XR UIs. Developers define the visual, interactive, and behavioral characteristics of each XR UI, complying to standard XR interaction paradigms and design principles. At this stage, UIs are constructed as modular and independent entities to ensure they can function autonomously, simplify integration, and facilitate flexible reuse across different XR applications. Each XR UI is clearly defined with the necessary metadata and behavioral logic that enables seamless integration and dynamic composition within XR environments.

Stage 2: XR UI Distribution. The second stage involves registering and distributing functional XR UIs to the cloud repository. Following their creation, XR UIs are packaged, versioned, and stored along with associated metadata and configuration settings, thus becoming accessible for dynamic retrieval and instantiation at runtime. This cloud storage mechanism ensures widget availability, simplifies version control, and promotes reusability across multiple XR environments.

Stage 3: XR Consolidation. In the third stage, XR Consolidation, integration of the XR UI into the main XR application takes place. At this point, a developer distinct from the original creator is typically responsible for synchronizing and integrating UI behavior definitions stored in the cloud repository. Specifically, the developer retrieves UI definitions from the framework's database, ensuring that the UI's intended behavior and interaction logic remain intact. After successful consolidation, the XR application is compiled into an Android Package Kit (APK) and subsequently deployed onto the target head-mounted display (HMD). This structured separation of roles enhances modularity, reusability, and promotes collaborative development practices across diverse teams and application contexts.

Stage 4: XR Synthesis. The final stage, XR Synthesis, encompasses the continuous, dynamic orchestration of XR UIs within an XR environment. Through continuous monitoring of context-sensitive events, user interactions, and external triggers, the XR Scene Orchestrator Server synthesizes the active widget composition, dynamically configuring and activating, adjusting, or removing XR UIs in real-time. This synthesis capability ensures the XR environment remains responsive, contextually relevant, and interactive, seamlessly adapting to evolving conditions.

Each stage in this workflow plays an integral role in enabling the effective distribution and dynamic management of interactive XR UIs, resulting in a flexible and modular framework capable of supporting diverse application scenarios and collaborative development workflows.

5   Implementation

The implementation of XRSynthesizer follows a modular and distributed architecture that facilitates the dynamic integration of XR UIs into runtime applications. This approach envisions an ever-expanding application ecosystem—comparable to an XR-oriented operating system—where software components remain persistently active and are contextually rendered on demand. Analogous to the World Wide Web model, in which web applications are continuously accessible through a browser, the XRSynthesizer paradigm enables the seamless manifestation of these applications as interactive 3D XR user interfaces. The framework separates creation, distribution, and execution of XR UIs into distinct components, each responsible for a specific stage in the lifecycle of an XR UI. This section provides an overview of the technical realization of these components, highlighting their roles within the system and describing how they collectively enable the modular and context-aware assembly of XR interfaces.

5.1   System Architecture

The overall architecture of the XRSynthesizer framework is depicted in Fig. 3, illustrating the relationships and interactions between its main components. At the highest abstraction level, the system comprises two core Unity plugins—the XRSynthesizer Creator and the XRSynthesizer Builder—which interact directly with the XRSynthesizer Cloud Repository and the XR Scene Orchestrator Server. Communication between these components is facilitated through a hybrid communication model utilizing both RESTful services for structured data transactions and the MQTT protocol for real-time, event-driven messaging.

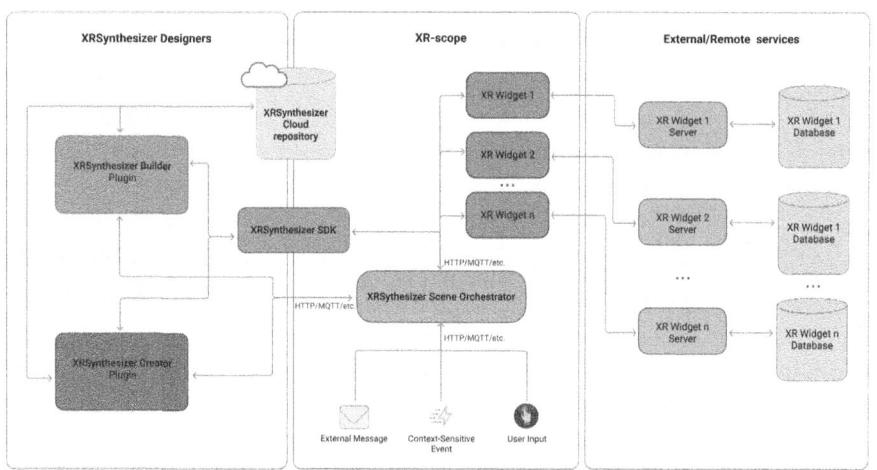

Fig. 3. The architecture of the XRSynthesizer framework

Additionally, UIs distributed via the framework may maintain independent communication channels with external, developer-defined servers—here referred to as widget-specific servers. For example, a weather UI may independently connect to a remote server to fetch up-to-date weather information. Within this context, the XRSynthesizer framework ensures that upon instantiation, XR UIs preserve their intended functionality, including maintaining communication with any external services they require. This architectural flexibility supports a wide spectrum of widget complexity, from elementary UI controls to sophisticated interactive three-dimensional environments, each potentially interacting with distinct external services to fulfill its designed purpose.

5.2   Core Software Components and Development Environment Plugins

As a developer-oriented tool, the framework is integrated in the Unity engine to ensure a seamless development experience. Through the use of dedicated Unity plugins, namely the *XRSynthesizer Creator* and *XRSynthesizer Builder*, the framework supports the entire lifecycle of XR UIs—from creation and packaging to retrieval and runtime integration—within the familiar Unity environment. This integration not only aligns with standard Unity development practices but also minimizes the need for extensive manual configuration or additional tooling, thereby streamlining both the development and deployment workflows. Furthermore, the framework enables seamless communication with external entities, such as the *XRSynthesizer Cloud Repository* and the *XRSynthesizer Scene Orchestrator*, directly from within Unity, removing the need for additional tools like browsers or standalone applications.

XRSynthesizer Creator Plugin. The XRSynthesizer Creator plugin serves as a development and packaging environment, enabling developers to design interactive XR UIs, specify their behaviors, and prepare them for registration and storage in the cloud repository. Moreover, developed as an easily importable package for Unity, the Creator plugin simplifies the UI development process, providing developers with a streamlined workflow through an intuitive toolbar integrated directly into the Unity editor interface. The plugin offers a set of defined actions aimed at guiding them step-by-step through the essential processes involved in preparing XR UIs for distribution.

The process of creating XR UIs within the XRSynthesizer framework closely aligns with standard XR application development practices, thereby minimizing additional complexity for developers. Consequently, developers can design and implement XR UIs using familiar development paradigms and workflows inherent to the Unity game engine, without significant deviations from conventional methods. Once functionality has been verified, the XR UI is packaged using Unity's Asset Bundle system[1]. Asset Bundles enable modular content management by allowing assets to be loaded and unloaded dynamically at runtime, rather than being statically embedded in the main application build. This approach reduces the application's initial size and supports lightweight, post-deployment content updates.

Within the XRSynthesizer pipeline, Asset Bundles serve as the primary distribution format for XR UIs. During registration, the developer attaches relevant metadata—including version identifiers, descriptions, and optional refer-

---

[1] https://docs.unity3d.com/Manual/AssetBundlesIntro.html.

ences to external APIs or services—to ensure that other developers can understand and effectively integrate the UI components into their own applications. This structured packaging process guarantees that each XR UI unit is modular, self-contained, and ready for seamless upload to and retrieval from the XRSynthesizer repository.

To ensure smooth integration and interoperability, XRSynthesizer includes functionality to manage and isolate code dependencies through selective assembly referencing. Developers can refine which dependencies are bundled with each XR UI, helping to prevent conflicts and reduce redundancy. By default, the system maintains a configurable list of common Unity, .NET, and internal framework assemblies to exclude from distribution, ensuring that only the necessary, unique components are packaged. This approach enhances modularity, improves build performance, and preserves compatibility across diverse deployment environments.

XRSynthesizer Builder Plugin. The XRSynthesizer Builder is a complementary Unity plugin that enables the dynamic retrieval, instantiation, and orchestration of XR UIs during application runtime. It forms the second half of the framework's workflow, building on the modular packaging achieved through the Creator plugin. Once integrated into a Unity project, the Builder simplifies the process of embedding external XR UIs into existing scenes without requiring changes to the core application code.

The plugin supports seamless communication with the XRSynthesizer cloud infrastructure and the runtime orchestrator. Developers can configure connection parameters and initiate the orchestration system directly within the Unity editor. This setup includes a centralized manager object that automatically handles runtime behavior such as asset retrieval, event-driven updates, and communication with external services. The architecture is designed to require minimal manual intervention, ensuring compatibility with existing Unity workflows.

To ensure that dynamically loaded XR UIs operate as intended, the plugin also provides mechanisms to import behavior definitions and accompanying dependencies. This allows for the inclusion of customized interaction logic and platform-specific features authored by the original widget developers. Before these behaviors are introduced into the scene, the system verifies and aligns all relevant dependencies to prevent conflicts and ensure runtime consistency.

Moreover, to support robust versioning and reduce deployment errors, the Builder plugin includes safeguards that alert developers if the latest versions of behavior definitions have not yet been synchronized before compiling the application. This ensures that the most up-to-date logic is always included in the final build, reducing the risk of runtime inconsistencies due to outdated assets.

Once registered in the cloud repository, XR UIs become accessible to developers through the Builder plugin, which enables their discovery, retrieval, and runtime integration. Additionally, while the core structure and logic of each XR UI are defined at creation time, developers integrating them into a scene retain control over layout, positioning, visibility, and high-level behavior through standard Unity interfaces and orchestration parameters, enabling contextual customization at runtime.

XRSynthesizer Scene Orchestrator. The XRSynthesizer Scene Orchestrator serves as the central coordination hub responsible for managing and orchestrating XR UI interactions and lifecycle events. Implemented as a Node.js application, the server integrates both HTTP and MQTT protocols to facilitate seamless communication between the cloud repository, external services, and XR runtime environments. By abstracting UI registration, dependency management, and runtime event handling into discrete, manageable components, the server provides a robust foundation upon which dynamic XR experiences can be built. Its ability to integrate HTTP-based configuration management with MQTT-based real-time communication exemplifies the hybrid communication model that is central to the XRSynthesizer framework, ensuring that XR UIs function as intended by their developers while dynamically adapting to contextual changes in the XR environment.

XRSynthesizer Cloud Repository. XRSynthesizer's Cloud Repository serves as the centralized storage solution for XR UI definitions, asset bundles, and associated metadata within the XRSynthesizer framework. This repository not only maintains UI assets but also manages versioning, dependency configurations, and other essential information required for the dynamic retrieval and integration of XR UIs at runtime.

The repository is designed to facilitate the rapid distribution and update of XR UIs by ensuring that all necessary files and configurations are stored in a secure and scalable cloud environment. By leveraging standard cloud storage mechanisms, the repository supports efficient content delivery and dynamic updates, which are critical for maintaining a responsive XR application. XR UIs registered in the repository include comprehensive metadata that specifies their operational parameters, version information, and any dependency requirements, thereby allowing the XRSynthesizer system to seamlessly synchronize and instantiate XR UIs as needed.

Furthermore, the repository's architecture emphasizes modularity and decoupling. Developers can update individual UIs or dependencies without affecting the broader ecosystem, enabling continuous integration and distribution workflows. This decoupled approach ensures that the main application can dynamically load and integrate widgets based on context-specific triggers and user interactions, thereby preserving the intended functionality as defined by the original developers.

XRSyntheizer SDK. The XRSynthesizer SDK constitutes the foundational layer that abstracts the complexities of integrating and managing XR UIs within the framework. By providing a uniform set of application programming interfaces

(APIs), the SDK simplifies communication among the framework's components and ensures that widgets can be developed and distributed with minimal overhead. The SDK thereby enables consistent, developer-friendly interactions across different system components, minimizing the integration effort required for developers utilizing the framework, thus enabling an agnostic two-way communication between the dynamically created XR UIs and the main XR application.

5.3   Technical Overview of the Orchestration of XR UIs Within a Meeting Room Scenario

To demonstrate the practical impact of XRSynthesizer, we present a technical walkthrough of the meeting room scenario described in Sect. 3, where multiple XR UIs—such as a to-do list, a weather widget, and a video conferencing interface—must be dynamically assembled into the XR environment.

Using XRSynthesizer, each of these XR UIs is developed independently through the Creator Plugin by different authors.

After development, these XR UIs are uploaded to the XRSynthesizer Cloud Repository by their creator along with their metadata and behavioral logic. The core application, which is built using the Builder Plugin, remains loosely-coupled from these interface components at compile time. During runtime, the XR Scene Orchestrator Server evaluates contextual signals—such as user location, activity state, or environmental conditions—and dynamically retrieves and instantiates the appropriate XR UIs. This approach allows each UI to be versioned and updated independently, without requiring changes to or recompilation of the main application. As a result, even small interaction-level updates can be deployed seamlessly by modifying only the affected XR UI. Furthermore, developers are able to work in parallel, with no need for coordination around a shared codebase, while integration logic remains centralized and flexible through the orchestration server.

In contrast, implementing this scenario using a conventional XR development workflow would involve embedding all UI elements directly within the main application's source code. Each variation of an interface would have to be manually coded into the logic of the application, including conditions for when and how UIs are activated or hidden. Developers working on separate widgets would need to tightly coordinate their efforts to avoid conflicts in scene structure, interaction logic, or resource usage. Any change to the behavior or layout of a single UI component would typically require a full recompilation and redeployment of the entire application. This not only increases overhead, but also significantly slows iteration and complicates maintenance.

Figure 4 demonstrates a comparative overview of the XRSynthesizer and traditional approaches. This comparison highlights several advantages introduced by XRSynthesizer's architecture. While this approach does not eliminate all complexities associated with XR development, it offers a practical pathway toward more flexible and maintainable workflows, particularly in scenarios where interfaces must frequently adapt to changing user contexts.

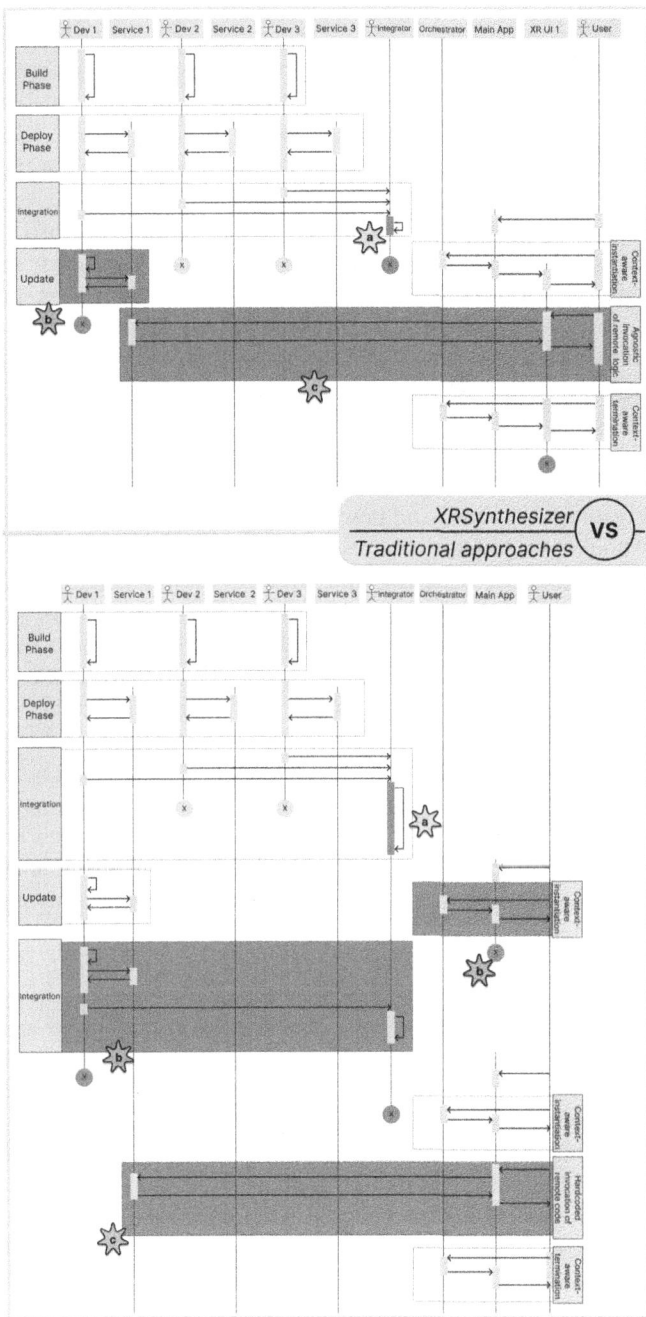

Fig. 4. Compared to traditional methods, our approach has 3 main advantages: (a) streamlined integration, (b) live updates without downtime, (c) agnostic invocation of service-specific remote functionality.

6   Evaluation

In evaluating the XRSynthesizer system, our approach was guided primarily by the evaluation principles proposed by Dan R. Olsen in [10]. This decision was motivated by the nature of our framework, which is not an end-user application but a developer-oriented toolkit designed to enable and streamline the synthesis, registration, and distribution of interactive XR UIs. Traditional usability testing methods—focused on metrics such as time-to-task-completion or error rates— are inadequate for evaluating systems of this kind. Olsen identifies the "usability trap" as a common misapplication of evaluation methods in systems research. He argues that usability studies are often built on assumptions that do not hold for developer toolkits, such as "walk-up-and-use" paradigms, the presence of standardized tasks, and small-scale evaluation timelines.

Demonstrations have been recognized as one of the most effective and widely used evaluation strategies in toolkit research. According to Ledo et al. [11], demonstrations serve as existence proofs and communicate a toolkit's capabilities by showing what it enables and how its components can be combined. Rather than testing small isolated features in controlled tasks, demonstrations contextualize the toolkit in realistic scenarios and allow for a more holistic understanding of its design goals and technical depth. Our choice of a demonstration-based, heuristic evaluation is consistent with several other HCI and toolkit research papers that adopted similar methods to assess system expressiveness and architectural value, including ChainForge (2024), Albrecht et al. (2023), and XSpace (2022) [12–14].

To ensure an appropriate evaluation approach, we performed a walkthrough demonstration with seven (7) HCI/XR experts. We recruited seven male participants from our HCI research lab, all with academic and research backgrounds in Computer Science. Their ages ranged from 20 to 47. All participants had substantial experience with Unity development, and the majority actively work with XR technologies in their research. This ensured that the evaluators were well-positioned to assess the technical relevance, architectural design, and practical integration potential of the XRSynthesizer framework.

During the walkthrough, the evaluators were encouraged to ask questions and offer comments. This was followed by a group discussion to gather further insights and foster critical reflection. Afterwards, the experts were asked to assess XRSynthesizer based on Olsen's set of heuristics via an online form. This form was based on a set of heuristic claims proposed by Olsen, which are widely used to evaluate UI systems and developer toolkits. These claims are particularly suited for developer-oriented frameworks and emphasize architectural, design, and practical concerns over traditional usability metrics. The set of heuristics proposed by Olsen are the following:

1. **Importance**: Evaluates whether the toolkit addresses a significant and relevant problem within its intended context of use. This includes assessing the significance of the user population, tasks, and situations the toolkit targets.

2. **Problem not previously solved**: Assesses whether the toolkit introduces a genuinely novel capability, enabling solutions that were difficult or impossible to achieve with existing tools.

3. **Generality**: Measures the breadth of applicability—how well the toolkit supports a diverse range of use cases, user groups, or tasks beyond a single narrow scenario.

4. **Reduction of Solution Viscosity**: Refers to the ease with which developers can iterate on or modify solutions. A low-viscosity toolkit makes experimentation and adaptation simple and efficient. There are at least three ways in which a tool can reduce solution viscosity: through flexibility, expressive leverage and expressive match.

5. **Empowering new design participants**: Considers whether the toolkit lowers the barrier of entry for non-experts or new contributors, enabling broader participation in the design or development process.

6. **Power in Combination**: Assesses whether the toolkit supports composability—i.e., how well it integrates with other systems or components to enable complex, scalable solutions.

7. **Can it scale up?**: The toolkit should be capable of handling complex or large-scale applications, not just small examples or demos.

6.1   Results

We analyzed participants' responses across claims by calculating both mean scores and standard deviations to understand the consistency of perceptions. The chart in Fig. 5 displays the mean expert evaluation scores and standard deviation for each of Olsen's heuristic claims as applied to the XRSynthesizer system. The results were aggregated to reflect the average perception of the system's performance in relation to each heuristic dimension. It is observed that Claims 1 and 2 showed high agreement with moderate variability (SD 0.53âĂŞ0.74), while Claims 3, 4, 5 and 6 showed good agreement with slightly higher variability (SD 0.68âĂŞ0.91), indicating some differences in user experiences. Claim 7, concerning compatibility and scalability, had the lowest average score and the highest variability (SD 0.89), suggesting this is an area with mixed perceptions and potential room for improvement.

Claims 1 (*Importance*) and 2 (*Problem not previously solved*) received the highest scores, with averages of 4.5 and 4.6, respectively. These scores suggest strong consensus among the experts that XRSynthesizer addresses a relevant and valuable challenge in the XR development space, and that it introduces novel capabilities that were previously difficult or impractical to achieve using traditional approaches. Similarly, Claim 6 (*Power in combination*) was positively evaluated (4.4), indicating that the system's architectural design—particularly its modularity and support for dynamic behavior registration—was seen as enabling effective composition and integration with existing tools such as Unity.

The lowest score was observed for Claim 7 (*Can it scale up?*), which received an average rating of 3.8. This score reflects expert concerns regarding the system's readiness for large-scale adoption and its ability to support increasingly

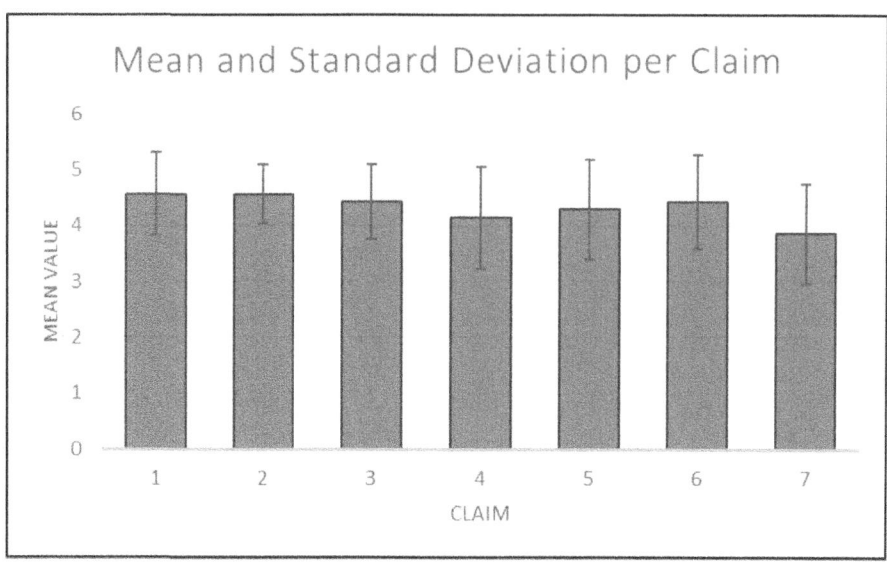

Fig. 5. Mean and Standard Deviation per Olsen Claim

complex deployment scenarios. The moderate score in response to these claims suggests that while XRSynthesizer was recognized as a functional and well-integrated solution for current use cases, experts expressed reservations about its long-term viability in more demanding contexts. Specifically, some evaluators noted that although the system encapsulates complexity effectively for straight-forward use cases, it may expose limitations when developers attempt to override default behaviors or customize functionality beyond the intended abstraction layer. Furthermore, while the framework is designed with Unity compatibility in mind, questions were raised about how well it would adapt to more heterogeneous software ecosystems, version migrations and overall compatibility.

During the group discussion, most evaluators expressed that the problem addressed by XRSynthesizer is highly relevant to their work and development practices. Several participants indicated that the framework aligns well with their existing workflows and would offer tangible benefits, particularly by streamlining repetitive integration tasks and facilitating collaboration in team-based development environments. Notably, concerns regarding the integration of the framework into daily practice were minimal; instead, evaluators emphasized its potential to save time and reduce overhead, especially when coordinating across teams with diverse roles and responsibilities. Furthermore, the evaluators suggested that the framework could be significantly enhanced by incorporating an asset store or community-driven interface. Such a feature would enable developers to explore, share, and reuse distributed XR UIs, thereby extending the utility of the system and fostering a broader ecosystem around modular XR components.

Overall, the evaluation results support the conclusion that XRSynthesizer provides a compelling and innovative approach to XR widget development and integration, with strong performance in terms of novelty, expressiveness, and composability. However, future work should address concerns around system generality, XR UI customization and especially complexity management, in order to position the framework for broader adoption and long-term impact in more complex XR development contexts.

7   Limitations

Despite its modular architecture and cloud-based flexibility, XRSynthesizer presents some limitations. Firstly, although asset and UI updates can be deployed without recompiling the application, any changes to behavior code require developers to synchronize their project with the framework's database and rebuild their application. Secondly, the use of underlying tools such as Unity asset bundles, while essential for modularity, presents a steep learning curve for beginners. This somewhat conflicts with the framework's goal of simplifying the integration process for developers without requiring in-depth knowledge of these tools. Thirdly, the current versioning and dependency management mechanisms need further improvement, posing challenges in maintaining consistency across evolving widget libraries and shared assets. Furthermore, while the orchestration server effectively supports runtime widget synthesis, its scalability in highly dynamic environments or in managing multiple simultaneous context shifts warrants further enhancement. Finally, end developers have limited flexibility in configuring widget behavior at runtime, as they cannot modify the underlying code of retrieved widgets, restricting full customization in certain scenarios.

8   Conclusions

We introduce XRSynthesizer, a modular framework that overcomes the limitations of static XR interface development by enabling dynamic synthesis, distribution, and reuse of XR UIs. Through a structured four-stage pipeline, XRSynthesizer decouples user interface development from application runtime. This architecture allows XR UI components to be uploaded, configured, managed, and instantiated on demand, supporting scalable and adaptable XR experiences in scenarios where user needs and contextual conditions frequently change.

In addition to enabling dynamic XR UI integration, XRSynthesizer aims to simplify the development and maintenance of intelligent XR applications. The framework is designed with a developer-centric focus, streamlining the reuse of XR UIs across different applications while supporting dynamic view composition for independent widgets. This flexibility makes it possible to construct responsive, context-aware interfaces without embedding UI elements directly into the application's codebase.

To evaluate the framework's usability and effectiveness, an expert-based heuristic evaluation was conducted using methods appropriate for the assessment of development frameworks and toolkits [10,11]. Through a guided walkthrough demonstration, HCI and XR experts explored the system and shared insights that underscored the framework's strengths in modularity and adaptability, while also identifying areas for further improvement.

By addressing key challenges in XR UI development, XRSynthesizer paves the way for more scalable, flexible, and user-adaptive XR applications, and anticipates a future in which XR UI development resembles web development: user interfaces are defined externally, loaded dynamically, and rendered at runtime. By supporting immersive 3D interfaces, multitasking across multiple active applications, and context-driven deployment, the framework lays groundwork for reusable, adaptive XR UIs that can scale beyond monolithic, app-centric design models.

Future work will focus on developing a windowed environment specifically designed to support XR user interfaces, enabling more flexible and intuitive management of multiple XR UI components within a single immersive workspace. Additionally, further evaluation of the framework is planned to validate its usability and effectiveness in diverse real-world scenarios.

Key challenges to be addressed include enhancing system generality to support a wider range of XR applications, improving runtime customization capabilities for greater developer control, and managing the complexity that arises from dynamic context-driven UI composition. In parallel, we are actively exploring how XRSynthesizer could enhance existing XR operating systems, such as Android XR, Meta Horizon OS, and Apple visionOS, by leveraging their APIs and SDKs to introduce system-wide UI composition capabilities.

References

1. Yeo, A., Kwok, B.W.J., Joshna, A., Chen, K., Lee, J.S.A.: Entering the next dimension: a review of 3D user interfaces for virtual reality. Electronics 13(3), 3 (2024). https://doi.org/10.3390/electronics13030600
2. Todi, K., Lafreniere, B., Jonker, T.: Computational Adaptation of XR Interfaces Through Interaction Simulation, 18 October 2022. arXiv: arXiv:2204.09162, https://doi.org/10.48550/arXiv.2204.09162
3. Grubert, J., Langlotz, T., Zollmann, S., Regenbrecht, H.: Towards pervasive augmented reality: context-awareness in augmented reality. IEEE Trans. Visual Comput. Graphics 23(6), 1706–1724 (2017). https://doi.org/10.1109/TVCG.2016.2543720
4. Murray, J.T., Johnson, E.K.: XR content authoring challenges: The creator-developer divide. Augmented and mixed reality for communities, pp. 245–264. CRC Press (2021)
5. Erdem, A.G.: The Hitchhiker's Guide to XR: Novel Methods to Lower the Barriers for Novice Developers (2024)
6. Nebeling, M.: XR tools and where they are taking us: characterizing the evolving research on augmented, virtual, and mixed reality prototyping and development tools. XRDS 29, 1 (Fall 2022), 32–38 (2022). https://doi.org/10.1145/3558192

7. J. M. Evangelista Belo et al., "AUIT – the Adaptive User Interfaces Toolkit for Designing XR Applications," in Proceedings of the 35th Annual ACM Symposium on User Interface Software and Technology, in UIST '22. New York, NY, USA: Association for Computing Machinery, Oct. 2022, pp. 1–16. https://doi.org/10.1145/3526113.3545651

8. Elvezio, C., Sukan, M., Feiner, S.: A framework to facilitate reusable, modular widget design for real-time interactive systems. In: 2016 IEEE 9th Workshop on Software Engineering and Architectures for Realtime Interactive Systems (SEARIS), pp. 1–7, March 2016. https://doi.org/10.1109/SEARIS.2016.7551586

9. Weber, S., et al.: Frameworks enabling ubiquitous mixed reality applications across dynamically adaptable device configurations. Front. Virtual Real. **3**, 765959 (2022). https://doi.org/10.3389/frvir.2022.765959

10. Olsen, D.R.: Evaluating user interface systems research. In: Proceedings of the 20th Annual ACM Symposium on User Interface Software and Technology, in UIST 2007, New York, NY, USA, pp. 251–258. Association for Computing Machinery, October 2007. https://doi.org/10.1145/1294211.1294256

11. Ledo, D., Houben, S., Vermeulen, J., Marquardt, N., Oehlberg, L., Greenberg, S.: Evaluation strategies for HCI toolkit research. In: Proceedings of the 2018 CHI Conference on Human Factors in Computing Systems, in CHI 2018. New York, NY, USA, pp. 1–17. Association for Computing Machinery, April 2018. https://doi.org/10.1145/3173574.3173610

12. Arawjo, I., Swoopes, C., Vaithilingam, P., Wattenberg, M, Glassman, E.L.: Chain-Forge: a visual toolkit for prompt engineering and LLM hypothesis testing. In: Proceedings of the 2024 CHI Conference on Human Factors in Computing Systems (CHI 2024). Association for Computing Machinery, New York, NY, USA, Article 304, pp. 1–18 (2024). https://doi.org/10.1145/3613904.3642016

13. Albrecht, M., Assländer, L., Reiterer, H., Streuber, S.: MoPeDT: a modular head-mounted display toolkit to conduct peripheral vision research. In: IEEE Conference Virtual Reality and 3D User Interfaces (VR). Shanghai, China 2023, pp. 691–701 (2023). https://doi.org/10.1109/VR55154.2023.00084

14. Herskovitz, J., Cheng, Y.F., Guo, A., Sample, A.P., Nebeling, M.: Space: an augmented reality toolkit for enabling spatially-aware distributed collaboration. Proc. ACM Hum. Comput. Interact. **6**, 568 (2022). https://doi.org/10.1145/3567721

Navigating Narratives: A Typology of Way-Finding Strategies for VR Storytelling

Soumya Agarwal$^{(\boxtimes)}$ and Jayesh S. Pillai

IDC School of Design, Indian Institute of Technology, Bombay, India
{24m2522,jay}@iitb.ac.in

Abstract. Way-finding is central to the user experience of narrative-driven virtual reality (VR), yet few frameworks systematically address how navigation supports story progression, spatial orientation, and presence. This paper proposes a typology of way-finding strategies grounded in a structured review of existing literature and an inductive analysis of four VR narrative experiences—*Goliath*, *The Key*, *Maya*, and *Impulse*. The study identifies recurring design patterns and classifies way-finding techniques across three key dimensions: adaptability, cognitive load, and spatial scale. The resulting ten-category typology captures the diversity of navigation approaches used in immersive storytelling and clarifies their experiential impacts. Applied to real-world case studies, the typology demonstrates practical relevance and analytical utility, offering a structured lens for evaluating and designing narrative-supportive navigation in VR. This work contributes to ongoing efforts to integrate spatial design and storytelling in immersive environments and lays groundwork for user-centred evaluation and adaptive system design.

Keywords: Virtual Reality (VR) · Narrative-Driven VR · Way-finding Strategies · Spatial Orientation · Narrative Progression · Sense of Presence · Interaction Design · Cognitive Load · Adaptive Navigation · VR Storytelling

1 Introduction

Movement shapes not just how we get from one place to another, but how we experience the world around us. It influences our memories, emotions, and even the stories we tell about places [15, 20, 36]. The familiar route through a childhood home, the winding streets of a new city, the way a spotlight focuses our gaze in a theatre, all of these experiences are deeply tied to how we navigate space. Fictional narratives often rely on this too: Hogwarts' shifting staircases don't just move characters from place to place, they control the pace and discovery of the story [26]; Sherlock Holmes' 221B Baker Street holds clues that shape how mysteries unfold [13].

Virtual reality (VR) brings this connection between movement and meaning to the forefront. Unlike traditional media, where users passively watch a story unfold, VR places them inside it. In six degrees of freedom (6DoF) VR, users

D. Michael-Grigoriou et al. (Eds.): EuroXR 2025, LNCS 16101, pp. 124–138, 2026.
https://doi.org/10.1007/978-3-032-03805-0_7

move along three spatial axes (x, y, and z), actively exploring virtual spaces [18]. This kind of embodied navigation introduces new possibilities for storytelling, but also new challenges. Users must not only follow a narrative but also stay oriented and engaged within complex, interactive environments. Designing these experiences requires an understanding of how users perceive and act on spatial cues in order to stay immersed in the story.

In this paper, we define narrative-driven VR as immersive environments in which story structure shapes how users explore, interact, and progress through space. Within this category, we use the term VR narratives more narrowly to describe authored, often linear or semi-linear experiences where spatial movement supports a pre-structured storyline. Ensuring that users stay engaged and oriented within these environments requires the careful design of affordances, i.e., potential actions offered by the environment and perceived by users [15,23].

In VR, affordances extend beyond visual cues to include interactive objects, environmental feedback, and dynamic storytelling elements that respond to user behaviour [16,37]. These shape not just attention and interaction, but also how users physically navigate the space. Affordances directly influence two interrelated processes: locomotion, which refers to the mechanics of movement, and way-finding, which involves maintaining spatial orientation and making navigation decisions [4]. Both are essential to ensuring that the user's movement remains coherent with the narrative progression (Table 1).

Table 1. Comparison of Locomotion and Way-finding in Virtual Environments

Aspect	Locomotion	Way-finding
Definition	The physical act of moving within a VE using specific movement methods	The cognitive process of deciding where and how to move within a VE
Focus	Movement methods such as teleportation or smooth walking	Spatial orientation, path selection, and decision-making
Key Methods	Teleportation, smooth movement, redirected walking	Use of landmarks, spatial layouts, path highlighting, Assisted guidance
Challenges	Motion sickness, VR fatigue	Disorientation, cognitive overload

Way-finding plays a crucial role in narrative-driven VR, where navigation is deeply intertwined with storytelling. Unlike linear media, VR narratives often require users to explore and make choices that shape the experience. Effective way-finding directs attention to key story elements while preserving a sense of autonomy. Games such as *Half-Life: Alyx* [38] and *The Under Presents* [8] demonstrate how environmental cues, lighting, and sound design can organically guide users through complex narrative spaces. In contrast, poor way-finding disrupts immersion and leads to confusion or frustration.

Beyond entertainment, VR-based navigation has critical applications in areas like military training, industrial safety, and emergency response. Simulations such as the *Virtual Battlespace* series prepare soldiers for combat environments where rapid decision-making and spatial awareness are vital [32]. Platforms like *STRIVR* use VR navigation training to improve workplace safety, allowing users to practice evacuation procedures and hazard identification in immersive, controlled environments [40]. Similarly, VR-based fire evacuation simulations demonstrate how realistic way-finding aids can improve response times and decision-making under stress [17].

Despite its central role in shaping user experience, most VR navigation research has focused narrowly on locomotion techniques, such as teleportation, redirected walking, and continuous movement, primarily addressing practical concerns like motion sickness and physical comfort [4,5]. While these studies offer valuable insights, they often overlook the cognitive and perceptual dimensions of navigation: how users develop spatial understanding, maintain narrative coherence, direct attention, and achieve a sense of immersion within VR environments [25,27,30], , and poor design in this area can leave users disoriented or disengaged [11,27].

This study explores that gap by examining how different way-finding techniques balance cognitive load, adaptability, and spatial scale to shape user experience in VR narratives. By reviewing existing literature, it proposes a typology of way-finding strategies in VR narratives and by using four VR narrative experiences—*Goliath* [22], *The Key* [35], *Maya* [2], and *Impulse* [6], it demonstrates the applicability of the proposed typology. This paper offers a structured vocabulary for describing and comparing way-finding techniques in immersive storytelling. By focusing on how these strategies align with narrative pacing, spatial layout, and user interaction, the typology supports both analysis of existing VR experiences and the intentional design of spatial guidance in narrative contexts.

2   Review of Way-Finding in Narrative-Driven VR

Understanding how users navigate VR narrative experiences, requires a multidisciplinary perspective. Drawing from cognitive science, environmental psychology, and human-computer interaction, this section outlines the theoretical and empirical foundations of way-finding in virtual environments. We also examine specific challenges posed by narrative structures in VR and highlight the absence of a unified framework that addresses the interplay between navigation, storytelling, and user experience.

2.1   Foundations of Spatial Cognition and Navigation in VR

Way-finding research in VR builds on cognitive and environmental psychology, particularly Lynch's spatial elements (paths, edges, districts, nodes, landmarks) and Tolman's concept of cognitive maps [19,34]. These concepts explain how users construct internal representations to navigate spaces. In virtual environments, these mental models rely heavily on visual cues, landmarks, lighting, and auditory feedback, due to the absence of physical proprioception and gravity [20, 39].

Users typically adopt one of two navigation strategies: egocentric, which orients from the user's point of view, or allocentric, which builds maps using spatial anchors and fixed landmarks. The challenge in VR is that environments lack inherent directionality, so designers must construct these cues intentionally [11].

2.2 Way-Finding Challenges in VR Narratives

Narrative-driven VR poses unique way-finding challenges. Unlike traditional navigation systems that prioritize task efficiency, VR narratives often aim to preserve immersion, emotional tone, and a coherent story rhythm. Overly explicit navigation aids can feel intrusive or artificial, disrupting the sense of presence and undermining user agency [30].

Disorientation is common in expansive or abstract narrative spaces where spatial anchors are limited. The disconnect between visual input and the absence of proprioceptive feedback increases cognitive load and can compromise narrative progression [9, 27]. Conversely, minimal guidance can lead users to miss key narrative moments or become stuck, breaking narrative flow and reducing engagement.

These challenges suggest that VR narratives require more than traditional spatial logic; demanding perceptual strategies that align with narrative beats, symbolic meaning, and emotional arcs. This makes way-finding in VR narratives fundamentally different from procedural or task-based environments.

2.3 Prior Typologies of Navigation and Way-Finding

While VR locomotion has been thoroughly categorized, such as Boletsis's classification of walk-in-place and gaze-based techniques [3], these models focus on physical input methods. Early work by Darken and Sibert [10] identified landmark-based, route-based, and survey-based strategies but lacked integration with narrative design.

Recent adaptive models such as Richardson et al. [25] explore real-time cueing, but their focus is on system responsiveness rather than narrative structure. There remains no cohesive model that links perceptual strategies with spatial reasoning and narrative flow—especially one that considers user effort, environmental responsiveness, and spatial scale together.

2.4 Synthesis and Transition to Typology

From the literature, three design dimensions consistently emerge as critical in shaping user navigation in VR: cognitive load, adaptability, and spatial scale. Cognitive load reflects the mental effort needed to interpret navigational cues

[39,41], while adaptability captures how spatial guidance responds to user actions [1,25]. Spatial scale refers to the complexity and extent of the navigable environment, influencing orientation and presence [19,20].

These dimensions were selected for their consistent appearance across spatial cognition, immersive design, and VR narrative studies. *Cognitive load* appears prominently in discussions of disorientation and effort [31,39,41], *adaptability* in systems that tailor cues dynamically [11,17], and *spatial scale* in foundational theories of spatial representation and VR navigation [27].

While other factors such as interactivity and narrative structure play a role in shaping user experience, we found that their impact is often mediated through these three dimensions. For instance, interaction complexity may increase cognitive load when users must frequently interpret cues or make decisions. Likewise, the adaptability of guidance systems often reflects the branching or linear nature of a narrative structure. Focusing on these dimensions offers a streamlined but inclusive typology that captures a wide range of perceptual and narrative design concerns without introducing overlapping variables.

Together, cognitive load, adaptability, and spatial scale form a foundational lens through which to examine how spatial guidance supports immersive storytelling. These dimensions frame our analysis of the literature and guide the development of a typology for way-finding in VR narratives.

3   Gaps in Current Research and Opportunities for VR Narratives

Despite extensive research on VR locomotion and spatial orientation, few studies directly examine how navigation design contributes to narrative coherence and emotional pacing in immersive storytelling [3,30]. Much of the existing work emphasizes utilitarian or task-driven environments, overlooking how navigation supports user engagement in authored, story-driven spaces [28].

Current frameworks often isolate spatial mechanics from narrative logic. While studies on adaptive guidance and cue responsiveness are growing [1,25], they rarely address how navigation shapes user agency, narrative transitions, or symbolic meaning; elements central to immersive narrative design [29]. Existing models typically focus on spatial accuracy or disorientation rather than on narrative immersion.

We address this gap by framing way-finding in VR narratives through three design dimensions: *cognitive load, adaptability*, and *spatial scale*—that shape how spatial cues function in immersive narratives. These dimensions also influence experiential outcomes like presence and narrative pacing, not as isolated effects, but as results of how navigation is structured within the environment.

The following section outlines the methodology used to construct our typology, drawing from a targeted literature review and a comparative analysis of four authored VR narrative experiences.

4   Methodology

The aim of this study was to examine how way-finding strategies in narrative-driven VR influence user experience and to construct the typology of way-finding strategies in VR narratives. Two guiding research questions were established:

1. **RQ1:** What are the defining characteristics of different way-finding strategies used in VR Narratives ?
2. **RQ2:** How can we best categorize these way-finding techniques?

To address these questions, we conducted a structured qualitative analysis comprising two phases: a targeted literature review and a comparative case application.

4.1   Literature Review and Pattern Identification

We initially retrieved 45 peer-reviewed articles published between 2010 and 2024 from the ACM Digital Library, IEEE Xplore, and SpringerLink using search terms - "VR navigation," "way-finding in virtual environments," "VR narratives," and "immersive storytelling." After applying inclusion criteria—English-language, peer-reviewed, and directly relevant to user navigation, perceptual cues, or spatial design in immersive environments—and excluding articles focused solely on hardware, locomotion algorithms, or generic theoretical overviews, we retained a final core set of 17 articles for full-text thematic analysis. These included works published between 2010 and 2025 that directly informed the construction of the typology. An additional 14 foundational texts were referenced for conceptual grounding across the introduction and review sections.

We conducted an inductive thematic analysis on the core set of 17 peer-reviewed articles to identify recurring way-finding strategies relevant to VR narrative contexts. Each article was coded for explicit or implicit descriptions of spatial cues, user guidance techniques, and navigation behaviours. These codes were then grouped into broader conceptual categories based on thematic similarity. These categories were iteratively refined to align with the three previously identified design dimensions: *cognitive load*, *adaptability*, and *spatial scale*. This process ensured that the derived typology was both grounded in literature and meaningfully structured to reflect the cross-disciplinary theories informing immersive spatial design.

4.2   Case Application in VR Narratives

To illustrate the relevance and applicability of the resulting typology, we applied it to four VR narratives: *The Key* (2019) [35], *Goliath* (2021) [22], *Maya* (2020) [2], and *Impulse* (2021) [6]. These cases were selected for their diversity across the three core design dimensions identified in the typology: *cognitive load*, *adaptability*, and *spatial scale*.

- *The Key* (2019) follows a user unlocking a series of memories to make a life-altering decision, set within a confined environment where metaphorical and symbolic cues demand interpretive effort—resulting in high cognitive load and low adaptability [35].
- *Goliath* (2021) tells the story of a man navigating schizophrenia through online games and digital relationships, unfolding across modular scenes with intermittent guidance that balance moderate cognitive load and medium adaptability on a medium spatial scale [22].
- *Maya* (2020) places the user in fragmented dream-like worlds exploring emotional trauma, using broad abstract environments with minimal guidance—leading to high cognitive load, low adaptability, and a large spatial scale [2].
- *Impulse* (2021) centers on rhythm-based movement to regain agency in a disrupted body, set in confined but highly reactive environments that demand continuous input and attention—resulting in high cognitive load, high adaptability, and limited spatial scale [6].

These varying formats allowed us to observe how different types of spatial cues and narrative alignments influence the deployment of way-finding strategies. We documented instances of each way-finding strategy in use and analysed how they aligned with the three design dimensions.

This phase was designed as an applied demonstration of the typology's relevance across diverse VR narrative formats. By applying the typology to authored experiences with different spatial and narrative structures, we observed how spatial cues support user movement and narrative continuity. This helped clarify how the three design dimensions translate into practical way-finding strategies.

5   Results

This section presents the findings of our structured review and analysis, aligned with the study's three research questions: (1) identifying key patterns in way-finding strategies used in VR narratives, (2) organizing them into a typology based on design characteristics, and (3) analysing how different strategies influence spatial orientation, narrative progression, and sense of presence.

5.1   Recurring Strategy Patterns in VR Narratives

Across the literature and case study review, we observed six recurring patterns in how navigation is implemented within VR narrative environments. These patterns varied in sensory modality (visual, auditory, haptic), user interaction demands, and degree of narrative embedding. While not a formal classification, they offer an empirical foundation for the typology proposed in the next section.

- **Ambient Cues:** Subtle elements like lighting, ambient sound, and environmental audio that gently guide attention with minimal cognitive effort [11, 21].

- **Landmark Cues:** Fixed visual elements—architectural structures, recurring objects, symbols—used to maintain spatial awareness and narrative cohesion [4,27].
- **Exploration Guides:** Overlays such as mini-maps, HUDs, or in-world signage that support orientation in expansive environments [28].
- **Path Indicators:** Explicit directional aids (e.g., glowing trails, arrows) that reduce error but may limit narrative agency [39].
- **Dynamic Landmarks:** Environmental elements that shift in response to narrative progression or user behaviour [25].
- **Virtual Guides:** NPCs or narrative agents that act as companions or guides, integrating movement cues within story events [7].

These patterns reflect frequently used approaches, but do not fully capture the variability in interaction complexity or spatial structure. To address this, we propose a typology based on underlying design dimensions.

5.2 A Typology of Way-Finding Strategies

To systematically classify way-finding strategies across VR narrative contexts, we developed a typology structured around three key design dimensions identified in prior research:

- **Cognitive Load** (low/ Medium/ High)—the mental effort required to process and act on navigational cues [39].
- **Adaptability** (Static/ Dynamic)—whether and how cues respond dynamically to user behaviour or narrative state [25].
- **Spatial Scale** (Limited/ Open)—the size and complexity of the environment in which way-finding occurs [27].

Intersecting these dimensions yielded ten distinct strategy categories. Two additional combinations—Dynamic strategies with Low Cognitive Load—were excluded, as dynamic guidance inherently demands interpretive effort and thus imposes at least medium cognitive load [11]. The detailed typology is discussed in Table 2.

The examples listed here are intended to illustrate how each strategy appears in real-world VR contexts, and not as sources used to construct the typology, which was developed independently through literature analysis. A select few of these examples are revisited in more detail in the next section.

For instance, 'Exploratory Mapping' in *Maya* invites users to make sense of abstract environments without overt guidance, requiring spatial reasoning and recall. In contrast, 'Character-Driven Guidance' in *Goliath* relies on reactive NPC behaviour to gently steer user attention. These examples show how each strategy aligns differently with the three design dimensions.

This typology is intended as a flexible comparative tool, supporting both the analysis of existing experiences and design reflection. It offers a structured vocabulary to describe how way-finding is integrated into VR narratives and how it shapes user experience through spatial, perceptual, and cognitive factors.

Table 2. Typology of VR narrative way-finding strategies

Adapta-bility	Cognitive Load	Spatial Scale	Category	Definition	Example
Static	Low	Limited	Ambient Cues	Subtle environmental cues, such as lighting or sound, that passively direct users with minimal effort.	*The Key*—flickering hallway lights subtly guide movement without breaking immersion [35].
		Open	Environmental Landmarks	Static landmarks placed within expansive environments to orient users without active input.	*Allumette*—glowing bridge and skyline anchor spatial memory in a floating city [33].
	Medium	Limited	fixed landmarks	Static, recognizable features that guide navigation through confined spaces.	*Goliath*—recurring arcade machines signal narrative shifts and orient users [22].
		Open	Exploration Guides	Non-diegetic aids such as maps or HUDs that assist exploration without adaptive elements.	*Maya*—glowing doorways and intuitive layout nudge navigation in open surreal spaces [2].
	High	Limited	Spatial Problem-Solving	Confined maze-like spaces that require complex reasoning, memorization, or problem-solving without adaptive cues.	*Impulse*—memory-based object tasks challenge spatial reasoning in dream-like rooms [6].
		Open	Exploratory Mapping	User-driven exploration requiring mental maps and spatial reasoning in open environments.	*Lone Echo*—players mentally map zero-G corridors without external guidance [12].
Dynamic	Medium	Limited	Narrative Branching	Adaptive guidance that responds to user decisions at key narrative junctures.	*Goliath*—NPC dialogue branches shape modular narrative paths and pacing [22].
		Open	Responsive Exploration	Cues that adapt in real-time to user exploration choices within expansive environments.	*Wraith: The Oblivion âÅŞ Afterlife*—reactive lights and sounds respond to user proximity in eerie spaces [14].
	High	Limited	Adaptive Spatial Challenges	Evolving navigation tasks requiring active problem-solving within confined spaces.	*The Last Clockwinder*—puzzle spaces evolve, requiring real-time spatial adaptation [24].
		Open	Adaptive Spatial Exploration	Complex, dynamic navigation tasks in large environments requiring active engagement and spatial reasoning.	*Maya*—shifting terrain reflects emotion and demands constant spatial recalibration [2].

The following section provides case examples to illustrate the practical applicability of the typology, demonstrating how different combinations of way-finding strategies shape user experience in real-world scenarios.

6   Case Studies: Applying the Typology to VR Narrative Experiences

To demonstrate the practical applicability of the proposed typology, this section analyses four VR narrative experiences: *Goliath, The Key, Maya,* and *Impulse* (see Table 3 for an overview). These were selected for their diversity in narrative structure, spatial scale, and interaction complexity as mentioned earlier in the methodology.

Each entry identifies key way-finding techniques, categorizes them according to the typology dimensions (adaptability, cognitive load, spatial scale), and reflects on their experiential implications across spatial orientation, narrative progression, and sense of presence. Analysing the four VR experiences through the typology reveals consistent patterns in how spatial guidance strategies are used:

- *The Key* and *Goliath* utilize static, low-load strategies like ambient cues and scene framing to maintain orientation in confined spaces.
- *Goliath* and *Impulse* apply dynamic strategies, such as branching interactions and reactive puzzles, to maintain engagement and narrative momentum.
- *Maya* emphasizes open spatial design and symbolic cues, depending on user-led exploration and abstract spatial reasoning.
- *Impulse* shows how high-load, adaptive strategies can sustain user attention even in compact environments, especially when balanced with perceptual cues.

Most of the strategy categories from the typology were observed across the four case studies, suggesting its relevance for analysing a range of VR narrative designs. However, not all combinations, particularly those involving highly adaptive strategies, were represented, reflecting the design constraints of the selected experiences.

Most techniques mapped clearly onto a single category within the typology. For example, static landmark cues and ambient audio were consistently categorized as low-load, static strategies in limited spatial scales, while procedural landmarks and adaptive transitions aligned with dynamic, high-load strategies in open environments. These patterns reaffirm the usefulness of the typology in classifying design strategies and predicting their impact on spatial orientation, narrative progression, and presence.

However, certain ambiguities emerged. Some techniques, such as gaze- triggered transitions in *Goliath* or dynamic feedback loops in *Impulse*, operated across multiple categories depending on scene pacing or user behaviour. Additionally, perceived spatial scale occasionally diverged from physical scale, particularly in emotionally abstract environments like *Maya*, challenging the binary of open vs. limited space.

These edge cases do not invalidate the typology but instead suggest areas for refinement, such as incorporating a more flexible notion of spatial perception or hybrid category recognition. Overall, the typology functioned as a reliable

Table 3. Way-finding Strategies in *The Key*, *Maya*, and *Impulse* (contd.)

Experience	Technique Used (Scene)	Typology Category	Experiential Implication
Goliath	Ambient spatial audio cues (Intro)	Static / Low / Limited (Ambient Cues)	Subtle orientation support that maintains sense of presence without disrupting narrative progression.
	Visual motifs (arcade machines)	Static / Medium / Limited (fixed landmarks)	Reinforces spatial memory and anchors story transitions through recurring landmarks.
	NPC dialogue branches (Choice points)	Dynamic / Medium / Limited (Narrative Branching)	Enhances narrative progression and user agency while requiring moderate cognitive input.
	Gaze-based object highlighting (Interactive scenes)	Dynamic / Medium / Limited (Narrative Branching)	Guides attention adaptively, balancing user control and narrative direction.
	Spatial memory cues (VR Chat sequence)	Static / High / Limited (Spatial Problem-Solving)	Requires sequential recall, increasing cognitive load but enriching engagement.
	Environment transitions (Closing scene)	Dynamic / High / Limited (Adaptive Spatial Challenges)	Drives narrative progression through reconfigured spatial layout; cognitively demanding.
The Key	Spatial audio cues (Dream scene)	Static / Low / Limited (Ambient Cues)	Maintains presence and subtly directs user attention during symbolic sequences.
	Recurrent key objects (All scenes)	Static / Medium / Limited (fixed landmarks)	Helps users track narrative state while anchoring them spatially.
	Triggered transitions via key interaction	Dynamic / Medium / Limited (Narrative Branching)	Allows active narrative progression through exploratory actions.
	Color-coded environments	Static / Medium / Limited (fixed landmarks)	Simplifies navigation decisions while preserving autonomy.
	Object placement memory task	Static / High / Limited (Spatial Problem-Solving)	Engages deeper spatial reasoning, increasing both cognitive load and narrative investment.
Maya	Recurring spatial locations (e.g., house, river)	Static / Medium / Open (Exploration Guides)	Maintains orientation in expansive environments without intrusive overlays.
	Gaze-triggered transitions (Birth scene)	Dynamic / Medium / Open (Responsive Exploration)	Provides adaptive guidance while supporting agency in abstract scenes.
	Absence of HUD or explicit map	Static / High / Open (Exploratory Mapping)	Encourages mental mapping; supports orientation but increases cognitive load.
	Adaptive lighting (City scenes)	Dynamic / Medium / Open (Responsive Exploration)	Supports orientation passively in visually dense settings.
	Procedural environmental changes (Climax)	Dynamic / High / Open (Adaptive Spatial Exploration)	Demands active spatial reasoning as space evolves with story; high cognitive engagement.
Impulse	Highlighted objects and ambient sound (Intro)	Static / Low / Limited (Ambient Cues)	Directs gaze smoothly; supports early orientation and presence.
	Sequential puzzle cues	Static / High / Limited (Spatial Problem-Solving)	Requires memory and attention sequencing; increases cognitive strain.
	Real-time layout shifts with decisions	Dynamic / High / Limited (Adaptive Spatial Challenges)	Reinforces narrative stakes through spatial consequences.
	Way-point highlighting post-failure	Dynamic / Medium / Limited (Narrative Branching)	Balances guidance and challenge adaptively; preserves flow and agency.
	Sound proximity feedback (Exploration scenes)	Dynamic / Medium / Limited (Responsive Exploration)	Maintains orientation in ambiguous spaces while preserving presence.

analytical lens, offering actionable structure while leaving room for narrative-specific adaptation.

7   Discussion

This work introduces a typology for understanding way-finding strategies in VR narratives, organised across three core dimensions: cognitive load, adaptability, and spatial scale. Rather than offering prescriptive guidance, the typology provides a structured vocabulary for comparing how spatial cues function within authored VR experiences.

The typology is intended as a lens for analysis, not a set of best practices. It surfaces the often implicit design choices that shape how users move through and interpret spatial storytelling. In doing so, it complements research in spatial cognition and narrative interaction by organizing technical strategies into comparable categories rather than evaluating their effectiveness.

7.1   Limitations and Scope

We acknowledge the interpretive nature of this work. Strategy classification involves subjectivity, especially when experiences use multiple strategies in tandem. The examples drawn from VR narratives are illustrative and exploratory and not empirical validations, but demonstrate the typology's descriptive potential.

7.2   Insights from Applying the Typology

Applying the typology across different VR experiences reveals several design patterns that offer new perspectives:

- **High-adaptability strategies in confined environments create the illusion of agency by reacting to user behaviour in real-time.** In *Impulse*, responsive spatial puzzles and environment-triggered events help users feel in control despite restricted space. This suggests that adaptability can be used to simulate openness, allowing designers to sustain engagement without needing large environments.
- **Exploratory mapping in open symbolic environments transforms way-finding into emotional interpretation rather than spatial orientation.** In open environments like *Maya*, where users explore without clear goals or structured prompts, navigation becomes a way to process ambiguity. The absence of direct guidance shifts way-finding into an interpretive act, where users construct emotional and symbolic meaning from movement itself. This turns spatial disorientation into a deliberate narrative device, foregrounding uncertainty, reflection, and subjective pacing.

- **Narrative branching benefits from spatial or narrative anchors that reduce disorientation without limiting choice.** In *Goliath*, NPC-led sequences and repeating visual motifs offer structure amid branching dialogues, allowing users to feel guided without constraining their narrative path. This reveals that successful branching design may rely less on interface clarity and more on embedded continuity.
- **Ambient cues are effective only when timed with narrative pauses or spatial stillness that prime the user to notice them.** In *The Key*, subtle lighting and sound cues were more likely to guide attention when the environment momentarily slowed down. This suggests that ambient cues work best when narrative pacing allows users the perceptual space to register subtle spatial signals.

These patterns suggest that the effectiveness of way-finding strategies often depends less on individual elements and more on how they are layered and sequenced within a narrative context. By aligning spatial cues with narrative intent, designers may better support both engagement and orientation.

7.3 Future Work

Future work could investigate how this typology supports design ideation or critique in real-world workflows. It may also serve as a foundation for user studies exploring the experiential outcomes of different strategy combinations— such as presence, comprehension, and emotional engagement.

8 Conclusion

This paper proposes a typology of way-finding strategies in VR narratives, organised across the dimensions of cognitive load, adaptability, and spatial scale. Developed through literature review and applied to four VR narratives, the typology offers a structured lens to describe, compare, and reflect on spatial guidance in immersive storytelling.

Rather than prescribing specific design rules, the typology reveals how different combinations of cues shape spatial orientation, narrative flow, and engagement. It supports the idea that no single strategy guarantees immersion, effective navigation depends on how spatial design aligns with story structure and user expectations.

As VR storytelling evolves, typologies like this can help creators think more critically about how navigation contributes to narrative clarity and emotional pacing. This work lays a foundation for ongoing research into spatial storytelling and opens pathways for adapting these strategies across genres, user groups, and cultural contexts.

References

1. Azmandian, M., Hancock, M., Benko, H., Ofek, E., Wilson, A.D.: Haptic retargeting: dynamic repurposing of passive haptics for enhanced virtual reality experiences. In: Proceedings of the 2016 CHI Conference on Human Factors in Computing Systems (CHI 2016), pp. 1968–1979. Association for Computing Machinery, New York, NY, USA (2016). https://doi.org/10.1145/2858036.2858226
2. Bhimji, S., Basu, P.: Maya: The birth of a superhero (2020). https://crossoverlabs.xyz/maya-vr, narrative VR film exploring gender and transformation. Premiered at Tribeca Immersive 2020. Produced by Crossover Labs
3. Boletsis, C.: The new era of virtual reality locomotion: a systematic literature review of techniques and a proposed typology. Multimod. Technol. Interact. **1**(4), 24 (2017)
4. Bowman, D.A., Kruijff, E., LaViola, J.J., Poupyrev, I.: 3D User Interfaces: Theory and Practice. Addison-Wesley (2004)
5. Bozgeyikli, E., Raij, A., Katkoori, S.E., Dubey, R.: Point & teleport locomotion technique for virtual reality. In: Proceedings of the 2016 Annual Symposium on Computer-Human Interaction in Play, pp. 205–216. ACM (2016). https://doi.org/10.1145/2967934.2968105
6. Burr, P., Heartscape, P.C.: Impulse (2021). https://www.acuteart.com/artist/porpentine-charity-heartscape/
7. Chen, S., Miranda, F., Ferreira, N., Lage, M., Doraiswamy, H., Brenner, C.: Urbanrama: navigating cities in virtual reality. IEEE Trans. Visual Comput. Graphics **28**(12), 4685–4699 (2022). https://doi.org/10.1109/TVCG.2021.3099012
8. Claws, T.: The under presents. Virtual Reality Game, Tender Claws (2019)
9. Cummings, J.J., Bailenson, J.N.: How immersive is enough? A meta-analysis of the effect of immersive technology on user presence. Media Psychol. **19**(2), 272–309 (2016)
10. Darken, R.P., Sibert, J.L.: A toolset for navigation in virtual environments. In: Proceedings of the 6th Annual ACM Symposium on User Interface Software and Technology, pp. 157–165. ACM (1993)
11. Darken, R.P., Sibert, J.L.: Wayfinding strategies and behaviors in large virtual worlds. In: Proceedings of the SIGCHI Conference on Human Factors in Computing Systems, pp. 142–149. ACM (1996)
12. Dawn, R.A.: Lone echo (2017). https://www.oculus.com/experiences/rift/1368187813209604/
13. Doyle, A.C.: The Adventures of Sherlock Holmes. George Newnes Ltd., London (1892)
14. Games, F.T.: Wraith: The oblivion – afterlife (2021). https://www.fasttravelgames.com/wraith-the-oblivion-afterlife/
15. Gibson, J.J.: The ecological approach to visual perception. Houghton Mifflin (1979). https://doi.org/10.4324/9781315740218
16. Janlert, L.E., Stolterman, E.: Things that Keep Us Busy: The Elements of Interaction. MIT Press, Cambridge (2017)
17. Kinateder, M., Ronchi, E., Nilsson, D., Kobes, M., Müller, M., Pauli, P.: Virtual reality for fire evacuation research. In: Applications of Virtual Reality, pp. 69–91. InTech (2014)
18. LaViola, J.J., Kruijff, E., McMahan, R.P., Bowman, D.A., Poupyrev, I.: 3d user interfaces for VR and AR. In: ACM SIGGRAPH 2017 Courses. p. 10 (2017)
19. Lynch, K.: The Image of the City. MIT Press, Cambridge (1960)

20. Montello, D.R.: Integrating cognitive, perceptual, and geographic approaches in human spatial orientation. Psychol. Sci. **4**(6), 372–378 (1993). https://doi.org/10.1111/j.1467-9280.1993.tb00598.x

21. Montello, D.R.: Navigating Large-Scale Space. Cambridge University Press, Cambridge (2005)

22. Murphy, B.G., Abdalla, M.: Goliath: Playing with reality (2021). https://www.anagram.io/goliath

23. Norman, D.A.: The Design of Everyday Things. Basic Books, New York (1998)

24. Pontoco: The last clockwinder (2022). https://pontoco.com/clockwinder/

25. Richardson, A.E., Powers, M., Bousquet, K.: Integrating locomotion and wayfinding in virtual environments: a unified framework. Virtual Real. **25**(3), 587–603 (2021)

26. Rowling, J.K.: Harry Potter and the Philosopher's Stone. Bloomsbury Publishing, London (1997)

27. Ruddle, R.A., Lessels, S.: The benefits of using a walking interface to navigate virtual environments. ACM Trans. Comput. Human Interact. **16**(1), 5 (2009)

28. Ruddle, R.A., Volk, S., Bülthoff, H.H.: Walking improves your cognitive map in environments that are large-scale and large in extent. ACM Trans. Comput. Human Interact. **18**(2), 1–20 (2011)

29. Ryan, M.L.: Narrative as Virtual Reality 2: Revisiting Immersion and Interactivity in Literature and Electronic Media. Johns Hopkins University Press (2015)

30. Slater, M., Sanchez-Vives, M.V.: Enhancing our lives with immersive virtual reality. Front. Robot. AI **3**, 74 (2016)

31. Slater, M., Wilbur, S.: A framework for immersive virtual environments (five): Speculations on the role of presence in virtual environments. Presence: Teleoper. Virtual Environ. **6**(6), 603–616 (1997)

32. Smith, A., Harrison, C.: Use of virtual reality battlespace simulations for military training. In: Proceedings of the 2018 Simulation and Training Conference (2018)

33. Studios, P.: Allumette (2016). https://penrosestudios.com/allumette/

34. Tolman, E.C.: Cognitive maps in rats and men. Psychol. Rev. **55**(4), 189–208 (1948)

35. Tricart, C.: The key (2019). https://www.luciddreamsprod.com/the-key

36. Tuan, Y.F.: Space and Place: The Perspective of Experience. University of Minnesota Press (1977). https://doi.org/10.1007/978-94-009-9394-5_19

37. Turner, P., Turner, S., Burrows, A.: Cognitive and social factors in the design of affordances in virtual environments. Int. J. Hum Comput Stud. **71**(3), 275–281 (2013)

38. Valve: Half-life: Alyx. Virtual Reality Game, Valve Corporation (2020)

39. Waller, D.: Individual differences in spatial learning from computer-simulated environments. J. Exp. Psychol. Appl. **6**(4), 307–321 (2000)

40. Weller, M.: Advances in VR training for industrial safety. Saf. Sci. **114**, 48–55 (2019)

41. Witmer, B.G., Singer, M.J.: Measuring presence in virtual environments: a presence questionnaire. Presence Teleoper. Virtual Environ. **7**(3), 225–240 (1998)

Guidelines for Biophilic Design in Immersive Virtual Reality Workspaces: A Spatial Approach

Sara Romano⬩, Luana Marangelli⬩, Enricoandrea Laviola⁽✉⁾⬩,
and Michele Gattullo⬩

Department of Mechanics, Mathematics, and Management, Polytechnic University of Bari,
via Orabona, 4, 70125 Bari, Italy
`enricoandrea.laviola@poliba.it`

Abstract. While the benefits of biophilic design, incorporating natural elements to promote well-being, are well-demonstrated in Immersive Virtual Reality (IVR) environments, its application remains underexplored. Specifically, no studies have clarified how biophilic elements should be spatially and contextually integrated into IVR environments. Most studies focus on the presence or type of elements rather than on design strategies or spatial criteria. This gap is critical in IVR, where the absence of real-world constraints enables a high degree of design freedom, potentially leading to ineffective or inauthentic integration. To address this issue, we engaged 13 expert designers in a focus group to develop guidelines for biophilic design in IVR workspaces. Each expert was asked to enrich four virtual offices using four types of indoor plants: floor plant, table plant, hanging plant, green wall. Their insights were synthesized into practical spatial design guidelines. These were then combined to generate 16 biophilic configurations, evaluated by 81 users. Results indicated no statistically significant preference among configurations, suggesting all combinations were similarly received. In a second evaluation phase, 117 participants compared four specific configurations: based on guidelines; with an unconstrained (but realistic) spatial arrangement; with an unrealistic spatial arrangement; without plants. The guidelines-based configuration significantly outperformed the others across subjective measures including willingness to work, focus, and comfort. These findings suggest the proposed guidelines are effective in supporting the design of engaging, pleasant biophilic IVR environments.

Keywords: Biophilic Design · Immersive Virtual Reality · Workspace · Well-being

1 Introduction

In recent years, the increasing integration of natural elements into workspaces has gained growing attention for its potential to enhance human well-being—a concept broadly referred to as biophilic design. Despite this growth in real workspace, its application in fully Immersive Virtual Reality (IVR) environments remains largely unexplored. The biophilia hypothesis, introduced by E.O. Wilson in 1984, suggests that humans have

© The Author(s), under exclusive license to Springer Nature Switzerland AG 2026
D. Michael-Grigoriou et al. (Eds.): EuroXR 2025, LNCS 16101, pp. 139–154, 2026.
https://doi.org/10.1007/978-3-032-03805-0_8

an innate connection with nature [1]. This concept has driven the adoption of biophilic design in physical spaces, where natural elements are incorporated to promote well-being [2]. When applied to IVR environments, biophilic design aligns with key theories from environmental psychology, such as Attention Restoration Theory (ART) [3, 4] and Stress Reduction Theory (SRT) [5]. Both emphasize that exposure to nature—whether physical or virtual—supports cognitive restoration, reduces stress, and enhances overall well-being.

Although emerging literature suggests that biophilic elements can improve psychological and subjective well-being [6], and physiological [7] even in virtual workspaces, no formal guidelines currently exist on how to implement such design strategies within IVR contexts. Existing studies typically report which biophilic elements are embedded in IVR environments. Many works specify which pattern of biophilic design [8] they used [6, 9], such as visual connection with nature, dynamic and diffuse light, and material connection with nature, or which type of biophilic elements [10] they used [7, 11, 12], such as walls and potted plants, water, and natural materials. Many works specify the species of potted plants used [13, 14]. Current studies have focused on the effect that biophilic elements have on users' well-being or users' performance [15], but no one clarifies the design followed to incorporate those elements into IVR environments.

Biophilic elements can be added in IVR environments without concern for physical constraints like cost, maintenance, or space, enabling exaggerated, arbitrary, or unrealistic implementations. Removing real-world limitations could lead to new possibilities for enhancing users' experiences and emotional connections to digital environments through an intensified and immersive expression of nature. While biophilic design in physical spaces is known to reduce stress and enhance well-being, it remains unclear whether unconventional or unrealistic implementations in IVR offer the same benefits.

Based on the analysis of the literature and considering the unconstrained design possibilities of IVR environments, it is essential to focus on three key characteristics of biophilic elements:

- Spatial: concerning their quantity and placement within the environment [7, 11].
- Temporal: involving dynamic effects, as their growth or leaves movement [16, 17].
- Appearance: referring to biophilic aesthetic and rendering elements that do not necessarily mimic real-life forms [18, 19].

Each of these aspects can significantly impact concentration, work performance, and overall human well-being. The lack of design guidance in literature becomes relevant in IVR, which is free from physical constraints. Therefore, exploring whether biophilic design in IVR should adhere to real-world principles or evolve toward new guidelines specific to digital contexts is essential. Investigating how expert designers approach the creation of virtual workspaces can reveal whether their strategies align with traditional design or take advantage of IVR possibilities. Equally important is understanding how end-users perceive and respond to such environments.

Considering this gap in literature, the research question guiding this study is: *"How can biophilic design be implemented in IVR workspaces?"*. In this paper, we focused specifically on the spatial properties of biophilic elements in the design of IVR workspaces, with the well-demonstrated consideration that biophilia increases well-being.

We tried to answer this research question by designing a user study, setting up a focus group of 13 experts in the field of Design. As a virtual workspace, we used an office because an increasing number of companies are adopting metaverse offices for telework [20]. We first asked experts to independently enrich four different virtual offices with biophilic elements. Among all the biophilic elements that characterize a biophilic environmental design [10], we focused only on the incorporation of plants commonly used indoors for their many beneficial characteristics [21]. The experts shared their design choices agreeing on the design we used to derive a set of guidelines. We developed a set of biophilic design configurations based on the proposed guidelines and implemented them in a newly designed office space. As a second step, we conducted a user evaluation involving a large sample of users. This evaluation unfolded in two phases involving subjective multi-dimensional metrics. In the first phase, participants evaluated each configuration, allowing us to assess which combinations of guidelines were perceived as more suitable. In the second phase, we validated these guidelines through an additional user study where participants evaluated a guideline-based biophilic office against configurations that did not adhere to the proposed guidelines. The results of the proposed user studies allowed us to extract a set of guidelines that can serve as a valuable resource for companies and designers, helping them easily integrate biophilic elements into IVR workspaces. The user studies and the guidelines represent the main contributions to this work.

The paper is organized into 5 sections. Section 2 presents the user study for the definition of guidelines for the design of biophilic elements into IVR workspaces and Sects. 3 the guidelines evaluation. Section 4 provides a discussion. In Sect. 5, a conclusion, with limitations and future works are provided.

2   Definition of Guidelines for Biophilic Design

To answer the RQ, we conducted a user study in which we chose the type of biophilic elements to focus on, then we used the methodological approach of Focus Group for the definition of the guidelines for designing workspaces with biophilic elements.

2.1   Plant Selection

We chose only green leafy plants classified into four categories: table plants, floor plants, hanging plants, and green walls. Looking at the average size of real plants, we used floor plants 1.5m high and table plants 20cm high with a 20cm pot. Except for green walls, for each plant category, we selected three distinct indoor species [22–24]:

- Table Plants: Schefflera arboricola, Marble Queen Pothos, and Chlorophytum comosum (spider plant).
- Floor Plants: *Dracaena marginata, Sansevieria trifasciata* (snake plant or mother-in-law's tongue), and *Ficus elastica.*
- Hanging Plants: *Hoya linearis, Epipremnum aureum,* and *Philodendron scandens Brazil.*
- Green walls: *Schefflera* (typical species).

2.2 Focus Group

The participants of the focus group were all experts in the field of Interior Design. The entire procedure was composed of two phases: in the first, designers were asked to enrich four different virtual workspaces by incorporating the chosen biophilic elements, i.e., the plants. They did this task individually. In the second part, the authors organized a meeting with all the participants together, in which they first reviewed each virtual office individually designed. Then, the participants discussed among themselves their design choices, with the goal of extracting the guidelines for the biophilic environmental design of virtual workspaces using the four selected categories of plants.

Participants. The focus group included 13 participants (6 females, 22 to 28 years old, mean = 25.2, SD = 2.80). They were volunteers recruited from our university, and they were 6 Ph.D. students with master's degree in industrial design and 7 master's degree students in industrial design. All of them had a deep knowledge of interior design principles. They were also experts in VR development, in fact their mean familiarity level with the use of the design software Unity was 6.31 (SD = 0.85, Min = 5, Max = 7) on a 7-point Likert scale (1: Not at all familiar – 7: Extremely familiar).

Virtual Workspace Development. We developed four virtual workspaces, representing four different open space offices which differed in the number of workstations, size, and furniture layout; to set the four offices, we based on real existing offices. Each virtual office was equipped with natural and artificial lighting to provide realistic illumination. Large windows were placed to increase natural light and provide a visual connection to the outside world, contributing to the overall realism. Overall, each office was equipped with traditional office furniture such as desk with swivel chair for workstation, bookcases, small cabinets, a yearly planner on the wall, coffee break items, a chalkboard, and so on. The atmosphere was almost "aseptic" and neutral with an arrangement of furniture in shades of gray not to influence the designers' subjective impressions of the environment in terms of colors and textures [25]. Each office included a relaxation area, furnished with sofas, coffee machine, a low table, and similar, and other areas designed for specific functions, like the brainstorming area with the clipboard. In all four offices, there were both shared and individual desks, reflecting a typical office setup. In detail, the four offices (see Fig. 1) are:

- Office 1: a square layout with an area of 20×20 m^2 and 15 individual workstations.
- Office 2: a square layout of 9×9 m^2 and 5 individual workstations.
- Office 3: an irregular layout covering approximately 180 m^2 and 12 workstations arranged in two shared desks of 2 users each, one shared desk of 3 users, and one shared desk of 5 users each.
- Office 4: a rectangular area of 10×13 m^2, and 8 workstations arranged in two shared desks of 4 users each.

Procedure. In the first phase of the focus group, each participant was invited to enrich the four virtual offices individually using the plants reported in Sect. 2.1, with no time constraints and no requirement to use all types of plants. Participants had complete freedom to choose spatial arrangements, whether realistic or unrealistic, without any

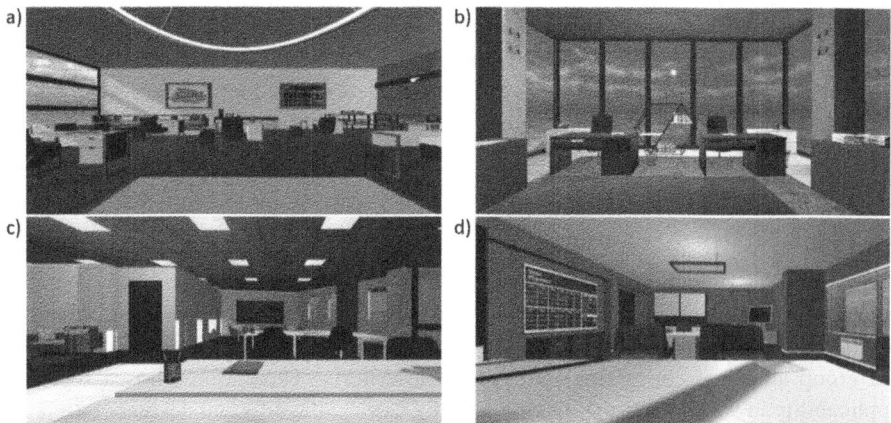

Fig. 1. The four virtual offices used by the designers involved the focus group for enrichment with plants: (a) Office 1, (b) Office 2, (c) Office 3, (d) Office 4.

suggestions or imposed constraints. This phase took place in our Lab, where each participant was provided with a desk and a PC. The task was accomplished using the VR design software Unity 3D Engine 2019.4.12. We used a PC Windows 11 Home, having a 64-bit operating system, an Intel Core i7-12700H, 2.30 GHz, 16 GB RAM, and an NVIDIA Ge-Force RTX 3070 Ti graphics card.

At the beginning of each session, the experimenter collected general user information and informed the user about the experiment procedure. Then, the participant was invited to use Unity to design the four virtual offices one at a time by including plants. CAD models of the ten plant species were positioned outside each virtual office in the Unity scene, so that the participants already had the available plants within the scene, and they just had to duplicate them and move/rotate them in the office at will. Before incorporating the plants into the Unity environment, we ensured that their rendering quality was high enough to avoid any impact on the frame rate. The plants were already scaled to the right size and there was not the possibility to change the scale. After this design phase, users had the possibility to explore the four personalized offices in VR, displaying them on a Head-Mounted Display (HMD), the HTC Vive Pro Eye, with the integration of Steam VR. In this way, participants could better realize whether they were satisfied with the enrichment they had done with the plants in the offices or whether they wanted to make further changes. This phase concluded with a brief individual interview where the experimenter documented the user's rationale behind the quantity and the placement of each plant type in the four offices.

The second phase consisted of carrying out a focus group meeting with all participants, which took place in the meeting room of the department of our university. The session lasted approximately two hours, with the authors attending; one author moderated the discussion while the others recorded the proceedings and took notes. Initially, all 52 (4 offices x 13 participants) designed offices were shown to the focus group, and this visual presentation aimed to provide an overview of the similarities and differences among the designs. Following, each participant was invited to explain his/her design choices and to discuss them with colleagues. This discussion facilitated a comparative analysis, allowing participants to articulate their positive and negative opinions regarding the designs. All the criteria used for the placement of the four types of plants were documented. The group then proceeded to define the most pertinent criteria for each type of plant category to draw up the final guidelines.

2.3 Biophilic Design Guidelines

The insights, comments, and opinions gained from the focus group were instrumental in defining biophilic design guidelines. Two mutually exclusive criteria per plant category resulted from the focus group. To ensure that none of the participants' ideas were omitted, the group aimed at converging into two basic criteria. These were chosen for their applicability in various settings and their ability to meet the different designer rationale. The defined guidelines for the integration of plants in virtual workspaces, extracted from the focus group, are outlined below, and subdivided by plant category. The integration of biophilic elements within the office followed the guidelines, with one criterion excluding the other. Since there were four plant categories and two criteria for each category, all possible combinations of these guidelines were obtained by performing the Cartesian product. Applying the guidelines to a virtual workspace, it is possible to create $2^4 = 16$ configurations, which are schematically shown in Fig. 2.

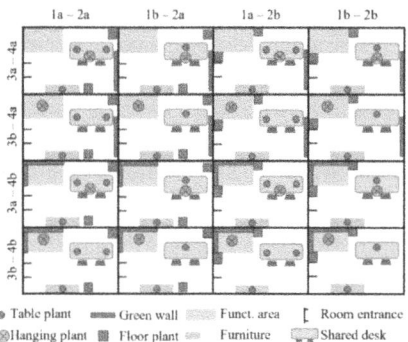

Fig. 2. Example of the floor plan of an IVR workspace composed of a work area with a desk for two workstations (grey), office furniture (orange), and a generic functional area (pink). We configured it with 16 biophilic configurations generated by all possible combinations of plant category criteria of the guidelines.

1. Table plants:
   a. Place one plant for each workstation, even with shared desks, positioned within the worker's visual task area but not necessarily directly on the desk (e.g., small cabinet). Additionally, a plant should be placed on every bookcase and on every piece of furniture in functional areas, if any in the room.
   b. Place one plant for each desk, even in the case of a shared desk, and place directly on the desk. Additionally, a plant should be placed on every bookcase and on every piece of furniture in functional areas, if any in the room.

2. Floor plants:
   c. Locate plants along the perimeter of empty walls and at corners where walls change direction.
   d. Locate plants along the room's perimeter, specifically at the separation between areas with different functions (e.g., entrance, relaxation area, work area, brainstorming area).
3. Hanging plants:
   e. Locate a plant above each desk while considering the ceiling lights, ensuring they do not obstruct the light cone.
   f. Locate a plant at the center of each specific functional area.
4. Green walls:
   g. Install green walls on empty walls, excluding specific functional areas.
   h. Install green walls only in areas with specific functions.

3   Biophilic Guidelines Evaluation

The guidelines derived from the focus group were subsequently evaluated in two phases using a new virtual office, similar to previous ones. In Phase 1 (ranking), we created 16 distinct biophilic configurations with all possible combinations of the two guidelines criteria to assess whether there are configurations more suitable than others. These configurations were inserted into the new office, one at a time, to be put to the vote by a large sample of users focusing on the willingness to work in these IVR workspaces. In Phase 2 (validation), based on the results of phase 1, we selected one configuration among the most suitable and we compared it against configurations developed without following the guidelines. These configurations were presented to another large sample of users. They were asked to evaluate the four configurations according to their willingness and comfort working in them, realism, and ability to stay focused.

3.1   Phase 1: Ranking

Design of Experiment.   The new virtual office (see Fig. 3a), called Office 5, was created with a rectangular layout of 150 m^2 and with the same characteristics and functional areas as other offices in Sect. 2.2. We created a unity scene with Office 5 for each of the 16 biophilic configurations described in Sect. 2.3.

A user-friendly 2D application was developed using Unity WebGL to be used on desktops, smartphones, and tablet devices, to avoid having users come to our lab to use the VR device, thus ensuring a large sample of users. Once the users clicked the link, they were automatically returned to the application available on ITCH.IO (see Appendix A1), a platform online on which we uploaded our app.

We performed a within-subjects design in which each participant evaluated all 16 biophilic configurations. They assessed each environment considering how much they would like to work in by varying the configurations in the same virtual office, voting using a rating scale of 1 (minimum) to 7 (maximum), represented by yellow star icons. By moving a slider, users were able to explore the entire office at 360 degrees. This feature allowed users to understand better the spatial arrangement and the impact of the biophilic elements. One biophilic configuration appeared at a time in Office 5, to give the users the possibility to evaluate it. A randomization script was implemented to ensure the reliability of the collected data by presenting the configurations in a non-fixed sequence. The user's point of view was positioned at a workstation as in Fig. 3.

Participants. The test involved 81 participants (50 females, 19 to 44 years old, mean = 23.32, SD = 4.06). They were 48 bachelor's degree students, 17 master's degree holders, 5 Ph.D. students, 3 researchers, and 8 employees. The mean familiarity level with VR was 4.35 (SD = 1.70, Min = 1, Max = 7).

Experimental Procedure. The application begins with a demographic form and then a window of instructions to guide users in understanding how to use the buttons to vote later. Upon clicking "Start", Office 5, with one biophilic configuration among all applied, appeared and users began evaluating the first configuration by clicking one among the 7 yellow stars representing the scores. Once the users made an evaluation, they could proceed to the next biophilic configuration by clicking the "Next" button and continuing to vote. Users had the opportunity to go back and change the vote given to a previous configuration if necessary. When users voted on all 16 configurations, a "Save and Exit" button appeared and by clicking it, the test ended.

Results. The data analysis focused on calculating the average scores provided by users for each biophilic configuration. The scores exhibited a narrow range, indicating that the evaluations of all 16 configurations were similar and the average of the mean scores given to each configuration was 4.63 (SD = 0.14, Min = 4.36, Max = 4.94). The Shapiro-Wilk test was performed showing that the data were not normally distributed. Hence, the non-parametric Friedman ANOVA test was performed to compare the 16 groups. We found no statistically significant differences among the 16 biophilic configurations ($\chi2(15)$ = 16.390, p = 0.357). It emerges that users perceived all 16 biophilic configurations equally well-received. There was no greater preference toward one configuration over another, whereby the lack of a clear preference for any specific biophilic configuration.

3.2 Phase 2: Validation

Design of Experiment. The results of phase 1 revealed that there was an equal preference among all configurations. Therefore, we identified the most easily replicable combination of guideline criteria, resulting in 1a-2a-3a-4a. In fact, in IVR environments, identifying functional areas or delineating area boundaries can be challenging, especially in more complex or irregular layouts.

To validate this guideline-based configuration (GB), we compared it to other developed without following any guidelines. In the focus group, we found that designers placed biophilic elements as they were in a real environment. Therefore, a first alternative configuration is a realistic biophilic design but with an unconstrained spatial arrangement (UCB). A second alternative configuration is an unrealistic spatial arrangement (URB). We also included in the comparison an office configuration without biophilic elements, used as baseline (NB). Office 5 was again used to be enriched with the four configurations (see Fig. 3). As in Phase 1, a user-friendly 2D application was developed using Unity WebGL and made accessible via the ITCH.IO platform (see Appendix A2). A within-subjects design was adopted, where each participant evaluated the four configurations by answering four questions each on willingness to work within (*"How would you like to work in this virtual office?"*), realism (*"How realistic do you think it is to work in this virtual office?"*), ability to focus (*"How well could you focus working in this virtual office?"*), and comfort (*"How comfortable would you feel working in this virtual office?"*) working in that virtual office. Responses were given using a 7-point scale represented by yellow stars. Users could explore the virtual office at 360 degrees through a slider, viewing one configuration at a time and in random order.

Participants. The test involved 117 participants (28 females, 18 to 36 years old, mean = 20.50, SD = 3.10). They were 104 bachelor's degree students, 8 Ph.D. students, 4 researchers, and 1 employee. The mean familiarity level with VR was 3.80 (SD = 1.70, Min = 1, Max = 7).

Experimental Procedure. The same procedural steps used in Phase 1 were adopted, involving four subjective questions (instead of one) for each configuration.

Fig. 3. Office 5 used for biophilic guidelines evaluation across the four configurations: (a) NB, (b) GB, (c) URB, and (d) UCB.

Results. The data analysis focused on comparing the average scores of the four configurations for each question. The Shapiro-Wilk test was performed showing that all the data were not normally distributed. Hence, the non-parametric Friedman ANOVA test was performed and, since statistically significant differences emerged in all four questions, the Wilcoxon Signed-Rank Test was performed to compare all pairs for each question. We found statistically significant differences (see Fig. 4) for the willingness to work between GB and NB ($Z = -6.460$, p < 0.001), GB and URB ($Z = -7.748$, p < 0.001), GB and UCB ($Z = -6.377$, p < 0.001), for realism between GB and URB ($Z = -8.055$, p < 0.001), GB and UCB ($Z = -7.515$, p < 0.001), for ability to focus between GB and NB ($Z = -3.846$, p < 0.001), GB and URB ($Z = -7.503$, p < 0.001), GB and UCB ($Z = -6.633$, p < 0.001), and for comfort between GB and NB ($Z = -4.596$, p < 0.001), GB and URB ($Z = -7.552$, p < 0.001), GB and UCB ($Z = -6.624$, p < 0.001).

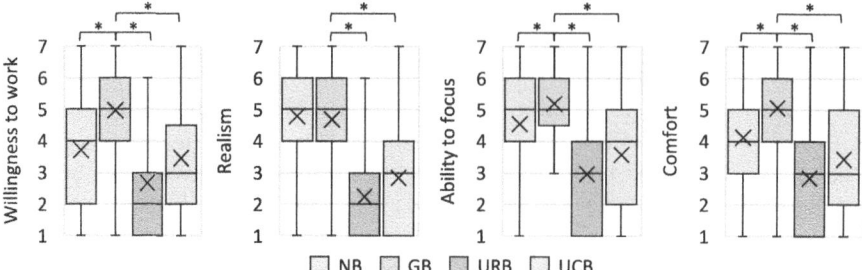

Fig. 4. Box plot for each question (willingness to work, realism, ability to focus, comfort) submitted to users comparing the average scores of the four configurations (NB, GB, URB, UCB) in Phase 2. The asterisks indicate statistically significant different conditions.

4 Discussion

The findings obtained in this work allow to answer our RQ: "*How can biophilic design be implemented in IVR workspaces?*". The focus group with the experts in the field of design allowed us to define a set of guidelines to be used for biophilic design in IVR workspaces. We made a preliminary evaluation of the end-user's willingness to work in the IVR biophilic configurations generated by combining the guidelines. The results of this first phase indicate that user preferences were equally favorable across all 16 configurations. This suggests that the proposed spatial guidelines led to visually coherent, agreeable outcomes that are flexible and robust. This finding is significant because it implies that, within the IVR, there is no singular best configuration for biophilic elements; rather, multiple design solutions based on our guidelines can equally support a pleasing and restorative workspace. The absence of a dominant preference indicated that all the plant criteria were thoughtfully and consistently integrated across all the configurations, resulting in uniformly positive perception. The second evaluation phase confirmed the effectiveness of the Guidelines-based Biophilic configuration, which received the highest ratings in the questions submitted to users. In particular, the willingness to work was significantly greater in GB than in all the other configurations. This suggests that the plant presence alone is not sufficient to elicit a positive response; the integration must follow rational, guideline-based principles to enhance user motivation and engagement. Regarding realism, a key factor in immersion and environmental quality, GB outperformed URB and UCB but no difference with NB, indicating that the integration of plants following structured design guidelines does not compromise the perception of realism, while unrealistic or arbitrary biophilic designs may break the cognitive coherence of the workspace. Results on realism and willingness to work indicate that both URB and UCB were perceived as inadequate for work. Their incoherent, exaggerated application disrupted realism, reducing users' motivation to engage within. Furthermore, GB significantly outperformed others in ability to focus and perceived comfort, suggesting that plants integrated according to guidelines enhance not only cognitive functioning but also the well-being.

One notable insight derived from this research is that the designers approached their task as if furnishing real physical spaces, despite no specific instructions and constraints on placement or quantity of plants. They considered practical aspects such as plant care and spatial dimensions, treating the virtual plants as real. According to focus group feedback, while IVR offers a degree of design flexibility, arranging plants in ways that diverge significantly from real-world configurations may diminish attentional focus and negatively impact worker performance. This tendency is reinforced by Phase 2 results, emphasizing the importance of having a biophilic design that visually and functionally resembles reality, avoiding exaggerated or unrealistic representations. This aspect can be generally interpreted based on the Savannah hypothesis: anthropoid apes, the ancestors of the human race, used to live not in dense forests but in grasslands, like savannahs. According to the savannah hypothesis by Gorden Orians [26, 27], the human race has difficulty in coping with situations in highly dense and dark forests, so they prefer a spacious natural space such as a savannah with few trees [28].

This work focused on an initial IVR workspace, specifically an office with typical furniture, due to the rise of metaverse offices among companies embracing telework [20]. Nonetheless, other scenarios merit exploration. Prior works involving biophilic elements in IVR rarely justify plant placement choices, though they demonstrate the benefits of biophilic enrichment. When comparing those to our guidelines, a general consistency in plant placement emerges. For instance, in [11] table plants are placed on desks and furnishings such as bookshelves and side tables, in quantities comparable to those suggested by our guidelines. Floor plants are positioned along perimeters and near relaxation areas, while green walls are mounted on empty walls. In [6] a larger number of table plants are grouped on shelves, hanging plants are located above desks, and green walls are again placed on empty walls. However, floor plants in this case are clustered in one area rather than distributed along the perimeter. In [7] the environment features a much denser plant presence, lacking hanging plants but including table and floor plants generally aligned with our guidelines, i.e. table plants on shelves, floor plants along the perimeter, and green walls on empty walls. Conversely, [9] includes only small table plants placed on shelves and cabinets. Moreover, [29] places floor plants along the perimeters, and table plants on shelves and cabinets. [30] positions floor plants along the perimeter, table plants on desks, and green walls on empty wall surfaces. Thus, there is coherence with our guidelines, especially when multiple plant types are included. Despite this consistency, replicating all guidelines across IVR workspaces may be challenging. Future research will aim to incorporate natural elements in varied work contexts, to generalize the proposed guidelines with the ultimate goal of simplifying biophilic design in these IVR environments, addressing not only spatial arrangement but also temporal dynamics and visual appearance.

5   Conclusion, Limitations and Future Works

Our work provides novel, expert-driven spatial design guidelines for integrating biophilic elements into IVR workspaces. While previous research has predominantly focused on the beneficial effects of biophilic elements in virtual environments, this study emphasizes the significance of spatial organization and contextual integration. Since in IVR, there are no spatial constraints, we investigated the method used by expert designers to design an IVR office with biophilic elements. The developed guidelines offer clear and actionable recommendations for incorporating indoor plants (table plants, floor plants, hanging plants, and green walls) into IVR offices. They suggest a biophilic design aligned with real-life workspaces, avoiding exaggerated design.

While these results are promising, limitations exist. Although expert designers used an HMD to draw recommendations, participants evaluated configurations via a more accessible web-based application. These participants engaged with the scenarios only briefly, primarily to provide initial impressions, which may have constrained the observed effects on perceived well-being. These decisions were made deliberately to facilitate participation from larger samples of users. Also, the study focused exclusively on offices, leaving out other potential scenarios, such as industrial warehouses. Future research could test the identified guidelines in other IVR environments, for example by placing table plants on workbenches without compromising the working area.

6 Appendices

A1. Screenshots made in itch.io platform in smartphone (up) and desktop (down) mode for Sect. 3.1 Phase 1 for the biophilic guidelines evaluation.

A2. Screenshots made in itch.io platform in smartphone (up) and desktop (down) mode for Sect. 3.2 Phase 2 for the biophilic guidelines evaluation.

Acknowledgments. This work was supported by the European Union - Next Generation EU, NATIONAL RECOVERY AND RESILIENCE PLAN (NRRP) - MISSION 4 Component 2 Investment 1.1 – "Fund for the National Research Program and for Projects of National Interest (NRP)" - CUP D53D23017380001. Finally, the authors would also like to acknowledge all the participants involved in this research.

References

1. Wilson, E.O.: Biophilia. Harvard University Press (1984)
2. Kellert, S.R.: Biophilic Design: The Theory, Science and Practice of Bringing Buildings to Life. John Wiley & Sons, Inc., Hoboken, NJ (2008)
3. Kaplan, R., Kaplan, S.: Restorative experience: the healing power of nearby nature. In: Francis, M., Hester, R.T. (eds.), The Meaning of Gardens: Idea, Place, and Action (1990)
4. Kaplan, S.: The restorative benefits of nature: toward an integrative framework. J. Environ. Psychol. **15**, 169–182 (1995). https://doi.org/10.1016/0272-4944(95)90001-2
5. Ulrich, R.S., Simons, R.F., Losito, B.D., Fiorito, E., Miles, M.A., Zelson, M.: Stress recovery during exposure to natural and urban environments. J. Environ. Psychol. **11**, 201–230 (1991). https://doi.org/10.1016/S0272-4944(05)80184-7
6. Yin, J., Arfaei, N., MacNaughton, P., Catalano, P.J., Allen, J.G., Spengler, J.D.: Effects of biophilic interventions in office on stress reaction and cognitive function: a randomized crossover study in virtual reality. Indoor Air **29**, 1028–1039 (2019). https://doi.org/10.1111/ina.12593
7. Yin, J., Yuan, J., Arfaei, N., Catalano, P.J., Allen, J.G., Spengler, J.D.: Effects of biophilic indoor environment on stress and anxiety recovery: a between-subjects experiment in virtual reality. Environ Int. **136** (2020). https://doi.org/10.1016/j.envint.2019.105427
8. Ryan, C.O., et al.: 14 patterns of biophilic design, 62–76 (2014)
9. You, J., Wen, X., Liu, L., Yin, J., Ji, J.S.: Biophilic classroom environments on stress and cognitive performance: a randomized crossover study in virtual reality (VR). PLoS One **18** (2023). https://doi.org/10.1371/journal.pone.0291355

10. Kellert, S.R., Calabrese, E.F.: The Practice of Biophilic Design - A Simplified Framework (2015)

11. Mostajeran, F., Steinicke, F., Reinhart, S., Stuerzlinger, W., Riecke, B.E., Kühn, S.: Adding virtual plants leads to higher cognitive performance and psychological well-being in virtual reality. Sci Rep. **13** (2023). https://doi.org/10.1038/s41598-023-34718-3

12. Latini, A., Marcelli, L., Di Giuseppe, E., D'Orazio, M.: Potential of biophilic design in workplaces: a pilot study with eye tracking in immersive virtual environments. Smart Innov. Syst. Technol. **378**, 355–365 (2024). https://doi.org/10.1007/978-981-99-8501-2_32

13. Choi, J.Y., et al.: Physiological and psychological responses of humans to the index of greenness of an interior space. Complement. Ther. Med. **28**, 37–43 (2016). https://doi.org/10.1016/J.CTIM.2016.08.002

14. Romano, S., Laviola, E., Uva, A.E., Gattullo, M.: METAGREENVERSE: exploring the user experience in a biophilic metaverse workspace. In: Di Stefano, P., Gherardini, F., Nigrelli, V., Rizzi, C., Sequenzia, G., Tumino, D. (eds.) Design Tools and Methods in Industrial Engineering IV. ADM 2024. Lecture Notes in Mechanical Engineering, pp. 287–294. Springer, Cham (2025). https://doi.org/10.1007/978-3-031-76594-0_33

15. Gattullo, M., Laviola, E., Romano, S., Evangelista, A., Manghisi, V.M., Fiorentino, M., Uva, A.E.: Biophilic enriched virtual environments for industrial training: a user study. In: Proceedings of the 2022 IEEE International Symposium on Mixed and Augmented Reality, ISMAR 2022, pp. 206–214 (2022). https://doi.org/10.1109/ISMAR55827.2022.00035

16. Corchado, M.A.R., Ruiz, J.C.S., Corchado, F.Francisco.R., Romero, J.R.M.: Growing plants for virtual 3D environments. In: Proceedings of the 2009 6th International Conference on Electrical Engineering, Computing Science and Automatic Control (CCE), pp. 1–6 (2009). https://doi.org/10.1109/ICEEE.2009.5393469

17. Slob, N., Hurst, W., van de Zedde, R., Tekinerdogan, B.: Virtual reality-based digital twins for greenhouses: a focus on human interaction. Comput. Electron. Agric. **208**, 107815 (2023). https://doi.org/10.1016/j.compag.2023.107815

18. Guo, J., Xu, S., Yan, D.-M., Cheng, Z., Jaeger, M., Zhang, X.: Realistic procedural plant modeling from multiple view images. IEEE Trans. Vis. Comput. Graph. **26**, 1372–1384 (2020). https://doi.org/10.1109/TVCG.2018.2869784

19. Awiszus, M., Schubert, F., Rosenhahn, B.: World-GAN: a generative model for minecraft worlds. In: Proceedings of the 2021 IEEE Conference on Games (CoG), pp. 1–8 (2021). https://doi.org/10.1109/CoG52621.2021.9619133

20. Park, S.M., Kim, Y.G.: A metaverse: taxonomy, components, applications, and open challenges. IEEE Access **10**, 4209–4251 (2022). https://doi.org/10.1109/ACCESS.2021.3140175

21. Sal Moslehian, A., Roös, P.B., Gaekwad, J.S., Van Galen, L.: Potential risks and beneficial impacts of using indoor plants in the biophilic design of healthcare facilities: a scoping review. Build. Environ. **233**, 110057 (2023). https://doi.org/10.1016/J.BUILDENV.2023.110057

22. KavyaJ Asst, A.: Interior design landscaping. Quest J. J. Archit. Civ. Eng. **8**, 2321–8193 (2023)

23. Smith, A., Pitt, M.: Healthy workplaces: plantscaping for indoor environmental quality. Facilities **29**, 169–187 (2011). https://doi.org/10.1108/02632771111109289

24. Fjeld, T., Veiersted, B., Sandvik, L., Riise, G., Levy, F.: The effect of indoor foliage plants on health and discomfort symptoms among office workers. Indoor Built Environ. **7**, 204–209 (1998). https://doi.org/10.1177/1420326X9800700404

25. McGee, B., Park, N.K.: Colour, light, and materiality: biophilic interior design presence in research and practice. Interiority **5**, 27–52 (2022). https://doi.org/10.7454/in.v5i1.189

26. Bender, R., Tobias, P.V., Bender, N.: The savannah hypotheses: origin, reception and impact on paleoanthropology. Hist. Philos. Life Sci. (2012). https://doi.org/10.7892/boris.13934

27. Hartsell, A.M.: Savanna hypothesis in the human–urban nature relationship. Open House Int. **46**, 18–29 (2021). https://doi.org/10.1108/OHI-05-2020-0024

28. Yeom, S., Kim, H., Hong, T.: Psychological and physiological effects of a green wall on occupants: a cross-over study in virtual reality. Build Environ. **204** (2021). https://doi.org/10.1016/j.buildenv.2021.108134

29. Seufert, C., Oberdörfer, S., Roth, A., Grafe, S., Lugrin, J.-L., Latoschik, M.E.: Classroom management competency enhancement for student teachers using a fully immersive virtual classroom. Comput. Educ. **179**, 104410 (2022). https://doi.org/10.1016/j.compedu.2021.104410

30. Latini, A., Torresin, S., Oberman, T., Di Giuseppe, E., Aletta, F., Kang, J., D'Orazio, M.: Virtual reality application to explore indoor soundscape and physiological responses to audio-visual biophilic design interventions: an experimental study in an office environment. J. Build. Eng. **87** (2024). https://doi.org/10.1016/j.jobe.2024.108947

SENSO3D: Structured Pipelines for AI-Based 3D Object Detection, Classification, and Texture Generation

Mohammad Mohammad Amini[1]([⊠]), Ali Hajqani[1], Mohammad Hasan Bahari[2], Davood Fanaei Sheikholeslami[1], Ali Mazaheri[1], and Mohammad Mohammadi[1]

[1] Researcher at Sensomatt Lda, 6000-767 Castelo Branco, Portugal
mm_amini@sensomatt.com
[2] Researcher at Sensifai BVBA, 1950 Kraainem, Belgium

Abstract. Creating high-quality, scalable 3D environments for Extended Reality (XR) applications is often labor-intensive, requiring manual modeling, mesh optimization, and texturing. This paper introduces a novel AI-powered pipeline—developed under the SENSO3D project—that automates the transformation of 2D photographs and textual prompts into fully textured 3D objects and immersive scenes. Leveraging advanced models such as F-Cube R-CNN for object detection and F-TripoSR for single-image 3D reconstruction, the system generates 3D assets enriched with AI-driven texture synthesis and semantic categorization. These assets are seamlessly integrated into Unity, enabling real-time deployment in XR contexts such as virtual conferences, product showcases, and interactive training environments. The pipeline achieved a reconstruction accuracy of 92% across varied environments, with object detection precision exceeding 95% across 50+ classes. Additionally, a prompt-based scene generator empowers non-technical users to create complete 3D environments from natural language input. The entire workflow is optimized for speed and scalability, reducing development time from days to minutes. This work demonstrates how AI can bridge the gap between static visual data and dynamic immersive experiences, enabling faster, more accessible XR content creation.

Keywords: 3D Reconstruction · AI Object Detection · Texture Synthesis · Unity XR · Prompt-Based Scene Generation · 2D-to-3D Modeling · Immersive Environments · Deep Learning for XR

1 Introduction

1.1 The Background

XR content development—spanning Virtual, Augmented, and Mixed Reality—relies heavily on the availability of high-quality 3D models and realistic environments. Traditionally, this process involves time-consuming manual steps such as object modeling, mesh optimization, UV mapping, and texture generation. This pipeline demands both artistic skill and technical expertise, posing significant barriers to scalability and democratization in sectors such as virtual meetings, retail, real estate, and training.

© The Author(s), under exclusive license to Springer Nature Switzerland AG 2026
D. Michael-Grigoriou et al. (Eds.): EuroXR 2025, LNCS 16101, pp. 155–166, 2026.
https://doi.org/10.1007/978-3-032-03805-0_9

With the rise of AI and deep learning, new opportunities have emerged to streamline and partially or fully automate XR content creation. However, most current approaches remain either narrowly focused on isolated tasks (e.g., object segmentation or texture transfer) or are limited to academic research without real-time XR deployment pathways.

1.2 Motivation for AI Automation

The SENSO3D project was launched to address these limitations by designing a structured, AI-driven pipeline capable of:

- Detecting and classifying objects from unstructured 2D inputs (images and photographs),
- Reconstructing their 3D geometry using monocular input,
- Automatically generating PBR-style textures based on AI descriptors,
- Assembling these objects into coherent, interactive scenes based on textual prompts,
- Exporting final assets directly into Unity for real-time XR rendering. This automation significantly reduces production time, supports rapid prototyping, and opens XR content creation to non-expert users.

1.3 How SENSO3D Addresses These Challenges

SENSO3D introduces a multi-stage system that begins with object detection using a fine-tuned F-Cube R-CNN and progresses through 3D reconstruction using F-TripoSR. The pipeline integrates a novel AI-based texture synthesis module and a prompt-based scene generation engine that maps user commands to spatial layouts through AI-supported asset retrieval and classification. All generated content is optimized and deployed within Unity XR environments.

Unlike fragmented solutions, SENSO3D provides a cohesive end-to-end approach with quantifiable accuracy, rapid execution times, and tested deployment in real XR applications including virtual business meetings and conference simulations.

1.4 Structure of This Paper

The remainder of this paper is organized as follows:

Section 2 reviews prior work in 2D-to-3D modeling, object detection, and scene generation.
Section 3 details the methodology and architecture of the SENSO3D pipeline.
Section 4 presents evaluation results, including reconstruction accuracy and XR integration metrics.
Section 5 discusses limitations, trade-offs, and potential areas of future improvement.
Section 6 concludes with reflections on the impact of this technology on scalable XR development.

2 Related Work

2.1 Monocular 3D Reconstruction from 2D Images

A growing body of research focuses on reconstructing 3D geometry from a single monocular image. For instance, Pan et al. [1] addressed soft-edge enhanced 3D depth estimation from historical 2D photos using a modified deep network tailored for cultural heritage applications, such as Borobudur relief reconstructions. Their work notably emphasized small depth gradients and low-curvature boundaries, which are critical for semantic depth integrity. Similarly, Mouawad et al. [2] introduced a novel self-supervised learning framework for monocular 3D object detection that capitalizes on temporal consistency across RGB video frames, thereby eliminating the need for LIDAR or labeled real-world datasets. Their model achieved competitive results with minimal supervision, aligning with structured image pipelines utilized in current automated approaches.

Zhang et al. [3] extended the field by developing 3DCascade-GAN, which utilizes a multi-stage GAN enhanced with 3D self-attention layers. This enables shape completion from partial depth images through global feature refinement—a core challenge also addressed in current pipelines. Notably, their architecture bridges local and non-local geometrical cues, paralleling goals of holistic 3D formation.

2.2 Virtual and Synthetic Dataset Usage

To address the challenge of limited annotated 3D data, Song et al. [4] proposed VONet, a deep learning model trained on synthetically generated organoid datasets. A fully convolutional network was employed to reconstruct 3D volumes from minimal z-stack inputs, thereby reducing the cost and time associated with confocal microscopy. This synthetic-data-first philosophy serves as an inspiration for controlled synthetic training pipelines used in 3D mesh reconstruction from annotated 2D projections.

Another innovative example is provided by Giannis et al. [5], who employed a 3D-CNN architecture to predict full 3D particle geometries from multiple 2D projections. Their pipeline emphasized the recovery of key morphological parameters (e.g., sphericity and flatness) and validated predictions using Fourier shape descriptors. Their work underscores the potential of CNN-based volumetric learning using procedurally generated synthetic data.

2.3 Texture Synthesis and Image Completion

In parallel with structural reconstruction, texture generation from incomplete or noisy images is pivotal. Zdunek [6] introduced a hybrid texture synthesis and image completion approach that combines radial basis function interpolation with patch-based synthesis. This methodology effectively handles both dense and sparse image corruption, a concept applicable to UV-based texture mapping modules where patch interpolation and synthesis are jointly optimized.

Wu and Liu [7] further enhanced realism in aggregate surface modeling using GPR-CNN fusion. Their deep model synthesized rough surface textures with varying scales using Catmull–Clark subdivision and displacement mapping. This multi-scale roughness augmentation presents clear parallels with physics-aware UV unwrapping and micro-texture fusion stages found in advanced pipelines.

2.4 Shape Retrieval and Representation Learning

Bickel et al. [8] proposed a deep-learning-based shape retrieval framework optimized for engineering parts. Their pipeline processes point clouds into shape descriptors using autoencoders and part-alignment heuristics. The framework provides significant insights for classifying 3D objects using learned feature vectors and descriptors following the reconstruction phase.

Van den Herrewegen et al. [9] focused on self-supervised learning for 3D object retrieval using a PointNet++ backbone and VICReg, demonstrating robustness to unseen domains. Their cross-domain performance and label-free architecture reinforce the feasibility of classifier components in handling real-world object classes derived from synthetic training data.

3 Methodology

3.1 Overall System Pipeline (from 2D Input to Unity Asset)

The SENSO3D pipeline transforms raw 2D inputs into textured, categorized 3D assets ready for integration into real-time XR environments built with Unity. The process is designed to be modular, scalable, and accessible to both technical and non-technical users. It is composed of five primary stages:

2D Image Ingestion & Preprocessing: Users upload photographs or screenshots of interior environments. These images may contain overlapping objects, partial views, and lighting inconsistencies. Preprocessing includes resolution normalization and noise filtering.

Object Detection and Classification: Using the F-Cube R-CNN model, objects are identified, segmented, and categorized into over 50 predefined XR-optimized classes. Bounding box data and semantic labels are extracted at this stage.

3D Shape Reconstruction: Cropped object segments are passed into the F-TripoSR module to infer full 3D geometry from a single view. The model supports soft-edge and occlusion compensation, allowing the system to accurately reconstruct partially visible objects.

Texture Generation: Texture synthesis is driven by AI descriptors extracted during classification. These descriptors are cross-referenced with a texture library and augmented with generative models to produce UV-ready textures.

Unity Asset Export: All reconstructed and textured objects are exported as.glb or.fbx files with optimized polygon counts and UV maps. These are directly importable into Unity and configured with collider and anchor settings for XR interaction.

3.2 AI Models Used

F-Cube R-CNN (Object Detection): A custom variant of R-CNN developed for XR-friendly object recognition, F-Cube R-CNN integrates spatial anchor awareness and class-bounded non-maximum suppression (NMS). It enables accurate bounding box generation in scenes with overlapping or complex object arrangements. The model handles 50+ object categories ranging from "conference table" and "glass wall" to "plant pot" and "TV screen."

F-TripoSR (2D-to-3D Reconstruction): F-TripoSR is a modified version of TripoSR fine-tuned to infer geometry from partial views. It performs well in scenarios where input images provide limited angle coverage. The model outputs mesh-level geometry that is then post-processed for smoothing and hollow detection, achieving an average accuracy of 92%, even in scenes with complex occlusion.

Texture Generator (Using AI Descriptors): Textures are generated by combining descriptor embeddings from the classification phase with statistical texture databases. The generator employs a blend of style transfer, image completion, and latent interpolation techniques to ensure textures match both the object class and visual context. All textures are applied with PBR maps (diffuse, normal, specular) and exported with unwrapped UVs.

3.3 Prompt-Based Scene Generator

Text-to-Scene Layout Mapping: The prompt-based generator allows users to define spatial scenes using natural language. Prompts such as "Create a conference room with eight chairs and a projector" are interpreted by a natural language processing (NLP) parser, which breaks down the request into spatial commands and object queries.

Search Engine and AI Integration: A hybrid semantic-keyword engine, augmented by an embedding-based AI layer, maps textual prompts to previously generated or reconstructed 3D assets. The system prioritizes size compatibility, class accuracy, and layout coherence. Scene graphs are generated and exported as Unity-compatible JSON configurations.

4 Results and Evaluation

4.1 Object Detection Accuracy

The F-Cube R-CNN model was tested on internal datasets containing labeled images of XR-targeted environments. It achieved an average precision of 95.7% and recall of 93.2% across more than 50 object categories. The model's ability to separate overlapping or nested objects significantly enhanced scene reconstruction fidelity.

4.2 2D-to-3D Reconstruction Accuracy

The F-TripoSR module demonstrated an average mesh fidelity of 92% when bench-marked against ground truth 3D scans. Accuracy remained robust even in scenes with 40–60% occlusion. Visual results indicated that the reconstructed shapes closely approximate proportions, curvature, and surface area.

4.3 Texture Generation

Texture fidelity was evaluated by comparing AI-generated UV maps with reference images. Results indicated:

– Visual realism rated 4.6/5 by expert reviewers.
– Average deviation in pattern fidelity was less than 7% from real-world textures.
– UV seams and distortion were minimized through automatic mapping using neural edge detection.

4.4 Performance Metrics

To evaluate the operational efficiency and scalability of the SENSO3D system, key performance indicators were measured across object processing, scene generation, mesh optimization, and integration into XR environments. Table 1 presents the results from a controlled evaluation on a representative dataset.

The system demonstrated an average object processing time of 3.2 s and was capable of generating complete scenes (with up to 5 objects) in under 20 s. Each reconstructed model maintained an optimized polygon count between 3,000 and 5,000, supporting high visual quality while preserving XR performance. Texture outputs included 1k and 2k PBR maps, and Unity integration achieved a 100% import success rate across a test suite of 40 distinct environments.

Table 1. Performance report of SENSO3D functions.

Metric	Value
Average object processing time	3.2 s
Scene generation (5 objects)	<20 s
Polygon count per model (optimized)	~3,000–5,000 polygons
Texture resolution	1k/2k PBR maps
Unity import success rate	100% (test suite of 40 scenes)

4.5 Visual Results

The SENSO3D system was visually validated through a series of end-to-end reconstructions encompassing object detection, 3D mesh generation, UV mapping, and full scene integration in Unity. Figures 1, 2, 3, 4 and 5 illustrate key stages and outcomes from the pipeline, emphasizing system performance in real-world XR use cases such as virtual meetings and interior layout design.

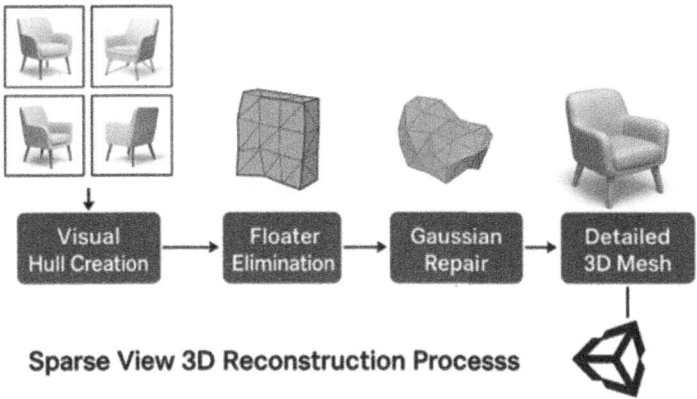

Fig. 1. Diagram of the sparse-view 3D reconstruction workflow using Gaussian splatting, enabling model generation from limited photo inputs.

SENSO3D 3D Model Creation Pipeline

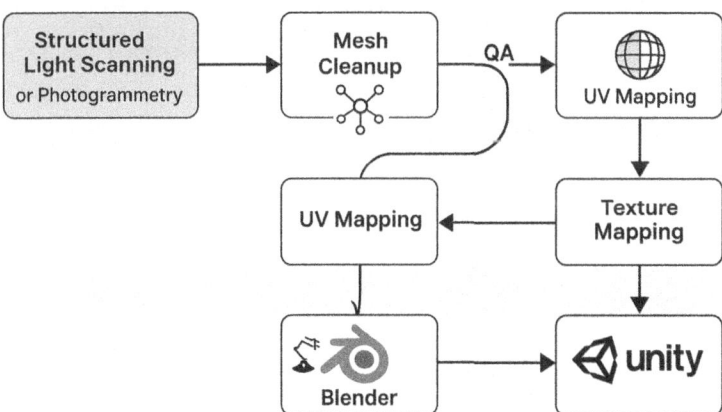

Fig. 2. SENSO3D's 3D model generation process includes scanning, cleanup, mapping, and optimization with QA loop integration.

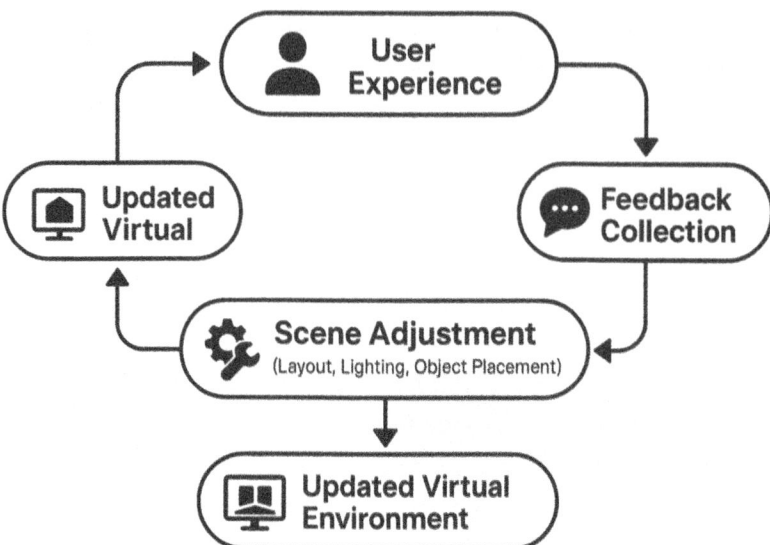

Fig. 3. Feedback loop illustrating how user input is collected and used to iteratively improve virtual scene quality and interactivity.

Fig. 4. Object Detection and Semantic Labeling in a Virtual Conference Room. This figure shows a rendered view of a virtual conference room used in SENSO3D, comparing the original scene

Fig. 5. Sample of 3D object mesh generation and texturing from 2D image description as the input

5   Discussion

5.1   Trade-Offs: Realism vs. Performance

The SENSO3D pipeline was designed to strike a deliberate balance between visual realism and real-time performance, particularly for deployment in XR environments such as Unity and WebXR. To support broad accessibility and rapid prototyping, the pipeline employs polygon-optimized meshes and lightweight PBR textures. While this configuration supports high frame rates and low load times—even on modest hardware—it introduces visual simplifications, especially in fine surface detailing and shading nuance.

For instance, objects reconstructed from a single photographic angle may exhibit minor geometric smoothness or flattening on occluded sides. Additionally, in order to maintain manageable polygon budgets, curvature features are typically approximated rather than fully modeled. These compromises are essential for maintaining interactive frame rates across devices (e.g., Meta Quest, browser-based XR), but may not satisfy the fidelity requirements of photorealistic rendering engines such as Unreal Engine.

5.2   Generalizability Across XR Applications

The SENSO3D system was validated across a range of scene types, including:

– Professional conference rooms
– Corporate lobbies
– Waiting areas and open interior spaces

The modularity of the object detection and reconstruction system enables reuse across a variety of XR applications, including:

– Remote business meetings (spatialized XR environments)
– Educational training rooms
– Showroom visualizations
– AI-assisted design prototyping

This generalizability is driven by the use of universal AI object categories and the abstraction of scene layout logic into prompt-based controls. The same pipeline can be repurposed for use in industrial training simulations or marketing VR experiences by adjusting prompt inputs and texture profiles.

5.3   Current Limitations

Despite its demonstrated strengths, the SENSO3D system presents several current limitations:

Complex Texture Fidelity: The texture generator exhibits reduced performance when processing images containing high-gloss, transparent, or intricately patterned materials (e.g., glass, marble with veins).

Scene Scale Awareness: While individual objects are well reconstructed, their spatial relationships are inferred rather than measured, which may necessitate manual adjustments for ergonomic accuracy.

Partial Occlusion Inference: Although F-TripoSR supports occlusion handling, reconstructions in highly cluttered scenes or of thin structures (e.g., chair legs, cables) may yield noisy outputs.

Lack of Live AR Preview: The current workflow exports assets for use in Unity-based VR or WebXR platforms but does not yet offer integrated live AR mapping for mobile or headset-based real-time visualization.

5.4   Future Enhancements

Based on technical evaluations from milestone D3, the following advancements are planned:

Level-Of-Detail (LOD) Models: Multiple mesh versions (LOD0–LOD3) will be exported to support scalable rendering tailored to user proximity and device capabilities.

High-Fidelity PBR Integration: The existing PBR texture generation system will be extended to include advanced lighting models, subsurface scattering simulation, and environment-aware shadow baking.

Scene-Scale Optimization: A SLAM-based scanning layer will be incorporated to align object coordinates with real-world scaled layouts, enhancing XR spatial fidelity.

Live AR Projection: Upcoming updates will introduce real-time AR overlays leveraging mobile depth APIs (e.g., ARKit, ARCore), allowing users to preview reconstructed environments in situ before exporting to Unity.

6 Conclusion

6.1 Summary of Innovations

SENSO3D introduces a fully integrated pipeline that transforms 2D images and natural language prompts into fully textured, categorized, and XR-ready 3D assets. Key innovations include:

– F-Cube R-CNN for high-accuracy multi-class object detection from photographs.
– F-TripoSR for rapid monocular-based 3D reconstruction with occlusion resilience.
– Prompt-based scene layout generation, enabling non-technical users to describe XR environments.
– Texture synthesis guided by AI descriptors and optimized UV mapping.

These components together form a structured and repeatable framework for scalable XR content creation..

6.2 Impact on XR Development

By reducing reliance on 3D modeling software and manual texturing, SENSO3D provides a significant advancement in XR asset generation speed and accessibility. The platform supports a wide array of use cases, including:

– Business conferencing in realistic virtual environments.
– Training room simulation for onboarding and scenario-based learning.
– Remote showroom visualization for real estate or product showcases.
– Interior design prototyping for architects and creative agencies.

The pipeline bridges the gap between content creators, developers, and domain experts by lowering the barrier to immersive design.

6.3 Final Performance Evaluation

Based on internal benchmarking conducted during the Cortex2-supported pilot phase:

– Object detection precision exceeded 95% across more than 50 classes.
– 2D-to-3D reconstruction accuracy reached 92% using partial-view inputs.
– Average processing time per scene (5–7 objects) was under 25 s.
– Unity integration achieved a 100% success rate in both import and interaction.

These performance metrics validate the system's readiness for commercial and research-grade deployment in XR scenarios that demand rapid, accurate, and visually coherent 3D environments.

Acknowledgments. This study was funded by the European Union's Horizon Europe research and innovation programme under CORTEX^2 Open Call 1, subgrant agreement number 101070192, in support of the SENSO3D project. The authors gratefully acknowledge the CORTEX^2 consortium for providing financial and technical support, and for facilitating collaboration across XR innovation communities.

Disclosure of Interests. The authors have no competing interests to declare that are relevant to the content of this article.

References

1. Pan, J., et al.: 3D reconstruction of Borobudur reliefs from 2D monocular photographs based on soft-edge enhanced deep learning. ISPRS J. Photogramm. Remote Sens. **183**, 439–450 (2022)
2. Mouawad, I., Brasch, N., Manhardt, F., Tombari, F., Odone, F.: View-to-label: Multi-view consistency for self-supervised monocular 3D object detection. Comput. Vis. Image Underst. **254**, 104320 (2025)
3. Alhamazani, F., Lai, Y.-K., Rosin, P.L.: 3DCascade-GAN: shape completion from single-view depth images. Comput. Graph. **115**, 412–422 (2023)
4. Song, E., et al.: VONet: a deep learning network for 3D reconstruction of organoid structures with a minimal number of confocal images. Patterns **5**, 101063 (2024)
5. Giannis, K., Thon, C., Yang, G., Kwade, A., Schilde, C.: Predicting 3D particles shapes based on 2D images by using convolutional neural network. Powder Technol. **432**, 119122 (2024)
6. Zdunek, R.: Hybrid texture synthesis and interpolated structure image completion. Procedia Comput. Sci. **207**, 2464–2473 (2022)
7. Wu, L., Liu, P.: Realistic aggregate based on rough textures with deep learning. Appl. Soft Comput. **164**, 111938 (2024)
8. Bickel, S., Schleich, B., Wartzack, S.: A novel shape retrieval method for 3D mechanical components based on object projection, pre-trained deep learning models and autoencoder. Comput.-Aided Des. **154**, 103417 (2023)
9. Van den Herrewegen, J., Tourwé, T., Wyffels, F.: Self-supervised learning for robust object retrieval without human annotations. Comput. Graph.. Graph. **115**, 13–24 (2023)

Human Factors and Perception

Assessing the Immersive Experience with Physiological Measures: A Systematic Literature Review

Athina Bosta⬤ and Spyros Vosinakis⁽⊠⁾ ⬤

University of the Aegean, Konstantinoupoleos 2, 84100 Ermoupoli, Greece

Abstract. User experience evaluation in Virtual Reality (VR) includes a variety of methods and practices that contribute to locating findings regarding the application design. Consequently, each evaluation procedure differs based on context, technology, participants, and design objectives. At the same time, an increasing number of researchers emphasize the need to utilize physiological measurements as evaluation input to provide a more objective view of the experience. Therefore, they require a multidisciplinary approach to plan and conduct evaluations in VR, including physiological data recording and processing as part of the evaluation procedure. There has been plenty of work towards this end in the last decade but given the variety of devices and physiological measures and the complicated nature of VR setup and interactions, there is a rising need for mapping the field and identifying prospects and limitations. This paper presents a literature review of user experience evaluations using physiological measures in virtual reality settings to aid VR experts in understanding the role, requirements, and limitations of these measures within their evaluation process. The results showcase insights based on five domains: 1) user experience aspect, 2) wearable recording devices, 3) physiological measures, 4) self-report methods, and 5) reliability and highlight future research areas in the utilization of the physiological measures in VR environments assist researchers in deriving meaningful feedback.

Keywords: User Experience Evaluation · Virtual Reality · Physiological Measures · Human-Computer Interaction · Assessment Practices

1 Introduction

User experience (UX) evaluation in virtual reality (VR) offers a variety of methods and practices to provide feedback about quality, performance, usability issues, risk of problems, and possible improvements to designers and developers. Evaluators have been using assessment methods in VR, incorporating standard tools and practices from the Human Computer Interaction (HCI) discipline [1, 2] or by adapting and customizing the existing ones to match the evaluation objectives [3]. The VR community is invested in clarifying the importance and the connections [4] between immersion, presence [5], and interactivity [6], thus, more and more evaluation tools have been utilized to measure

D. Michael-Grigoriou et al. (Eds.): EuroXR 2025, LNCS 16101, pp. 169–187, 2026.
https://doi.org/10.1007/978-3-032-03805-0_10

aspects of the UX. The standard evaluation methods are based on observation and self-report questionnaires [7]. These evaluation tools are categorized as subjective feedback providers because they depend on how researchers understand the interaction between VR environment and the participant or how users express and describe their experience retrospectively. Previous studies have outlined the limitations of these tools and discussed that physiological data can collect insights during the interaction without interfering with the experience. Physiological data can provide information about the affective response from the users, offering objective measurements about the VR experience. These measurements may be particularly valuable in immersive VR contexts, where maintaining a rich interactive environment without disrupting presence is critical. Additionally, their collection method is described as nonintrusive and user-friendly, allowing the user to remain immersed in the experience without disruptions [8].

A number of reviews have been carried out up to date related to UX and usability evaluations using physiological measures in HCI and VR application evaluation field. A group of studies focused on the integration of physiological measures as a means of collecting UX evaluation insights in more generic settings, without taking into account the special circumstances of the immersive VR experience (embodiment, immersion, etc.) [7, 9, 10]. A second group of reviews explore the UX evaluation of a VR environment through physiological and behavioral metrics emphasizing in the emotional aspect of the experience [11, 12]. Further publications examine the evaluation of UX experience regarding specific factors related to VR environments, such as perception, presence, spatial navigation, and cybersickness, combining physiological measures and standard UX or usability evaluation methods [13–16]. Whilst these works shed much light into specific aspects of the experience and the analysis of physiological features, there is still a lack of knowledge about evaluation protocols and practices in VR environments that incorporate these measures in generic UX evaluations. Therefore, it becomes imperative to conduct a literature review about the utilization of physiological measures in Virtual Reality application evaluations and how the UX evaluation protocols are shaped.

This review explores researchers' choices on UX evaluation in VR with physiological measures, mapping the variety of evaluation approaches. The main objective is to reveal common or unexpected patterns or trends of the UX evaluation practice in VR. At the same time, this review will record the different approaches in the user experience evaluation field, providing insights about the UX aspects that occur as metric types, the wearable recording devices that are usually involved, the different categories of physiological data utilized as objective feedback, the integrated self-report methods, and the reliability of physiological measurements in UX evaluation in VR. A literature review [17, 18] is employed to present how UX evaluations using physiological data in VR are being implemented and if they offer meaningful assessment procedures to the HCI evaluation practices.

2   Theoretical Background

This section briefly introduces the relevant terminology, mainly terms of physiological measures, signals, and sensors, raw data and data features, as well as the meaning of UX metrics. Measuring the user experience and, more specifically, the participants' effective states or body responses is a particularly complex and difficult process due to the broad spectrum of human emotions and body states and the challenge of accurately capturing them [94]. The fluctuations of physiological data are related to the involuntary changes in emotional states that usually are not perceivable by individuals. Therefore, biosensors are a reliable method of recognizing emotional or behavioral states because they can monitor different parts of the human body [19].

Furthermore, physiological measurements are derived from physiological signals, through the sensors of wearable devices. Firstly, the researcher decides which physiological measurement is going to be utilized in an evaluation, narrowing their choices in wearable devices. When the raw data has been processed, features are derived. Features are quantified values, numerical attributes of the monitored body functions. For example, if heart rate (HR) data is the physiological measure for an evaluation, a wristband or a heart strap is going to be utilized potentially. A photoplethysmogram (PPG) sensor provides information about the Heart Rate (HR) [20]. Often, the interbeat interval time (IBI) measures the changes in the blood volume and determines the variability in the timing of the heartbeat (Heart Rate Variability or HRV) [21]. A PPG sensor is considered a more suitable option than the electrocardiogram (ECG) [22], which also provides details about heart-related features. The PPG sensor is embedded in a variety of wearable devices such as in the Empatica E4 [23], Huawei Watch 2 [24], and Shimmer3 [25], which are wristband-type wearables in contrast with other PPG-based devices (forehead-type and ear-type) [26]. Certain devices, such as the Empatica wristbands [27], include more than one sensor, enabling the parallel recording of different signals.

Additionally, UX metrics provide insights into the experience itself, describing how the participant perceives the use of a VR application. UX metric depicts a finding about the user's interaction with a virtual environment that is being evaluated, disclosing information about people's behavior, attitude, or perspective. It is pertinent to note that each UX evaluation differs in terms of the research objectives and the users' goals, the technology available and accessible to collect, analyze, and present the data, and the time and expertise required for the appropriate processing of the findings. UX researchers highlight that to understand the users, as well as their interaction with the system, evaluators should focus on three key aspects of the user experience which are performance, preferences, and emotions [28].

3   Research Methodology

3.1 Review Planning

The objectives of this literature review are: a) to investigate the procedures used by researchers when evaluating the user experience of a virtual reality application using physiological measures, b) to identify which aspects of the user experience, particularly those unique to immersive VR, researchers prioritize in their assessments, c) to explore the physiological measures and wearables that are commonly utilized, d) to ascertain whether and which self-report methods are involved in such evaluations and e) to discover potential opportunities for future research. As a result, the main research questions (RQ) are shaped as follows:

RQ1: Which aspect of the UX (metric) in VR is assessed?

RQ2: Which wearable devices are integrated into UX evaluations in VR?

RQ3: What physiological measures are being included in user experience evaluations in virtual reality settings?

RQ4: If self-report methods are integrated, which are commonly used among the research studies?

RQ5: Which reliability issues arise during the evaluation?

We decided to limit our search to high-quality articles published between 2010 and 2024. The reason for this limitation is that immersive VR systems were not widely available before the release of affordable consumer head-mounted displays, whilst physiological measurement devices had not yet reached full maturity.

3.2 Review Implementation

We followed the PRISMA methodology for implementing our review. A thorough search was implemented on the following digital databases: ACM, Frontiers, IEEE, IGI Global, MDPI, PLOS One, PubMed Central, SAGE Publications, ScienceDirect, Scientific Reports, SpringerLink, Taylor & Francis. The primary search phrase was "Evaluation" AND ("Physiological Signals" OR "Physiological Measurements") AND ("Virtual Reality" OR "Virtual Environments"). The inclusion and exclusion criteria that we used involve the language, the publication date and the relevance to the aims of the review. And are presented in Table 1.

Table 1. Inclusion and Exclusion Criteria to determine review material

	Criteria
Inclusion	1. Research papers in English 2. Papers published between 2010–2024 3. The papers present the evaluation of at least an aspect of the user experience 4. The research article assesses an experience that occurs in a VR setting 5. The paper includes at least one physiological measurement in the evaluation of VR experience
Exclusion	1. Research articles unrelated to the topic of the literature review 2. Papers presenting UX evaluation with physiological measures in different settings (not in virtual reality)

The screening process led to 70 research articles. Figure 1 presents the detailed PRISMA flow diagram of the reviewing process. The body of articles included in the review offered intriguing insights, outlining five main domains for data extraction based on the research questions. These domains are: 1) UX Aspect: The subject of the VR application evaluation, 2) Wearable Recording Devices: The equipment employed for physiological signal recording, 3) Physiological measures: The different categories of body response data types, 4) Self-report methods: Researchers' approaches to request feedback from the participants about their intentions, beliefs, behavior, physical state, and attitude, and 5) Reliability: researchers' perspective on physiological measure involvement in UX evaluation in VR. Finally, quantitative and qualitative data were gathered based on the review material concerning these five domains. A spreadsheet was created including all the selected review research articles, to analyze the data more quickly and efficiently as well as to generate charts and diagrams accurately.

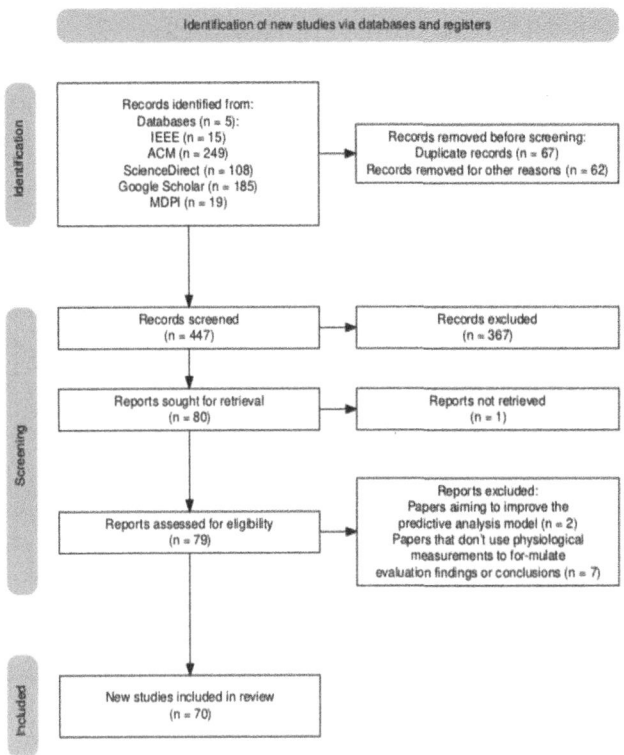

Fig. 1. PRISMA Flow Diagram.

4   Review Results

This section presents the findings shaped by this literature review. It consists of five more subsections, each offering insights into the research questions as stated in the Research Methodology section. It is important to mention that the articles included in this review had differences regarding their research objectives and can be grouped as follows. A group of works aimed to develop evaluation software [29–32] emphasizing aspects such as physiological data processing and data visualization. The next group consists of papers that aimed to design an evaluation methodology [33–35], creating a framework that future researchers can repeat and follow. The third group involves comparative studies between VR and other interfaces (devices) [36–41]. The fourth group consists of works that study the most effective data model or data management process. The remaining works are the ones that focus on UX evaluation of a commercial or custom (self-developed) VR environment.

4.1 UX Aspect

Fifty-six different unique descriptions were detected as metric types, which were assigned into five categories: 1) Emotional State, 2) User Status, 3) Physiological Feature, 4) Social Skills, and 5) Other. Figure 2 presents a conceptual map of the categories and the associated metrics.

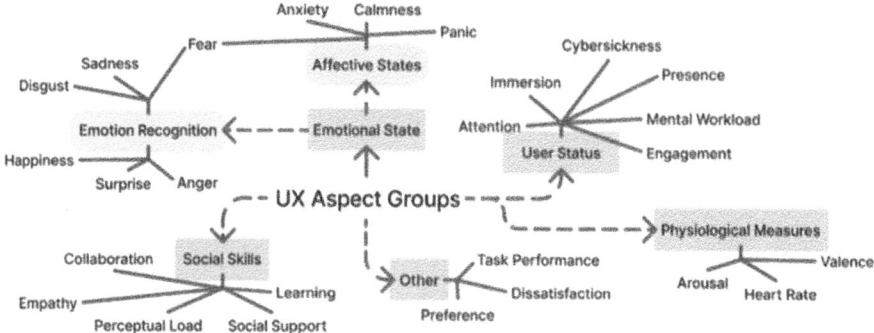

Fig. 2. Conceptual mapping of UX Aspect Groups.

The *Emotional State* metric category (23 articles) refers to studies focused on recognizing a specific emotion or affective state of a participant. Anxiety or other stress-related types or conditions (e.g., social stress, stress recovery) [31, 42–44], calmness [45, 46], fear [47–49], and panic [50] were used as terms to express the selected emotion monitoring during the VR evaluation. A broad description, which was also utilized to describe the UX aspect of this group, is emotion recognition [51, 52]. Various sets of emotions were included in different papers that referred to emotion recognition. For example, happiness, surprise, fear, anger, disgust, and sadness were the six main emotions Xie et al. [51] focused on identifying in contrast to Xu et al. [52] who classified emotions positive and negative, labeling the positive ones as happy or peace, and the negative ones as fear or disgust.

The second category, *User Status* (26 articles), is named after the measurable senses the participant generated during an experience in a VR environment. All the studies that characterized their UX metric based on the user state are included in this group. These states are associated with metrics encountered in other evaluation frameworks, such as mental workload [53] and attention [32], or are connected to metrics commonly affiliated with the VR evaluation applications, for example, cybersickness [53–56], presence [41] immersion, and engagement [29]. It is noteworthy that physiology can interpret these UX metrics with quantitative data, matching each measurement with specific human body responses. Once more, the descriptions for a metric of a study in this group overlap.

In the third category of 8 articles, the UX aspect was described based on the *Physiological Features*. These features are interlinked with Russell's circumplex model of affect [57] without further processing. In this way, researchers used measurements or the features that can be derived from them as metrics. For example, researchers defined their metric as arousal [40], influence of experience on heart rate (increase/decrease)

[58], or in general, body responses [59] or emotional reactions [60] to refer to physiological changes monitoring during the VR evaluation. This group reflects the conceptual overlap researchers have made between the notion of evaluation metrics and the method of measuring these metrics.

Next, the *Social Skills* category (9 articles) includes studies evaluating the competencies related to understanding and interacting with others or how the users perceive and interpret the information from the virtual environment. In VR, users may have to communicate either with actual players or non-playable characters (NPCs) in verbal and nonverbal ways, or they may utilize VR for learning. Researchers are interested in investigating collective experiences, in particular the user interactions to assess collaboration [61], social factors such as empathy [35], and the influence of social support [62]. Additionally, metrics such as perceptual load [63] and learning in VR [33] are metrics that represent how the users process information while exposed to digital external factors aiming to trigger the user's response.

The last category, *Other*, includes four studies that do not fit the previous groups. These are studies regarding the measurements based on user's satisfaction level characterized in generalized descriptions expressing a range of metrics, and activities that a participant must perform, i.e., Task Performance [64], encountered in usability tests. Observations indicated that user gratification or dissatisfaction is often referred to as quality of experience and is related to the UX evaluation of different interface devices, for example Desktop, or AR applications including always into the assessment procedure one VR application [38], or the evaluation of content resolution displayed into the virtual space [65, 66].

At this point, it has to be mentioned that researchers used different descriptions for their measurement, even if they were measuring the same aspect of the experience. More specifically, cybersickness is also mentioned as VR sickness, quality of experience assessment seems to have a different meaning from the UX evaluation, arousal relates to a variety of terms (e.g., Relaxation–Arousal, Emotional Arousal, etc.), and affective state recognition has multiple descriptions. A range of emotions interest researchers, with some focusing on certain emotions or states (e.g., stress, fear) and others on the user's overall emotional mood. Meanwhile, the word used more frequently in UX aspect descriptions among the studies included in this review is "Emotional", followed by "Experience" and "Stress". It is, therefore, evident that UX researchers need to use common terminology to present their evaluations in VR.

4.2 Wearable Recording Devices

In a UX evaluation of a VR application using physiological measurements, more than one body response recording device may be employed, based on the 70 reviewed articles. Figure 3 presents the most commonly used devices among those studies. Devices with a single occurrence have been grouped as Other.

The most frequently used brand devices are the Vive Pro Eye HMD for eye tracking, the Empatica wristband for EDA, HR, IBI, and skin temperature monitoring, and the Biopac systems, which, based on their sensor combination, can monitor a wide range of physiological measures. Additionally, only 3% of studies utilized custom devices in their evaluations [30, 34, 67], emphasizing the researcher's preference for commercial devices. The detected types of commercial wearables devices are wristbands [39, 48, 67–73], (EEG) sensors in caps [8, 37, 51, 55, 74, 75], patch sensors [35, 40, 50, 54, 60, 61, 76], VR headset integrated sensors [42, 53, 56, 63, 77], (eye-tracking) glasses [68, 73], EEG headset [32, 46, 78, 79], and chest straps [29, 47, 80, 81].

Most studies simultaneously employed more than one body response recording device, especially in the case of patch sensors, which, along with (EEG) sensors in caps, represent advanced and challenging device options, as in these types of wearables, researchers have to choose either the appropriate combination of the sensors involved and transmission setup, or the cap configuration (EEG sensor placement). Wristbands, VR headset integrated sensors, (eye-tracking) glasses, and chest straps are more ready-to-use options due to ease of setup with minimal configuration.

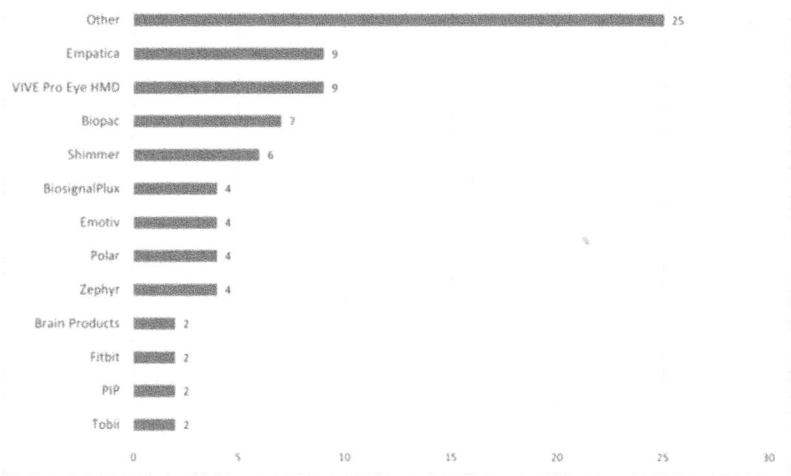

Fig. 3. Wearable brands among the studies.

4.3 Physiological Measures

Sixteen distinct physiological measure types were detected through this literature review, and their occurrence is depicted in Fig. 4.

Attributes related to cardiac activity are the most common type of measurements (50 occurrences). However, this is not a single measurement, but a group that includes a number of distinct features that can be extracted using biosensors: electrocardiography (ECG), heart rate (HR), blood volume pulse (BVP), and photoplethysmogram (PPG). The most common among those is ECG with 18 occurrences. On the other hand, among distinct measurements the most prevalent physiological types are GSR (33 occurrences) and Electroencephalography (EEG) (19 occurrences).

It is important to note that only 27 studies integrated only one physiological measure into their evaluation procedure. While there were also terminology variations, the data science and medicine community relating to the physiological responses analysis have clarified which terms are associated with each other. As a result, breathing rate is expressed as respiration rate, and electrodermal activity, or skin conductance, is stated as galvanic skin response (GSR). Attributes related to cardiac activity are electrocardiography (ECG), heart rate (HR), blood volume pulse (BVP), and photoplethysmogram (PPG).

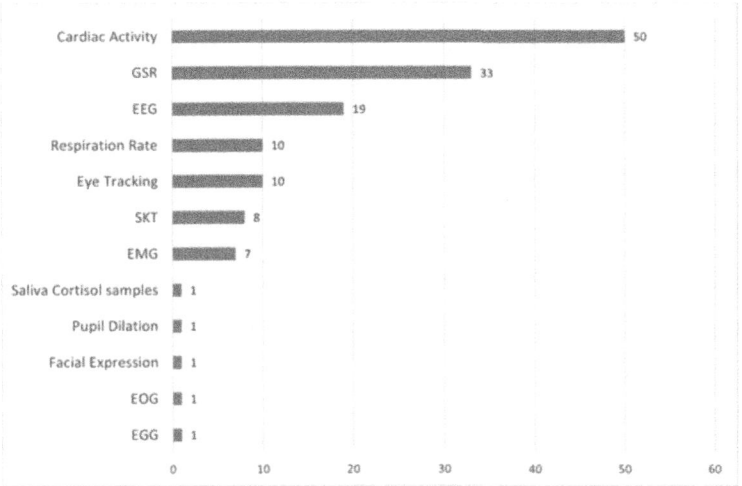

Fig. 4. Physiological Measure Types among the studies.

Each study follows a unique data management pipeline, regardless of their similarities. Recording, preprocessing (filtering), sampling, synchronizing, and feature extraction can be identified as the main steps of their data management pipeline. Also, depending on the evaluation category of each paper, the data management pipeline and the software utilized for running this pipeline varies. Although researchers use commercial software, for example, Matlab [30, 37, 41, 46, 51, 68, 74, 82], they usually include more procedures and practices to run the data management pipeline. To perform either statistical analysis or prepare the machine learning (cleaning, transforming, normalizing data), train or use a machine learning model, they involve open source tools such as Python [43, 71, 74], R [42, 44], or TensorFlow [55]. As a result, researchers utilize a variety of tools and practices to fulfil their data management pipeline objectives. Additionally, the studies of data models or data management processes (see grouping at the beginning of Sect. 4) seem to present in detail all their procedures involved than the works in which the main interest was the evaluation results and VR experience feedback. Finally, observations indicated that a particular physiological signal can be processed into generating a variety of features, and researchers did not always choose the same features to draw their conclusions [45, 56, 72, 81].

All research articles reported information about the physiological measures that are being used in VR UX evaluations, outlining the UX researchers' engagement with other research fields and particularly that of data science. The involvement of wearable devices and the integration of physiological data in the evaluation findings force researchers to develop new skills to be able to manage the collected data, affecting the evaluation procedure in structure, which is frequently characterized as experimental among the research studies. Ultimately, this study demonstrates that UX researchers need to gain expertise in human body physiology, sensors and wearable devices, and data analysis. In addition, requirements and standards for the utilization of physiological data have not yet been benchmarked, allowing researchers to select their preferred physiological measure of their choice.

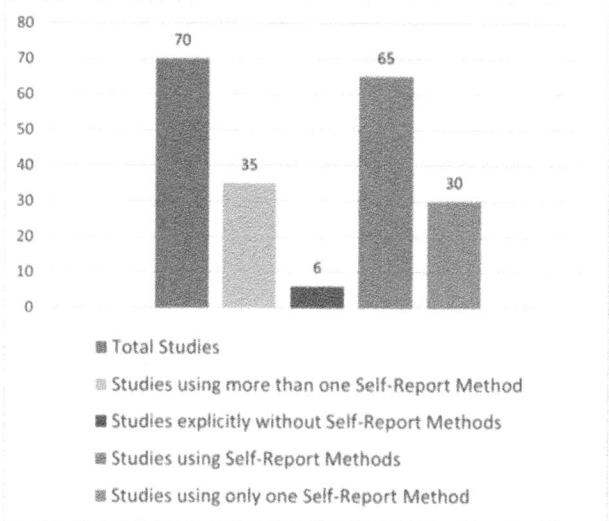

Fig. 5. Self-report Methods in Research Articles.

4.4 Self-report Methods

The majority of research papers integrate self-report methods in UX evaluations that utilize physiological methods in VR applications. Figure 5 presents information on the degree to which self-report methods are incorporated in the research studies. It's important to acknowledge that thirty studies used only one self-report method, and thirty-five studies used more than one self-report method. Moreover, 74% of research articles employed standard methods to collect subjective feedback, using tools that have already been established and documented for their data reliability and validity. A total of 65 different self-report questionnaires were detected in VR UX evaluations. The questionnaire that appears to be used most widely is the Simulator Sickness Questionnaire [83], followed by the Self-Assessment Manikin [84], the Nasa Task Load Index [85], and the State-Trait Anxiety Inventory [86]. The importance of self-report methods is emphasized in cases of unexpected errors, such as server failures or occasional disconnections, during the pipeline, or data loss in general [87].

Researchers combine different data to gather insights using both physiological and self-report data. The employment of self-report methods depends on the context and, thus, the application topic explaining the range of different questionnaires identified. Furthermore, the integration of self-report methods in VR UX evaluations with physiological measures reflects the intention of researchers to include additional resources for collecting evaluation data. Taken together, the findings suggest that self-report methods are going to be part of the evaluation procedure, so the importance of how the self-report methods are integrated within the procedure and their correlation with the physiological data recording becomes increasingly evident to be elucidated. For example, it needs to be specified whether physiological recording stops when the user offers self-report feedback or whether there should be a self-report method before or during baseline recording.

4.5 Reliability

Research communities involved with the utilization of physiological data have already highlighted the objectivity that these types of data offer, and thus, this literature review seeks to discuss researchers' perspectives and positions on the reliability of these data. Physiological signal monitoring is considered objective not only because their fluctuations cannot be directly triggered but also because they are an actual representation of the physiological status of the human body and are not invasive [41, 55]. Researchers argue that the VR headset should not be removed once the evaluation has started and should remain as stable as possible to reduce noise in the recordings when the VR headset is near the wearable device (e.g., when the user wears an EEG monitoring device) [88]. Moreover, some wearable devices are not so compatible with the VR headset, affecting the quality of physiological data recordings [47]. Also, researchers emphasize that users should minimize the movement of the wearable device to avoid creating noise in data recordings [31, 33, 49, 87], affecting the flow of interaction with the VR controllers. At the same time researchers struggle to identify precisely the origin of the physiological data fluctuations, meaning that they can decide easily whether the evaluation stimulus caused the changes to the participants' body, or some other condition influenced them [35, 42].

Meanwhile, many evaluation conditions affect physiological data reliability. The displayed stimulus impact on users is also an important factor that may influence physiological data fluctuations, and it is essential to be curated and organized appropriately [33, 37, 65]. The familiarity level of participants with VR experiences may make a difference in the changes of body responses [82]. Intense physical activity causing sweating or heart rate increase, device placement and wearable configuration limitations, such battery power, sensor conductivity or frequency recording [39, 52, 69, 89] can distort the data. Last but not least, the sample of participants involved can interfere with physiological signals recording and processing due to factors like age, heath status, and age [31]. Finally, several researchers argue that the reliability of physiological measures is being assessed or is going to be assessed by researchers that seek to locate concrete evidence on their objectivity and usability either in the laboratory or another evaluation environment [54, 56, 90]. More and more studies report technical difficulties, which may affect physiological data reliability [87, 91, 92].

5 Discussion

Based on this literature review, it is essential to highlight the needs and requirements that can assist researchers to establish knowledge and acquire resources necessary for these evaluations in VR while reflecting on the expertise they need from other research fields, such as affective computing, data science, and UX research. In contrast to other reviews that focused mostly on effective ways of analyzing data (e.g. in [15]), we aimed to create a wider map that attempts to identify trends and limitations in evaluation protocols and procedures. The issues for discussion are grouped in three topics: the selection of physiological features and devices, the evaluation process, and the need for universal practices and solutions.

5.1 Selection of Physiological Features and Devices

The review results provided some noteworthy trends regarding the use of physiological measures in VR evaluations. It is evident that the most common measure utilized is Electrodermal Activity (EDA), as it has been used in 33 of the cases. Its analysis can provide insight about the levels of emotional arousal of the user, indicating how stimulating an experience is, and can also be used to detect affective states like stress, anxiety, fear and engagement. However, it is important to notice that in the majority of cases (29 out of 33) EDA is combined with additional measures. In the works that are based on a sole measurement (28 articles), the majority of them (11 articles) are relying on Electroencephalography (EEG). Although the setup and preparation of these devices is significantly more tedious and time-consuming compared to wrist-worn devices used for measuring EDA, they provide a rich set of results about a variety of emotional states, including excitement, stress and attention. This output might be useful for assessing the impact of the VR environment on the user in educational [79] or entertainment [37] settings.

A further observation is that nature of immersive VR hardware and the tasks executed in the environment can have an impact on the choice of measurement devices and the reliability of the identified features. Some commercial EEG headsets cannot be easily combined with the VR headsets and may cause user discomfort or sensor misplacement. Evaluators need to prepare and test appropriate setups that effectively support both devices without significant impact on the experience. Additionally, the pace and intensity of the user interaction may also affect the quality of sensor readings. Frequent head rotations, e.g. in exploratory environments, may introduce noise in EEG values or cause sensor drift, and respectively rapid hand movements may reduce the quality of measurements of wrist-worn devices. Thus, more relaxed and slow-paced environments may be more appropriate for using these types of measurements. Probably these risks of lower-quality output are the reason that in many case studies multiple concurrent measures (42 articles) and additional self-reports (65 articles) have been used. On the other hand, the fact that there are commercial VR headsets available with integrated eye-tracking sensors provides the opportunity of using this measure in evaluations without extra preparation or additional user-worn devices. Eye tracking measurements have been used in 11 articles featured in this review, in four of which as a single source. It provided insights about aspects such as quality of experience [66], mental [53] and perceptual workload [63], which may be important in several application areas of VR.

5.2 UX Evaluation Procedure

The evaluation procedure is often characterized as experimental, outlining the need to establish requirements and standards. This review acknowledges that VR experts do not follow a common evaluation protocol. Findings reveal that the role of the evaluator during the procedure should be investigated because it's important to clarify how a researcher can intervene in the evaluated experience, for example, by giving instructions and how they identify and manage the data recordings that seem unrelated to the VR experience. Additionally, researchers should have access to self-report questionnaires (digitized or paper), and in case an external device is involved, coordination is required for distribution and completion time. Lastly, the evaluation procedure should be thoroughly described due to ethical restraints, ensuring that researchers know what information must be concealed and which security and privacy protocols they must follow.

Physiological measures in virtual reality evaluations raise several ethical concerns. Experts should consider the impact on the handling of personal data and be aware of data privacy legislation. They should ensure respect for cultural and individual differences, using unbiased software based on fair data processing models. Additionally, the role of the data handler emerges as the legal entity that has the data and is responsible for its storage and protection. Body measurements may include personally identifiable and sensitive health information, so anonymization and encryption procedures should be followed thoroughly.

5.3 Need for Universal Practices and Solutions

While the data science field is still evolving, there is a notable absence of universal standard practices or models [93] for data processing and analysis for UX evaluations in VR. Based on this review, data management varies even if the UX aspect and physiological signals are the same, and data recording and processing differs on the context based on the UX metric and physiological data type used. Future research should focus on defining the procedures that are essential for drawing conclusions in UX VR evaluations by investigating and justifying which measures should be preferred in case scenarios. At the same time, commercial wearable devices and software make it more difficult for researchers to intervene because raw data are not compatible with other data processing software. Therefore, there is an immediate need for learning resources to guide UX researchers to integrate physiological measures in VR evaluations.

Furthermore, commercial device adoption illustrates the dependency between researchers and distribution device companies. This reveals the need for transparency in the process of physiological raw data recording, administration, distribution, and processing. Most of the device brands mentioned have converted data recordings into a service (licensing option). As a result, researchers must now consider the raw data access fee with the equipment expenses. At the same time, wearable devices function more smoothly with their native software, increasing the complexity for evaluators who would like to use open-source software. Furthermore, it should be noted that raw data transfer from the recording device to the researcher's processing and management unit is perceived as a black box, resulting in a lack of information for security and encryption procedures, raw data storage location, and servers' communication and transmission [94]. This highlights the need for open-source resources. It's important to provide VR experts with tools and practices to achieve their objectives promoting fair and ethical physiological data usage without additional restrictions and limitations [95].

6 Conclusions

This literature review aimed to explore the experimental procedures researchers currently follow to evaluate UX in a VR application using physiological measurements, offering valuable insights about the type and conditions of the UX evaluations in VR. It has been motivated by the absence of universally accepted evaluation protocols and frameworks that guide researchers about the utilization of physiological measurement devices in immersive settings. The works examined in this review assess a wide range of UX aspects in VR, focusing on emotion monitoring, the physiological measurement recording, the user state that is formed based on what the participant is sensing, the social skills the user is acquiring during the activity, and the quality of the experience. Also, this review investigated the commercial brands of wearables that are usually used, the categories of body response recordings during a VR experience, and the self-report methods that researchers prefer to incorporate in the evaluation. Lastly, the review summarized researchers' opinions about the credibility of physiological data. Ultimately, the key takeaway of this literature review is to acknowledge the need for further research in a framework that presents a comprehensive overview of physiological measures utilization in immersive environments during a VR evaluation.

Acknowledgements. This work has received funding from HORIZON-CL2-2022-HERITAGE-01 (Grant Agreement Number 101094998), under the HeritACT project.

References

1. Sutcliffe, A., Gault, B.: Heuristic evaluation of virtual reality applications. Interact. Comput. **16**(4), 831–849 (2004)
2. Sutcliffe, A.G., Kaur, K.D.: Evaluating the usability of virtual reality user interfaces. Behav. Inf. Technol. **19**(6), 415–426 (2000)
3. Harms, P.: automated usability evaluation of virtual reality applications. ACM Trans. Comput.-Hum. Interact. **26**(3), 14:1–14:36 (2019)
4. Chr. Nilsson, N., Nordahl, R., Serafin, S.: Immersion revisited: a review of existing definitions of immersion and their relation to different theories of presence. Hum. Technol. **12**(2), 108–134 (2016)
5. Slater, M., Lotto, B., Arnold, M.M., Sanchez-Vives, M.V.: How we experience immersive virtual environments: the concept of presence and its measurement. Anuario de psicología **40**(2), 193–210 (2009)
6. Mütterlein, J.: The three pillars of virtual reality? Investigating the roles of immersion, presence, and interactivity. In: Proceedings of the 51st Hawaii International Conference on System Sciences (2018)

7. Maia, C.L.B., Furtado, E.S.: A systematic review about user experience evaluation. In: Marcus, A. (ed.) Design, User Experience, and Usability: Design Thinking and Methods, pp. 445–455. Springer International Publishing, Cham (2016)
8. Kober, S.E., Neuper, C.: Using auditory event-related EEG potentials to assess presence in virtual reality. Int. J. Hum.-Comput. Stud. **70**(9), 577–587 (2012)
9. Inan Nur, A., Santoso, H.B., Hadi Putra, P.O.: The method and metric of user experience evaluation: a systematic literature review. In: Proceedings of the 2021 10th International Conference on Software and Computer Applications, in ICSCA '21, pp. 307–317. Association for Computing Machinery, New York, NY, USA (2021)
10. Zaki, T., Islam, M.N.: Neurological and physiological measures to evaluate the usability and user-experience (UX) of information systems: a systematic literature review. Comput. Sci. Rev. **40**, 100375 (2021)
11. Kim, Y.M., Rhiu, I., Yun, M.H.: A systematic review of a virtual reality system from the perspective of user experience. Int. J. Human-Computer Interact. **36**(10), 893–910 (2020)
12. Marín-Morales, J., Llinares, C., Guixeres, J., Alcañiz, M.: Emotion recognition in immersive virtual reality: from statistics to affective computing. Sensors **20**(18), Art. no. 18 (2020)
13. Weech, S., Kenny, S., Barnett-Cowan, M.: Presence and cybersickness in virtual reality are negatively related: a review. Front. Psychol. **10**, 158 (2019)
14. Rebenitsch, L., Owen, C.: Review on cybersickness in applications and visual displays. Virtual Real. **20**(2), 101–125 (2016)
15. Chang, E., Kim, H.T., Yoo, B.: Virtual reality sickness: a review of causes and measurements. Int. J. Hum.-Comput. Interact. **36**(17), 1658–1682 (2020)
16. Mishra, S., Kumar, A., Padmanabhan, P., Gulyás, B.: Neurophysiological correlates of cognition as revealed by virtual reality: delving the brain with a synergistic approach. Brain Sci. **11**(1), Art. no. 1 (2021)
17. Kitchenham, B., Charters, S.M.: Guidelines for performing Systematic Literature Reviews in Software Engineering, Technical report, ver. 2.3 ebse (2007)
18. Kitchenham, B.: Procedures for performing systematic reviews, vol. 33. Keele, UK, Keele University (2004)
19. Calvo, R.A., D'Mello, S.: Affect detection: an interdisciplinary review of models, methods, and their applications. IEEE Trans. Affect. Comput. **1**(1), 18–37 (2010)
20. Choi, E.J., Kim, D.K.: Arousal and valence classification model based on long short-term memory and DEAP data for mental healthcare management. Healthc. Inform. Res. **24**(4), 309–316 (2018)
21. Thayer, J.F.: A neurovisceral integration model of heart rate variability. In: ResearchGate
22. Sayed Ismail, S.N.M., Ab. Aziz, N.A., Ibrahim, S.Z.: A comparison of emotion recognition system using electrocardiogram (ECG) and photoplethysmogram (PPG). J. King Saud Univ. - Comput. Inf. Sci. **34**(6), Part B, 3539–3558, (2022)
23. Bulagang, A.F., Mountstephens, J., Wi, J.T.T.: Tuning support vector machines for improving four-class emotion classification in virtual reality (VR) using heart rate features. J. Phys. Conf. Ser. **1529**(5), 052069 (2020)
24. Kim, K.B., Baek, H.J.: Photoplethysmography in wearable devices: a comprehensive review of technological advances, current challenges, and future directions. Electronics **12**(13) Art. no. 13 (2023)
25. Udovičić, G., Đerek, J., Russo, M., Sikora, M.: Wearable emotion recognition system based on GSR and PPG signals. In: Proceedings of the 2nd International Workshop on Multimedia for Personal Health and Health Care, in MMHealth '17, pp. 53–59. Association for Computing Machinery, New York, NY, USA (2017)
26. Castaneda, D., Esparza, A., Ghamari, M., Soltanpur, C., Nazeran, H.: A review on wearable photoplethysmography sensors and their potential future applications in health care. Int. J. Biosens. Bioelectron. **4**(4), 195–202 (2018)

27. EmbracePlus, Empatica. https://www.empatica.com/embraceplus. Accessed 3 Apr 2025
28. Albert, B., Tullis, T.: Measuring the user experience: collecting, analyzing, and presenting usability metrics. Newnes (2013)
29. Quintero, L., Muñoz, J.E., de Mooij, J., Gaebler, M.: Excite-O-meter: software framework to integrate heart activity in virtual reality. In: 2021 IEEE International Symposium on Mixed and Augmented Reality (ISMAR), pp. 357–366 (2021)
30. Lin, K.-H., Peng, B.-X.: wearable technology and visual reality application for healthcare systems. Electronics 11(2), Art. no. 2 (2022)
31. Mateos-García, N., Gil-González, A.-B. Luis-Reboredo, A., Pérez-Lancho, B.: Driver stress detection from physiological signals by virtual reality simulator. Electronics 12(10), Art. no. 10 (2023)
32. You, C.-W., Chen, H.-A., Chen, P.-C., Lai, W.-N., (Tina) Yuan, C.W., Bi, N.: Toward understanding the impact of visualized focus levels in virtual reality on user presence and experience. Proc ACM Hum-Comput Interact 8(MHCI), 280:1–280:30 (2024)
33. Collins, J., Regenbrecht, H., Langlotz, T., Said Can, T., Ersoy, C., Butson, R.: Measuring cognitive load and insight: a methodology exemplified in a virtual reality learning context. In: 2019 IEEE International Symposium on Mixed and Augmented Reality (ISMAR), pp. 351–362. (2019)
34. Granato, M., Gadia, D., Maggiorini, D., Ripamonti, L.A.: An empirical study of players' emotions in VR racing games based on a dataset of physiological data. Multimed. Tools Appl. 79(45), 33657–33686 (2020)
35. Lucifora, C., Schembri, M., Poggi, F., Grasso, G.M., Gangemi, A.: Virtual reality supports perspective taking in cultural heritage interpretation. Comput. Hum. Behav. 148, 107911 (2023)
36. Keighrey, C., Flynn, R., Murray, S., Murray, N.: A physiology-based QoE comparison of interactive augmented reality, virtual reality and tablet-based applications. IEEE Trans. Multimed. 23, 333–341 (2021)
37. Tian, F., Zhang, W.: The difference of emotional arousal between traditional 2D and VR movies: a comparative study based on EEG signals. In: 2021 6th International Conference on Intelligent Computing and Signal Processing (ICSP), pp. 734–737 (2021)
38. Choy, S.-M., Cheng, E., Wilkinson, R.H., Burnett, I., Austin, M.W.: Quality of experience comparison of stereoscopic 3D videos in different projection devices: flat screen, panoramic screen and virtual reality headset. IEEE Access 9, 9584–9594 (2021)
39. Keighrey, C., Flynn, R., Murray, S., Brennan, S., Murray, N.: Comparing User QoE via physiological and interaction measurements of immersive AR and VR speech and language therapy applications. In: Proceedings of the on Thematic Workshops of ACM Multimedia 2017, in Thematic Workshops '17, pp. 485–492. Association for Computing Machinery, New York, NY, USA (2017)
40. Bayro, A., Ghasemi, Y., Jeong, H.: A physiological approach to assess arousal in virtual reality and computer-based remote collaboration. Proc. Hum. Factors Ergon. Soc. Annu. Meet. 66(1), 2202 (2022)
41. Higuera-Trujillo, J.L., López-Tarruella Maldonado, J., Llinares Millán, C.: Psychological and physiological human responses to simulated and real environments: a comparison between Photographs, 360° Panoramas, and Virtual Reality. Appl. Ergon. 65, 398–409 (2017)
42. Rubo, M., Munsch, S.: Social stress in an interaction with artificial agents in virtual reality: effects of ostracism and underlying psychopathology. Comput. Hum. Behav. 153, 107915 (2024)
43. Chauhan, U., Reithinger, N., Mackey, J.R.: Real-time stress assessment through PPG sensor for VR biofeedback. In: Proceedings of the 20th International Conference on Multimodal Interaction: Adjunct, in ICMI '18, pp. 1–5. Association for Computing Machinery, New York, NY, USA (2018)

44. Weibel, R.P., et al.: Virtual reality-supported biofeedback for stress management: Beneficial effects on heart rate variability and user experience. Comput. Hum. Behav. **141**, 107607 (2023)
45. Paredes, P.E., et al.: Driving with the fishes: towards calming and mindful virtual reality experiences for the car. Proc ACM Interact Mob Wearable Ubiquitous Technol. **2**(4), 184:1–184:21 (2018)
46. D'Errico, F., Leone, G., Schmid, M., D'Anna, C.: Prosocial virtual reality, empathy, and EEG measures: a pilot study aimed at monitoring emotional processes in intergroup helping behaviors. Appl. Sci. **10**(4), Art. no. 4 (2020)
47. Zhang, H., Li, X., Sun, Y., Fu, X., Qiu, C., Carroll, J.M.: VRMN-bD: a multi-modal natural behavior dataset of immersive human fear responses in VR stand-up interactive games. In: 2024 IEEE Conference Virtual Reality and 3D User Interfaces (VR), pp. 320–330 (2024)
48. Baldini, A., Frumento, S., Menicucci, D., Gemignani, A., Scilingo, E.P., Greco, A.: Subjective fear in virtual reality: a linear mixed-effects analysis of skin conductance. IEEE Trans. Affect. Comput. **13**(4), 2047–2057 (2022)
49. Bălan, O., Moise, G., Moldoveanu, A., Leordeanu, M., Moldoveanu, F.: An investigation of various machine and deep learning techniques applied in automatic fear level detection and acrophobia virtual therapy. Sensors **20**(2), Art. no. 2 (2020)
50. Gutiérrez-Martín, L., et al.: Fear detection in multimodal affective computing: physiological signals versus catecholamine concentration. Sensors **22**(11), Art. no. 11 (2022)
51. Xie, J., Luo, Y., Wang, S., Liu, G.: Electroencephalography-based recognition of six basic emotions in virtual reality environments. Biomed. Signal Process. Control **93**, 106189 (2024)
52. Xu, T., Yin, R., Shu, L., Xu, X.: Emotion recognition using frontal EEG in VR affective scenes. In: 2019 IEEE MTT-S International Microwave Biomedical Conference (IMBioC), pp. 1–4 (2019)
53. Grootjen, J.W., Thalhammer, P., Kosch, T.: Your eyes on speed: using pupil dilation to adaptively select speed-reading parameters in virtual reality. Proc ACM Hum-Comput Interact **8**(MHCI), 284:1–284:17 (2024)
54. Dennison, M.S., Wisti, A.Z., D'Zmura, M.: Use of physiological signals to predict cybersickness. Displays **44**, 42–52 (2016)
55. Liu, M., Yang, B., Xu, M., Zan, P., Xia, X.: Exploring quantitative assessment of cybersickness in virtual reality using EEG signals and a CNN-LSTM network. In: 2023 IEEE Conference on Virtual Reality and 3D User Interfaces Abstracts and Workshops (VRW), pp. 827–828 (2023)
56. Jeong, D., Han, K.: PRECYSE: predicting cybersickness using transformer for multimodal time-series sensor data. Proc. ACM Interact Mob. Wearable Ubiquitous Technol. **8**(2), 42:1–42:24 (2024)
57. Russell, J.A.: A circumplex model of affect. J. Pers. Soc. Psychol. **39**(6), 1161–1178 (1980)
58. Albert, I., Burkard, N., Queck, D., Herrlich, M.: The effect of auditory-motor synchronization in exergames on the example of the VR rhythm game beatsaber. Proc. ACM Hum.-Comput. Interact. **6**(CHI PLAY), 253:1–253:26 (2022)
59. Bayro, A., Buneo, C., Jeong, H.: Emotion recognition in virtual reality: investigating the effect of gameplay variations on affective responses. Proc. Hum. Factors Ergon. Soc. Annu. Meet. **67**(1), 1516–1517 (2023)
60. Bayro, A., Jeong, H.: Quantum computational modeling for affective assessment in virtual reality systems. In: 2024 IEEE Conference on Virtual Reality and 3D User Interfaces Abstracts and Workshops (VRW), pp. 277–279 (2024)
61. Bayro, A., Ghasemi, Y., Jeong, H.: Subjective and objective analyses of collaboration and co-presence in a virtual reality remote environment. In: 2022 IEEE Conference on Virtual Reality and 3D User Interfaces Abstracts and Workshops (VRW) (2022)
62. Neumann, I., Käthner, I., Gromer, D., Pauli, P.: Impact of perceived social support on pain perception in virtual reality. Comput. Hum. Behav. **139**, 107490 (2023)

63. Chiossi, F., et al.: Understanding the impact of the reality-virtuality continuum on visual search using fixation-related potentials and eye tracking features. Proc. ACM Hum.-Comput. Interact. **8**(MHCI), 281:1–281:33 (2024)
64. Chiossi, F., Turgut, Y., Welsch, R., Mayer, S.: Adapting visual complexity based on electrodermal activity improves working memory performance in virtual reality. Proc. ACM Hum.-Comput. Interact. **7**(MHCI), 196:1–196:26 (2023)
65. Li, Z., Geng, B., Tao, X., Duan, Y., Li, T., Huang, J.: EEG-based VR video quality measurement for resolution reduction. In: 2023 IEEE International Conference on Communications Workshops (ICC Workshops), pp. 1872–1876 (2023)
66. Zhu, H., et al.: EyeQoE: a novel QoE assessment model for 360-degree videos using ocular behaviors. Proc. ACM Interact Mob. Wearable Ubiquitous Technol. **6**(1), 39:1–39:26 (2022)
67. Mevlevioğlu, D., Murphy, D., Tabirca, S.: Visual respiratory feedback in virtual reality exposure therapy: a pilot study. In: Proceedings of the 2021 ACM International Conference on Interactive Media Experiences, in IMX '21, pp. 1–6. Association for Computing Machinery, New York, NY, USA (2021)
68. Bigne, E., Ruiz, C., Curras-Perez, R.: Furnishing your home? The impact of voice assistant avatars in virtual reality shopping: a neurophysiological study. Comput. Hum. Behav. **153**, 108104 (2024)
69. Katsigiannis, S., Willis, R., Ramzan, N.: A QoE and simulator sickness evaluation of a smart-exercise-bike virtual reality system via user feedback and physiological signals. IEEE Trans. Consum. Electron. **65**(1), 119–127 (2019)
70. Lopes, R.P., et al.: Digital technologies for innovative mental health rehabilitation. Electronics **10**(18), Art. no. 18 (2021)
71. Gupta, K., et al.: Total VREcall: using biosignals to recognize emotional autobiographical memory in virtual reality. Proc. ACM Interact Mob. Wearable Ubiquitous Technol. **6**(2), 55:1–55:21 (2022)
72. Martin, N., Mathieu, N., Pallamin, N., Ragot, M., Diverrez, J.-M.: Virtual reality sickness detection: an approach based on physiological signals and machine learning. In: 2020 IEEE International Symposium on Mixed and Augmented Reality (ISMAR), pp. 387–399 (2020)
73. Wilson, J.C., Nair, S., Scielzo, S., Larson, E.C.: Objective measures of cognitive load using deep multi-modal learning: a use-case in aviation. Proc. ACM Interact Mob. Wearable Ubiquitous Technol. **5**(1), 40:1–40:35 (2021)
74. McDermott, E.J., Raggam, P., Kirsch, S., Belardinelli, P., Ziemann, U., Zrenner, C.: Artifacts in EEG-based BCI therapies: friend or Foe?. Sensors **22**(1), Art. no. 1 (2022)
75. Zhang, Y., Su, Y., Sun, X.: A QoE physiological measure of VR with vibrotactile feedback based on frontal lobe power asymmetry. IEEE Trans. Multimed. **26**, 2932–2942 (2024)
76. Bermúdez i Badia, S., et al.: Toward emotionally adaptive virtual reality for mental health applications. IEEE J. Biomed. Health Inform. **23**(5), 1877–1887 (2019)
77. Jeong, D., Jeong, M., Yang, U., Han, K.: Eyes on me: investigating the role and influence of eye-tracking data on user modeling in virtual reality. PLoS ONE **17**(12), e0278970 (2022)
78. Lee, S., Kim, S., Kim, H.G., Ro, Y.M.: Assessing individual VR sickness through deep feature fusion of VR video and physiological response. IEEE Trans. Circuits Syst. Video Technol. **32**(5), 2895–2907 (2022)
79. Carofiglio, V., Ricci, G., Abbattista, F.: User brain-driven evaluation of an educational 3D virtual environment. In: 2015 10th Iberian Conference on Information Systems and Technologies (CISTI), pp. 1–7 (2015)
80. Blum, J., Rockstroh, C., Göritz, A.S.: Heart rate variability biofeedback based on slow-paced breathing with immersive virtual reality nature scenery. Front. Psychol. **10** (2019)
81. Lee, R., Kim, Y.S.: VR sickness evaluation method using recurrence period density entropy. Appl. Sci. **14**(11), Art. no. 11 (2024)

82. Charoensook, T., Barlow, M., Lakshika, E.: Heart rate and breathing variability for virtual reality game play. In: 2019 IEEE 7th International Conference on Serious Games and Applications for Health (SeGAH), pp. 1–7 (2019)

83. Kennedy, R.S., Lane, N.E., Berbaum, K.S., Lilienthal, M.G.: Simulator sickness questionnaire: an enhanced method for quantifying simulator sickness. Int. J. Aviat. Psychol. **3**(3), 203–220 (1993)

84. Bradley, M.M., Lang, P.J.: Measuring emotion: the self-assessment manikin and the semantic differential. J. Behav. Ther. Exp. Psychiatry **25**(1), 49–59 (1994)

85. Hart, S.G.: Nasa-task load index (NASA-TLX); 20 years later. Proc. Hum. Factors Ergon. Soc. Annu. Meet. **50**(9), 904–908 (2006)

86. Spielberger, C.D., Gonzalez-Reigosa, F., Martinez-Urrutia, A., Natalicio, L.F.S., Natalicio, D.S.: The state-trait anxiety inventory. Rev. Interam. Psicol. J. Psychol. **5**(3 & 4), Art. no. 3 & 4 (2017)

87. Steinhaeusser, S.C., Eckstein, B., Lugrin, B.: A multi-method approach to compare presence, fear induction and desensitization in survival horror games within the reality-virtuality-continuum. Entertain. Comput. **45**, 100539 (2023)

88. Gao, H., Yue, K., Yang, S., Liu, Y., Guo, M., Liu, Y.: Exploring depth-based perception conflicts in virtual reality through error-related potentials. In: 2024 IEEE Conference Virtual Reality and 3D User Interfaces (VR), pp. 774–784 (2024)

89. Geraets, C.N.W., et al.: Virtual reality facial emotion recognition in social environments: an eye-tracking study. Internet Interv. **25**, 100432 (2021)

90. Marín-Morales, J., et al.: Affective computing in virtual reality: emotion recognition from brain and heartbeat dynamics using wearable sensors. Sci. Rep. **8**(1), 13657 (2018)

91. Mancuso, V., et al.: IAVRS—international affective virtual reality system: psychometric assessment of 360° images by using psychophysiological data. Sensors **24**(13), Art. no. 13 (2024)

92. Cho, D., et al.: Detection of stress levels from biosignals measured in virtual reality environments using a kernel-based extreme learning machine. Sensors **17**(10) Art. no. 10 (2017)

93. Luecken, L.J., Gallo, L.C.: Handbook of physiological research methods in health psychology. SAGE (2008)

94. Edgar, T.W., Manz, D.O.: Research methods for cyber security. Syngress (2017)

95. World Medical Association. World medical association declaration of helsinki: ethical principles for medical research involving human subjects. JAMA **310**(20), 2191–2194 (2013)

Almost There: Evaluating the Psychological and Motor Impact of Near-Miss "White Lie" Feedback in Virtual Rehabilitation

Haruka Murakami$^{(\boxtimes)}$ and Tetsunari Inamura

Tamagawa University, Machida, Tokyo 194-8610, Japan
`hmurakami0418@gmail.com`

Abstract. Feedback systems often aim to boost user motivation in virtual rehabilitation through performance-enhancing visual manipulations. While previous studies have shown that positively biased feedback can improve engagement, few have examined how such strategies affect long-term motor learning and user perception once the input is removed. This study explores the psychological and motor effects of a novel "White Lie" feedback design, which simulates the experience of "almost succeeding" rather than outright success. During a virtual ball-throwing task, thirty-two participants were assigned to one of four groups—Control, Fixed Support, Variable Support, and Ball-throwing. The support manipulated the perceived distance between the thrown ball and the target without altering physical input. Results showed that participants in the White Lie conditions reported significantly lower perceived task difficulty and greater reduction in difficulty over time. Regression analyses indicated that perceived support and early task performance were key predictors of psychological engagement. Notably, the variable support group, which mimicked the fading of training wheels, achieved reduced difficulty without explicit awareness of the support. Although the intervention did not significantly improve motor performance, early success was strongly linked to later motivation. These findings suggest that "near-miss" feedback can enhance subjective experience and promote sustained engagement, providing a psychologically safe support method without impairing motor fidelity. This strategy may hold promise for applications in motivational rehabilitation design.

Keywords: Virtual Reality · White Lie · Rehabilitation

1 Introduction

In recent years, virtual reality (VR) technologies have attracted growing attention as tools for supporting physical activity and rehabilitation. Especially in interventions targeting older adults or individuals with motor decline, not only physical outcomes but also the acquisition of sustained motivation has become a critical factor in successful rehabilitation [1, 2]. However, in the early stages of rehabilitation or exercise, experiences of "not being able to perform" due to a lack of skill often lead to frustration, which can hinder continued engagement in the task [3].

© The Author(s), under exclusive license to Springer Nature Switzerland AG 2026
D. Michael-Grigoriou et al. (Eds.): EuroXR 2025, LNCS 16101, pp. 188–199, 2026.
https://doi.org/10.1007/978-3-032-03805-0_11

Previous studies have shown that VR systems can intentionally modify performance outcomes to increase user motivation. For example, expanding the range of motion or exaggerating hitting accuracy in avatars can enhance users' sense of competence [4, 5], which has been shown to increase engagement and immersion during tasks [6, 7]. Positive visual feedback has also been reported to help maintain participation, especially in the early stages of rehabilitation for stroke and neurological patients [8, 9]. Such strategies often involve deliberate misinformation—what may be called White Lie. Positively biased feedback has been shown to enhance users' sense of agency, satisfaction, and task persistence [10, 11]. Moreover, perception of physical performance can be altered through visual feedback. For example, phantom limb therapy creates the illusion that a non-functioning limb is moving [13], while VR-based exergames often manipulate hit accuracy or feedback timing to foster a sense of achievement [14, 15].

However, despite these encouraging psychological effects, very few studies have investigated whether such feedback actually affects the quality of motor performance or sensorimotor accuracy. In the context of rehabilitation, feedback strategies that improve motivation must also be validated in terms of their effects on physical control and learning. Therefore, it is essential to evaluate whether these interventions support both the mental and physical aspects of rehabilitation without introducing negative trade-offs.

2 Related Work

A number of studies have explored the use of modified or positively biased feedback in virtual reality (VR) systems to support motivation and engagement, particularly in motor rehabilitation. These approaches, which we refer to broadly as benevolent deception, "White Lie"-type strategies, have been shown to improve users' subjective experience. However, relatively few studies have investigated their effects on objective motor performance or proprioceptive accuracy. This section reviews prior research in two parts: (1) studies that demonstrated psychological and behavioral benefits, and (2) studies that addressed physical performance outcomes—highlighting the need for more integrated evaluations.

2.1 Psychological and Behavioral Effects of Biased Feedback

White Lie-type feedback, where performance is made to appear better than it is, has been repeatedly shown to enhance engagement, enjoyment, and persistence in VR-based rehabilitation. For instance, Granqvist et al. [4] showed that exaggerating avatar flexibility in a martial arts game improved perceived capability and task enjoyment. Similarly, Marwecki et al. [22] demonstrated that assigning short-term, ego-oriented goals increased participation in stroke rehabilitation. Montoya et al. [20] and Dias et al. [23] also reported improved user engagement when feedback was adaptively tuned to provide a sense of success.

These studies collectively support the psychological utility of biased feedback: they demonstrate that users are more likely to continue participating when they feel successful. However, their focus remains predominantly on subjective or behavioral outcomes—such as enjoyment or frequency of task repetition—while the quality of movement execution or underlying motor adaptation is rarely assessed.

2.2   Effects on Motor Accuracy and Control

A smaller body of work has begun to address how manipulated feedback influences actual motor outcomes. Nataraj et al. [16] showed that biased positive feedback in a reaching task altered not only perceived agency but also kinematic movement profiles. Amin et al. [17] reported improved motor performance using immersive VR hand rehabilitation games, although the direct contribution of feedback manipulation was not isolated. Similarly, Bortone et al. [18] and Nardi et al. [19] reported gains in motor execution with gamified or reward-based VR systems, but did not specifically assess whether exaggerated feedback might interfere with accurate motor learning or proprioceptive calibration.

While these studies imply that visual feedback manipulation might assist motor skill development, there is a lack of rigorous investigation into whether such benefits come at the cost of degraded motor fidelity or unrealistic movement perception. Furthermore, few studies compare exaggerated feedback against accurate feedback in controlled conditions, making it difficult to evaluate the trade-offs.

2.3   Research Gap and Objectives of This Study

Taken together, existing research supports the potential of White Lie to improve psychological outcomes, but leaves unanswered questions regarding its safety and effectiveness from a motor control perspective. In physical rehabilitation, where the goal is to encourage participation and promote accurate and transferable motor skills, biased feedback must be evaluated with caution. One particularly underexplored issue is what happens after the removal of biased feedback—especially in the case of White Lie interventions. While such feedback may successfully encourage engagement during initial practice, its long-term consequences remain unclear. There is a risk that once the White Lie is removed, users may experience a psychological backlash due to a mismatch between their inflated confidence and actual ability. This could undermine their motivation or lead to frustration when real performance fails to meet expectations. Moreover, many existing systems provide biased feedback in the form of "success"—for example, exaggerated hit rates or visual extensions of motion—but these are often arbitrarily defined and difficult to quantify across applications. The degree of bias is usually hard-coded and lacks an interpretable scale, which complicates both implementation and empirical evaluation.

To address these limitations, this study proposes a new conceptualization of the White Lie as a form of supportive guidance rather than outright deception—more akin to training wheels on a bicycle. In this approach, users still feel the challenge of performing the task but are subtly assisted in a way that suggests "you're getting close," thereby fostering autonomous engagement without presenting overt success. To implement this idea, we drew inspiration from the structure of addictive reward systems in games and gambling, particularly the concept of a "near miss." The psychological appeal of the near miss—commonly exploited in Japanese pachinko machines and slot games—relies not on success itself, but on the illusion of being just short of success. We hypothesize that this same mechanism, when repurposed for good, could effectively motivate users to persist in a rehabilitation task even without actual success.

In this study, we developed a White Lie feedback system that deliberately manipulates the perceived proximity to success, rather than success itself. This was achieved by presenting the outcome of a motor task as being close to a target, regardless of its actual accuracy, thereby evoking the psychological state of "almost there." This allows us to both stimulate continued task engagement and quantitatively control the degree of feedback bias, by defining it as a percentage of apparent progress toward the goal. The objective of this study is to evaluate the psychological and motor consequences of introducing and then removing such a White Lie feedback system. By measuring both subjective and objective effects across different phases of the intervention, we aim to assess whether this subtle form of deception can promote sustainable engagement without impairing motor accuracy or leading to negative psychological effects when withdrawn.

3 Implementation

3.1 Implementation Strategy

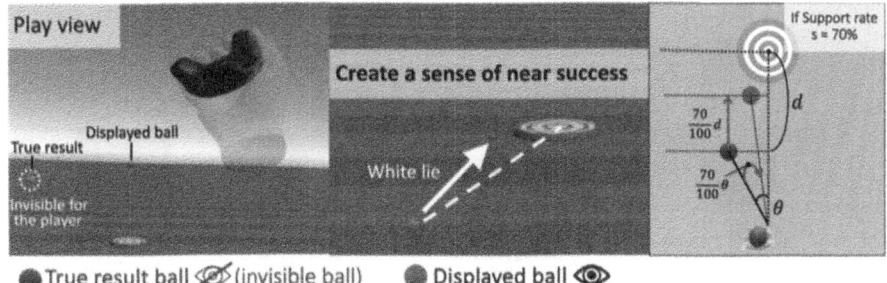

Fig. 1. The White Lie mechanism visualizes ball landings as closer to the target center, generating a sense of "almost hitting" rather than outright success.

We implemented a VR-based underhand ball-throwing task to facilitate performance evaluation and target a muscle group essential for daily life—the upper arm—within a relatively safe seated posture. The system comprises two main components: one task involves throwing a ball as far as possible, with verbal feedback on distance; the other is a target-hitting task in which audiovisual feedback (a burst of white smoke and a satisfying sound) informs the player of a successful hit.

To enhance user motivation in the target-hitting task, we implemented a "White Lie" system designed to provide players with a feeling of "almost hitting" the target (Fig. 1). The system introduces a support coefficient, s, representing the level of performance exaggeration. When the user throws the ball, the system instantly calculates the distance and angle between the actual landing point and the center of the target. It then adjusts the ball's visual trajectory and landing position to make it appear s% closer to the center in both dimensions. A support rate of 0% indicates that the user's throw is shown without any correction, while 100% indicates full system control—every throw appears to hit the target directly.

3.2 System Setup

Fig. 2. Play view from player's side.

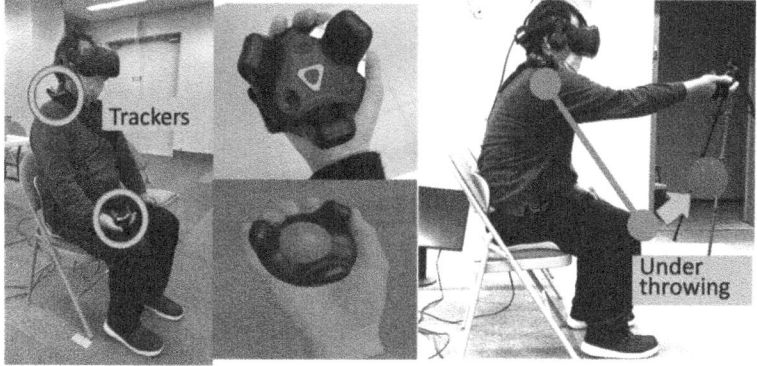

Fig. 3. The tracker's settings for underthrowing.

The VR setup consisted of an HTC Vive Pro headset, two HTC Base Stations, and Vive Tracker (ver. 2.0) units. The application was developed in Unity (Fig. 2). To track throwing motion without impeding user movement, two trackers were attached to the dominant shoulder and hand. For enhanced immersion, participants physically held the hand tracker, which was also visually rendered in VR (Fig. 3). A throw was triggered when the following conditions were met:

- The angle between the shoulder's vertical vector and the vector from shoulder to hand exceeded 45°
- The hand's forward angle was aligned with the player's facing direction

- The velocity of the hand tracker exceeded 1.5 m/s

In the VR view, the hand and tracker appeared to cradle the ball, although in physical space, the palm was flat and in contact with the ball. When the throw was triggered, the ball inherited the current velocity of the hand tracker, producing a sensation similar to pushing a ball off a flat surface.

4 Experiment

4.1 Experimental Design

To examine the effect of the White Lie system on motor performance, we recruited healthy adult participants capable of repeated throws and divided them into four groups: two without the White Lie (Control and Throwing), and two with the White Lie (Fixed Support and Variable Support). All but the Throwing group performed the target-hitting task. The ball had a radius of 3 cm, and the target had a radius of 30 cm. Each participant threw 50 balls in total. The first 10 throws (Phase 0) were used as a familiarization phase with the VR throwing environment and to assess each participant's throwing power to appropriately set the target distance. The Throwing group continued to focus solely on maximizing throwing distance. In the remaining three groups, the target was placed at a distance calculated as 1.2 times their longest Phase 0 throw. From the 11th to the 20th throw (Phase 1), all three groups performed the same unassisted target-hitting task. In throws 21–40 (Phase 2), group-specific interventions were introduced:

a) Control group: No support
b) Fixed Support group: Constant support rate of 70%, based on pre-study preference ratings
c) Variable Support group: Support increased from 20% to 70% over 10 throws, then decreased from 70% back to 20% over the next 10 throws (Fig. 4)
d) Throwing group: Continued distance throwing without targets or support

Regarding c), this gradual modulation of support was designed to offer subtle assistance that participants might not consciously notice. The choice of the 70% support rate for the Fixed Support group was based on results from a preliminary pilot study involving ten participants not included in the main experiment. In this pre-study, participants were presented with a series of visually manipulated ball trajectories using support rates ranging from 0% to 100% in 10% increments. They were asked to rate how motivating or psychologically helpful each condition felt. The most commonly preferred support levels fell between 60% and 80%, with 70% emerging as the median and most favorably rated value. By contrast, support levels below 40% were often not consciously noticed, and throws in those conditions were typically perceived as mere misses rather than "almost successful." Based on these findings, 70% was selected as the fixed support level to ensure the illusion of near-success was both noticeable and positively reinforcing, while remaining below complete success.

The aim was to simulate a natural improvement process and investigate whether such imperceptible White Lie feedback could maintain motivation and enhance performance without disrupting the perception of self-agency. Finally, from throws 41 to

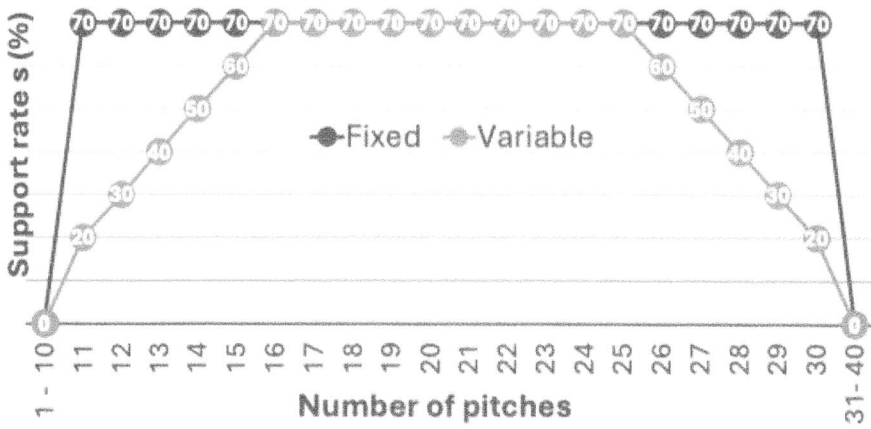

Fig. 4. The settings of the support rate value.

50 (Phase 3), all three target-hitting groups reverted to the same no-support condition. Participants were informed beforehand that the system may include a White Lie mechanism that makes results appear more favorable. While Phase 1 was the same for all groups, participants were told that in Phase 2 and/or Phase 3, some may receive White Lie support.

4.2 Participants

Thirty-two healthy adult participants (19 male, 13 female) took part in the study. Their ages ranged from 19 to 51 years (M = 25.5, SD = 8.6). Participants were assigned to one of four experimental groups: 10 in the Control group, 8 in the Fixed Support group, 10 in the Variable Support group, and 4 in the Throwing group. All participants provided informed consent prior to participation, and the study protocol was approved by the ethics committee. Following the experiment, each participant completed a questionnaire assessing their subjective and psychological responses across the different phases. The questionnaire included items rated on 4- or 5-point Likert scales covering the following dimensions: perceived task difficulty for each phase, operability of the VR system, physical and mental fatigue at the end of the session, perceived duration, perceived number of throws, enjoyment, willingness to retry the task, and preference for the VR-based task experience compared to a real-world equivalent. These measures were intended to capture various affective and cognitive responses to the White Lie feedback conditions.

5 Performance Evaluation Metrics

To evaluate the quality and accuracy of motor performance under different feedback conditions, we decomposed the throwing outcome into three distinct metrics reflecting distance accuracy, directional accuracy, and lateral deviation. These metrics were selected to decompose the throwing error in polar coordinates, enabling separate evaluation of radial (distance-related) and directional (angular) accuracy. Additionally, since the distance to the target varied across conditions, all metrics were normalized appropriately to ensure comparability between trials.

A. Normalized Radial Error (Reach Rate)

This metric evaluates the extent to which the ball reached the target along the depth (z-axis) direction. It is calculated as the deviation of the landing position y from the target center z, normalized by the target distance:

$$\text{Normalized lateral Deviation} = \frac{x}{z} \tag{1}$$

Positive values indicate undershooting, while negative values indicate overshooting. The result is a dimensionless value representing the proportional deviation in distance.

B. Angular error (°)

To assess the directional accuracy of the throw, the angular deviation between the actual landing point and the intended straight-ahead direction was calculated. This error is expressed in degrees:

$$\text{Angular Error} = \arctan\left(\frac{x}{z}\right) x \frac{180}{\pi} \tag{2}$$

Here, x is the lateral deviation and z is the distance to the target. This metric was included primarily to reflect a subjectively intuitive measure of performance from the participant's point of view, in contrast to the objective physical deviation captured by the following metric.

C. Normalized Lateral Deviation

To complement the angular error with a distance-based measure of directional accuracy, we defined the normalized lateral deviation as the ratio of horizontal error to the target distance:

$$\text{Reach Rate} = \frac{z - y}{z} \tag{3}$$

This metric accounts for the same angular deviation, which results in more significant lateral error as the target distance increases. It thus provides a normalized, dimensionless measure of physical deviation in the lateral direction.

6   Results

6.1   Group Differences in Perceived Task Difficulty

The perceived difficulty at each phase as reported by participants in each experimental group is shown in Fig. 5. In the Fixed Support group, all participants noticed the absence of support in Phase 3, while in the Variable Support group, half of the participants were able to correctly identify the phase during which they received support. To assess the impact of White Lie feedback on subjective experience, we compared perceived task difficulty across groups using ANOVA and independent t-tests. In Phase 2, a significant group effect was observed ($F(2,25) = 13.613$, $p < .001$). The control group reported the highest difficulty ($M = 4.30$, $SD = 0.68$), while the fixed support ($M = 2.38$, $SD = 0.74$) and variable support groups ($M = 2.80$, $SD = 1.03$) reported significantly lower difficulty. A t-test comparing White Lie (WL) conditions (fixed and variable) against the control confirmed this difference ($t(26) = 5.562$, $p < .001$).

In Phase 3, difficulty ratings remained lower in the WL groups. ANOVA revealed a significant difference ($F(2,25) = 4.96$, $p = .015$), and the t-test again showed lower difficulty in the WL group ($t(26) = 3.161$, $p = .004$). Additionally, the change in perceived difficulty from Phase 1 to Phase 3 (ΔDifficulty) was significantly different across groups ($F(2,25) = 3.65$, $p = .041$), with the variable support group showing the greatest reduction ($M = -1.00$). The t-test comparing WL vs. control groups also indicated a significant improvement ($t(26) = 2.13$, $p = .047$).

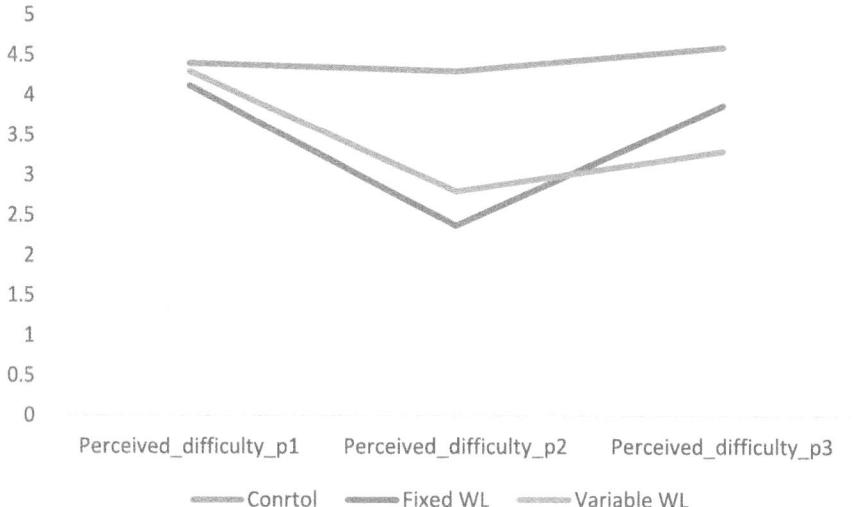

Fig. 5. Participants' perceived difficulty by phase.

6.2 Correlational Findings

Correlation analysis revealed high consistency in performance across phases. Hit rates and distance error rates between Phase 1 and subsequent phases were strongly correlated ($r > .63$, $p < .001$), suggesting stable motor tendencies within individuals. Furthermore, poor early performance (low hit rate or high distance error in Phase 1) was associated with increased perceived difficulty in Phase 2 ($r = -0.378$, $p = .048$) and reduced enjoyment ($r = -0.419$, $p = .026$). Enjoyment, in turn, positively predicted replay intention ($r = 0.713$, $p < .001$), indicating a close link between affective experience and motivation.

6.3 Multiple Regression: Predicting Difficulty Reduction

To explore what factors contributed to the reduction in perceived difficulty, we conducted a multiple regression analysis using the difference in difficulty from Phase 1 to Phase 3 as the dependent variable. The model was statistically significant ($F = 2.936$, $p = .027$), with $R^2 = 0.647$ (adjusted $R^2 = 0.427$). Significant predictors included:

- Hit rate in Phase 2 ($\beta = -3.586$, $p = .002$): better motor performance predicted greater difficulty reduction.
- VR hand comfort ($\beta = 2.459$, $p = .026$): higher usability predicted greater perceived improvement.
- Perceived support in Phase 2 ($\beta = -2.193$, $p = .043$): those who felt supported showed greater reduction in difficulty.

These results suggest that motor success, system operability, and subtle psychological support each contributed uniquely to the perceived ease of task completion.

7 Discussions

The present study investigated whether a White Lie feedback system, designed to create a sense of "almost succeeding," could enhance subjective experience and preserve motor performance in a VR rehabilitation task. The results provide strong support for the psychological effectiveness of this approach. Participants who received White Lie feedback reported significantly lower perceived difficulty, particularly in the variable support condition, which gradually increased and then decreased the level of support. This group showed the most pronounced improvement in subjective difficulty, even though they were not explicitly aware of the changes in feedback. This pattern aligns with the metaphor of "training wheels," where subtle, fading support promotes the perception of autonomous progress.

Crucially, while the White Lie feedback significantly improved subjective evaluations—such as difficulty, enjoyment, and motivation—it did not distort or enhance motor accuracy. Correlation analyses demonstrated strong intra-individual consistency across performance phases, suggesting that feedback manipulation did not interfere with genuine skill development. However, early task success was a key factor in shaping later enjoyment and willingness to continue, underscoring the importance of fostering early engagement.

The multiple regression results further emphasized that subjective difficulty is not shaped by motor outcomes alone, but by a combination of support perception and system usability. Notably, the perception of being subtly supported (even without overt success feedback) emerged as a significant predictor of improved experience. This finding illustrates that the psychological framing of effort—feeling that one is "almost there"—can enhance motivation without relying on deception through artificial success.

Taken together, the results support the viability of near-miss style White Lie feedback as a motivational design strategy in physical rehabilitation. By subtly guiding users toward goal states without distorting performance metrics, such feedback may sustain effort and reduce discouragement, potentially improving long-term adherence in motor recovery tasks.

8 Conclusion and Future Work

This study investigated the psychological and motor effects of a "White Lie" feedback mechanism in a virtual rehabilitation task. Unlike conventional success-biased feedback, our approach emphasized the illusion of "almost succeeding," aiming to evoke intrinsic motivation without distorting actual performance. Participants in both fixed and variable support conditions reported significantly lower perceived task difficulty than those in the control group. Importantly, participants in the variable support condition—who experienced support increasing and then decreasing without explicit awareness—showed the greatest reduction in perceived difficulty from baseline. Regression analyses further revealed that task engagement and the perception of subtle support were key predictors of improved subjective experience. Although no clear performance advantage was observed for the White Lie groups in terms of hit rate or error reduction, early task success was strongly associated with later enjoyment and motivation. These results suggest that well-designed, psychologically subtle feedback can facilitate continued engagement while preserving the integrity of motor learning. The findings support the use of near-miss-based White Lie strategies in rehabilitation systems as a means of sustaining user effort without compromising performance fidelity.

Acknowledgement. This research was supported by JST [Moonshot R&D][Grant Number JPMJMS2034].

References

1. Snider, L., Majnemer, A.: Virtual reality: we are virtually there. Phys. Occup. Ther. Pediatr. **30**(1), 1–3 (2010)
2. Gougeh, R.A., Falk, T.: Head-mounted display-based virtual reality and physiological computing for stroke rehabilitation: a systematic review. Front. Virtual Real. **3**(1) (2022)
3. Lewis, G., Rosie, J.: Virtual reality games for movement rehabilitation in neurological conditions. Disabil. Rehabil. **34**(1), 1880–1886 (2012)
4. Granqvist, B., et al.: Exaggeration of avatar flexibility in virtual reality. IEEE Trans. Vis. Comput. Graph. **24**(1) (2018)
5. Wang, L., et al.: Weight perception and controlling experience in loaded virtual rehabilitation. In: IEEE SeGAH, pp. 1–6 (2023)
6. De Keersmaecker, E., et al.: Virtual reality for multiple sclerosis rehabilitation. Cochrane Database Syst. Rev. **1**(1) (2025)
7. Kiper, P., et al.: Virtual reality for upper limb rehabilitation in subacute stroke. Arch. Phys. Med. Rehabil. **99**(5), 834-842.e4 (2018)
8. Dores, A., et al.: Significance of virtual reality-based rehabilitation in acquired brain injury. IGI Global (2016)
9. Hashim, N.A., et al.: On the use of virtual reality for individuals with upper limb loss: a scoping review. Eur. J. Phys. Rehabil. Med. **58**(1) (2022)
10. Gouveia, M., et al.: Correlates of presence in a virtual reality gamification rehabilitation system. Front. Psychol. **14**(1) (2023)
11. Alonso-Enr√/≠quez, L., et al.: Effectiveness of virtual reality and feedback in DPN patients. Healthcare **11**(1) (2023)

12. Zhang, J., et al.: TacPoint: partial visuo-tactile feedback on sense of embodiment. In: IEEE VRW, pp. 1–2 (2024)
13. Aung, Y., Al-Jumaily, A.: AR-based Illusion System with Biofeedback. In: IEEE MEC-BME, pp. 1–2 (2014)
14. Stammler, B., et al.: Negami: AR app for spatial neglect after stroke. JMIR Serious Games **11**(1) (2023)
15. Johnston, T., et al.: Virtual reality for IPV prevention and rehabilitation. Front. Psychol. **13**(1) (2023)
16. Nataraj, R., et al.: Disproportionate positive feedback facilitates sense of agency and performance. PLoS ONE **15**(1) (2020)
17. Amin, F., et al.: Effectiveness of immersive virtual reality-based hand rehabilitation games. IEEE Trans. Neural Syst. Rehabil. Eng. **32**(1), 2060–2069 (2024)
18. Bortone, I., et al.: Integration of serious games and wearable haptic interfaces. In: Proceedings of the ICORR, pp. 1094–1099 (2017)
19. Nardi, F., et al.: Bill-EVR: embodied virtual reality framework. In: Proceedings of the ICORR, pp. 1–6 (2023)
20. Montoya, M., et al.: Enhancing virtual rehabilitation with muscle fatigue estimation. IEEE Trans. Neural Syst. Rehabil. Eng. **28**(1) (2020)
21. Wei, W.: Virtual reality enhanced robotic systems for disability rehabilitation. Technical Report (2019)
22. Marwecki, S., et al.: Goal-oriented feedback in virtual reality stroke therapy. In: Rehabilitation Gaming System, pp. 36–45 (2017)
23. Dias, P., et al.: Using virtual reality to increase motivation in stroke patients. JMIR Serious Games **7**(1) (2019)
24. Ballester, B., et al.: Including social interaction in stroke VR-based motor rehabilitation enhances performance. PRESENCE **21**(5), 490–501 (2012)

Seeing Cold, Eating Warm: Food Perception in Imaginative Storytelling and Immersive Virtual Reality Winter Contexts

Jiayan Zhao[1]([✉]) [iD], Xi Zhang[2], and Garmt Dijksterhuis[3] [iD]

[1] Laboratory of Geo-Information Science and Remote Sensing, Wageningen University & Research, Wageningen, the Netherlands
jiayan.zhao@wur.nl
[2] Experimental Psychology, Helmholtz Institute, Utrecht University, Utrecht, the Netherlands
[3] Faculty of Psychology and Neuroscience, Section Teaching and Innovation of Learning, Maastricht University, Maastricht, the Netherlands

Abstract. Food intake is a fundamental daily activity. Its relationship to external factors such as social and environmental contexts has been widely investigated in consumer studies. Virtual reality (VR) technology enables the realistic simulation of real-life conditions and, therefore, holds promise as an ecologically valid method for understanding eating intentions and behavior. This study examines whether contextual exposure to VR or text-based storytelling influences food liking and desire in alignment with the presented environment. A total of 117 participants, either online or in a laboratory setting, viewed and rated eight food items varying in calorie density while exposed to one of three conditions: a VR-simulated winter forest, a text-based storytelling winter forest, or a control group without winter cues. Accounting for individual characteristics such as eating habits and body mass index, the results showed that participants' food perceptions —defined here as evaluative responses toward digitally presented food items—followed a similar pattern across both winter forest contexts, with a stronger desire and liking for high-calorie over low-calorie foods. However, the intensity of their perceptual responses varied significantly between conditions. Participants in the VR forest reported greater familiarity, liking, and desire for all food items, as well as a stronger sense of spatial presence, compared to those in the storytelling condition. While VR elicited heightened and more affective responses, both VR and storytelling seem to be useful interventions for assessing contextual effects on product consumption. These findings provide insights into how different modes of contextual presentation shape food perception and encourage the integration of multiple sensory modalities to further bridge the gap between virtual and real food experiences.

Keywords: Immersive Technologies · Eating Context · Immersion · Food Preferences · Calorie Density

D. Michael-Grigoriou et al. (Eds.): EuroXR 2025, LNCS 16101, pp. 200–219, 2026.
https://doi.org/10.1007/978-3-032-03805-0_12

1 Introduction

Eating is a fundamental biological function, and food has always been a necessary part of our daily life. For humans living in an ancient or hostile environment with scarce food resources, such as during the Stone Age or Ice Age, consuming foods rich in calories allowed for efficient energy acquisition, thereby improving the individual survival rate. As we now live in a world with easy access to a wide range of food products, modern history has witnessed a shift from eating for survival to hedonic eating [1]. However, due to the increasing obesity rate and the pressure of climate change, there is a strong demand for healthy and sustainable food intake [2]. Despite continuous societal efforts to promote healthy food products, some people still opt for foods high in sugar, fat, and calories, like fried chicken and donuts, even when they already know that such products may overburden their bodies with unbalanced nutrition and negatively impact their physical health [3]. Consequently, it is critical to examine what internal and external factors, such as eating habits and the food situation (i.e., the environment where the food is located), may influence individuals' food perception and preferences as well as their eating decisions. Results from the current research can provide evidence to inform the design of interventions effective in promoting healthy food choices and eating behavior.

1.1 Eating as a Multisensory Experience

Our perception of food is complex and inherently multisensory, involving the integration of visual, auditory, olfactory, gustatory, and tactile cues. According to the conceptual framework proposed by Spencer and Ho [4], these sensory inputs converge to form a coherent perceptual experience that shapes our expectations and guides eating behavior. For example, the visual appearance of a dish can influence people's evaluation of its taste, while auditory cues, such as the crunching sound produced during eating, can alter feelings of texture and freshness [5]. Given the multisensory nature of food perception, researchers have increasingly sought to disentangle the relative contributions of each sensory modality to the overall food experience.

Although many studies have investigated the psychological and behavioral aspects of food intake, most findings are obtained in standardized laboratory experiments. As with the traditional sensory booth, participants assess a small portion of food within a succinct lab environment, ensuring that confounding factors have little influence on the outcome [6]. However, such testing systems lack external validity and do not necessarily reflect real-life consumption behavior. External validity refers to the extent to which the results of a study can be generalized to a broader context encompassing real-life conditions [7]. Sufficient external validity is paramount when the experiment aims to elicit in participants perceptual and affective responses similar to those experienced in the real-world. The home use test allows participants to evaluate food products at home over an extended period [8]. Due to the incorporation of daily life contexts, the data gathered are more externally valid and offer a more accurate representation of consumer opinion than the sensory booth setting. However, manipulating the ingredients and visual characteristics of a real food product is challenging in practice, and the experimental setup can be expensive and often results in food waste.

1.2   The Use of Simulation Technology in Food-Related Research

To overcome the limitations of traditional laboratory setups, researchers have increasingly turned to mediated approaches, among which immersive technologies stand out as some of the most progressive. Immersive technologies like virtual reality (VR) and mixed reality (MR) offer an efficient means of realizing design options in laboratory environments without incurring the cost of food or other physical resources. As an emerging visualization technique, the vividness, interactivity, and 3D interface of VR provide an ecologically valid experience that creates an illusion of being physically present in the mediated space (i.e., spatial presence [9]). Furthermore, recent advances in chemo- and thermo-sensory augmentation interfaces, such as utensils with digital gustation and olfactory-assist masks, enable the integration of smell, taste, and thermal feedback into VR, allowing for even more immersive and realistic food experiences [10].

The ecological validity of VR in food-related research is illustrated by Lombart et al. [11], who found strong consistency in participants' selection of fresh produce between VR and real-world store environments. Likewise, Schnack et al. [12] reported that participants in a virtual convenience store exhibited behaviors—such as preferring food items placed on higher shelves—that align with patterns commonly observed in physical retail settings. Evidence from nutrition education also suggests that interactive 3D food models provide more realistic representations than 2D on-screen images, aiding in a better understanding of portion sizes and food types [13]. Together, these findings highlight the potential of VR to replace real-life environments (e.g., a buffet or supermarket) and support the validity of using 3D models to assess the impact of food type and appearance on individuals' preferences and eating intentions (see [14, 15] for reviews).

Another potential usefulness of VR lies in its high degree of flexibility—everything in a virtual environment, from object locations and appearances to the way of interacting with virtual space and objects within it, is programmable and controllable [16]. Given the advantages of VR in simulating real-world scenarios and manipulating variables, a growing number of studies have begun to employ this technology to examine factors such as food shape, portion size, and environmental elements that are difficult to manipulate or control in conventional experimental setups [17–20]. For example, Wang et al. [21] explored whether changing the visual appearance of coffee in VR could affect its perceived flavor. Participants consumed cold brew coffee while wearing a VR headset that displayed the coffee as either dark brown or light brown. Results showed that the lighter-colored coffee was perceived as creamier despite no change in its actual composition. In another study, Goedegebure et al. [22] examined the influence of popularity cues (e.g., a slogan reading "sold the most") on food choices in a VR supermarket. Labeling healthy products as popular significantly increased their selection, whereas popularity cues had no effect on the choice of regular alternatives.

It is important to note that VR, as a high-end and high-immersion technology, is not the only medium capable of transporting users away from physical reality. Traditional storytelling—such as viewing pictures, reading stories from a book, or listening to audiobooks—can also be considered an "immersive" technique, as it permits individuals to engage their imaginations in scenarios that may or may not exist in the real world [23, 24]. This low-tech, low-immersion approach provides an imaginative and affective experience without the need for any digital technology or hardware. While experiencing stories through text has been found effective for sustainability-related engagement [25], whether this approach evokes consumer perceptions about food products remains an open question. Furthermore, only one study has directly compared the effectiveness of text-based storytelling and immersive VR. Huang et al. [26] investigated the impact of nostalgic storytelling across these two modalities and found that VR elicited higher enjoyment, social connectedness, and state-level well-being than text-based storytelling. The extent to which this positive affective influence holds for food consumption scenarios is still unclear.

1.3 Effect of Contextual Congruence

Evolution theory suggests that humans, like other mammals, have developed a mechanism for adapting dietary habits to weather and temperature conditions. In tropical regions, lighter foods that help regulate body temperature may be preferred, whereas in colder climates, people tend to protect themselves against the potential scarcity of food resources by consuming calorie-dense foods for warmth and energy [27, 28]. In line with this theoretical perspective, a study on lifestyle habits found that Americans consume fewer healthy foods and engage in less physical activity in the fall and winter compared to the spring and summer, leading to increased obesity during the colder months [29]. Liu et al. [30] introduced the concept of sensory correspondence between food features and contextual information, referred to as *contextual congruence*. They stated that consumers prioritize the choice of a food product with intrinsic and extrinsic properties (e.g., texture and label claims) perceptually congruent with environmental variables (e.g., eating location and social ambiance). This congruence effect was further studied by Schouteten et al. [31], who found that participants' liking of watermelon was significantly higher in a video-based congruent beach setting than in an incongruent winter context. Similarly, Folwarczny et al. [32] demonstrated that watching videos depicting a winter forest walk elicited thoughts related to food scarcity and energy-dense foods (e.g., burgers and fries). Although several studies have explored contextual effects on food perception, it remains unclear to what extent immersive VR simulations and traditional text-based storytelling can immerse consumers in environmental contexts that are appropriate for food evaluation.

1.4 The Current Study

The current study aims to explore the impact of environmental cues and media use on food perception. Here, food perception is defined as participants' evaluative responses to digitally presented food items. To investigate this, a winter forest environment was presented in a VR headset or as a text-based story. Participants were guided through one of these winter forest contexts or received no environmental cue if assigned to the control group, and then rated their familiarity, eating desire, and liking for food items varying in calorie density. It is hypothesized that both VR and storytelling can elicit contextually congruent responses to food products (i.e., a preference for high-calorie foods in a winter context), and that the differences in desire and liking between contextually congruent and incongruent foods will be more pronounced among participants immersed in the VR winter environment.

The contribution of this paper is twofold. First, Spence and colleagues' framework of multisensory processing [4, 5] emphasizes the influence of multiple sensory inputs, particularly those related to the intrinsic properties of food items (e.g., color, texture, and smell), on perception and behavior. Our study advances research on food as a multisensory experience by examining how the context of food presentation affects desire and liking, thereby highlighting the importance of extrinsic situational factors in shaping food perception. Second, we introduced text-based storytelling as a low-tech approach for simulating environmental cues and directly compared it with immersive VR. This comparison offers insights into how different types of media can be leveraged to evoke contextually congruent food evaluations, with implications for scalable, flexible, and effective health intervention design.

2 Methodology

This section describes the experimental design, participant characteristics, materials used for the food evaluation task, as well as the procedures followed by participants in the VR, storytelling, and control groups. It also outlines the measures and data analysis methods employed to examine the effects of environmental cues and media use on food-related evaluations.

2.1 Participants and Design

This study compared three groups in a between-subjects design: the VR group, in which participants wore a VR headset and experienced a simulated winter forest environment with trees and the ground covered in snow; the storytelling group, in which participants read a narrative text describing a winter forest; and the control group, in which no environmental cues were provided. Participants in the VR group were recruited from the campus of Utrecht University in the Netherlands and completed the experiment in a laboratory setting. In contrast, participants in the storytelling and control groups were recruited online and completed the experiment via a Qualtrics survey.

A total of 120 participants aged between 18 and 34 years took part in the study. To increase the quality of data collected from different groups, we inserted a simple math question ("$1 + 5 = ?$") in the online survey to ensure that participants were actively reflecting on the material rather than responding randomly; this resulted in the exclusion of one participant. Additionally, two participants who reported allergies to any of the foods evaluated in this study were excluded. After applying these criteria, the final sample included 31 participants in the VR group (19 females; average age 23.5 years), 49 in the storytelling group (23 females; average age 28.0 years), and 37 in the control group (31 females; average age 24.2 years).

2.2 Materials

VR Winter Forest and Food Evaluation. The VR forest environment was developed in the Unity Game engine and was based on ready-to-use models from the Unity asset "Winter Environment - Nature Pack." the scene featured a realistic 3D depiction of a winter forest scene, complete with snow-covered terrain and ambient sounds of howling wind (Fig. 1, top left). Participants wore an Oculus Rift VR headset while standing within a 2m-by-2m fenced area (Fig. 1, top right), and used the controller's thumbstick to move continuously in the virtual environment. The Oculus Rift headset offers a display resolution of 1080 x 1200 pixels per eye, a horizontal field of view of 87°, and a maximum refresh rate of 90Hz. The laboratory in which the VR experiment was conducted was controlled for temperature (20–25 °C) and lighting conditions, using sunshade curtains and overhead illumination to ensure consistent ambiance.

While in an empty virtual room, participants were first guided to view and rate three everyday items (e.g., a toy car) to familiarize themselves with the interaction mechanics. Following this training phase, participants were placed in the winter forest and instructed to navigate through it by following red arrows on the ground (Fig. 1, top left). The path was about 150 m long and took approximately 1–2 min to finish. At the end of the path, participants encountered eight photorealistic food models, each placed on a pillar and covered with a cloche, positioned around a flat iced area (Fig. 1, bottom). These food items were familiar to most participants and were classified into two categories based on calorie density, according to data from the Dutch National Institute for Public Health and the Environment (https://nevo-online.rivm.nl/Home/En). Low-calorie density foods included cucumber (13 kcal/100 g), asparagus (19 kcal/100 g), tomato (20 kcal/100 g), and apple (55 kcal/100 g). High-calorie density foods included grilled chicken thigh (209 kcal/100 g), burger (255 kcal/100 g), cheesecake (330 kcal/100 g), and doughnut (358 kcal/100 g). These high-calorie items were ready-to-eat and presented in forms that closely resembled how they are typically consumed. In contrast, most low-calorie foods used in this study, such as cucumber, apple, and tomato, were raw and shown in both sliced and whole forms, reflecting common ways these foods are prepared and visually encountered in everyday contexts.

Participants viewed and evaluated the food items in a random order. At each evaluation round, the participant approached a pillar and used the hand controller to open the cloche covering a food model. Once the food item was revealed, a questionnaire popped up on the left-hand controller, asking the participant to rate their liking, eating desire, and familiarity with the food using a continuous slider (Fig. 2, left). To elicit intuitive and affective responses, no numeric feedback was displayed during the task (which applied to the storytelling and control groups as well). After submitting their responses, the participant proceeded to another pillar and repeated the same steps until all eight food items had been evaluated.

Narrative Winter Forest and Food Evaluation. Participants in the storytelling group completed the experiment online, where they read a 326-word first-person narrative describing a person wandering through a cold winter forest. For example, one paragraph from the story reads: *"The ground beneath my feet was covered in a thick layer of crisp, powdery snow. Each step I took sent a jolt of coldness through my boots as if the very ground itself held a frosty secret. The branches above me creaked under the weight*

Fig. 1. Top left: the winter forest virtual environment with directional arrows on the ground guiding participants' navigation. Top right: Laboratory setup for the VR experiment. Bottom: Eight food items covered by cloches.

of frost, their delicate icicles threatening to plummet at any moment." The story was generated by ChatGPT and verified by the authors to appropriately match the scene in the VR group (see Appendix for the full narrative). After reading the story, participants were shown screenshots—presented on a computer screen and in a random order—of the same collection of food items used in the VR group. They rated each item using the same questions, including liking, eating desire, and familiarity (Fig. 2, right). Similarly, participants in the control group received the same series of food items and evaluation questions on a computer screen, but without the narrative provided to the storytelling group. The characteristics of food images, such as contrast, brightness, and shooting angle, were standardized partially following the recommendations outlined in [33].

2.3 Procedure and Measures

The entire experiment lasted about 20 min for participants assigned to the VR and storytelling groups, and about 12 min for those assigned to the control group. Participants in the VR group received a piece of chocolate as an incentive after completing the session. Data collection began in late May 2023 and continued for two weeks. The study was

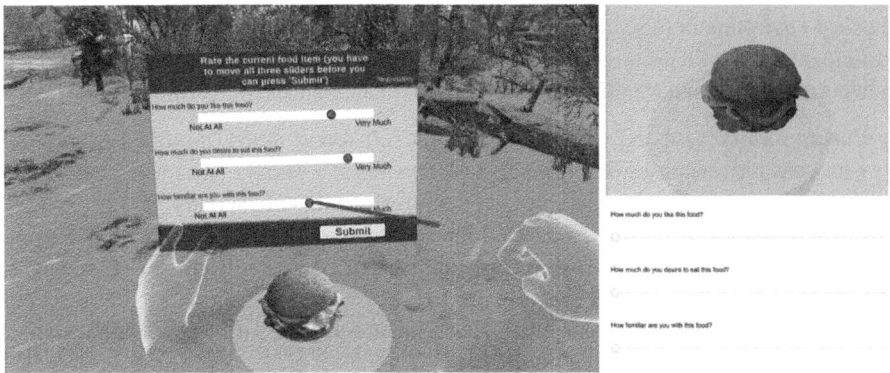

Fig. 2. Evaluation of food perception in VR (left) and, in the storytelling and control groups on a computer screen (right).

approved by the Ethics Review Board of the Faculty of Social & Behavioural Sciences at Utrecht University.

Upon giving informed consent, participants reported any food allergies and completed an online survey consisting of the following components:

- **Demographics:** including age, gender, hometown, and education level
- **Hunger level:** a single-item 5-point Likert scale question, "how hungry are you?" with possible responses ranging from 1(*"very full"*) to 5 (*"starving"*)
- **Video game familiarity:** three 5-point Likert scale questions ranging from 1 (*"not at all familiar"*) to 5 (*"extremely familiar"*). For example, *"how familiar are you with video games of any kind (gaming consoles, PC, or on phones)?"* [34]
- **VR familiarity:** a single-time 5-point Likert scale question, *"how familiar are you with virtual reality experiences (HTC Vive, Oculus Rift, Samsung GearVR, Google Cardboard, etc.)"* [34]

Participants then experienced either the VR or narrative winter forest environment, or skipped the environmental exposure if assigned to the control group. In the subsequent food evaluation phase, participants rated their familiarity with, desire for, and liking of four low-calorie and four high-calorie food items using 100-point slider scales, with higher scores indicating stronger levels of the corresponding perception. Participants in the VR group viewed and rated food items directly within the virtual forest, whereas for participants in the storytelling and control groups, the same set of food items were presented as still images on a computer screen and rated via the Qualtrics online survey.

After the food evaluation, participants in the VR and storytelling groups reported their sense of spatial presence using four 5-point Likert scale items (e.g., *"I felt like I was actually there in the environment."*), with higher average scores indicating a stronger sense of presence [35]. Participants in the VR group also completed two 5-point Likert scale questions assessing simulator sickness (e.g., *"How much general discomfort are you experiencing right now?"*), with higher average scores reflecting more intense symptoms [36]. For participants in the storytelling and control groups, they were additionally asked to estimate the ambient temperature, that is, the temperature of the surrounding physical environment (e.g., the room) that they were in during the experiment. Finally, participants across all groups provided information about their eating habits and reported their current height and weight, which were used to calculate the Body Mass Index (BMI).

- **Eating habits**: assessed using eight 3-point self-report items (modified from [37]) with possible responses of 1 (*"no"*), 2 (*"sometimes"*), and 3 (*"yes"*): 1) I eat a good breakfast, 2) I eat fresh vegetables, 3) I eat fresh fruit, 4) I eat dairy, 5) I eat sweets, 6) I eat fast food, 7) I eat fried food, and 8) I eat salty food. Questions 5–8 were reverse coded, and a higher total accumulative score (ranging from 3 to 24) indicates healthier eating habits.
- **Vegetarian status**: assessed using a self-report statement: *"I eat meat,"* with response options of *"no"*, *"sometimes,"* and *"yes."*
- **BMI**: a long-established measure of obesity and malnutrition, commonly used as a survey factor to assess whether a person has a healthy body weight [38, 39]. In this study, BMI was calculated as weight in kilograms (kg) divided by height squared in meters (m^2). According to the World Health Organization [40], a BMI between 18.5 and 25 kg/m^2 is considered the normal weight range for adults.

2.4   Data Analysis

All statistical analyses were conducted using RStudio version 2024.04.2. We first compared spatial presence scores between the VR and storytelling groups using Welch's two-sample t-test. To evaluate comparability across the media groups (VR, storytelling, and control), we performed a correlation analysis to identify demographic and individual factors associated with participants' food ratings. Given the presence of continuous, polytomous, and dichotomous variables, we used the *mixedCor* function from the *psych* package in R [41], which applies appropriate correlation methods based on the type of variable involved.

To test the study hypotheses, we constructed three generalized linear mixed models (GLMMs) using the *nlme* package in R [42] to analyze the effects of media type (VR, storytelling, control) and food calorie density (low, high) on eating desire, food liking, and food familiarity. The GLMM for food familiarity was conducted as an exploratory analysis to examine whether differences in presentation format (i.e., 2D images on a computer screen versus 3D models in VR) influenced participants' ability to recognize food items.

In each GLMM, media type (a between-subject factor) and calorie density (a within-subject factor) were taken as fixed effects. Participant was entered as a random intercept and modeled with a random slope for calorie density. Individual food item was also entered as a random intercept with a random slope for media type. Additionally, demographic or individual factors that showed significant correlations with the dependent variable were included as covariates to account for individual differences within and between media groups. Missing values on covariates were handled using multiple imputation via the *mice* package in R [43]. Pairwise comparisons with Tukey correction were conducted to break down significant main effects and interactions. All *p*-values and estimated marginal means from the GLMMs were adjusted for covariates using the *emmeans* package in R [44].

3 Results

Participants in the VR group reported an average simulator sickness score of 1.58 (*SD* = .47), indicating little to no discomfort while experiencing the virtual winter forest environment. In terms of spatial presence, participants in the VR group (*M* = 3.78, *SD* = .77) reported significantly higher scores than those in the storytelling group (*M* = 2.96, *SD* = .72), $t(60.8) = 4.77, p < .001$, *Cohen's d* = 1.11.

Table 1 presents the correlation coefficients between participants' demographic and individual factors and their evaluations of food perception. Eating desire was significantly correlated with video game familiarity, VR familiarity, hunger level, ambient temperature, and food familiarity. Food liking was significantly correlated with eating habits, ambient temperature, and food familiarity. Food familiarity was significantly correlated with video game familiarity. Based on these results, the corresponding variables were included as covariates in the subsequent GLMM analyses of food evaluation outcomes.

Table 1. Correlations between variables included in the analysis.

Variables	Mean	SD	Eating desire	Food liking	Food familiarity
Gender	—	—	0.04	-0.07	0.11
Age	25.6	4.69	-0.14	-0.11	0.12
Hometown	—	—	0.01	0.06	0.13
Education level	—	—	0.00	0.04	0.13
Video game familiarity	2.68	1.21	0.18*	0.14	0.27**
VR familiarity	1.73	0.89	0.18*	0.12	0.03
Eating habits	17.8	2.34	0.07	0.22*	0.10
Vegetarian status	—	—	0.13	0.07	-0.13
BMI	21.9	3.94	0.01	-0.02	0.02
Hunger level	2.83	0.87	0.21*	0.13	0.01
Ambient temperature	—	—	-0.35***	-0.26**	-0.03
Food familiarity	75.8	17.8	0.36***	0.46***	

Note. Gender was coded 0 = female and 1 = male. Hometown was coded 1 = rural, 2 = suburban, 3 = urban. Education level (including degrees in progress) was coded 1 = secondary education or lower, 2 = bachelor's degree, 3 = master's degree, 4 = doctoral degree. Vegetarian status was coded 0 = does not eat meat, 1 = eats meat or sometimes eats meat. Ambient temperature was coded 1 = below 5 °C, 2 = 5–15 °C, 3 = 15–25 °C, 4 = 25–35 °C, 5 = above 35 °C. * $p < .05$, ** $p < .01$, *** $p < .001$

For eating desire, the main effects of calorie density ($F(1,4) = 20.2, p = .01, f^2 = .17$) and media type ($F(2, 4) = 14.4, p = .01, f^2 = .06$) were significant as well as the interaction between calorie density and media type ($F(2, 4) = 12.2, p = .02, f^2 = .05$; Fig. 3, top left). Pairwise comparisons on the interaction revealed that both the VR group and the storytelling group showed significantly stronger desires for high-calorie foods than low-calorie food (VR: $t.ratio(113) = 3.86, p = .003$; storytelling: $t.ratio(113) = 4.45, p < .001$), whereas there was no significant difference in the control group, $t.ratio(113) = -.21, p = .99$. The pairwise comparisons also revealed that participants in the VR group showed significantly stronger desires for high-calorie foods than those in the storytelling ($t.ratio(110) = 3.25, p = .02$) and control groups ($t.ratio(110) = 3.89, p = .002$); no other difference was significant ($p = .96$). Similarly for low-calorie foods, VR participants showed significantly stronger desires than storytelling participants ($t.ratio(110) = 3.01, p = .04$), while participants in the control group were in between with no significant differences ($ps > .09$).

There were significant main effects of calorie density ($F(1, 4) = 29.6, p = .006, f^2 = .25$) and media type ($F(2, 4) = 9.29, p = .03, f^2 = .04$) on food liking. The interaction between calorie density and media type was not significant ($F(2, 4) = 1.75$,

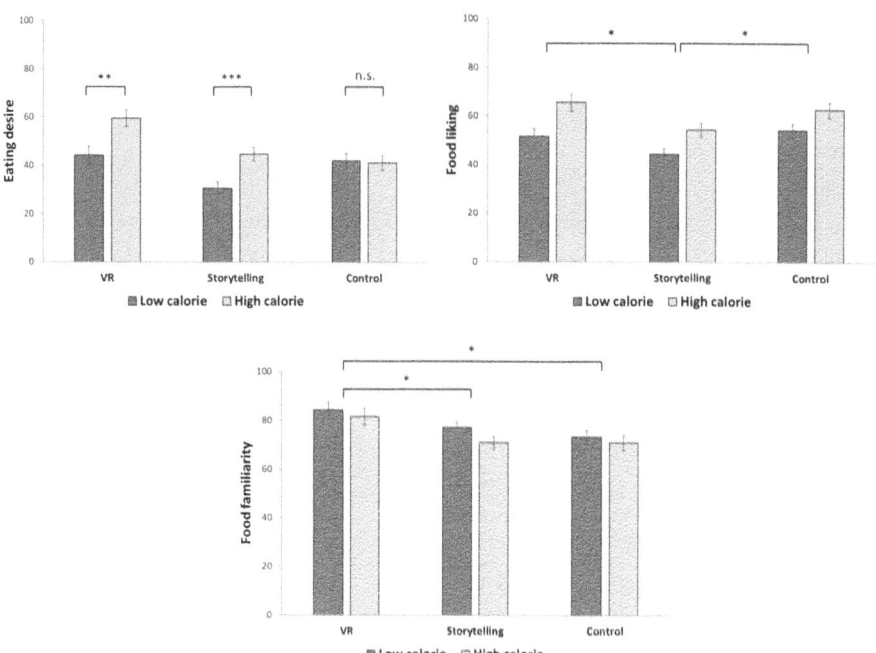

Fig. 3. Eating desire (top left), food liking (top right), and food familiarity (bottom) for low- and high-calorie foods across VR, storytelling, and control groups. Error bars represent ± 1 standard error of the mean. Means and standard errors are adjusted for relevant covariates. The short vertical lines at the base of each significance line denote the bars involved in the comparison. In cases where these lines are centered between two adjacent bars, the comparison reflects the average of those two conditions. n.s. not significant, $*p < 0.05$, $**p < 0.01$, $***p < 0.001$.

$p = .28, f^2 = .007$; Fig. 3, top right). These results showed that participants across all media groups reported significantly higher liking for high-calorie foods than low-calorie foods. Pairwise comparisons on the effect of media type revealed that participants in both the VR and control groups reported significantly higher food liking than those in the storytelling group ($ps = .05$ and $.02$ respectively).

Regarding food familiarity, the main effects of calorie density ($F(1, 4) = 8.10, p = .05, f^2 = .07$) and media type ($F(2, 4) = 7.77, p = .04, f^2 = .03$) were significant, but the interaction was not significant ($F(2, 4) = 1.77, p = .28, f^2 = .008$; Fig. 3, bottom). These results showed that participants across all media groups were significantly more familiar with low-calorie foods than high-calorie foods. Pairwise comparisons on the effect of media type revealed that participants in the VR group reported significantly higher food familiarity than those in the storytelling group ($p = .05$) and the control group ($p = .03$).

4 Discussion

When interpreting our findings, it is important to consider the potential confounding bias caused by individual differences and experimental settings. Participants varied in characteristics such as gender, age, and eating habits, and were tested either in a laboratory or an online environment, which may have introduced uncontrolled variables such as differences in room temperature. While these variables were not balanced across the three experimental conditions due to practical constraints, we collected self-reported data on key demographic and individual factors. Correlation analyses revealed that some of them did influence food evaluations. However, the core patterns of the results, particularly the contextually congruent effect of environmental cues and the heightened responses elicited by VR stimuli, remained significant after statistically controlling for these variables. This suggests that, although individual differences played a role, the observed effects on food perception are primarily attributable to the contextual presentation itself.

When experiencing the VR and storytelling winter forests, participants reported a higher eating desire for high-calorie foods than for low-calorie foods, but this difference was not observed in the control group where no environmental cues were present (Fig. 3 top left). These results suggest that consumers' desire for food is closely linked to the appropriateness of the environmental context, which agrees with previous research on the congruence effect of food characteristics and further confirms that eating desire is context-dependent [31, 32, 45, 46]. In line with our finding, the predictive coding theory posits that the human brain generates predictions about how a food will smell and taste based on past experiences [47]. That is to say, consumers' perceived quality of a food product does not merely depend on the food's sensory properties (e.g., appearance and texture) but also on extrinsic information, such as product descriptions and the situational context in which the product is typically consumed [46]. In the current study, the snow- and wind-induced contextual cues embedded in the winter forest environment may have triggered participants' memories of foods that were often eaten during colder months. These contextual associations, in turn, likely shaped their expectations about how much motivation and desire they would possess to obtain certain types of food.

However, unlike eating desire, we found that participants consistently rated high-calorie foods as more liked than low-calorie foods across all media groups including control. This general preference for high-calorie foods may be explained from an evolutionary perspective. Historically, in times of food scarcity, high-calorie foods provided the energy needed for physically demanding activities such as hunting and gathering. Our ancestors who preferred and prioritized high-calorie foods were more likely to survive and pass on this adaptive preference to future generations [48, 49]. Meanwhile, the absence of contextual congruence effect on food liking does not support our initial hypothesis but corroborates the notion that desire and liking represent different dimensions of the human relationship with food. Whereas desire is about the motivation to obtain and consume food, liking reflects the sensory pleasure and enjoyment derived from food [50]. Our finding indicates that food liking is less context-dependent and therefore a more stable long-term trait compared to eating desire, particularly when consumers have sufficient prior experience to inform their acceptance of a food product [46].

Regarding the effect of media use, we hypothesized that VR would produce a more pronounced perceptual difference between low- and high-calorie foods than text-based storytelling. However, this hypothesized effect was not supported. Response patterns in the VR and storytelling groups were similar for all food perception measures, including the congruent association between eating desire and contextual cues, as well as the stronger liking for high-calorie foods. To our knowledge, only one previous study by Andersen et al. [51] has explicitly examined the effect of media type on eating desire, finding that a VR-simulated summer beach fostered a stronger congruence effect between cold beverages and environmental cues compared to a photo-visualized beach context. In contrast to their study, the results of our study suggest that text-based storytelling, as a low-tech and low-immersion medium, can be just as effective as immersive VR in eliciting food-related perceptual responses akin to those observed in real-world environments (see also [23]). The discrepancy between their and our results might be because the winter cues used in our study are more salient and easier to detect and process than summer cues, making even the traditional storytelling approach sufficient to evoke cold feelings. This interpretation is supported by more a recent finding showing that watching videos of a winter forest walk—but not a summer one—can alter food preferences [32]. Another factor that may have influenced the results is the presentation format of the food stimuli. Manippa et al. [52] found that the position of food images on a screen can affect participants' attitudes toward high- versus low-calorie foods. In our study, participants in the storytelling group viewed static screenshots of food items consistently displayed on the top of the computer screen (Fig. 2, right). Conversely, with a head-tracked headset participants in the VR group were able to freely explore the 3D food models from different angles and distances, thereby eliminating the potential confounding impact of fixed viewing positions.

Besides calorie-related context effects, differences between media groups showed that immersive VR elicited a stronger sense of spatial presence than text-based storytelling. Wirth et al. [53] proposed a two-step process for the formation of spatial presence. The first step is to develop a mental model of the mediated situation (imagined or simulated) by encoding spatial relationships among depicted elements, i.e., the construction of a spatial situation model (SSM). Emerging from the SSM, the second step, self-location, involves mentally shifting one's perceived location from the physical to the mediated environment and recognizing possible actions within that environment. In light of Wirth's spatial presence theory, the heightened spatial presence reported by VR participants of this study was an expected outcome. A substantial body of research has demonstrated that VR is more effective than desktop screens or other traditional media in enhancing the accuracy of SSM construction (through realistic 3D representations) and supporting natural self-location (through head-tracking and body-based interactions) [35, 54].

According to the food evaluation results, participants in the VR group reported higher ratings of familiarity, liking, and desire for all food items compared to those in the storytelling and control groups. There are at least two possible explanations for this finding. First, the perception of familiarity involves recognizing the appearance and texture of a food item and matching these properties with past experiences of tasting [55]. Unlike static images, VR allows participants to examine realistic 3D food models from various perspectives and distances, which may facilitate recognition especially for food items with fewer distinctive visual features (e.g., tomato and apple). This interpretation is further supported by Ramousse et al. [56], who found that the visual quality of food stimuli significantly influences the desire to eat, with more realistic models eliciting greater desire. Second, most participants had never used VR before. Their curiosity might have driven them to explore this novel medium enthusiastically, leading to increased enjoyment and heightened responses to food items [57, 58]. The impact of user bias due to the novelty effect could be mitigated by offering more extensive training or including participants with prior VR experiences. Moreover, comparing participants' responses to food dishes in VR and real-world settings could help isolate and control for the novelty effect associated with VR exposure.

5   Limitations and Future Research Directions

This study has several limitations. First, the experimental data for the VR group were collected in a laboratory setting, whereas data for the storytelling and control groups were collected online with remote participants. Research indicates that the demographic characteristics of online participants often differ from those recruited in laboratory settings [34]. Moreover, due to the unsupervised nature of remote experimentation, participants may not consistently attend to experimental stimuli or complete questionnaires with sufficient care [59]. Although individual difference factors were statistically controlled in the analysis of food perception, the differences in procedures and behaviors between laboratory and online environments may have weakened the reliability of the conclusions.

Second, this study did not fully account for the diverse physical and cultural environments of online participants in the storytelling and control groups. These participants provided subjective estimates of their room temperature, which may not accurately reflect the temperature of the actual outdoor environment or the seasonal context they were experiencing. Moreover, we did not collect information on participants' country of residence or culture background, both of which could influence interpretations of environmental cues, seasonal eating norms, and familiarity with specific foods. These uncontrolled individual factors may have introduced unexpected variability in how participants responded to the contextual manipulation.

Third, the number of participants included was relatively small, particularly for a between-subject design with modest effect sizes and substantial individual variability in eating behavior [60]. Therefore, the results reported in this study need to be interpreted with caution. Future research should increase the sample size covering a broader age range and geographic region, and investigate how more complex consumer character-istics—such as personality traits, emotional states, environmental beliefs, specific food preferences or aversions, and regional or cultural background—influence individuals' food-related attitudes and preferences.

Fourth, all high-calorie foods used in this study were ready-to-eat items, whereas the low-calorie foods typically required additional preparation or accompaniments to be consumed. While this approach likely enhanced the recognizability of food identity, differences in meal-readiness may have influenced participants' liking or desire ratings. In addition, all low-calorie foods were typically served cold, which may have made them feel less seasonally appropriate within the simulated winter environment. This raises the possibility that the observed higher desire and liking for high-calorie over low-calorie foods was driven not only by caloric density but also by perceived temperature suitability. Future studies should consider including prepared or warm versions of low-calorie foods (e.g., salads, vegetable soup) or using matched pairs to minimize potential confounds related to food temperature and preparation level.

Fifth, participants in the storytelling group proceeded to the food evaluation imme-diately after reading the text story, whereas participants in the VR group evaluated food items embedded within the virtual winter forest. This procedural difference may have affected the comparability of the two groups. To better align participants' experiences, future studies could either conduct the food evaluation task outside the VR environment or more directly integrate it into the narrative structure of the story.

Sixth, we only employed self-report questionnaires to measure related constructs. Although this method is convenient and widely used in consumer studies [61], it would be interesting to include eye-tracking, electroencephalography, and other physiological or behavioral measures to implicitly assess the effects of media use and contextual factors on food consumption.

Lastly, the food stimuli used in this study were restricted to visual information only (3D models and screenshots). Other senses such as smell, touch, and taste also play a crucial role in shaping our food perception [62]. In this regard, some emerging MR headsets enable the integration of multiple sensory modalities into simulated eating scenarios due to their ability to seamlessly blend digital and real-world elements [63]. Future research may consider using this technology to further bridge the gap between virtual and real food experiences.

6   Conclusions

The present study created winter forest environments using both VR simulation and text-based storytelling to assess their impact on individuals' perceptions of high- ver-sus low-calorie foods. The results indicate that both VR and storytelling can effectively immerse consumers in a context that influences their desire for food, with items con-gruent with the environmental context being more strongly wanted than incongruent ones. We also demonstrate that VR, compared to storytelling, triggers a stronger sense of spatial presence and higher sensory evaluations of food products. While VR is powerful in delivering interactive and emotionally engaging experiences, traditional low-tech storytelling may serve as a sufficient and accessible alternative for mimicking contextual cues in food evaluation tasks (see also [23]), considering that VR systems are remarkably more expensive and complex to set up. Together, our findings confirm the influence of environmental context on food perception and demonstrate that both high-fidelity immersive media and low-tech imaginative storytelling can shape evaluative responses to food. These insights contribute to the conceptual framework of multisensory processing and inform the future design of effective and scalable health interventions.

Acknowledgments. The authors would like to thank Jan Oliver Wallgrün for contributing to the development of the VR experience.

Disclosure of Interests. The authors have no competing interests to declare that are relevant to the content of this article.

Appendix

Winter is Coming In the heart of a barren forest, nestled beneath a slate-gray sky, a desolate winter scene unfolded. The icy jungle stretched out before me, its frozen embrace sending shivers down my spine. As I ventured deeper into this stark landscape, the chilling wind howled through the skeletal trees, its mournful whispers echoing in the stillness. The ground beneath my feet was covered in a thick layer of crisp, powdery snow. Each step I took sent a jolt of coldness through my boots as if the very ground itself held a frosty secret. The branches above me creaked under the weight of frost, their delicate icicles threatening to plummet at any moment.

As I peered into the distance, the world seemed drained of color. The once vibrant greens were replaced by a palette of grays and whites, the monotony was broken only by the occasional glimpse of a deep, frozen blue. The air was so cold that it felt tangible, each breath a frigid reminder of the inhospitable environment.

The wildlife, adapted to survive in this harsh realm, remained elusive. Occasionally, a fleeting shadow darted between the trees, its presence barely registering before disappearing into the frost-laden underbrush. The animals knew better than to linger in the open, seeking shelter from the relentless winter cold.

In this frigid realm, silence prevailed. The stillness seemed to seep into my bones, making them ache with the cold. The wind whispered haunting melodies, carrying with it a sense of isolation and solitude. I bundled up in my thickest layers, trying to shield myself from the biting gusts that seemed determined to penetrate every inch of exposed skin.

The sunlight, feeble and distant, struggled to break through the thick cloud cover. Its weak rays cast long, distorted shadows across the icy ground, offering little respite from the bone-chilling cold. The landscape appeared frozen in time, suspended between the icy grip of winter and the distant hope of warmth.

References

1. Manippa, V., Padulo, C., van der Laan, L.N., Brancucci, A.: Gender differences in food choice: effects of superior temporal sulcus stimulation. Front. Hum. Neurosci. **11**, 597 (2017). https://doi.org/10.3389/fnhum.2017.00597
2. Bustamante, V.M.O., Aguirre, S.I.H., Moreno, A.M.M., Hermida, C.E.C.: Trends in food processing: innovations for healthy and sustainable eating. JNS **33** (2023). https://doi.org/10.59670/jns.v33i.1038
3. Carels, R.A., Konrad, K., Harper, J.: Individual differences in food perceptions and calorie estimation: an examination of dieting status, weight, and gender. Appetite **49**, 450–458 (2007). https://doi.org/10.1016/j.appet.2007.02.009
4. Spence, C., Ho, C.: Multisensory information processing. In: Boehm-Davis, D.A., Durso, F.T., Lee, J.D. (eds.) APA handbook of human systems integration, pp. 435–448. American Psychological Association, Washington (2015). https://doi.org/10.1037/14528-027
5. Zampini, M., Spence, C.: Assessing the role of visual and auditory cues in multisensory perception of flavor. In: Murray, M.M., Wallace, M.T. (eds.) The neural bases of multisensory processes. Frontiers in neuroscience, vol. 20111651, pp. 739–758. CRC Press, Boca Raton (2012). https://doi.org/10.1201/9781439812174-47
6. Hartmann, C., Siegrist, M.: 16 - Virtual reality and immersive approaches to contextual food testing. In: Meiselman, H.L. (ed.) Context, pp. 323–338. Woodhead Publishing (2019). https://doi.org/10.1016/B978-0-12-814495-4.00016-7
7. McDermott, R.: Internal and external validity. In: Druckman, J.N., Greene, D.P., Kuklinski, J.H., Lupia, A. (eds.) Cambridge Handbook of Experimental Political Science, pp. 27–40. Cambridge University Press (2011)
8. Park, S., Heo, J., Oh, J., Chung, S.-J., Sub Kwak, H.: Consumer testing away from a sensory facility: application of home-use test and no-contact home-use test. Food Qual. Prefer. **109**, 104905 (2023). https://doi.org/10.1016/j.foodqual.2023.104905
9. Pallavicini, F., Pepe, A., Minissi, M.E.: Gaming in virtual reality. what changes in terms of usability, emotional response and sense of presence compared to non-immersive video games? Simulation & Gaming **50**, 136–159 (2019). https://doi.org/10.1177/1046878119831420
10. Brooks, J., et al.: Smell, taste, and temperature interfaces. In: Kitamura, Y., Quigley, A., Isbister, K., Igarashi, T. (eds.) CHI EA'21: Extended Abstracts of the 2021 CHI Conference on Human Factors in Computing Systems, pp. 1–6. Association for Computing Machinery, New York NY (2021). https://doi.org/10.1145/3411763.3441317
11. Lombart, C., Millan, E., Normand, J.-M., Verhulst, A., Labbé-Pinlon, B., Moreau, G.: Effects of physical, non-immersive virtual, and immersive virtual store environments on consumers' perceptions and purchase behavior. Comput. Hum. Behav. **110**, 106374 (2020). https://doi.org/10.1016/j.chb.2020.106374
12. Schnack, A., Wright, M.J., Holdershaw, J.L.: An exploratory investigation of shopper behaviour in an immersive virtual reality store. J. Consum. Behav. **19**, 182–195 (2020). https://doi.org/10.1002/cb.1803
13. Ho, D., Lee, Y.-C., Chiu, W.-C., Su, H.-Y., Chang, J.-S.: A pilot study of integrating interactive digital 2D and 3D food models for virtual dietary assessment training in dietetic course. Clinical Nutrition ESPEN **54**, 514–515 (2023)
14. Xu, C., Siegrist, M., Hartmann, C.: The application of virtual reality in food consumer behavior research: a systematic review. Trends Food Sci. Technol. **116**, 533–544 (2021). https://doi.org/10.1016/j.tifs.2021.07.015
15. Schöniger, M.K.: The role of immersive environments in the assessment of consumer perceptions and product acceptance: a systematic literature review. Food Qual. Prefer. **99**, 104490 (2022). https://doi.org/10.1016/j.foodqual.2021.104490

16. Zhao, J., Riecke, B.E., Kelly, J.W., Stefanucci, J., Klippel, A.: Editorial: human spatial perception, cognition, and behaviour in extended reality. Front. Virtual Real. **4** (2023). https://doi.org/10.3389/frvir.2023.1257230

17. Siegrist, M., et al.: Consumers' food selection behaviors in three-dimensional (3D) virtual reality. Food Research International (Ottawa, Ont.), **117**, 50–59 (2019). https://doi.org/10.1016/j.foodres.2018.02.033

18. Ung, C.-Y., Menozzi, M., Hartmann, C., Siegrist, M.: Innovations in consumer research: the virtual food buffet. Food Qual. Prefer. **63**, 12–17 (2018). https://doi.org/10.1016/j.foodqual.2017.07.007

19. Taufik, D., Kunz, M.C., Onwezen, M.C.: Changing consumer behaviour in virtual reality: a systematic literature review. Computers in Human Behavior Reports **3**, 100093 (2021). https://doi.org/10.1016/j.chbr.2021.100093

20. Long, J.W., et al.: Portion size affects food selection in an immersive virtual reality buffet and is related to measured intake in laboratory meals varying in portion size. Appetite **191**, 107052 (2023). https://doi.org/10.1016/j.appet.2023.107052

21. Wang, Q.J., Meyer, R., Waters, S., Zendle, D.: A dash of virtual milk: altering product color in virtual reality influences flavor perception of cold-brew coffee. Front. Psychol. **11**, 595788 (2020). https://doi.org/10.3389/fpsyg.2020.595788

22. Goedegebure, R.P., van Herpen, E., van Trijp, H.C.: Using product popularity to stimulate choice for light products in supermarkets: an examination in virtual reality. Food Qual. Prefer. **79**, 103786 (2020). https://doi.org/10.1016/j.foodqual.2019.103786

23. Köster, E., Mojet, J.: Complexity of consumer perception. In: Ares, G., Varela, P. (eds.) Methods in consumer research. Woodhead Publishing Series in Food Science, Technology and Nutrition, pp. 23–45. WP Woodhead Publishing an imprint of Elsevier, Duxford United Kingdom (2018). https://doi.org/10.1016/B978-0-08-102089-0.00002-9

24. Dijksterhuis, G., Wijk, R. de, Onwezen, M.: New consumer research technology for food behaviour: overview and validity. Foods (Basel, Switzerland) **11** (2022). https://doi.org/10.3390/foods11050767

25. Sundermann, A., Fischer, D., Fücker, S., Hanss, D., Selm, H.: Does storytelling for sustainability work? an experiment. In: Fischer, D., Fücker, S., Selm, H. (eds.) Narrating sustainability through storytelling. Routledge-SCORAI Studies in Sustainable Consumption Series, pp. 26–44. Routledge, New York (2023). https://doi.org/10.4324/9781003326144-5

26. Huang, Y., Benford, S., Spence, J., Blake, H.: Exploring effects of a nostalgic storytelling virtual reality experience beyond hedonism. Cyberpsychol. Behav. Soc. Netw. **27**, 221–226 (2024). https://doi.org/10.1089/cyber.2023.0183

27. Prentice, A.M., Rayco-Solon, P., Moore, S.E.: Insights from the developing world: thrifty genotypes and thrifty phenotypes. Proc. Nutr. Soc. **64**, 153–161 (2005). https://doi.org/10.1079/PNS2005421

28. Humphries, M.M., Studd, E.K., Menzies, A.K., Boutin, S.: To everything there is a season: summer-to-winter food webs and the functional traits of keystone species. Integr. Comp. Biol. **57**, 961–976 (2017). https://doi.org/10.1093/icb/icx119

29. Mendes, E.: U.S. Health Habits Continue Sharp Winter Decline. GALLUP (2011)

30. Liu, R., Hannum, M., Simons, C.T.: Using immersive technologies to explore the effects of congruent and incongruent contextual cues on context recall, product evaluation time, and preference and liking during consumer hedonic testing. Food research international (Ottawa, Ont.), **117**, 19–29 (2019). https://doi.org/10.1016/j.foodres.2018.04.024

31. Schouteten, J.J., van Severen, A., Dull, D., de Steur, H., Danner, L.: Congruency of an eating environment influences product liking: a virtual reality study. Food Qual. Prefer. **113**, 105066 (2024). https://doi.org/10.1016/j.foodqual.2023.105066

32. Folwarczny, M., Otterbring, T., Sigurdsson, V., Gasiorowska, A.: Seasonal cues to food scarcity and calorie cravings: winter cues elicit preferences for energy-dense foods. Food Qual. Prefer. **96**, 104379 (2022). https://doi.org/10.1016/j.foodqual.2021.104379

33. Blechert, J., Meule, A., Busch, N.A., Ohla, K.: Food-pics: an image database for experimental research on eating and appetite. Front. Psychol. **5**, 617 (2014). https://doi.org/10.3389/fpsyg.2014.00617

34. Zhao, J., et al.: CrowdXR - pitfalls and potentials of experiments with remote participants. In: 2021 IEEE International Symposium on Mixed and Augmented Reality (ISMAR), pp. 450–459 (2021). https://doi.org/10.1109/ISMAR52148.2021.00062

35. Zhao, J., Klippel, A.: Scale - unexplored opportunities for immersive technologies in place-based learning. In: Teather, R., Itoh, Y., Gabbard, J. (eds.) Proceedings of the 26th IEEE Conference on Virtual Reality and 3D User Interfaces, pp. 155–162. IEEE, Piscataway, NJ (2019). https://doi.org/10.1109/VR.2019.8797867

36. Helland, A., Lydersen, S., Lervåg, L.-E., Jenssen, G.D., Mørland, J., Slørdal, L.: Driving simulator sickness: Impact on driving performance, influence of blood alcohol concentration, and effect of repeated simulator exposures. Accident; Analysis and Prevention **94**, 180–187 (2016). https://doi.org/10.1016/j.aap.2016.05.008

37. Keller, V.: Segmenting Hungarian people based on healthy eating. Apstract **13**, 65–72 (2019). https://doi.org/10.19041/APSTRACT/2019/3-4/8

38. World Health Organization: A healthy lifestyle - WHO recommendations (2010). https://www.who.int/europe/news-room/fact-sheets/item/a-healthy-lifestyle---who-recommendations

39. Prentice, A.M., Jebb, S.A.: Beyond body mass index. Obesity Reviews : an Official J. International Association for the Study of Obesity **2**, 141–147 (2001). https://doi.org/10.1046/j.1467-789x.2001.00031.x

40. World Health Organization: Obesity: preventing and managing the global epidemic (1998)

41. Revelle, W.: psych: Procedures for Psychological, Psychometric, and Personality Research [R package]. R package version 2.5.3. Northwestern University, Evanston, Illinois. https://CRAN.R-project.org/package=psych (2025)

42. Pinheiro, J., Bates, D.: nlme: Linear and Nonlinear Mixed Effects Models. R package version 3.1–168. https://CRAN.R-project.org/package=nlme (2025)

43. van Buuren, S., Groothuis-Oudshoorn, K.: mice : Multivariate Imputation by Chained Equations in R. J. Stat. Soft. **45** (2011). https://doi.org/10.18637/jss.v045.i03

44. Lenth, R.V.: Emmeans: Estimated Marginal Means, aka Least-Squares Means. R package version 1.11.0. https://rvlenth.github.io/emmeans/ (2025)

45. Li, S., Zeng, Y., Zhou, S.: The congruence effect of food shape and name typeface on consumers' food preferences. Food Qual. Prefer. **86**, 104017 (2020). https://doi.org/10.1016/j.foodqual.2020.104017

46. van Bergen, G., Zandstra, E.H., Kaneko, D., Dijksterhuis, G.B., de Wijk, R.A.: Sushi at the beach: effects of congruent and incongruent immersive contexts on food evaluations. Food Qual. Prefer. **91**, 104193 (2021). https://doi.org/10.1016/j.foodqual.2021.104193

47. Higgs, S., Spetter, M.S.: Cognitive control of eating: the role of memory in appetite and weight gain. Curr. Obes. Rep. **7**, 50–59 (2018). https://doi.org/10.1007/s13679-018-0296-9

48. Breslin, P.A.S.: An evolutionary perspective on food and human taste. Current biology : CB **23**, R409–R418 (2013). https://doi.org/10.1016/j.cub.2013.04.010

49. Drewnowski, A., Almiron-Roig, E.: Human perceptions and preferences for fat-rich foods. In: Montmayeur, J.-P., Le Coutre, J. (eds.) Fat detection. Taste, texture, and post ingestive effects. Frontiers in neuroscience, vol. 20096070, pp. 265–291. CRC Press/Taylor & Francis, Boca Raton (2010). https://doi.org/10.1201/9781420067767-c11

50. Finlayson, G., King, N., Blundell, J.E.: Liking vs. wanting food: importance for human appetite control and weight regulation. Neuroscience and Biobehavioral Reviews **31**, 987–1002 (2007). https://doi.org/10.1016/j.neubiorev.2007.03.004

51. Andersen, I.N.S.K., Kraus, A.A., Ritz, C., Bredie, W.L.P.: Desires for beverages and liking of skin care product odors in imaginative and immersive virtual reality beach contexts. Food Research International (Ottawa, Ont.) **117**, 10–18 (2019). https://doi.org/10.1016/j.foodres.2018.01.027

52. Manippa, V., Ferracci, S., Pietroni, D., Brancucci, A.: Can the position on the screen of an image influence its judgment? The case of high- and low-calorie foods. Food Qual. Prefer. **96**, 104407 (2022). https://doi.org/10.1016/j.foodqual.2021.104407

53. Wirth, W., et al.: A process model of the formation of spatial presence experiences. Media Psychol. **9**, 493–525 (2007). https://doi.org/10.1080/15213260701283079

54. Coxon, M., Kelly, N., Page, S.: Individual differences in virtual reality: are spatial presence and spatial ability linked? Virtual Reality **20**, 203–212 (2016). https://doi.org/10.1007/s10055-016-0292-x

55. Birch, L.L.: Development of food preferences. Annu. Rev. Nutr. **19**, 41–62 (1999). https://doi.org/10.1146/annurev.nutr.19.1.41

56. Ramousse, F., et al.: Does this virtual food make me hungry? effects of visual quality and food type in virtual reality. Front. Virtual Real **4** (2023). https://doi.org/10.3389/frvir.2023.1221651

57. Zhao, J., et al.: Longitudinal effects in the effectiveness of educational virtual field trips. J. Educational Computing Research, pp. 1–27 (2021). https://doi.org/10.1177/07356331211062925

58. Makransky, G., Lilleholt, L.: A structural equation modeling investigation of the emotional value of immersive virtual reality in education. Education Tech. Research Dev. **66**, 1141–1164 (2018). https://doi.org/10.1007/s11423-018-9581-2

59. Stewart, J., et al.: Comparison of racial, ethnic, and geographic location diversity of participants enrolled in clinic-based vs 2 remote COVID-19 clinical trials. JAMA Netw. Open **5**, e2148325 (2022). https://doi.org/10.1001/jamanetworkopen.2021.48325

60. Jeltema, M., Beckley, J., Vahalik, J.: Model for understanding consumer textural food choice. Food Sci. Nutr. **3**, 202–212 (2015). https://doi.org/10.1002/fsn3.205

61. Bell, L., Vogt, J., Willemse, C., Routledge, T., Butler, L.T., Sakaki, M.: Beyond self-report: a review of physiological and neuroscientific methods to investigate consumer behavior. Front. Psychol. **9**, 1655 (2018). https://doi.org/10.3389/fpsyg.2018.01655

62. Colebrooke, L.: The perfect meal: the multisensory science of food and dining. The International Journal of Sociology of Agriculture and Food, **22**(2) (2015). https://doi.org/10.48416/ijsaf.v22i2.133

63. Chai, J.J., O'Sullivan, C., Gowen, A.A., Rooney, B., Xu, J.-L.: Augmented/mixed reality technologies for food: a review. Trends Food Sci. Technol. **124**, 182–194 (2022). https://doi.org/10.1016/j.tifs.2022.04.021

A User Experience Evaluation of Volumetric Capture Within the Performing Arts

Eoghan Hynes[1]($\boxtimes$), Bryan Dunphy[1], Conor Keighrey[1], Niall Murray[1], Gareth Young[2], and Colm O'Feaghail[2]

[1] Technological University of the Shannon, Midlands and Midwest, Athlone, Ireland
Eoghan.Hynes@TUS.ie
[2] Trinity College Dublin, Dublin, Ireland

Abstract. Volumetric capture (VolCap) systems are advanced technologies used to capture three-dimensional representations of people, objects, or environments in motion. They provide a means of creating high-quality content essential for professional immersive performing arts experiences. Nascent VolCap systems have not yet resulted in a single standard with few commercial offerings available. In this paper, performer, technician and director user experience (UX) was evaluated using three state-of-the-art VolCap systems in thirteen live performance capture configurations. The performances were volumetrically captured on site, outside of the controlled studio environment. Semi-structured post-experience interviews were conducted. A modified system usability scale was used to record UX. A thematic analysis of the data revealed six themes, strengthened by sentiment analysis. This included significant themes of operational and logistical learnings that resulted in a set of guidelines for use by professionals embarking on volumetric capture of live performances.

Keywords: Volumetric Capture · User Experience · Performing Arts

1 Introduction

Volumetric capture (VolCap) systems push the boundaries of creativity and expression in the performing arts by enabling the creation of lifelike digital characters, content for interactive storytelling experiences, and innovative stage productions. Such content can be enjoyed in real-time or as pre-recorded extended reality (XR) productions [1]. The realism of these productions aims to provide the attention and emotional engagement of truly immersive experiences [2]. Systems using RGB and RGB-D cameras combined with volumetric video (VV) reconstruction techniques are the predominant VolCap solutions [3]. However, due to the relatively recent emergence of volumetric capture systems, there is no standard specification, resulting in a variety of custom-made systems [4, 5]. Evaluation of live performance VolCap user experience (UX) other than the audience is absent from the literature.

This paper investigated how Volcap UX impacted the stakeholders' (technicians', director, and performers') ability to create high quality immersive performances by posing the research question: *How does the user experience of performers, directors, and technicians influence their ability to create volumetric video representations of live performances?* This was achieved by means of a thematic and sentiment analysis of stakeholder UX of the three separate systems, in thirteen different configurations. Two of the systems were based on RGB-D cameras (Kinects™) [6] while the third was based on RGB cameras (Blackmagic™, see Fig. 1) combined with cutting edge VV reconstruction techniques [7]. These systems were chosen because they represented the full spectrum of state-of-the art VV production, from accessible, low-cost solutions (Kinect-based [6]) to high-fidelity, studio-grade setups (Blackmagic-based). By selecting these systems, we were able to capture a broad range of UX across varying levels of technical complexity, fidelity, and production scalability. This diversity was critical to understanding how stakeholders' creative and technical agency is influenced not only by system performance but also by practical constraints such as setup time, calibration demands, and reliability during live performance contexts. The 13 different configurations consisted of 1:1 linear meter to performer increments, each requiring sensor and lighting calibrations. The camera and lighting configurations gave rise to additional experimental configurations such as $210°$ and rectangular camera arrangements.

The stakeholders completed written and oral interviews after each capture, leading to two key guidelines: one on the design or acquisition of VolCap systems, and one on their implementation for live multi-performer capture. Through iterative testing, we identified a spatial limitation of approximately 5 m^2 for RGB-D systems in circular setups. Performer feedback indicated that exceeding a density of one performer per 1.3 m^2 led to feelings of confinement, particularly in choreographies requiring full limb extension. However, this could be mitigated through practice, synchronization, and the use of spatial reference points, such as lights or cameras, to anchor performers during disorienting movements. In rectangular configurations, RGB-D systems suffered from blind spots beyond 7×4 m due to limited sensor overlapping. This constraint was not present in the RGB camera-based system (see Fig. 1), which offered broader spatial coverage through focal length adjustments and required less physical repositioning of hardware. However, this benefit came with longer calibration times and increased power usage. Systems that included real-time graphical feedback, either via dedicated monitors or custom GUIs, were strongly preferred, whereas a command line interface (CLI)-based system was perceived as less supportive for artistic direction.

In summary, this evaluation probed the boundaries of contemporary VolCap in terms of spatial limits, performer density, and UX support. It yielded practical guidelines for professionals: VolCap systems should offer real-time feedback and spatial flexibility to accommodate familiar stage formats, and usage practices should limit performer density or support movement synchronization to maintain comfort and expression in confined volumes. Future work will explore how UX relates to post-processed capture quality, with a focus on integrating advanced reconstruction techniques such as GPS-Gaussian and 4K4D to further enhance volumetric fidelity. To contextualize this evaluation and highlight the gap it addresses, the following section critiques the prior state-of-the-art in Volcap UX research in performance contexts.

Fig. 1. An 8m^2 capture area containing 5 performers conducting a standardized choreography of lateral limb extensions, featuring DSLR studio cameras combined with floor and tripod lighting.

2 Related Work

VolCap systems [8] have emerged as a revolutionary technology in the performing arts, offering new possibilities for immersive and interactive experiences [9]. In the performing arts, VolCap systems enable the recording and playback of three-dimensional representations of live performances, allowing audiences to engage with the content from their chosen perspectives [10]. The need for evaluation of stakeholder engagement with VolCap systems in order to ensure and democratize the realization of their potential benefits is an open question [11]. While many studies have used audience feedback to inform VolCap system design, the influence of VolCap system usage on the performer, director and technicians' ability to create engaging content for these target audiences is notably absent from the literature. This paper addresses this shortcoming by investigating performer, director and technician UX in the context of volumetric capture of the performing arts.

Prior works have established the importance of volumetrically capturing the essence of live performances [12, 13]. However, due to the relatively recent emergence of VolCap systems, a single standard end-to-end process does not exist. The focus has been on efficient and effective solutions for multi-sensor calibration [14], capture and reconstruction [15, 16]. One example of technical refinement is the pipeline by Prada et al. [22], which constructed motion graphs from unstructured, textured meshes by matching similar segments, fitting a common template, and synthesizing intermediate frames via mesh-based optical flow and deformation. Tested on multiple datasets (up to 2,000 + frames), it supported seamless loops and user-driven playback. However, despite its impact on volumetric content manipulation, it did not examine the experiences of the creative professionals who operate these tools, exemplifying a focus on system performance over practitioner engagement. Where research in this field focuses on the refinement of VolCap solutions, it is largely guided by audience UX [3, 7, 9, 11]. For example, Lischer-Katz et al. recently evaluated student engagement, highlighting the impact of VV on emotional engagement, storytelling authenticity, and learning enhancement compared to traditional texts and videos [11]. Similarly, K. Wise [9] used audience feedback to evaluate how volumetric performances in virtual reality (VR) resonated with end users. Although the author did reflect on how technical constraints informed choreographic and audience experience designs, the work focused on analyzing audience feelings of intimacy and empathy to assess the emotional and narrative impact of the performance.

While the user trials critiqued in this related work section reflect how audience UX can inform volumetric content creation, the focus of our work is to understand how VolCap system usage influences the performing art professional's ability to produce the engaging content for these target audiences. To examine these UX considerations in practice, three state-of-the-art VolCap systems were deployed outside of the controlled laboratory. The following section details the technical specifications and capture configurations of the systems used in this study.

3 Volumetric Capture Systems: Specifications and Experimental Configurations

This section outlines the hardware and software specifications of the three different volumetric capture systems used in this evaluation. It details the camera setups, their specifications and their settings. It provides a comprehensive technical context within which this research evaluated the stakeholders' UX of working with these systems.

3.1 System 1

The components of System 1 and their settings are presented in Table 1 of supplementary materials for the interested reader [17]. The Kinects™ and NUCs™ were connected by means of Ethernet RJ45 cables. These were connected in turn to a MacBook™ via the cisco switch. The 13″ 2019 MacBook™ had an Intel™ Core i5™ quadcore processor, 16 GB RAM, Intel™ Iris 645™ graphics with 1536 MB of dedicated RAM. The CPU was clocked at 1.4 GHz and the RAM was clocked at 2.1 MHz. The cameras were positioned 1.5 m above the ground at 45° of separation, 360° around a central focal point as per Fig. 2. These were connected to mains power and the NUCs via USB. Additionally, studio lights were arranged around the recording area to provide ample illumination and maintain a predictable white balance. Shutter synchronization between cameras was achieved by wiring the SYNC™ ports of the Kinect™ cameras in a daisy chain, with the first camera being the sync master. The laptop started the recordings on all cameras by invoking a Shell script on each of the NUC machines connected to the cameras. Performing this process from a central machine via a CLI enabled the system to start camera recordings in close sequence with the exact same values for settings such as white balance, exposure time, gain, frame rate and file format. After each recording, the recorded files were collected from the NUCs on the central machine via SSH. The files were verified and backed up on external storage.

3.2 System 2

This system consisted of similar equipment to System 1 but was differentiated from it by the settings of the Kinects™ and the laptop used as seen in Table 1 or supplementary material [17]. The laptop was an MSI Katana™ with an Intel™ Core i7™ 11800h processor clocked at 2.3Ghz, 16GB of RAM and an Nvidia™ 3060 graphics card. In addition to this, the custom software differentiates this system in capture and post processing of the volumetric data. System 2 was designed as a distributed system, where eight Intel™ NUCs™ manage and collect data from a single sensor. The set of sensors was orchestrated by a centralized application featuring a custom-made GUI [6]. Communication is handled by a RabbitMQ broker. System 2 performs temporal (software synchronization) and spatial calibration between the cameras.

Multi-sensor spatial calibration was performed using QR codes attached to a structure made from stacking 4 IKEA™ JATTENE™ boxes on top of each other oriented at 90° to one another. All the sensors were perimetrically oriented towards this structure which acted as the global coordinate system anchor. This was a two-step approach for volumetric sensor alignment. In the first step, the a-priori geometric knowledge of the box structure facilitated 3D coordinate estimation using the depth sensors by establishing 3D-point correspondences between the sensor's point cloud and the structure's virtual model. The second step completes the volumetric alignment of multiple sensors by performing a dense optimization refinement using each sensor's initial pose estimate, reaching a global solution. This calibration was performed by the system technician using the custom-made GUI.

3.3 System 3

The hardware components of this system can be seen in Fig. 1. The system specifications and settings of this system's components are shown in Table 2 of the supplementary material [18]. The performances were captured using 6 HD and 64 K DSLR cameras as seen in Fig. 1. These were positioned in alternation with 30o of separation, 360° around a central focal point. The cameras were placed at alternating heights of 1.1m and 3m above the floor in different capture configurations during the workshop. Table 2 shows the Blackmagic™ monitors that provided real time feedback to system technicians and the artistic director. This model is capable of interpreting depth information from the multiple perspectives of the DSLR video cameras. The calibration of the system during the workshop required that audio, ColorChecker® and calibration objects were recorded. The calibration objects consisted of a ChArUco board for intrinsic calibration [19], a ChArUco box for extrinsic calibration, and a calibration totem. The color correction and synchronization based on audio were applied in post-processing through DaVinci Resolve™. In practice, the cameras were calibrated through COLMAP [20] using footage of the calibration totem.

With the systems defined, the following section outlines the experimental protocol used to evaluate stakeholder experiences across multiple configurations.

4 Experimental Protocol

This section describes sample demographics and the experimental protocol. This section also describes the post-production semi-structured interview methodology, including a Reflexive Thematic Analysis (RTA) method based on Braun and Clarke's approach [21]. The data was collected at the Horizon Europe TRANSMIXR project's performance workshop, January 12th - 14th 2024. This workshop brought together four partners from the Centre for Research Technology (CERTH) Hella, Greece, Technological University of the Shannon (TUS) Athlone Ireland, Centrum Wiskunde Informatica (CWI) Amsterdam, Satore Studios Lisbon and Trinity College Dublin to perform collaborative experiments to test the limits of state-of-the-art depth-sensor and photogrammetry-based volumetric capture systems. Over the course of the 3-day workshop, a total of thirteen configurations (see Table 3 of supplementary material [22]) were explored in the systems.

On day 1, an initial lead-in set up and calibration for the first capture area of 2 m^2 was performed. After each production, each system was set-up and calibrated prior to capturing the performance in the subsequent configuration. There were two different styles of dance used during the workshop. The first style, referred to as the standard performance in Table 3 of the supplementary material, consisted of full lateral extension of the left and right arms to each side in turn, with the feet remaining stationary. Then the left and right feet were extended laterally along the ground while keeping their arms stationary. Next, the performers combined both movements by fully extending their limbs laterally in turn to the left and to the right as per Fig. 1. Finally, a double 360° spin completed the choreography. The alternative dance style used during the evaluation was a common Irish dance known to the competitive performers. The experimental protocol was conducted as follows.

1. The artistic director signaled the performer's entry into the capture space. The performer entered and executed the choreography in time with the director's counting.
2. An additional performer then entered the performance area, and the performance was repeated.
3. Step 2 was repeated until the number of performers in the space was equal to the metric length of the capture space i.e., 3 performers for 3 m^2, 4 performers for 4 m^2 etc.
4. After each performance, the performers, technicians and director completed a questionnaire and an oral interview.
5. Following this, the capture areas were expanded by 1 m^2. The system was calibrated for the larger area while the performers enjoyed refreshments and rest.
6. This protocol was repeated up to 8m^2 area. Experiments 5,6,7 and 11 of Table 3 in the supplementary material used rectangular configurations.

Having described how the captures were staged and executed, the next section outlines the methods used to evaluate stakeholder experiences and analyze the data collected.

4.1 Evaluation Methodology

This section describes the participants, the questionnaire and the semi-structured interviews. This is followed by a description of the data analysis methods for the questionnaire and interview responses. Sentiment analysis of the performers' open-ended questionnaire responses was used to support and enrich the thematic analysis of interview transcripts. While themes were developed inductively from the interviews, sentiment scores provided a parallel signal, helping to validate or highlight contrast in the emotional tone of specific topics. This triangulation ensured that insights reflected both what participants said and how they felt about each system. In addition to this, a descriptive analysis of the within- (technicians) and between-groups (performers and the director) modified system usability scale (SUS) responses was undertaken.

4.2 Participants

The participants consisted of award-winning competitive dancers (the performers), published technicians in the volumetric capture field and an award-winning director. This range of roles and expertise areas reflect the key stakeholders involved in immersive VV production. These partners were brought together under the auspices of the Horizon Europe TRANSMIXR project. The performers sample consisted of six females and two males of Irish nationality ranging in age from late teens to early twenties. The sample of 8 performers provided an ample selection of rested performers for each configuration. The technician sample consisted of six males hailing from the Netherlands, Greece, Italy and Ireland ranging in age from mid-twenties to mid-fifties. The Mexican-born male director was aged in his late forties. Each participant was designated with a unique identifier to provide complete anonymity (e.g. Performer 01).

4.3 Questionnaire

The modified SUS questionnaire [23] consisted of three five-point Likert-scale questions that were chosen and adapted from the IBM system usability questionnaire [24] to cover ease-of-use (EOU), usability and learnability. The questionnaire also included open-ended questions that were completed by all stakeholders after each capture and served as a prompt for the semi-structured interview questions.

4.4 Interviews

Two independent interviewers conducted oral interviews and ensured that the questionnaires were completed after each capture. One interviewer interviewed the performers while the other interviewed the technicians and the director. The interviews consisted of the three open-ended questions which the interested reader can find here [23].

4.5 Data Analysis Methods

The performers and the artistic director experienced all three systems in a within-groups study design. The technicians used only their own systems in a between-groups study design. Sentiment analysis was performed on the performers' written responses to the open-ended questions. A Python script was developed to leverage TensorFlow™ 2.17 with the cardiffnlp/twitter-roberta-base-sentiment model, available from the Hugging

Face repository [25]. This model was used because it provides classifications for neutral sentiments in addition to negative and positive sentiments. This was important where the performers responses were often relative to previous productions in the workshop running order, which were often mis-attributed with negative sentiment despite being neutral by other models (e.g., distilbert-base-uncased-finetuned-sst-2-english). Nuanced neutral sentiment, such as a phrase like 'tight space', is not explicitly negative out of context, and was treated cautiously. Despite this, explicitly negative and positive sentiment provided a good indication of system preference amongst the performers.

As a first step of the RTA, the oral interviews were transcribed using a speech-to-text transformer-based web service [26]. These transcripts were then validated by the interviewers. The transcripts were then analyzed by two independent reviewers. This was done to ensure the robustness of theme development while eliminating bias. Each independent reviewer undertook the following ten thematic analysis steps:

1. **Familiarization with the data:** Thoroughly reviewed the transcripts to get a sense of the content and context.
2. **Data Preparation:** Removal of any identifiable information to ensure anonymity and confidentiality.
3. **Initial Coding:** Generation of initial short labels that summarize meaningful concepts, ideas, and phrases.
4. **Create a Codebook:** A list of each code, its definition, and examples of its application, to maintain consistency.
5. **Sorting Codes into Categories:** Identify commonalities between codes that represent broader concepts.
6. **Theme Development:** Refine the categories to identify interpretive themes that capture the essence of the data.
7. **Review and refine themes:** Ensure coherent, distinct themes that are relevant to the research objective.
8. **Data retrieval:** Retrieve interview quotes that provide evidence for the theme.
9. **Data analysis:** Look for patterns, variations or sub-themes to support interpretations.
10. **Interpretation:** Reflection on the meaning and significance of the themes.

The following section presents the results of the modified SUS questionnaire, sentiment and thematic analysis of stakeholder feedback across the three systems.

5   Results

This section describes the results of the questionnaire responses emanating from analysis of the modified SUS responses. Sentiment analysis was performed on the performers' open-ended questionnaire responses (see [23]). This section also discusses the results of an RTA analysis of the verbal interview responses across the thirteen configurations of the three volumetric capture systems.

5.1 Questionnaire Results

This section reports the modified SUS responses descriptively using mean values by stakeholder type across the three systems. The stakeholder types were performer, technician and director. A description of this data between the systems allows for the indication of the influence of the different systems on stakeholder UX considering the 13 configurations experienced in each system.

Modified SUS Results. All stakeholders rated System 3 highest for EOU. The performers and the director also rated System 3 as the most usable and learnable. The following thematic analysis section discusses how a perception of restriction caused by quantity of performers co-located in the capture area was the greater influencing factor than system configuration on performer UX. The technicians found System 2 the easiest to learn. Bearing in mind this was a within-groups repeated measure, this reflects the technicians' familiarity with their own systems despite the experimental nature of usage outside of the controlled laboratory environment. Full mean scores are available in Table 4 of supplementary material [27]. The following thematic analysis section shows that the director and technicians' aversion to System 1 was related in part to its lack of a GUI.

Open-ended Question Sentiment Analysis. Performer sentiment showed a minor preference for System 3 as seen in Fig. 2. This coincides with a preference for larger performance spaces afforded by adjustment of lens focal length only in this system. This sentiment is broken down within each system by configuration in Fig. 3.

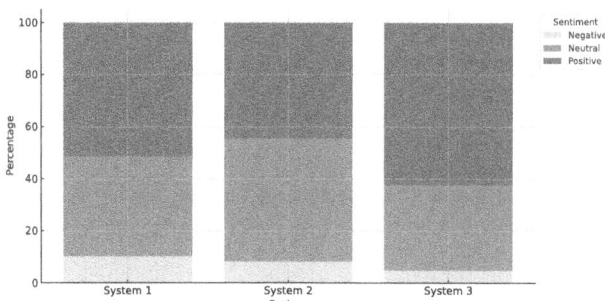

Fig. 2. A Stacked Bar Chart of overall performer sentiment across all three systems showing less negative and neutral sentiment and more positive sentiment for System 3.

This shows that the performers' configuration preference was informed not only by larger capture space but also by performance type. The performers reported more positive sentiment towards the more energetic Irish Dancing performance.

5.2 Thematic Analysis of Interviews

An RTA of data gathered from the semi-structured interviews revealed six overarching themes. This section defines each theme and provides illustrative examples from the participants.

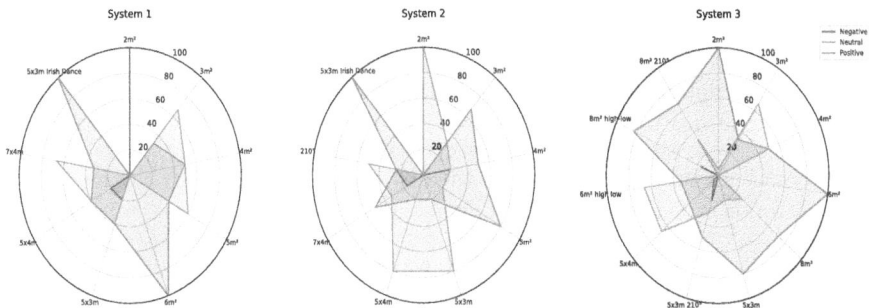

Fig. 3. Percentage of performer sentiment towards the 13 configurations of the 3 systems, showing consistency in positive sentiment towards larger spaces and dancing performances.

1. **Challenges and solutions to spatial awareness on performance quality**

   This theme combines the influence of spatial layout and spatial perception on performance quality and performer emotional state. Performers consistently reported that their sense of space - affected by system configuration, choreography style, and positioning - had a direct influence on their ability to perform confidently and comfortably.

   Key factors included:

- The number of performers co-located in the capture space.
- The performer's position in the choreography.
- Choreography style (arm movement or footwork).
- Anxiety around unintentionally colliding with others and equipment.

   Performers reported increased anxiety in tighter formations due to the quantity of collocated performers.

   "It got more squished when there were people either side of me." – Performer 05 (System 3, 6 m^2, 360o, high-low).

   This led to an impact on emotional state, with performers reporting feelings of tension or restraint when space was limited:

   "I took a tiny step back. Even just the outline, a tiny bit. Just so there'd be more room for me, so I'm not hitting anyone." – Performer 03 (System 2, 4x4 m).

   This tension can be relieved by choreography type, for example the Irish dancing choreography, which involved limited upper body movement, which felt less restricted:

   "The first performance was tight on the arm movements, but the Irish dancing was grand, there was a lot of space." – Performer 04 (System 3, 5x3 m, Irish Dance).

   Performer anxiety can also be relieved by starting position in the choreography, with Performer 05 reporting that they felt less anxious about unintentional collisions when they had good peripheral visibility of the group, and Performer 03's preference for an edge position:

"I could kind of see where things were at my side" – Performer 05 (System 2, 5x3 m).

"There was enough space for that one. There was no one to the left of me this time." – Performer 03 (System 3, 5x3 m, 210°).

Performer anxiety can also be alleviated by synchronicity, which can result from careful direction or familiarity with the choreography through practice:

"We're still flowing together, kind of, so we didn't move into each other" – Performer 02 (System 1, 7x4 m).

2. **Challenges and solutions to environmental and hardware influences on performer experience**

This theme addresses how lighting, cameras, system layout, and the physical environment influenced performer experience. The sub-themes included in this theme are:

- Influence of lighting on the performer
- Influence of cameras on the performer
- Perception of the general system

The lighting rig affected different performers in different ways. Some performers reported that the lighting didn't affect their ability to perform:

"The lighting was good. I'm used to it from the stage, so it didn't affect me." – Performer 05 (System 3, 6x6 m, high-low).

"When the lights are on, you focus." – Performer 01 (System 2, 6x6 m).

"I thought it looked more professional of a shoot because of more lighting in it." – Performer 07 (System 3, 5x3 m, 210°).

"Blinding enough." – Performer 02 (System 3, 8x8 m).

"The only thing I will say was that the lights were a bit disorientating." – Performer 08 (System 3, 3x3 m).

Similarly, the presence and configuration of cameras impacted performer behaviour. Those near the periphery were particularly affected:

"I had to go a bit behind them [cameras] or past them. I didn't notice them, just except for trying to avoid them, like the one on my side" – Performer 05 (System 2, 5x4 m).

"At the side, I think I was a bit too close to the one I was afraid of whacking it" - Performer 07 (System 2, 5x5 m).

Performer 07 also noted how a change in camera configuration led to dizziness as they had previously been using them as a reference point during disorientating movements. This highlights how using the VV systems components for reference point may inadvertently lead to dependency.

"I actually found I got dizzier this time, and I think it's because the cameras are at different heights than they were at yesterday" – Performer 07 (System 3, 6x6 m, High-Low)

Physical cues such as floor markings and socks were used to assist alignment and comfort:

> "The lines that were drawn on the floor. Very helpful." – Performer 07 (System 3, 2x2 m).

> "I take off my shoes, I wear my socks. I think it's just so I don't get stuck on my shoes." – Performer 01 (System 3, 8x8 m)

> "I'm more used to dancing in socks, because you can turn better and you can feel all the muscles in your feet rather than in shoes." – Performer 07 (System 3, 4x4 m).

Performers could rely on co-performers and the director for spatial orientation and reassurance:

> "I'm looking at the person. I'm kind of like lining myself up." – Performer 03 (System 2, 5x3 m).

> "I felt like I knew where all the hands were and all the movements were. I just felt very controlled." - Performer 04 (System 1, 6x6 m).

> "The fact that the director stood in front of [sic] each camera helped with the direction as well. So it was easier to be straightforward and not be changing and looking for somewhere to look because he was on top of that as well." – Performer 07 (System 3, 2x2 m).

3. Learning curve and reflection on experience

This theme captures the evolving understanding and comfort levels of performers, technicians, and the director as they engaged with the VolCap systems over the course of the workshop. It includes individual reflections on system familiarity, operational efficiency, and the process of discovery through experimentation. This theme is applicable to all system stakeholders. The sub-themes included here are:

- Increased familiarity with process and effect on performance
- Operational learning curve
- Increased understanding of possibilities of the systems
- Discovery through experimentation
- Importance of visual feedback

Performers described increased confidence and fluency as they became more familiar with both the choreography and their co-performers. This led to greater freedom of movement and reduced focus on individual steps:

> "I think I'd feel more comfortable to stretch out more if it was someone I knew rather than someone I didn't know." -Performer 04 (System 3, 6x6 m).

"I got a lot more used to the movements, so I focus less on the steps and more on the structure of it and making my arms linear." – Performer 07 (System 3, 5x3 m).

The technicians reported a clear operational learning curve with increasing efficiency and better coordination during setup and capture as the workshop progressed:

"We're getting a bit more into the flow now and what things need to be done in which order. The setup is easier now because we've done it a couple of times." – Technician 04 (System 1, 5x5 m).

"It is getting better. There is clearly improvement, but there is room for more improvement" – Technician 03 (System 1, 2x2 m).

Over time, technicians also developed insights into system limitations and strategies for more efficient reconfiguration and calibration. For example, they recognized the need for pre-planning and identified hardware constraints, such as limited SD card storage during longer captures:

"There's some pre-managerial decisions that need to go on in order to make things smoother, which is an interesting thing to think about." – Technician 05 (System 3, 8x8 m High-Low).

"We're running out of space in our cards very quickly. Data transfer becomes an issue at this point. We have an hour record time that's split in two because we have two sets of cards, but now we're getting 15 minutes per capture space, which means that our cards will be full, after this next shoot." - Technician 05 (System 3, 6x6 m, High-Low).

The director also reflected on how iterative experimentation contributed to a growing understanding of the systems' capabilities and limitations: demonstrated a desire to attain an increased understanding of the possibilities of the systems:

"I think by the time we walk away from all of this, we're actually going to have enough data to make a decision about what is the best way of doing it." – Director (System 3, 5x5 m, High-Low).

"We're trying to experiment and see where the sweet spot will land. I think we have enough data now that we'll have a little more data to figure out exactly what we're trying to do." – Director 01 (System 3, 5x5 m, High-Low).

Visual feedback through the system interface was identified as an important factor in guiding setup and decision-making:

"We can tell with the monitors everything that's going on, we can see what's happening. Very simple in terms of views. It's nice to be able to see everything working." – Director 01 (System, 3 3x3 m).

4. System configuration, operation and calibration challenges

This theme explores the practical challenges and technical considerations involved in configuring, operating, and calibrating the VolCap systems, particularly in experimental and variable spatial arrangements. It includes the perspectives of technicians and the director, who navigated the logistical constraints and technical limitations of system setup in real time.

Technicians frequently highlighted how spatial layout and camera placement directly impacted system calibration. Rectangular capture areas introduced blind spots that required compromise or reconfiguration:

"We found out that the field of views of the cameras have a slight blind spot in between the cameras. So, we had to go a little bit closer, so there are no blind spots." – Technician 01 (System 2, 7x4 m).

Calibration procedures were especially sensitive in larger or asymmetrical setups. Technicians described needing to adjust angles iteratively to achieve an acceptable result:

"For the calibration we needed to place some of the cameras together because some of them were too close to the boxes. So, we had to find the specific angle for the calibration to work." – Technician 01 (System 2, 5x3 m)

"If for example in the beginning the first calibration was not correct, we had to re-do the first one in a different way." – Technician 01 (System 2, 7x4 m)

Technical limits of the hardware also became apparent during testing. System 2, which used Kinect™ sensors, reached its functional range limit at around 3 m:

"Our calibration algorithm does not work above 3m, because it was trained in maximum distance." – Technician 01 (System 2, 5x5 m)

System 1 faced challenges due to cable lengths and sensor constraints in larger configurations:

"We're slowly but surely reaching the limit of what we can do and being it in terms of cameras and also cables maybe." – Technician 04 (System 1, 5x5m)

In response to these constraints, technicians improvised solutions to mitigate issues with lighting interference and sensor performance:

"We had a problem that we've never experienced before... we put some shadow, put some things here and there to shadow the whole lighting and everything worked quite well." – Technician 02 (System 2, 5x3 m, 210°).

Technicians also noted that the complexity of the systems, particularly System 3 with high-low sensor arrangements, made configuration unsuitable for novice users without prior experience:

"Regarding the system as it set up now, there's all very experimental. I would feel uncomfortable doing this for the first time if I was a novice." – Technician 05 (System 3, 2x2 m).

Hardware features like zoom lenses on DSLR cameras were seen as advantageous for adapting to changing space requirements without moving rigs:

"We would have been in trouble if we had fixed camera lenses. We would have had to move our rig a lot more." – Technician 05 (System 3, 5x4 m).

Finally, participants reflected on the unpredictable outcomes introduced by these experimental configurations. While some setups aimed to maximise capture volume or resolution in targeted zones, the effect on output quality remained uncertain:

"It'll be interesting to see if the footage comes out in a resolution that's usable... Everything in the centre is a little bit smaller and a little bit lower resolution." – Technician 05 (System 3, 4x4 m).

"Now we're squeezing it even more to see if we can get more resolution out of the front and back while maintaining the width of the distance. We are literally blind at the moment. We have no idea what's going to work." – Director 01 (System 3, 5x3 m).

In summary, this theme highlights the real-world operational complexity of deploying and tuning VolCap systems, particularly in contexts outside of controlled lab environments. It underscores the importance of iterative calibration, spatial awareness, and technical flexibility in achieving functional capture setups.

5. Implications of 'in the wild' environment

This theme captures the consequences of deploying VolCap systems outside a controlled lab environment. Technicians and the director reflected on how real-world constraints, such as lighting, surfaces, and speed of assembly, affected the reliability and practicality of system operation. This theme explores the following sub-themes:

- Improvised solutions to system issues
- Issues arising from 'in-the-wild' context
- In-the-wild vs lab contexts
- Observations on the capture environment

Unpredictable issues emerged in the workshop setting that had not appeared in previous lab trials. For instance, ambient lighting in the sports hall created interference with depth sensors, prompting improvised solutions:

"It's about the same, except from the fact that we haven't met such a problem with lighting or with the constant running of the sensors." – Technician 02 (System 2, 5x3 m, 210°)

"We put some shadow, put some things here and there to shadow the whole lighting and everything worked quite well." – Technician 02 (System 2, 5x3 m, 210°)

Other challenges included the time pressure of reconfiguring systems quickly in the field:

"That is just the hassle of having to quickly assemble the thing." – Technician 03 (System 1, 2x2 m)

Participants acknowledged the shift from lab-style precision to field-based adaptability. Technician 05 described the realism of the environment compared to the artificial control of lab conditions:

"It's like doing brain surgery in a back alley to describe the clinical nature of lab-based research. I'd say it's unrealistic. Whereas this is very real. This is very sort of like on the ground." – Technician 05 (System 3, 2x2 m)

Some aspects of the environment, such as the floor, were beneficial. Others, like lighting or vertical camera placement, required further adjustment:

"My preference for the sports hall is the ground is solid here. There's no camera bounce, no movement. But we don't have the lighting." – Technician 05 (System 3, 5x5 m, High-Low)

The director also noted how camera visibility issues during calibration led to further spatial experimentation:

"Yesterday we realized that we couldn't get the checkered board when all the cameras were low." – Director 01 (System 3, 6x6 m, High-Low)

Technicians reflected on how partial capture configurations like 210° might be more applicable to performance contexts such as theatre, where full 360° coverage is not always necessary:

"If you're in an arena you get 210 degrees seats. So, I think that for a seated event, you're probably going to get an accurate representation using this set-up." – Technician 05 (System 3, 5x3 m, 210°)

In summary, this theme illustrates how working in real-world conditions exposed both the practical constraints and the necessary flexibility required for deploying volumetric capture technologies in authentic performance settings.

6. **Potential for future development**

This theme explores the potential for further development of the systems based on observations made by the technicians and the director.

Technician 03 reported that System 1 was not currently suited to deployment for multiple camera models. This could be a direction for future development. They also reported that the system is not self-configuring, which would help with system operation in the future:

"At the moment, if I'm honest, the system is undeployable with multiple cameras. At the moment it is complicated to set up and requires a lot of training. It's not really self-configuring. There is a whole lot of things that you have to think of and that you have to all do in the right order to have a chance of getting it going." – Technician 03 (System 1, 2x2 m).

Technician 05 observed that a large interaction space with multiple people is desirable. They also postulated that volumetric capture could be the future of media capture where there is still room for high-definition equipment. They suggested that this could be an augmentation of the traditional Outside Broadcast industry:

"This is closer to what I would expect from a capture system. This sort of interaction space with more than one person using it. It's getting closer to realization." – Technician 05 (System 3, 4x4 m).

"This is how I can imagine the future of media capture. It's like it's no longer just one person with an iPhone doing their on-the-ground reporting. You still got a place for high tech high-definition capture setup. I don't think that it's the death of the outside broadcast industry. I just think it's an augmentation." – Technician 05 (System 3, 2x2 m).

These findings are now interpreted in relation to the research question, drawing on stakeholder feedback to identify broader implications for VolCap system design and deployment.

6 Discussion

The sentiment and thematic analysis of the subjective data captured during this evaluation highlights several recurring themes common to RGB- and RGB-D-based volumetric capture within a performing arts context. A–3 m diameter range limitation of RGB-D cameras poses a challenge to the volumetric capture of multiple performers. Emerging from this limitation was a performer preference for an average linear metric ratio of 1 performer to 1.3 m squared for a linear choreography consisting of full lateral limb extensions. A general system preference amongst performers for the space and convenience afforded by the system featuring focal length adjustments should be taken into consideration by professionals involved in the volumetric capture of live performances. It was discovered that careful choreography achieved through practice and repetition can alleviate a perception of restriction in finite volumetric capture areas. These findings not only contribute to answering the research question by showing how perceived spatial freedom and technical layout directly influenced the performers' ability to deliver volumetric performances but also offer solutions to allow them to do this in an expressive and well-coordinated way. Such spatial considerations are critical to ensuring both technical feasibility and artistic fluidity in live performance capture.

Common to all evaluated systems was that the performers can use elements of the volumetric captures systems themselves (e.g., lights and cameras) as reference points to maintain choreography during disorienting movements such as spinning, although this could lead to dependency as seen in the thematic analysis. All negative feedback related to lighting was due to System 3 which was unique in that it included floor lighting as seen in Fig. 1. A preference for the real time feedback afforded by GUIs emerged as another important sub theme for the artistic direction of volumetric capture of performances.

The deployment of these systems outside of controlled lab conditions presented challenges that should be taken into consideration when attempting on-location captures. These include a technician preference for systems based on focal length adjustments, as these require less physical effort and calibration between varying performance configurations. However, longer focal lengths used comparatively more memory and time during calibration. Technician feedback suggested that for VolCap to become more flexible and accessible it will be important to design for portability, providing more convenient systems that can be efficiently deployed 'in the wild'. Having said that, technician familiarity improved perceptions of comfort as the workshop progressed. These findings further answer the research question by showing how system usability, specifically in terms of portability, calibration efficiency, and field-readiness, influenced the technicians' ability to support live volumetric performance capture. The successful deployment of robust VolCap systems outside the lab may ultimately enable more authentic creative practice, allowing capture to take place where performances naturally occur, rather than relocating them to controlled environments.

Experimentation with rectangular configurations of depth sensors presented some interesting possibilities for capturing stage-like performances. For our VolCap systems configured with 8 RGB-D cameras, an upper rectangular capture area of 7x4m was established. This was due to the emergence of blind spots (lack of sensor overlaps) in larger rectangular spaces. This indicates future research paths relating to the RGB-D-based VolCap systems' ability to accommodate non-standard capture spaces (i.e. circular).

In summary, this work contributes to the body of research in VolCap of live performances by offering a heretofore absent set of performer, director and technician informed guidelines to aid in navigating the volumetric capture of the performing arts.

These broadly concern i.) design and ii.) use of VolCap systems in the performing arts. Regarding VolCap system design, artistic direction is facilitated by the real time feedback afforded by VolCap systems that feature a GUI. Systems based on focal length adjustments may capture larger rectangular stage like productions more readily. Furthermore, VolCap systems featuring focal length adjustment are preferred by technicians due to reduced physical labor involved in camera movement and re-calibration, and by performers due to the additional space they can afford regardless of the intimacy of the capture. Regarding use of VolCap systems to capture multiple performers, a maximum capture area capacity of 1 performer per $1.3m^2$ is recommended for choreographies involving full lateral extension of the performers' limbs. Alternatively, synchronization of movements can alleviate perceptions of confinement, achieved through artistic direction, practice and reference points provided by the VolCap systems themselves. These insights are consolidated into the following conclusion, which summarizes the contributions and outlines guidelines for future VolCap deployments in live performance contexts.

7 Conclusion

This paper presented a side-by-side evaluation of how three state-of-the-art volumetric capture systems influenced performing arts professionals' ability to create immersive live performances. Thirteen system configurations; two RGB-D-based and one RGB-based, were deployed to test the spatial and experiential limits of live choreographed capture. The experiences of eight performers, six technicians, and one director were analysed through interviews and open-ended questionnaires.

By addressing the research question, this study demonstrated that system usability, spatial layout, and real-time feedback mechanisms directly affected the ability of stakeholders to produce high-quality volumetric content. Sentiment analysis of open-ended questionnaire responses provided an additional signal that complemented the thematic analysis of interview transcripts. While neutral sentiment was treated cautiously, trends in positive and negative responses aligned closely with stakeholder preferences expressed in interviews. This triangulation strengthened the interpretation of system usability and performer comfort across configurations.

The findings led to two practical guidelines for professionals using VolCap systems. First, regarding system design, artistic direction is supported by real-time GUI feedback. Focal length–based calibration reduces physical setup effort, offers greater performer freedom, and better supports rectangular stage layouts—though it may increase calibration time and energy use. Second, regarding system use, a maximum density of 1 performer per 1.3 m^2 is recommended for choreographies involving full limb extension. Where this is not feasible, synchronisation achieved through rehearsal, reference points, or inter-performer communication can mitigate perceived confinement.

Future work will build on these in-the-wild deployments by evaluating how perceived user experience relates to the quality of post-processed volumetric output, with the aim of establishing practical links between subjective UX and objective capture fidelity. This will involve experimentation with advanced GPS-Gaussian and 4K4D reconstruction techniques.

Acknowledgments. This research was funded by the Horizon Europe TRANSMIXR project under grant agreement 101070109.

Disclosure of Interests. The authors declare no conflict of interests.

References

1. Pandey, R., et al.: Volumetric capture of humans with a single RGBD camera via semi-parametric learning. In: 2019 IEEE/CVF Conference on Computer Vision and Pattern Recognition (CVPR), pp. 9701–9710. IEEE, Long Beach, CA, USA (2019). https://doi.org/10.1109/CVPR.2019.00994

2. Young, G.W., O'Dwyer, N., Moynihan, M., Smolic, A.: Audience experiences of a volumetric virtual reality music video. In: 2022 IEEE Conference on Virtual Reality and 3D User Interfaces (VR), pp. 775–781. IEEE, Christchurch, New Zealand (2022). https://doi.org/10.1109/VR51125.2022.00099

3. Smolic, A., et al.: Volumetric video content creation for immersive XR experiences. London Imaging Meeting **3**, 54–59 (2022). https://doi.org/10.2352/lim.2022.1.1.13

4. Pires, F., et al.: The Fushimi Inari Experience: An Interactive Volumetric Film (2022). https://doi.org/10.1145/3505284.3533027

5. Schulz, A., Eder, A., Tiberius, V., Solorio, S.C., Fabro, M., Brehmer, N.: The digitalization of motion picture production and its value chain implications. Journalism and Media **2**, 397–416 (2021). https://doi.org/10.3390/journalmedia2030024

6. Sterzentsenko, V., et al.: A low-cost, flexible and portable volumetric capturing system. In: 2018 14th International Conference on Signal-Image Technology & Internet-Based Systems (SITIS), pp. 200–207 (2018). https://doi.org/10.1109/SITIS.2018.00038

7. Volumetric Video in Augmented Reality Applications for Museological Narratives: A User Study for the Long Room in the Library of Trinity College Dublin: Journal on Computing and Cultural Heritag **14**(2), https://dl.acm.org/doi/abs/https://doi.org/10.1145/3425400. Accessed 18 Nov 2024

8. Irlitti, A., et al.: Volumetric mixed reality telepresence for real-time cross modality collaboration. In: Proceedings of the 2023 CHI Conference on Human Factors in Computing Systems, pp. 1–14. Association for Computing Machinery, New York, NY, USA (2023). https://doi.org/10.1145/3544548.3581277

9. Wise, K.: Dancing invisible duets: using volumetric capture to create one-to-one performance in virtual reality. International Journal of Performance Arts and Digital Media **20**, 50–59 (2024). https://doi.org/10.1080/14794713.2024.2336638

10. Pagés, R., Amplianitis, K., Monaghan, D., Ondřej, J., Smolić, A.: Affordable content creation for free-viewpoint video and VR/AR applications. J. Vis. Commun. Image Represent. **53**, 192–201 (2018). https://doi.org/10.1016/j.jvcir.2018.03.012

11. Lischer-Katz, Z., Braggs, R., Carter, B.: Investigating volumetric video creation and curation for the digital humanities: a white paper describing findings from the project: Preserving BIPOC Expatriates' Memories During Wartime and Beyond. The University of Arizona Libraries (Tucson, AZ) (2024). https://doi.org/10.2458/10150.674673

12. Pietroszek, K., Eckhardt, C.: Volumetric capture for narrative films. In: Proceedings of the 26th ACM Symposium on Virtual Reality Software and Technology, pp. 1–3. Association for Computing Machinery, New York, NY, USA (2020). https://doi.org/10.1145/3385956.3422116

13. Zollhofer, M., Nießner, M., Izadi, S., Rhemann, C.: Real-time non-rigid reconstruction using an RGB-D camera. ACM Transactions on Graphics. https://doi.org/10.1145/2601097.2601165

14. Easy to Calibrate: Marker-Less Calibration of Multiview Azure Kinect. CMES - Computer Modeling in Engineering and Sciences **136**, 3083–3096 (2023). https://doi.org/10.32604/cmes.2023.024460

15. Saito, S., Huang, Z., Natsume, R., Morishima, S., Li, H., Kanazawa, A.: PIFu: pixel-aligned implicit function for high-resolution clothed human digitization. In: 2019 IEEE/CVF International Conference on Computer Vision (ICCV), pp. 2304–2314. IEEE, Seoul, Korea (South) (2019). https://doi.org/10.1109/ICCV.2019.00239

16. Remelli, E., Han, S., Honari, S., Fua, P., Wang, R.: Lightweight multi-view 3D pose estimation through camera-disentangled representation. In: 2020 IEEE/CVF Conference on Computer Vision and Pattern Recognition (CVPR), pp. 6039–6048. IEEE, Seattle, WA, USA (2020). https://doi.org/10.1109/CVPR42600.2020.00608

17. Hynes, E.: Supplementary Material Table 1: System 1 and System 2 hardware component specifications and workshop settings. https://osf.io/5w4zv. Accessed 22 May 2025

18. Hynes, E.: Supplementary Material Table2 The System 3 hardware components with their specifications and workshop settings. https://osf.io/3dn96. Accessed 22 May 2025

19. An, G.H., Lee, S., Seo, M.-W., Yun, K., Cheong, W.-S., Kang, S.-J.: Charuco board-based omnidirectional camera calibration method. Electronics **7**, 421 (2018). https://doi.org/10.3390/electronics7120421

20. Fisher, A., Cannizzaro, R., Cochrane, M., Nagahawatte, C., Palmer, J.L.: ColMap: a memory-efficient occupancy grid mapping framework. Robot. Auton. Syst. **142**, 103755 (2021). https://doi.org/10.1016/j.robot.2021.103755

21. Braun, V., Clarke, V.: Using thematic analysis in psychology. Qualitative Research in Psychology (2006)

22. Hynes, E.: Supplementary Material Table 3: The evaluation test configurations, including capture area, sensor setup, number of performers and type of performance. https://osf.io/bhfjy. Accessed 22 May 2025

23. Hynes, E.: Supplementary Material: Performing Arts Workshop Modified SUS Questionnaire. https://osf.io/zfhmq. Accessed 22 May 2025

24. Lewis, J.R.: IBM computer usability satisfaction questionnaires: psychometric evaluation and instructions for use. International Journal of Human-Computer Interaction. **7**, 57–78 (1995). https://doi.org/10.1080/10447319509526110

25. Jain, S.M.: Hugging face. In: Jain, S.M. (ed.) Introduction to Transformers for NLP: With the Hugging Face Library and Models to Solve Problems, pp. 51–67. Apress, Berkeley, CA (2022). https://doi.org/10.1007/978-1-4842-8844-3_4

26. Good Tape — Secure and Automatic Transcription. https://goodtape.io/. Accessed 7 Sep 2024

27. Hynes, E.: Supplementray Material Table 4: Mean Modified SUS Questionnaire Responses by Stakeholder for the Three Systems Across All Thirteen Configurations. https://osf.io/ma7ys. Accessed 22 May 2025

Cross-System Virtual Reality (VR) Authentication Using Transformer-Based Trajectory Forecasting

Mingjun Li[1], Natasha Kholgade Banerjee[2], and Sean Banerjee[2(✉)]

[1] University of Hartford, West Hartford, CT, USA
minli@hartford.edu
[2] Wright State University, Dayton, OH, USA
{natasha.banerjee,sean.banerjee}@wright.edu

Abstract. Ubiquitous devices, such as smartphones and tablets, have pervaded critical applications in education, healthcare, and military, with users having systems for their home, office, clinic, or job site. As virtual reality (VR) systems become more affordable, they are likely to gain similar multi-system adoption in critical applications where sensitive user data must be protected from malicious users. Recent work has shown that deep learning techniques are usable for cross-system authentication where enrollment data is provided in one system, e.g. an HTC Vive, and use time data on another, e.g. a Meta Quest. However, these approaches require complete or near complete trajectories of user behavior and show lower performance when smaller portions of user behavior from the start of the activity are used. In prior work, motion forecasting has been used to predict future motion and use it for VR authentication. However, this work works on a single VR system, and requires a distinct authentication model per user. We present the first generalized authentication framework for cross-system VR biometrics using a forecasting neural network based on the Transformer, and an authentication neural network based on a fully convolutional network. To validate our approach, we use a publicly available dataset that provides motion trajectories from a ball-throwing task using multiple VR systems. We show that our approach reduces the equal error rate (EER) by an average of 53.16% across all VR system combinations when compared to existing state-of-the-art approaches on cross-VR-system authentication. Our approach enables interoperability across VR systems that use lighthouse- and camera-based tracking and provides early authentication without requiring the full user trajectory. Link to code: https://bit.ly/44DafAD.

Keywords: VR biometrics · behavioral biometrics · deep learning · motion forecasting · interoperability

1 Introduction

As VR gains acceptance into domains such as education [6,10], healthcare [16, 44], and military [4,55], one expects a proliferation of sensitive user data.

D. Michael-Grigoriou et al. (Eds.): EuroXR 2025, LNCS 16101, pp. 240–264, 2026.
https://doi.org/10.1007/978-3-032-03805-0_14

Sensitive data must be protected from malicious agents and deliberate attacks by the user. Existing approaches that rely on PIN, password, or multi-factor authentication will fail when a user intentionally hands over their credentials. Password sharing is a universal problem faced by everyone ranging from middle school students [27], older adults [31], and couples [26]. Deliberate circumvention of security measures by users leads to challenges in domains such as education or healthcare. A student taking a remote VR-based exam may provide their university credentials to a friend to complete the exam. While video-based proctoring systems are in use for remote examinations, privacy related challenges remain a problem [43]. In healthcare, a patient who has been assigned an at-home VR-based therapy may log in and give their system to an able-bodied ally to complete the recommended activities or non-adherence to the protocol. Non-adherence is estimated to be around of 30–50% after injury or surgery [3] and up to 70% for musculoskeletal outpatient settings [14]. While immersive VR shows promise to combat non-adherence [17], such studies are performed in controlled settings with limited data on post study retention. Thus, in domains such as education or healthcare, early detection of deliberate malicious use or non-adherence is critical using approaches that cannot be easily circumvented.

Given the known issues with traditional credentials, there is a growing demand to look beyond the password [2]. One approach is to use the behavior of the user in VR, via their motions, activities, and interactions, as a security measure. In behavior-based VR biometrics, one can either perform authentication, i.e., determining if the user is who they claim to be, or identification, i.e., determining who the user is, using the movement data provided by the user. A large body of work has emerged on using human movement in VR to provide secure access [1, 19, 21–25, 28–30, 32, 33, 35–37, 45, 49, 51, 57], and surveyed in 2024 by Giaretta [9]. Prior work in behavior-based biometrics for VR has explored task-based activities that are repeatable with predictable steps such as throwing a ball, manipulating a cube, playing golf, lifting weights, or watching a video. Work by Rack et al. [53], shows that learning-based techniques used in task-based environments are also effective for user identification on arbitrary motion sequences and in longer gameplay-based environments [52].

The current body of work in behavior-based VR biometrics suffers from two challenges. **First**, there exists a limited body of work on performing cross-system VR biometrics [36,37]. In cross-system VR biometrics, the user has multiple VR systems and enrollment and use-time data is provided in different systems. Today, the ubiquity of smart devices means that an average person can be using a broad spectrum of devices at their work, home, clinic, or school. With reducing cost and size, one can expect the same with VR systems in the near future. Thus, a user could interact with one VR system at their workplace, school, or clinic, and have an alternate personal VR system at home. The challenge is further exacerbated by the lack of cross-system VR datasets, where multiple users provide data using a variety of VR systems. To date, the publicly available dataset of Miller et al. [36,37] is the only cross-system dataset. While Miller et al. [37] have shown the effectiveness of Siamese neural networks for cross-system VR biometrics, their approach presents our **second** challenge wherein the deep learning algorithms require nearly complete trajectories to attain the high security levels. Requiring nearly complete trajectories poses a security threat as a malicious agent will be able to launch an attack in the time taken for the user to complete the security task. While work by Li et al. [21] shows the feasibility of forecasting the future motion of a user to acquire a prediction of their longer range behavior for VR biometrics, their approach only works on a single VR system and requires a distinct authentication model per user. Thus, their approach cannot be generalized for cross-system scenarios.

In this paper, we present a Transformer-based framework for cross-system VR authentication. **Our work is the first to provide a generalized framework that forecasts user behavior across VR systems, thereby simultaneously enabling interoperability and early authentication.** Similar to Miller et al. [37], we assumes that a user, e.g., User A, has provided prior complete enrollment data using an enrollment VR system, e.g., a Meta Quest at the office, and is using a separate VR system, e.g., an HTC Vive at home. We perform authentication using a user's partial trajectory in the use-time system in two steps. Given the input partial trajectory at use-time, we use a forecasting neural network model to hypothesize the user's expected complete trajectory. In the second step, we use the hypothesized complete trajectory to authenticate the user using an authentication neural network model. We evaluate our approach using the only multi VR system dataset collected by Miller et al. [36, 37] and compare to their Siamese neural network approach. We show that our approach reduces the equal error rate (EER), a standard biometric measure for evaluating user authentication, by an average of 53.16% across all VR system combinations.

2   Related Work

Over the past half-decade a growing body of work has emerged on using the behavior of the person in the VR space as a biometric signature as surveyed by Giaretta [9] in 2024. Prior to the emergence of the hand-controllers for VR, work by Rogers et al. [56] explored blink patterns and head-movements as users watched a series of rapidly changing images using a Google Glass. Mustafa et al. [45] use support vector machines to classify users based on head movement as they listened to music on a Google Cardboard-based VR system. Work by Kupin et al. [19] uses nearest neighbors to identify users on a pilot dataset of 14 subjects performing a ball-throwing task. Their approach used positional information from the dominant hand controller. Using the Kupin et al. ball-throwing task, Ajit et al. [1] use position and orientation features from the headset and hand controllers to train a perceptron to classify distances in input and library sessions from a user. Work by Liebers et al. [23] explores activities, such as bowling and archery, to classify users using recurrent neural networks.

Pfeuffer et al. [51] explore generalized behavior in VR such as picking, pointing, typing, and grabbing. Random forests and support vector machines are trained and evaluated on aggregate statistics from unary features and pairwise relationships between the controllers, headset, and targets. Work by Olade et al. [49] investigates nearest neighbors and support vector machines for classification as users engage in activities that involve grabbing, rotating, and dropping objects in a virtual space. Mathis et al. [28] show that hand movement patterns when users grab and manipulate a virtual 3D cube can be used for authentication. Using a fully convolutional network (FCN) they achieve up to 98.91% accuracy on a dataset of 23 participants. Rack et al. [53], shows that learning-based techniques are effective for user identification on arbitrary motion sequences and in longer gameplay-based environments [52]. Work by Baldoni et al. [5] shows the effectiveness of learning-based techniques across an array of games using both movement and traffic. Work by Miller et al. [33] investigates approaches for identification using random forests as participants watch 5 videos and answer questions. However, users exhibited limited large-scale movements due to the relatively sedentary nature of watching videos in the VR environment.

Despite a growing market of VR systems, most VR datasets [1,19,23,24,28, 33,41,46,49,51] have users providing data using a single VR system. The earliest instance of cross-system VR biometrics is the work of Miller et al. [36] who extend the work of Ajit et al. [1] to include new features in the form of velocity, angular velocity, and trigger pressure. Work by Miller et al. [37] demonstrates that Siamese networks can learn cross-system relationships to provide high identification accuracy and low authentication EER. High assurance cross-system and cross-session VR biometrics is critical as work by Moore et al. [41] and Pfeuffer et al. [51] show that classifier performance degrades across sessions. Recent work by Miller et al. [39], Lieber et al. [25], and Miller et al. [32,34] shows that user behavior changes over time and can impact behavioral biometrics for VR. Recent work by Liebers et al. [24] has explored user identification using uni- and bi-manual finger movements. As VR systems move away from the traditional controller to enable seamless hands-free interactions, the ability to continue identifying users based on controller free activities is vital. The authors show up to 95% accuracy on a pilot dataset of 16 users interacting with eight different interaction elements. Using the Talking with Hands dataset [20] collected in a full-body motion capture environment, Schell et al. [57] compare performance of random forest, multi-layer perceptron, fully recurrent neural network, long short term memory, and gated recurrent unit architectures. However, as Schell et al. demonstrate high accuracy is only possible when using longer duration activities leaving the system vulnerable to attacks.

While iris and eye tracking may enable cross system security measures, the use of iris and eye tracking poses privacy challenges as iris images can get leaked with recent work encouraging the need for privacy guarantees [7] while maintaining the usefulness of eye tracking for immersive VR. In real-world settings iris scanners are unlikely to capture high quality iris images when users interact with dynamic content where iris or periocular regions show specular reflections from the onboard VR displays.

The extant body of work in VR has explored repeatable tasks that have clear start and end goals such as shooting an arrow, bowling, or throwing a ball or are action primitives such as grabbing, picking, or moving. In this paper, we leverage the repeatability of tasks to develop models to predict future behavior within the task given the user's prior actions. Li et al. [21] is the only approach that uses motion forecasting for VR biometrics. However, their approach works on a single VR system and requires a distinct authentication model per user.

3   Forecasting-Based Cross-System Authentication

Similar to Miller et al. [37], our approach assumes that a user, e.g., User A, has provided prior complete enrollment data using an enrollment VR system, e.g., a Meta Quest at the office, and is using a separate VR system, e.g., an HTC Vive at home. Our approach addresses the goal of using a user's partial trajectory in the use-time system based on the enrollment data in two steps. Given the input partial trajectory at use-time, our work uses a forecasting model to hypothesize the user's expected complete trajectory. In the second step, we use the hypothesized complete trajectory to authenticate the user using an authentication neural network model. We outline the overall architecture in Fig. 1.

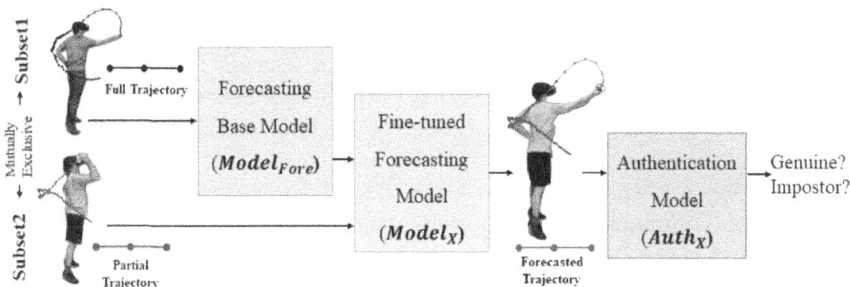

Fig. 1. We use two mutually exclusive datasets, **Subset1** and **Subset2**, for training and testing of the proposed method. **Subset1** is used to train the forecasting base model, $Model_{Fore}$, enabling it to learn the general ability to forecast future trajectories. Subsequently, **Subset2** is used to fine-tune the pre-trained base model (for details, see Sect. 6) to obtain models $Model_X$, enhancing its prediction accuracy and effectiveness across different enrollment- and use-time VR systems. Finally, the trajectory predictions generated by the fine-tuned model are used as input to the authentication model, $Auth_X$, for user authentication.

While training the forecasting neural network model, our work needs to ensure that forecasting can be conducted without requiring knowledge of the specific user's motion in the use-time VR system, but with knowledge of general motion using that use-time VR system. E.g., though we cannot assume that User A has used the HTC Vive before providing their Meta Quest enrollment, we need to be able to forecast how their movement is likely to evolve in the future using the HTC Vive from their partial Vive trajectory. We train the forecasting model to be cognizant of generalized user future motion across multiple VR systems by training the forecasting model using a holdout subset of users that do not contain User A. We use the data of the holdout users using a variety of VR systems—particularly, the Quest, Vive, and Cosmos from the publicly available Miller et al. multi-VR-system dataset [36,37]—to train the forecasting model. The resulting forecasting model, termed $\mathbf{Model_{Fore}}$ predicts complete motion from partial trajectories while lacking awareness of User A. We construct the holdout set, **Subset1**, to consist of half the users in the Miller et al. dataset.

The remaining half of the users, which would include User A, form **Subset2**. We use **Subset2** to train the authentication neural network model, with one model trained per user per enrollment VR system in **Subset 2**. For a given user in **Subset2**, the user's authentication model is trained by ground-truth labeling samples the user's enrollment VR system as genuine and samples from all other users in **Subset2** as impostor. We test the user's authentication model using use-time VR system trajectories from the intended user and all other users, with the objective that the intended user's trajectories are labeled as genuine and the rest of the users as impostor.

Since User A provides complete data using the enrollment VR system, e.g., Quest, we have the opportunity of building in awareness of User A into the forecasting model by fine-tuning $\mathbf{Model_{Fore}}$ using User A's enrollment data. We term this model $\mathbf{Model_X}$, where X represents the VR system in which User A provides enrollment data, e.g., $X =$ Quest. $\mathbf{Model_X}$ builds in user-specific awareness and general cross-VR system awareness, without needing knowledge of User A's use-time data. To strengthen $\mathbf{Model_X}$'s generalization, we fine-tune it using the enrollment data from all **Subset2** users.

We discuss the dataset used, partitioning of the dataset in **Subset1** and **Subset2**, preparation of trajectory samples, and impostor data generation in Sect. 4. We discuss the forecasting neural network $\mathbf{Model_{Fore}}$, particularly a Transformer in Sect. 5. In Sect. 6, we discuss our approach for fine-tuning $\mathbf{Model_{Fore}}$. Section 7 discusses the authentication neural network. We evaluate 12 enrollment/use-time cross-system pairs from the Miller dataset, respecting chronological order of data provision, namely Q1V1, Q1V2, Q1C1, Q2C2, Q2V1, Q2V2, Q2C1, Q2C2, V1C1, V1C2, V2C1, and V2C2 (in XaYb, enrollment is provided on day a of device X and day b of device Y). We also evaluate same-system pairs Q1Q2, V1V2, and C1C2.

4   Dataset

We utilize the publicly available 41 right-handed subject ball-throwing dataset collected by Miller et al. [36,37] in our study as it is the only dataset with multiple VR systems. While the lack of left-handed participants poses a generalizability challenge, since only around 10% of the population is left-handed [50] it is unlikely that a typical data collection will have enough left-handed participants to provide usable training and test data splits. Each user provides data using the Meta Quest, HTC Vive, and HTC Vive Cosmos. For each system, the user provides 10 sessions of data on two separate days. The dataset contains 20 features in total for each user/system pairing, with 7 features each for the hand controllers and 6 for the headset. The 7 features for the hand controllers are the x, y, and z physical coordinates, orientation values expressed as Euler rotations along the x, y, and z axes, as well as the trigger pressure values. The headset only includes the physical coordinates and orientations. In this paper, we use the abbreviations Q1, Q2, V1, V2, C1, and C2 to represent the data from the **Q**uest, **V**ive, and **C**osmos with the numeric signifying the day (day 1 vs. day 2).

Data Preparation. We generate the user subsets from the data **Subset1** of 21 participants and **Subset2** of 20 participants through a random partitioning by users. **Subset1** and **Subset2** are mutually exclusive in terms of users. Each subset contains all data for the users in the subset from Q1, Q2, V1, V2, C1, and C2. For each user, we obtain complete trajectory samples by extracting sliding windows of window size T_c timestamps from the entire ball-throwing motion of size T timestamps. The use of sliding windows enables our model to perform continuous authentication. For each trajectory, we retain the position coordinates x, y, and z for the headset and hand controllers, and the trigger pressure for the controllers. We convert the Euler angles provided in the original dataset for the headset and controllers to quaternions to circumvent Gimbal lock. With 3 position and 4 quaternion features for all 3 devices, and 1 trigger pressure value for the controllers, we have a total of 23 features per trajectory. The forecasting neural network is trained to generate the complete trajectory sliding windows as output from the initial part of the sliding window as input.

Impostor Data Sampling. For the authentication model of a particular user in **Subset2**, we need a set of impostor trajectories from the enrollment VR system for training and from the use-time VR system for testing. To ensure balanced training and testing, we need to keep the impostor trajectory counts the same as the count of genuine trajectories from the intended user. One approach for impostor data generation is to select complete trajectory sliding windows at random from the non-intended users in **Subset2**. However, this approach violates temporal consistency as the random windows are unlikely to be from the same time point when compared to the genuine user. The resulting impostor samples may not be temporally representative for training or testing. Instead, we obtain impostor data colocated with the intended user's time point, by randomly sampling the remaining users for sliding windows that share the start and end time point with the intended user's sliding window.

5   Transformer for Time Series Forecasting

We use the Quest, Vive, and Cosmos sliding window trajectories from all 21 users in **Subset1** to train the forecasting model, **Model$_{\text{Fore}}$**. We use a time-series forecasting Transformer [60,63]. The Transformer takes in the partial trajectory information from a user as a matrix of size $f \times T_p$ where f is the number of features (23) and T_p is the number of timestamps in the partial trajectory. Assuming the number of timestamps in the complete trajectory is T_c, the Transformer outputs the matrix $f \times T_{\text{Fore}}$ of forecasted trajectory, i.e., the latter portion of the complete trajectory of size $T_{\text{Fore}} = T_c - T_p$.

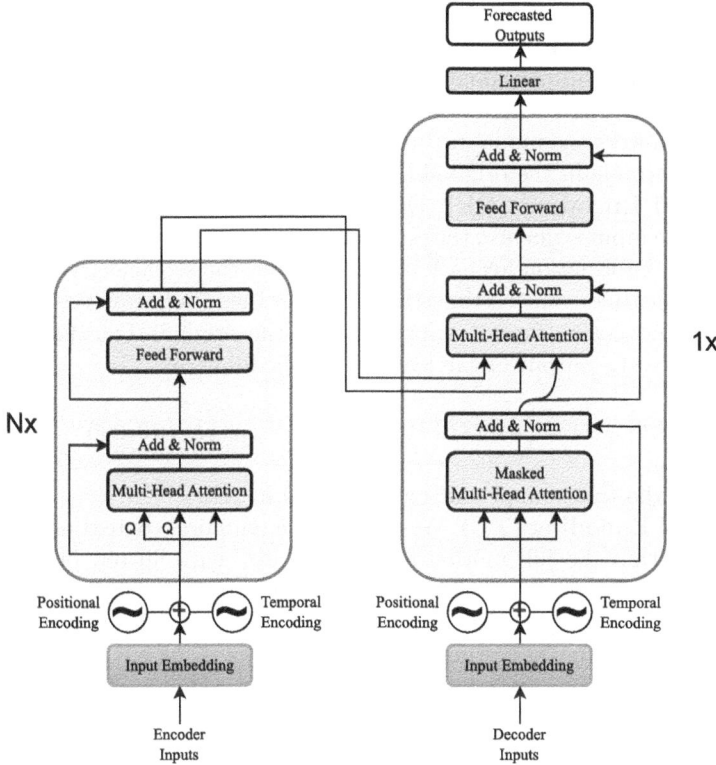

Fig. 2. Architecture of the forecasting model.

Following the architecture from Vaswani et al. [60], the Transformer consists of a multi-head self-attention encoder and a multi-head self-attention decoder, both of which use query, key, and value feature maps at intermediate layers to capture relationships between various parts of the trajectory at multiple hierarchies. The encoder takes in the $f \times T_p$ trajectory-feature matrix and generates key-value encodings as its output. The decoder combines the encoder's key-value encodings with query vectors, enabling the decoder to attend to various positions of the input sequence. The $f \times T_{\text{Fore}}$ forecasted trajectory output is generated at the output of the decoder. To generate query vectors that combine with the encoder, the decoder takes in a shifted version of the input of size $f \times T_o + T_{\text{Fore}}$. The first $f \times T_o$ portion of the shifted matrix overlaps with the last $f \times T_o$ portion of the input, whereas the remaining $f \times T_{\text{Fore}}$ section is filled with zeros, and enables the decoder to predict the forecasted region, as shown in Fig. 3.

Input Feature Embedding: Instead of operating directly on the input trajectory, we apply the Transformer encoder and decoder to an embedding of the feature space, as typical for Transformer architectures used in language and time series modeling [60,63]. We generate the embedding by summing a learnable embedding, a positional encoding (PE), and a temporal encoding (TE).

- **Learnable Embeddings**: We use learnable embeddings to transform the pre-processed 23-dimensional data into a higher-dimensional space with a dimensionality of F, where F is set to 512. The higher-dimensional representation empowers the model to capture patterns that might be latent but not easily discernible in the original low-dimensional space.
- **Positional Encoding (PE)**: During the process of extracting the feature maps of the input sequence, the parallelization of the Transformer leads to loss of position information for each element within the sequence. We encode the positional features of each timestamp data in the input sequence by applying the sine and cosine formulas discussed in the original Transformer framework [60] to the output of the learnable embedding, as

$$PE(t, 2i, 2i + 1) = \left(\sin \left(t / \left(10,000^{2i/F} \right) \right), \cos \left(t / \left(10,000^{2i/F} \right) \right) \right), \quad (1)$$

where t is the timestamp, and i goes from 0 to 255.
- **Temporal Encoding (TE)**: We capture the temporal context of each sliding window within the full motion for an activity—e.g., lift-off, pull-back, and forward-fling being early, intermediate, and latter parts of the ball-throwing action—by encoding a normalized version of the timestamp within the full activity. We obtain the normalized timestamp as

$$TE(t) = t/T - 0.5, \quad (2)$$

where t represents the timestamp within the original activity, and T is the total number of timestamps in the original data.

Transformer Encoder: Consists of a stack of 3 identical layers as shown in Fig. 2 (left), each comprising two sub-modules: a multi-head self-attention mechanism and a position-wise fully connected feed-forward network. We employ residual connections [12] and layer normalization within each layer to enhance gradient flow and improve training stability. The multi-head self-attention module has 8 scaled single-head dot product self-attentions defined as

$$Attention(Q, K, V) = \text{softmax} \left(QK^T / \sqrt{d_K} \right) V, \quad (3)$$

where Q, K, and V are the query, key, and value vectors of each element in the input sequence, and d_K represents the dimensionality of K. We set Q, K, and V to have a dimensionality of 64. We apply a softmax function to obtain a probability distribution as the resulting attention scores. Each scaled single-head dot product self-attention computes the correlations among elements in the input sequence from different perspectives, facilitating the model to have a holistic and comprehensive understanding of the input sequence. We use a residual connection operation [12], by adding the output of the multi-head attention module to its initial input. The position-wise dense feed-forward sub-layer uses a two-layer fully connected neural network. The dimension of the layers is 2,048.

Decoder Input

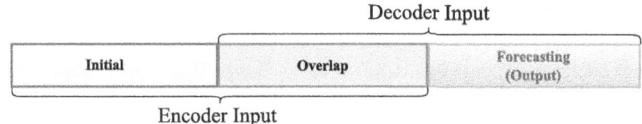

Encoder Input

Fig. 3. Input and output of the forecasting model. The encoder input consists of the initial sequence (in gray) and the overlap sequence (in blue), and the input of the decoder consists of the overlap sequence (in blue) and the sequence to be forecasted initialized with zeros (in yellow). (Color figure online)

Transformer Decoder: Consists of 1 layer as shown in Fig. 2 (right). We use a masked self-attention sub-layer that allows each element in the decoder input sequence to attend to only the previous elements, so as to take into account only the information available at prior timestamps. Attention is implemented using Eq. 3. We use the same dimensionality of 64 for the decoder query, key, and value vectors as the encoder. We use a masked cross-attention sub-layer to establish correlations between the decoder input and the encoder output, facilitating the extraction of relevant information from both sources. We apply the residual connection [12] and layer normalization after each sub-layer as well in the decoder to maintain effective learning.

The conventional Transformer decoder [60] is designed to perform step-by-step predictions, where each prediction is performed for a single element of the output sequence. Subsequent elements have to be predicted using a single-element prior prediction. Step-by-step single-element predictions are likely to introduce cumulative errors by dependence of each forecast output on prior predicted forecast outputs, causing drift. We instead employ the approach utilized in Informer [63] to restructure the decoder to predict the entire forecast sequence of size $f \times T_{\text{Fore}}$ in a single step.

Loss. We train **Model$_{\text{Fore}}$**, by optimizing the loss

$$L = L_{\text{pos}} + \lambda_{\text{quat}} L_{\text{quat}} + \lambda_{\text{trig}} L_{\text{trig}} \qquad (4)$$

over the Transformer model parameters. In Eq. 4, L_{pos}, given as,

$$L_{\text{pos}} = (1/|W|) \Sigma_{w \in W} MSE(\text{Pos}_{\text{pred}}, \text{Pos}_{\text{gt}}) \qquad (5)$$

quantifies the discrepancy, in terms of mean-square error (MSE), between the forecasted and ground truth trajectory positions, Pos_{pred} and Pos_{gt}, for the headset and controllers. $|W|$ represents the number of training sliding windows. The term L_{quat}, defined as

$$L_{quat} = (1/|W|)\Sigma_{w \in W} GEO(Quat_{pred}, Quat_{gt}), \tag{6}$$

measures the geodesic distance (GEO) between the forecasted and ground truth quaternion orientations, $Quat_{pred}$ and $Quat_{gt}$, for the right-hand controller, left-hand controller, and headset. We compute GEO using Du et al. [13] as

$$GEO(Quat_{pred}, Quat_{gt}) = cos^{-1}(|Quat_{pred} \cdot Quat_{gt}|). \tag{7}$$

The term L_{trig}, given as

$$L_{trig} = (1/|W|)\Sigma_{w \in W} BCE(Trig_{pred}, Trig_{gt}), \tag{8}$$

represents the match in terms of binary cross-entropy (BCE) between the predicted and ground truth trigger pressure values, $Trig_{pred}$ and $Trig_{gt}$, for the controllers. We use λ_{quat} and λ_{trig} in Eq. 4 to denote the weights for the loss terms L_{quat} and L_{trig}, respectively. We use Adam [18] for parameter optimization with a learning rate of 0.0001.

6 Fine-Tuning Forecasting Using Enrollment Data

We conduct fine-tuning of the **Model_Fore** with the purpose of improving user-awareness for **Subset2** users using their enrollment data only. We perform fine-tuning for each enrollment device to provide fine-tuned models for all enrollment / use-time pairs. For the 12 cross-system and 3 same-system pairs, we evaluate enrollment from all systems and days except Cosmos Day 2, i.e., C2, necessitating 5 fine-tuned models as shown in Fig. 4:

- **Model_Q1** obtained by fine-tuning **Model_Fore** using Q1 data from **Subset2** users, and used in forecasting for Q1Q2, Q1V1, Q1V2, Q1C1, and Q1C2.
- **Model_Q2** obtained by fine-tuning **Model_Fore** using Q2 data from **Subset2** users, and used in forecasting for Q2V1, Q2V2, Q2C1, and Q2C2.
- **Model_V1** obtained by fine-tuning **Model_Fore** using V1 data from **Subset2** users, and used in forecasting for V1V2, V1C1, and V1C2.
- **Model_V2** obtained by fine-tuning **Model_Fore** using V2 data from **Subset2** users, and used in forecasting for V2C1 and V2C2.
- **Model_C1** obtained by fine-tuning **Model_Fore** using C2 data from **Subset2** users, and used in forecasting for C1C2.

Fine-tuning of **Model_X** involves Adam-based optimization of the loss in Eq. 4 starting from the weights of **Model_Fore** and using the **Subset2** users' data from the respective VR system **X**.

7   Authentication Neural Network

We use an FCN as the authentication neural network model, following the find-ing of high performance of FCNs in VR authentication by Mathis et al. [28]. However, other networks can be used by replacing the FCN for the authentica-tion step. Similar to the fine-tuning, we use enrollment data from **Subset2** users to train one authentication FCN per enrollment VR system per user, resulting in 5 (enrollment VR systems) × 20 (users) or 100 authentication networks. The 5 per system authentication models are as follows:

- **Auth$_{Q1}$** trained Q1 data from **Subset2** users, used for Q1Q2, Q1V1, Q1V2, Q1C1, and Q1C2 authentication.
- **Auth$_{Q2}$** trained Q1 data from **Subset2** users, used for Q2V1, Q2V2, Q2C1, and Q2C2 authentication.
- **Auth$_{V1}$** trained Q1 data from **Subset2** users, used for V1V2, V1C1, and V1C2 authentication.
- **Auth$_{V2}$** trained Q1 data from **Subset2** users, used for V2C1 and V2C2 authentication.
- **Auth$_{C1}$** trained Q1 data from **Subset2** users, used for C1C2 authentication.

Each authentication model takes in the concatenation of the original $f \times T_p$ partial trajectory and $f \times T_{\text{Fore}}$ forecasted output from the Transformer as the input, and provides a label of genuine or impostor as the output. Figure 5 shows the network architecture used for the FCN. We apply three convolutional blocks

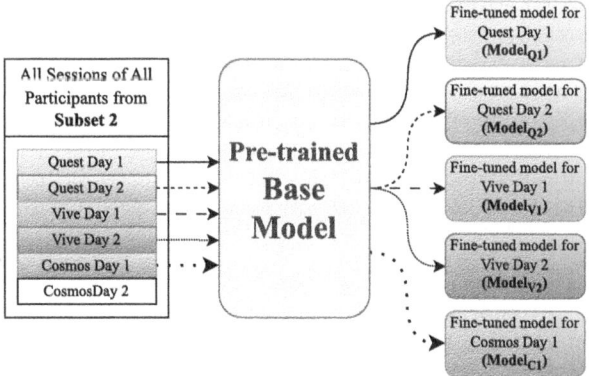

Fig. 4. We fine-tune the pre-trained base model by feeding diverse input data to it, generating distinct and specialized models with specific objectives. We input Quest Day 1 data (in yellow on the left) to the base model to obtain the fine-tuned model **Model$_{Q1}$** (in yellow on the right), similar to the input data Quest Day 2 (in gray on the left), Vive Day 1 (in green on the left), Vive Day 2 (in red on the left), and Cosmos Day 1 (in blue on the left) to obtain models **Model$_{Q2}$** (in gray on the right), **Model$_{V1}$** (in green on the right), **Model$_{V2}$** (in red on the right), and **Model$_{C1}$** (in blue on the right). (Color figure online)

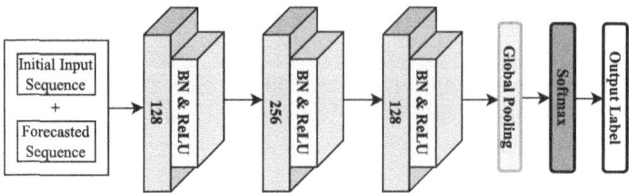

Fig. 5. We apply the FCN [61] as the classifier to authenticate users. We concatenate the forecasting input sequence and the forecasting output sequence to feed in the FCN. Pink boxes represent the filter sizes, i.e., 128, 256, and 128. BN is the batch normalization operation, and ReLU the activation function.

Table 1. We compute MSE between the ground truth and forecasted trajectories for the right-hand controller (R_{pos}), left-hand controller (L_{pos}), and headset (H_{pos}). We compute GEO between the ground truth (GT) and forecasted quaternion orientations for the right-hand controller (R_{quat}), left-hand controller (L_{quat}), and headset (H_{quat}). We compute BCE between GT and forecasted trigger positions for the right- (R_{trig}) and left-hand controller (L_{trig}).

	R_{pos}	L_{pos}	H_{pos}	R_{quat}	L_{quat}	H_{quat}	R_{trig}	L_{trig}
Q1Q2	0.082±0.047	0.042±0.014	0.020±0.002	0.035±0.004	0.019±0.005	0.026±0.004	0.012±0.014	0.688±0.002
Q1V1	0.062±0.018	0.033±0.008	0.019±0.001	0.033±0.005	0.022±0.005	0.026±0.004	0.045±0.030	0.685±0.002
Q1V2	0.067±0.020	0.040±0.013	0.022±0.003	0.031±0.005	0.021±0.004	0.024±0.004	0.040±0.016	0.684±0.003
Q1C1	0.099±0.029	0.052±0.012	0.024±0.002	0.034±0.004	0.024±0.005	0.023±0.004	0.011±0.014	0.688±0.002
Q1C2	0.091±0.023	0.049±0.009	0.023±0.002	0.035±0.004	0.022±0.004	0.025±0.005	0.005±0.005	0.689±0.002
Q2V1	0.062±0.020	0.035±0.010	0.022±0.002	0.033±0.005	0.024±0.005	0.024±0.005	0.048±0.030	0.685±0.002
Q2V2	0.068±0.016	0.035±0.008	0.020±0.002	0.030±0.006	0.019±0.005	0.024±0.005	0.041±0.017	0.685±0.002
Q2C1	0.095±0.026	0.051±0.011	0.025±0.003	0.034±0.005	0.022±0.006	0.023±0.005	0.008±0.007	0.686±0.002
Q2C2	0.092±0.020	0.050±0.010	0.025±0.003	0.034±0.005	0.020±0.004	0.024±0.003	0.007±0.009	0.687±0.002
V1V2	0.051±0.012	0.032±0.009	0.018±0.002	0.028±0.006	0.019±0.004	0.021±0.004	0.042±0.017	0.681±0.002
V1C1	0.098±0.031	0.049±0.012	0.024±0.002	0.034±0.004	0.025±0.005	0.022±0.004	0.011±0.010	0.686±0.002
V1C2	0.084±0.021	0.047±0.009	0.025±0.003	0.034±0.005	0.024±0.004	0.023±0.004	0.006±0.006	0.687±0.002
V2C1	0.094±0.026	0.047±0.012	0.022±0.002	0.033±0.004	0.025±0.005	0.022±0.004	0.008±0.007	0.688±0.003
V2C2	0.088±0.020	0.046±0.011	0.023±0.002	0.033±0.004	0.022±0.004	0.023±0.004	0.006±0.008	0.688±0.002
C1C2	0.087±0.020	0.046±0.010	0.023±0.002	0.032±0.005	0.021±0.004	0.022±0.004	0.007±0.009	0.685±0.002

in the FCN, each comprising a convolutional layer with a 1D kernel. The first convolutional block has a filter size of 128 and a 1D kernel size of 8, the second block utilizes a filter size of 256 and a 1D kernel size of 5, and the third block employs a filter size of 128 and a 1D kernel size of 3. To promote convergence and enhance generalization, we use batch normalization layers after each convolutional layer, followed by ReLU activation layers at the end of each block. We use a global average pooling layer after the three blocks, and generate the final output using a softmax layer.

During training, we optimize the FCN model by minimizing the BCE loss

$$\mathrm{L}_{\mathrm{auth}} = (1/|W|)\Sigma_{w \in W} BCE(y_{\mathrm{pred}}, y_{\mathrm{gt}}), \tag{9}$$

where y_{pred} and y_{gt} represent the predicted and ground truth authentication labels. The ground truth label is 1 for a genuine user and 0 for an impostor. We use Adam [18] for optimization with a learning rate of 0.001.

Table 2. Forecasting losses of original trajectories and normalized trajectories, where R_{pos}, L_{pos}, and H_{pos} represent the trajectory positions of the right-hand controller, left-hand controller, and headset. $Norm - R_{\mathrm{pos}}$, $Norm - L_{\mathrm{pos}}$, and $Norm - H_{\mathrm{pos}}$ denote the normalized trajectory positions of the right-hand controller, left-hand controller, and headset.

	R_{pos}	L_{pos}	H_{pos}	$Norm - R_{\mathrm{pos}}$	$Norm - L_{\mathrm{pos}}$	$Norm - H_{\mathrm{pos}}$
Q1Q2	0.082±0.045	0.046±0.017	0.020±0.007	0.368±0.204	0.544±0.196	0.399±0.178
Q1V1	0.063±0.024	0.038±0.014	0.019±0.006	0.410±0.193	0.578±0.198	0.387±0.174
Q1V2	0.068±0.026	0.044±0.016	0.022±0.008	0.388±0.187	0.547±0.204	0.419±0.181
Q1C1	0.100±0.054	0.055±0.023	0.024±0.008	0.471±0.212	0.605±0.200	0.458±0.188
Q1C2	0.096±0.047	0.052±0.023	0.023±0.008	0.479±0.213	0.623±0.200	0.448±0.180
Q2V1	0.063±0.024	0.034±0.012	0.022±0.007	0.408±0.197	0.538±0.191	0.424±0.177
Q2V2	0.069±0.027	0.039±0.014	0.022±0.007	0.358±0.189	0.532±0.194	0.443±0.175
Q2C1	0.094±0.052	0.051±0.023	0.025±0.008	0.453±0.207	0.589±0.188	0.494±0.181
Q2C2	0.092±0.045	0.050±0.020	0.031±0.009	0.478±0.207	0.646±0.176	0.480±0.170
V1V2	0.055±0.023	0.032±0.011	0.018±0.006	0.345±0.181	0.521±0.191	0.438±0.175
V1C1	0.102±0.052	0.051±0.024	0.025±0.008	0.476±0.206	0.606±0.195	0.466±0.185
V1C2	0.087±0.046	0.047±0.022	0.027±0.008	0.479±0.211	0.647±0.182	0.513±0.170
V2C1	0.096±0.054	0.049±0.022	0.025±0.008	0.467±0.210	0.612±0.190	0.516±0.172
V2C2	0.090±0.046	0.048±0.021	0.025±0.007	0.470±0.211	0.623±0.186	0.479±0.173
C1C2	0.093±0.041	0.046±0.021	0.027±0.008	0.456±0.211	0.607±0.198	0.470±0.175

8   Experimental Results

We conduct evaluations of the 12 cross-sytem and 3 within-system enrollment/use-time pairs for the 20 users in **Subset2**, and report results for the use-time data of **Subset2** users.

8.1   Forecasting Model Results

We perform ablation testing of the forecasting models by evaluating various combinations of T_p and T_{Fore}. During ablation testing, we vary T_p from 25 to 85 in increments of 10, and T_{Fore} from 10 to 70 in increments of 10. Different choices of T_p and T_{Fore} enable us to span a range of values for $T_c = T_p + T_{\mathrm{Fore}}$. We choose a maximum value of 85 for ablation testing of T_p as this exceeds more than half of the original data length of 135 timestamps. We also evaluate various values of T_o, ranging from 5 to $T_p - 5$, with a stride of 5 for each pair of T_p and T_{Fore}. We conduct ablation testing per enrollment system, and retain the parameters that provide the lowest loss value on the use-time set of **Subset2** users for each of the 5 enrollment system models.

We conduct evaluations using the fine-tuned models, as they are expected to have superior performance over **Model_{Fore}** in representing user-awareness. As evaluation metrics, we report the outputs of the individual terms in the loss function from Eq. 4, i.e., MSE, GEO, trigger pressure BCE value, and the total value of the loss. Table 1 summarizes the results of the metrics. Columns show per-device metrics, and rows show values for each enrollment/use-time pair. We report the values for each individual device where available, MSE, GEO, trigger BCE, and total loss for the hand controllers, and MSE, GEO, and total loss for the headset. We summarize the metrics for each enrollment/use-time pair, averaged over all users for that pair in **Subset2**. From Table 1, we observe that the right-hand controller MSE and GEO values exceed those of the left-hand controller and headset. The larger MSE and GEO of the right controller can be attributed to larger spatial movement from the right-handed user set evaluated in this work.

To further refine our evaluation, we employ a normalization step to ensure comparability between the ground truth and forecasted trajectories of the hand controllers and headset, i.e., we scale all trajectories proportionally to fit within a unit cube with a side length of one, then we compute the MSE loss for each of them. As shown in the last three columns of Table 2, the MSE loss of normalized right-hand controller's trajectory is lower than that of the left-hand controller and headset for nearly all the enrollment/use-time pairs, indicating the higher precision of our forecasting model for the right-hand controller's trajectory. This implies that during the training phase, optimizing the model parameters along the gradient direction of the right-hand controller trajectory yields substantial benefits in reducing the overall loss.

In order to gain deeper insights into our model's forecasting performance, we partition the trajectory into four chunks, i.e., grasping the virtual ball, elevating the ball above the shoulder, throwing the ball toward the designated target, and returning the controller to the initial neutral position. A pictorial description of the chunks can be found in Kupin et al. [19]. Subsequently, we classify the individual windows into the corresponding chunks based on the temporal range, enabling us to calculate the average loss for each metric within these chunks. We present the chunk ID associated with the smallest loss in Table 3. From Table 3, we observe that the trajectory of the right-hand controller, R_{pos}, is the feature that is the most consistent with the overall loss. Across almost all enrollment/use-time pairs, with the exception of Q1V2 and C1C2, the chunks displaying the lowest loss for R_{pos} are identical to those exhibiting the lowest overall loss. It suggests that accurate R_{pos} prediction contributes to overall forecasting, which also indicates R_{pos} is playing a critical role in driving the overall accuracy of the model's forecasting performance. In the majority of enrollment/use-time pairs, except for Q1Q2 and C1C2, the chunks exhibiting the lowest overall loss consis-

Table 3. Chunk IDs that exhibit the lowest average loss of each metric. R_{pos}, L_{pos}, and H_{pos} represent the trajectory positions of the right-hand controller, left-hand controller, and headset. R_{quat}, L_{quat}, and H_{quat} denote the quaternion orientation of the right-hand controller, left-hand controller, and headset. R_{trig} and L_{trig} mean the trigger pressure of the right- and left-hand controllers. 'Overall' and 'EER' represent the overall loss of forecasting results as Eq. 4 and authentication equal error rate, respectively.

	Q1Q2	Q1V1	Q1V2	Q1C1	Q1C2	Q2V1	Q2V2	Q2C1	Q2C2	V1V2	V1C1	V1C2	V2C1	V2C2	C1C2
R_{pos}	2	4	3	4	4	4	4	4	4	4	4	4	4	4	4
L_{pos}	3	3	4	2	3	3	1	4	3	2	4	3	2	2	2
H_{pos}	1	2	4	2	3	3	3	2	4	3	4	3	4	3	3
R_{quat}	1	4	4	2	4	3	4	1	4	4	4	4	4	3	3
L_{quat}	4	4	3	4	4	4	4	4	4	4	3	3	4	4	3
H_{quat}	3	4	4	4	4	3	4	4	1	3	4	3	4	3	4
R_{trig}	4	4	3	3	4	4	3	4	4	4	3	4	3	4	3
L_{trig}	1	1	1	1	1	1	1	4	1	4	4	4	1	1	1
Overall	2	4	4	4	4	4	4	4	4	4	4	4	4	4	3
EER	3	3	1	1	2	2	1	3	2	4	2	2	2	2	2

tently correspond to the fourth chunk of the motion sequence, which suggests that the final phase of the motion, the return of the controller to its initial neutral position, is relatively easier to forecast accurately.

From the last two rows of Table 3, we see that the chunks exhibiting the lowest overall loss in the forecasting results do not align with the chunks exhibiting the lowest EER in the authentication results. The chunks with lower forecasting loss tend to occur towards the later stage of the complete throwing motion (chunk 4), while the chunks associated with lower authentication EER predominantly belong to the mid-front portion of the entire throwing motion (chunks 2 and 3). This discrepancy can be attributed to the inherent dissimilarities in the data and objectives of the two models. The fourth chunk is the end stage of the ball-throwing behavior, returning the controller to its initial position. This phase displays minimal variation among different users compared to the middle and front segments involving the elevation and throwing of the ball. Consequently, the data in the last chunk exhibit high similarity across users, resulting in the forecasting model seeing more on this specific segment during training and achieving higher accuracy in predicting this part of the behavior. Conversely, the authentication model prioritizes the middle and front sections characterized by higher specificity, as these regions enable more precise differentiation among different users. Accordingly, during the training process, the model assigns greater weight to these segments, leading to more precise classification outcomes in these particular chunks.

8.2 Cross-System Authentication

Similar to the forecasting model, we conduct ablation testing for the authentication FCN models by varying T_c, T_{Fore}, and T_o, and show results for the parameter

Table 4. Equal Error Rate (EER) of cross-system authentication.

	Q1V1	Q1V2	Q1C1	Q1C2	Q2V1	Q2V2	Q2C1	Q2C2	V1C1	V1C2	V2C1	V2C2	Mean
Siamese [38]	0.167	0.172	0.193	0.175	0.132	0.164	0.185	0.144	0.229	**0.112**	0.173	0.161	0.158
Ours	**0.083**	**0.087**	**0.123**	**0.124**	**0.022**	**0.041**	**0.076**	**0.078**	**0.087**	0.115	**0.083**	**0.105**	0.074
Reduce %	50.29	49.42	36.27	29.14	83.33	75.00	58.92	45.83	62.01	-2.68	52.02	34.78	53.16

combinations that provide best performance in terms of equal error rate (EER). The EER, a standard measure in biometric authentication [15], represents the threshold at which the false acceptance rate (FAR) equals the false rejection rate (FRR). Lower EER indicates higher capability of genuine versus impostor distinction. In Table 4, we compare against the prior best cross-system authentication approach, i.e., that of Miller et al. [38]. The original work acts directly on the entire ball-throwing trajectory. To ensure equitable comparison to our work operates on complete window trajectories of size T_c as input, we re-train their approach using T_c-sized window trajectories from the same **Subset1** users' sliding windows as used to train our forecasting model. We use the value of T_c lowest EER as per ablation testing on our authentication FCNs.

We obtain the lowest EERs for the 3 within-system combinations as follows: 0.044 for Q1Q2, 0.012 for V1V2, and 0.030 for C1C2. In comparison, the Siamese network-based approach of Miller et al. [38] show a higher EER of 0.146 for Q1Q2, 0.116 for V1V2, and 0.104 for C1C2. Combining with the cross-system results shown in Table 4, we observe that our method outperforms the Siamese network in terms of EER for 14 out of the 15 system pairs, i.e., all except V1C2. Reductions in EER for our work compared to the Siamese network range from 29.14% to 89.66%, with an average reduction of 53.16%. The Siamese networks likely perform worse owing to two concerns with their architecture—(1) since they use convolutions, they are ineffective at modeling long-range dependencies at lower levels as attention mechanisms do, and (2) since they are designed to compare pairs of trajectories, they suffer from a class imbalance issue, since trajectory pairs from the same class are fewer than from different classes. We performed testing using an AMD 12-core 3.7GHz CPU powered machine with an NVIDIA RTX 4090 GPU. Using our pre-trained authentication model, we find that forecasting and then authentication takes on average 8.5ms per sample.

9   Discussion

In critical VR scenarios in education and healthcare, deliberate misuse by the user or non-adherence must be detected early. As VR becomes more pervasive, one may expect users to have access to different VR system in their homes, offices, schools, and clinics. Our approach provides the first mechanism to forecast motion behavior across multiple VR systems enabling early detection of misuse. We envision VR developers creating the base forecasting model in our work. While we demonstrated our approach using windows of data from the task beginning, this can be extended to any segment of user data and predicting forward. VR developers may recruit users to provide usage data to train the base model, similar to Mozilla Studies [42], in addition to usage data collected in-house through analysis of the operational profile. The application developer should also include an enrollment framework that enables the end user to provide data using their VR system to perform fine tuning as described in our work. External certification should be used to certify the base and fine tuned models to increase trust. The Responsible AI Institute [54] and TrustArc [59] offer such services. Once enrollment is complete our cross system motion forecasting model would predict the future motion of the user and determine if the user is genuine or a malicious agent even if the user moves to an alternate VR system. The application developer can choose to either lockdown usage immediately or request alternate credentials if a malicious agent is detected. Updates to the model due to release of new VR systems or evolving user behavior would be performed using new certified patches, similar to updates on operating systems and other software. Recent work by Baldoni et al. [5] raises concerns of network traffic data being used to identify users in VR-based environments. To prevent malicious use of the network traffic or motion data during transmission, VR system manufacturers should enable the creation of motion masking and de-masking frameworks in collaboration with application developers.

Early work by Miller et al. [39] using the same ball throwing dataset shows that behavior changes occur at varying time-scales. A remote field study shows the robustness of behavioral biometrics to changing user behavior [25]. The concept of changing user models and retraining for behavioral biometrics have also been explored for touch-based devices [58]. Our proposed approach can use similar guidelines that incorporate periodic retraining as the user model changes. The longitudinal field study of Liebers et al. [25] and the real-world classroom study of Miller et al. [34] demonstrates that behavior-based measures are robust over changing conditions, such as environment lighting or user fatigue. The dataset used in our work, though collected in a lab-based setting, encompasses multiple sessions/days where natural user and environment variability is present.

One of the fundamental challenges of research in cross-system VR biometrics is the lack of large-scale benchmark datasets that span multiple VR systems, users, user demographics, and tasks. We used the only known multi VR system dataset, that of Miller et al. [36,37] with 41 right-handed subjects using 3 VR systems. While the dataset provides a starting point, the lack of left-handed subjects, subjects from diverse demographics, and additional tasks makes generalizability challenging. Data collection from left-handed subjects is challenging, as 10% of the population is left-handed [50]. One strategy is to perform dominant hand detection. For the ball throwing task the detection of the dominant hand, i.e., the one picking up and throwing the ball, can be performed by measuring movement variance as the dominant hand will show larger scale movements. Future research can explore hand mirroring strategies to train networks in the absence of sufficient samples from left-handed subjects. Research in behavioral biometrics for smartphones, keyboards, and mice has benefited from the low overhead needed to collect data at scale. Downloadable apps or websites are deployed to collect user behavior data at scale. Similar mechanisms cannot be used for VR due to the setup time needed. As a result, most VR datasets are collected in lab-based settings. While attempts have been made to collect data at scale by researchers working in conjunction with game developers [48], the process of collection raises concerns as users may not have been made aware that their data would be used for biometrics. Large-scale collection efforts, such as that of Miller et al. [33], where 511 subjects watched a series of videos and answered questions is possible only due to the shorter duration of the task and the usage of public spaces for data collection. A collective effort is needed by the research community to collect large-scale multi VR system datasets.

Fig. 6. Examples of freeform VR applications we are currently developing for complex study of activity. Left: A virtual classroom [40]. Right: A virtual bank.

The ball throwing task in our dataset is broken into a starting point, i.e., picking up the ball, an action, i.e., throwing the ball, and an end goal, i.e., hitting the target. While some users may interpret the action of throwing the ball as overhanded or underhanded, these differences are biomechanical as opposed to changing the action needed or other intermediary steps. For example, it is highly unlikely that a user would lift the ball and then physically walk to the target as the action of walking to the target is uncommon for the given task. For more complex tasks, such as going to a virtual class and taking a quiz, there are likely to be higher degrees of variability in the intermediary steps. For example, a student may take virtual notes during one lecture to reinforce knowledge and forego taking notes for a different lecture if they are familiar with the material. The intermediary action, i.e., taking notes, is likely to be different across users and even within users. As part of future work, we will investigate the effectiveness of our approach when tasks become more complex with multiple possible choices of action by collecting and releasing novel cross-system datasets on more freeform tasks across multiple VR systems. In Fig. 6, we show examples of applications in banking and education that we are currently developing. A natural concern is whether the forecasting-based approach can effectively predict future behavior in an unstructured or complex task setting. Our work is inspired by the use of motion forecasting in autonomous driving, whether predicting the motion path and future positions of agents such as vehicles, animals, and pedestrians is critical to ensure hazardous situations do not arise. We direct interested readers to a recent survey by Fu et al. [8] that details pedestrian trajectory prediction for autonomous driving. Our future work will build on these forecasting approaches, already in use in unstructured real-world settings, to conduct movement prediction with awareness of user behavior in more complex VR environments.

The chosen dataset encompasses three VR system—Vive, Cosmos, and Quest, where each system uses a different tracking mechanism. The Vive uses external lighthouse-based tracking, while the Quest and Cosmos use camera-based tracking. We demonstrate the scope for generalizability across different tracking mechanisms and hardware designs. From our results we find that within-system EER is lowest for the Vive and highest for the Cosmos and Quest. We expect a higher EER for the Cosmos and Quest as they use camera-based tracking, which can be influenced by factors such as lighting, field-of-view, and rapid movement. On the other hand, the Vive uses lighthouse-based tracking which is less likely to be influenced by the same factors. The Cosmos shows a lower EER than the Quest due to a documented issue with the tracking [11]. The physical characteristics of the controllers and headset may influence how users adjust when performing long duration tasks. As part of future work, we will use the external cameras and sEMG sensors to understand how the biomechanics change as users move from system to system when performing tasks of varying durations.

In our work, forecasting the future behavior of the human enables us to generate plausible trajectories and use them for authentication. That said, if future VR systems are to incorporate behavior forecasting for behavior-based biometrics, then users must be informed in advance that the system is predicting the future behavior of the user. In the wrong hands, our approach may be used to hijack user sessions. For instance, recent work on future 3D indoor scene generation from human movement [62] may be leveraged to manipulate the virtual scene and enable an attacker to send the genuine user further from the authentication task goal while the attacker utilizes our approach to forecast the user's expected behavior and gain access. As part of our future work we will explore the system level noise model when tracking to determine whether a trajectory has been forecasted or is from a real system. For example, in the case of camera-based tracking systems, given the environment in which the person is interacting with the VR system, one can profile the tracking errors as the person's actions move beyond the viewpoint of the camera or during rapid motions. A forecasting approach may not be able to accurately represent such errors, thereby enabling the detection of real vs. attacker generated trajectories. Motion masking techniques can be employed to obfuscate user movements at the source [47] to ensure rogue agents do not intercept raw movement data.

10   Conclusion

In this paper, we present the first Transformer-based framework for cross-system VR authentication that enables early recognition of genuine or impostor users. Work in cross-system VR biometrics has been limited to the work of Miller et al. [36,37] that used a generic distance metric [36] and Siamese neural networks [37]. Prior approaches for cross-system behavior-based authentication required complete or near complete trajectories for high assurance security measures which leaves the environment vulnerable to attacks. Using the only known multi-VR-system dataset of Miller et al. [38,39], we demonstrate that our approach outperforms metric learning approaches, such as Siamese neural networks. Our approach outperformed the Siamese network of Miller et al. [37] in all system pairings with an EER reduction ranging from 29.14% to 89.66%, expect for Vive Day 1/Cosmos Day 2 when the EERs were nearly identical. Across all system pairings we show an average EER reduction of 53.16%. While our approach enables high assurance authentication with limited data, we must caution on the potential threats of generative AI models. A malicious agent could easily use our approach to generate plausible user motion behavior and attack an application before the genuine user has completed their authentication task.

References

1. Ajit, A., Banerjee, N.K., Banerjee, S.: Combining pairwise feature matches from device trajectories for biometric authentication in virtual reality environments. In: Conference on Artificial Intelligence and Virtual Reality (AIVR). IEEE (2019)
2. Alt, F., Schneegass, S.: Beyond passwords—challenges and opportunities of future authentication. IEEE Secur. Priv. **20**(1) (2022)
3. Argent, R., Daly, A., Caulfield, B., et al.: Patient involvement with home-based exercise programs: can connected health interventions influence adherence? JMIR Mhealth Uhealth **6**(3), e8518 (2018)
4. de Armas, C., Tori, R., Netto, A.V.: Use of virtual reality simulators for training programs in the areas of security and defense: a systematic review. Multimedia Tools Appl. **79** (2020)
5. Baldoni, S., Benhamadi, S., Chiariotti, F., Zorzi, M., Battisti, F.: Movement- and traffic-based user identification in commercial virtual reality applications: threats and opportunities. In: 2025 IEEE Conference Virtual Reality and 3D User Interfaces (VR), pp. 72–81 (2025)
6. Bozkir, E., Stark, P., Gao, H., Hasenbein, L., Hahn, J.U., Kasneci, E., Göllner, R.: Exploiting object-of-interest information to understand attention in VR classrooms. In: 2021 IEEE Virtual Reality and 3D User Interfaces (VR). IEEE (2021)
7. David-John, B., Butler, K., Jain, E.: Privacy-preserving datasets of eye-tracking samples with applications in XR. IEEE Trans. Vis. Comput. Graph. **29**(5), 2774–2784 (2023)
8. Fu, Z., Jiang, K., Xie, C., Xu, Y., Huang, J., Yang, D.: Summary and reflections on pedestrian trajectory prediction in the field of autonomous driving. IEEE Trans. Intell. Veh. (2024)
9. Giaretta, A.: Security and privacy in virtual reality: a literature survey. Virtual Reality **29**(1) (2024)

10. Hasenbein, L., Stark, P., Trautwein, U., Queiroz, A.C.M., Bailenson, J., Hahn, J.U., Göllner, R.: Learning with simulated virtual classmates: effects of social-related configurations on students' visual attention and learning experiences in an immersive virtual reality classroom. Comput. Hum. Behav. **133** (2022)

11. Hayden, S.: Vive cosmos rated least accurate among top headsets in controller tracking test. RoadToVR. https://www.roadtovr.com/htc-vive-cosmos-accuracy-test-controller/

12. He, K., Zhang, X., Ren, S., Sun, J.: Deep residual learning for image recognition. In: IEEE Conference on Computer Vision and Pattern Recognition (2016)

13. Huynh, D.Q.: Metrics for 3D rotations: comparison and analysis. J. Math. Imaging Vis. **35** (2009)

14. Jack, K., McLean, S.M., Moffett, J.K., Gardiner, E.: Barriers to treatment adherence in physiotherapy outpatient clinics: a systematic review. Man. Ther. **15**(3), 220–228 (2010)

15. Jain, A.K., Flynn, P., Ross, A.A.: Handbook of biometrics. Springer Science & Business Media (2007)

16. Karaosmanoglu, S., Kruse, L., Rings, S., Steinicke, F.: Canoe VR: an immersive exergame to support cognitive and physical exercises of older adults. In: CHI Conference on Human Factors in Computing Systems Extended Abstracts (2022)

17. Kern, F., Winter, C., Gall, D., Käthner, I., Pauli, P., Latoschik, M.E.: Immersive virtual reality and gamification within procedurally generated environments to increase motivation during gait rehabilitation. In: 2019 IEEE Conference on Virtual Reality and 3D User Interfaces (VR), pp. 500–509. IEEE (2019)

18. Kingma, D.P., Ba, J.: Adam: a method for stochastic optimization. arXiv (2014)

19. Kupin, A., Moeller, B., Jiang, Y., Banerjee, N.K., Banerjee, S.: Task-driven biometric authentication of users in virtual reality (VR) environments. In: Kompatsiaris, I., Huet, B., Mezaris, V., Gurrin, C., Cheng, WH., Vrochidis, S. (eds) MultiMedia Modeling. Springer, Cham (2019). https://doi.org/10.1007/978-3-030-05710-7_5

20. Lee, G., Deng, Z., Ma, S., Shiratori, T., Srinivasa, S.S., Sheikh, Y.: Talking with hands 16.2 m: A large-scale dataset of synchronized body-finger motion and audio for conversational motion analysis and synthesis. In: IEEE/CVF International Conference on Computer Vision (2019)

21. Li, M., Banerjee, N.K., Banerjee, S.: Using motion forecasting for behavior-based virtual reality (VR) authentication. In: Conference on Artificial Intelligence & Extended and Virtual Reality. IEEE (2024)

22. Li, M., Banerjee, N.K., Banerjee, S.: Predicting 3D motion from 2D video for behavior-based VR biometrics. In: Conference on Artificial Intelligence and eXtended and Virtual Reality (AIxVR). IEEE (2025)

23. Liebers, J., et al.: Understanding user identification in virtual reality through behavioral biometrics and the effect of body normalization. In: CHI Conference on Human Factors in Computing Systems. ACM (2021)

24. Liebers, J., Brockel, S., Gruenefeld, U., Schneegass, S.: Identifying users by their hand tracking data in augmented and virtual reality. Int. J. Hum.–Comput. Interact. (2022)

25. Liebers, J., Burschik, C., Gruenefeld, U., Schneegass, S.: Exploring the stability of behavioral biometrics in virtual reality in a remote field study: towards implicit and continuous user identification through body movements. In: Symposium on Virtual Reality Software and Technology (2023)

26. Lin, J., Hong, J.I., Dabbish, L.: "It's our mutual responsibility to share" the evolution of account sharing in romantic couples. ACM Hum.-Comput. Interact. **5**(CSCW1) (2021)

27. Martin, F., Hunt, B., Wang, C., Brooks, E.: Middle school student perception of technology use and digital citizenship practices. Comput. Schools (2020)
28. Mathis, F., Fawaz, H.I., Khamis, M.: Knowledge-driven biometric authentication in virtual reality. In: Ext. Abstracts of the 2020 CHI Conference on Human Factors in Computing Systems. ACM, New York, NY (2020)
29. Mathis, F., Williamson, J., Vaniea, K., Khamis, M.: Rubikauth: fast and secure authentication in virtual reality. In: Ext. Abstracts of the 2020 CHI Conference on Human Factors in Computing Systems. ACM, New York, NY (2020)
30. Mathis, F., Williamson, J.H., Vaniea, K., Khamis, M.: Fast and secure authentication in virtual reality using coordinated 3D manipulation and pointing. ACM Trans. Comput.-Hum. Interact. **6**(1) (2021)
31. Mentis, H.M., Madjaroff, G., Massey, A.K.: Upside and downside risk in online security for older adults with mild cognitive impairment. In: CHI Conference on Human Factors in Computing Systems, pp. 1–13 (2019)
32. Miller, M.R., Han, E., DeVeaux, C., Jones, E., Chen, R., Bailenson, J.N.: A large-scale study of personal identifiability of virtual reality motion over time. arXiv preprint arXiv:2303.01430 (2023)
33. Miller, M.R., Herrera, F., Jun, H., Landay, J.A., Bailenson, J.N.: Personal identifiability of user tracking data during observation of 360-degree VR video. Sci. Rep. **10**(1), 1–10 (2020)
34. Miller, M.R., et al.: Effect of duration and delay on the identifiability of VR motion. In: 2024 IEEE 25th International Symposium on a World of Wireless, Mobile and Multimedia Networks (WoWMoM), pp. 70–75. IEEE (2024)
35. Miller, R., Ajit, A., Banerjee, N.K., Banerjee, S.: Realtime behavior-based continual authentication of users in virtual reality environments. In: IEEE International Conference on Artificial Intelligence and Virtual Reality (AIVR). IEEE (2019)
36. Miller, R., Banerjee, N.K., Banerjee, S.: Within-system and cross-system behavior-based biometric authentication in virtual reality. In: 2020 Conference on Virtual Reality and 3D User Interfaces Abstracts and Workshops. IEEE (2020)
37. Miller, R., Banerjee, N.K., Banerjee, S.: Using Siamese neural networks to perform cross-system behavioral authentication in virtual reality. In: 2021 IEEE Virtual Reality and 3D User Interfaces (VR). IEEE (2021)
38. Miller, R., Banerjee, N.K., Banerjee, S.: Combining real-world constraints on user behavior with deep neural networks for virtual reality (VR) biometrics. In: 2022 IEEE Conference on Virtual Reality and 3D User Interfaces (VR). IEEE (2022)
39. Miller, R., Banerjee, N.K., Banerjee, S.: Temporal effects in motion behavior for virtual reality (VR) biometrics. In: 2022 IEEE Conference on Virtual Reality and 3D User Interfaces (VR). IEEE (2022)
40. Minnekanti, J., Banerjee, N.K., Banerjee, S.: ClassesInVR: an immersive VR-based classroom. In: 2024 IEEE International Conference on Artificial Intelligence and eXtended and Virtual Reality (AIxVR), pp. 310–314. IEEE (2024)
41. Moore, A.G., McMahan, R.P., Dong, H., Ruozzi, N.: Personal identifiability and obfuscation of user tracking data from VR training sessions. In: 2021 IEEE International Symposium on Mixed and Augmented Reality (ISMAR). IEEE (2021)
42. Mozilla: About Studies. Mozilla. https://support.mozilla.org/en-US/kb/shield
43. Mukherjee, S., Distler, V., Lenzini, G., Cardoso-Leite, P.: Balancing the perception of cheating detection, privacy and fairness: a mixed-methods study of visual data obfuscation in remote proctoring. In: Proceedings of the 2024 European Symposium on Usable Security, pp. 337–353 (2024)

44. Muñoz, J., et al.: Immersive virtual reality exergames for persons living with dementia: user-centered design study as a multistakeholder team during the COVID-19 pandemic. JMIR Serious Games **10**(1), e29987 (2022)
45. Mustafa, T., Matovu, R., Serwadda, A., Muirhead, N.: Unsure how to authenticate on your VR headset? come on, use your head! In: Fourth ACM International Workshop on Security and Privacy Analytics. ACM (2018)
46. Nair, V., Guo, W., Mattern, J., Wang, R., O'Brien, J.F., Rosenberg, L., Song, D.: Unique identification of 50,000+ virtual reality users from head & hand motion data. arXiv preprint arXiv:2302.08927 (2023)
47. Nair, V., Guo, W., O'Brien, J.F., Rosenberg, L., Song, D.: Deep motion masking for secure, usable, and scalable real-time anonymization of ecological virtual reality motion data. In: 2024 IEEE Conference on Virtual Reality and 3D User Interfaces Abstracts and Workshops (VRW), pp. 493–500. IEEE (2024)
48. Nair, V., Guo, W., Wang, R., O'Brien, J.F., Rosenberg, L., Song, D.: Berkeley open extended reality recordings 2023 (BOXRR-23): 4.7 million motion capture recordings from 105,000 XR users. IEEE TVCG (2024)
49. Olade, I., Fleming, C., Liang, H.N.: BioMove: biometric user identification from human kinesiological movements for virtual reality systems. Sensors **20**(10) (2020)
50. Papadatou-Pastou, M., et al.: Human handedness: a meta-analysis. Psychol. Bull. **146**(6) (2020)
51. Pfeuffer, K., Geiger, M.J., Prange, S., Mecke, L., Buschek, D., Alt, F.: Behavioural biometrics in VR: identifying people from body motion and relations in virtual reality. In: CHI Conference on Human Factors in Computing Systems. ACM (2019)
52. Rack, C., Fernando, T., Yalcin, M., Hotho, A., Latoschik, M.E.: Who is Alyx? A new behavioral biometric dataset for user identification in XR. Front. Virtual Reality **4**, 1272234 (2023)
53. Rack, C., Hotho, A., Latoschik, M.E.: Comparison of data encodings and machine learning architectures for user identification on arbitrary motion sequences. In: 2022 IEEE International Conference on Artificial Intelligence and Virtual Reality (AIVR), pp. 11–19. IEEE (2022)
54. ResonsibleAI: The Responsible AI Institute. https://www.responsible.ai/
55. Rettinger, M., Rigoll, G.: Defuse the training of risky tasks: collaborative training in XR. In: 2022 IEEE International Symposium on Mixed and Augmented Reality (ISMAR). IEEE (2022)
56. Rogers, C.E., Witt, A.W., Solomon, A.D., Venkatasubramanian, K.K.: An approach for user identification for head-mounted displays. In: ACM International Symposium on Wearable Computers (2015)
57. Schell, C., Hotho, A., Latoschik, M.E.: Comparison of data encodings and machine learning architectures for user identification on arbitrary motion sequences. In: Conference on Artificial Intelligence and Virtual Reality (AIVR). IEEE (2022)
58. Syed, Z., Helmick, J., Banerjee, S., Cukic, B.: Touch gesture-based authentication on mobile devices: the effects of user posture, device size, configuration, and intersession variability. J. Syst. Softw. **149**, 158–173 (2019)
59. TrustArc: Responsible AI Certification. TrustArc. https://trustarc.com/products/assurance-certifications/responsible-ai/
60. Vaswani, A., et al.: Attention is all you need. In: Advances in Neural Information Processing Systems, vol. 30 (2017)
61. Wang, Z., Yan, W., Oates, T.: Time series classification from scratch with deep neural networks: a strong baseline. In: 2017 International Joint Conference on Neural Networks (IJCNN), pp. 1578–1585. IEEE (2017)

62. Yi, H., Huang, C.H.P., Tripathi, S., Hering, L., Thies, J., Black, M.J.: MIME: human-aware 3D scene generation. In: IEEE/CVF Conference on Computer Vision and Pattern Recognition, pp. 12965–12976 (2023)
63. Zhou, H., et al.: Informer: beyond efficient transformer for long sequence time-series forecasting. In: AAAI Conference on Artificial Intelligence, vol. 35 (2021)

Interaction Techniques

Triggering Immersion in Public Spaces: A Comparative Study of Interactive Digital Art Installations

Tim Schneider[1,4]([⊠]) [ID], Céline Clavel[1], Gérard Kubryk[2,4], Michèle Gouiffès[1], Emmanuelle Frenoux[1], Matthieu Courgeon[3], Gaële Misiak[3], Vincent Hulot[4], and Xavier Maître[2,4]

[1] Université Paris-Saclay, CNRS, Laboratoire Interdisciplinaire des Sciences du Numérique (LISN), Orsay, France
`tim.schneider@lisn.fr`
[2] Université Paris-Saclay, CEA, CNRS, BioMaps, Orsay, France
[3] Cervval, Brest, France
[4] La métonymie, Le sas, Orsay, France

Abstract. Immersion is part of any human experience, whether it is governed by the surrounding contingent world or by artificial, virtual spaces. In the cultural sector, immersive technologies are increasingly employed in contemporary artworks, installations, exhibitions and live performances. In this paper, we present and compare four multi-user interactive digital art installations, which are characterised by their varying degrees of technical immersivity (VR headsets, 360-degree space, video wall with floor projection, or sphere projection), their sensing capabilities (hand and head tracking, centre of gravity and joint tracking, motion tracking and multi-touch), their inherent interactivity (single or multi-user interaction, human-machine interaction), and the supporting stimuli (audio, visual, or tactile). These installations were exhibited in different public environments (art gallery, third place/cultural centre, shopping mall, museum), where the subjective user experience of 532 volunteers was studied along different immersion factors (spatial presence, affordance, enjoyment, and cybersickness among others). The impact of user characteristics like gender, age and prior experience with immersive technology was also evaluated. While spatial presence increases with the technical immersivity of the installation, the results suggest that factors like affordance and realness are more impacted by aspects such as interaction design and installation aesthetics. The evaluated user characteristics were found to have little or no impact on the immersion experience.

Keywords: immersion · multi-user · installation · art · VR · public space · museum · comparative study · user study

Supplementary Information The online version contains supplementary material available at https://doi.org/10.1007/978-3-032-03805-0_15.

1 Introduction

The use of immersive technologies is becoming more and more widespread across different sectors of the cultural and creative industries, ranging from live performances such as concerts [4] and dance shows [24] to exhibitions and entire museums dedicated to immersive art installations [43]. While many user studies in this context focus on the application to educational [15,25,47], museum-based [1,20,45] and touristic [34] purposes, little research, so far, has investigated how different technologies impact the way in which users engage with immersive art works.

Moreover, the existing literature predominantly emphasizes experiences using head-mounted displays (HMDs), privileging individualized and enclosed forms of immersion. In contrast, a growing number of public installations employ open, shared, and spatialized immersive configurations that allow for collective engagement. These include room-scale projections, sensor-based environments, or interactive screens embedded in architectural settings. Yet, these configurations remain underexplored in XR research, particularly in terms of how they shape presence, engagement, and social interaction. In this study, we adopt the concept of presence as the psychological sense of "being there" in the mediated environment [41], and engagement as the sustained attention and affective involvement of the user in the experience [31]. Social interaction refers here to the observable communicative and behavioural exchanges between co-present users, including both verbal and non-verbal cues [12]. These dimensions are central to understanding immersive art as they mediate how users relate to the environment, to the artwork, and to each other.

In this study, we present a comparative field investigation of four distinct interactive digital art installations, each featuring multi-user interaction in public or semi-public environments. These installations were exhibited in an art gallery, a museum, a shopping centre, and a community cultural venue. By comparing these diverse setups, we aim to identify how specific immersive features (e.g., type of interface, openness of the space, narration) influence user engagement, emotional responses, and patterns of social behaviour. This work contributes to a better understanding of how immersion is constructed in shared cultural settings, and offers insights for the design of future XR-based artistic experiences.

2 Related Work

2.1 Definition and Dimensions of Immersion

The terms *immersion* and *immersive (experience)* have become ubiquitous in recent years and generally refer to the sensation of *being plunged into* or *feeling surrounded* by a different reality or environment, akin to the feeling of being immersed or submerged in water. However, a precise and universally accepted definition (especially within the academic discourse) is still lacking [11]. Moreover, there are several related concepts that are often mentioned in connection with immersion, or even used synonymously.

In this paper, we will follow the proposition put forth by Freitag et al. [11] who distinguish *immersion* (referring to the subjective experience or psychological state of a user) from *immersivity* (describing the technical characteristics of an installation or artwork that can elicit immersive experiences) and we will use the term *(spatial) presence* in this study (cf. Sect. 4.1) to describe the feeling of "being inside" the virtual or mediated environment [18,40].

More broadly, we rely on the theoretical framework proposed by Khenak, Vézien, and Bourdot [17,18], who conceptualize immersion as a dynamic construction involving the user, the system, and the context. Their model proposes a multi-layered view of immersion, encompassing several interrelated dimensions: *sensory* (e.g., display fidelity, audio-visual quality), *motor* (e.g., gestural interaction, spatial navigation), *cognitive* (e.g., situational understanding, attentional engagement), and *social* (e.g., co-presence, interpersonal interaction).

In addition, Skarbez et al. [39] emphasize three key elements in the creation of immersive experiences: *plausibility* (the sense that events are credible and respond coherently), *spatial presence* (the feeling of being located within the mediated environment), and *user engagement.* According to this perspective, immersion is not solely a function of technological complexity, but also of the extent to which the virtual environment aligns with users' perceptual and cognitive expectations.

Finally, Grassini and Laumann [13] highlight the role of individual differences in shaping immersive experiences. Their review shows that factors such as attention, mental absorption capacity, and personality traits (e.g., openness to experience) significantly influence how immersed a user feels. They argue for greater consideration of these psychological variables in immersion research.

Taken together, these perspectives suggest that immersion cannot be reduced to a purely technical property or a uniform psychological state. Rather, it emerges from a complex interplay of system features, environmental context, social configuration, and individual user characteristics. This view is particularly relevant for understanding immersive experiences in multi-user interactive installations deployed in real-world cultural settings, such as those examined in the present study.

2.2   Immersive Technologies in Cultural and Public Spaces

Cultural spaces, such as museums and galleries, are increasingly adopting immersive technologies to enrich visitor experiences [20]. They combine 360-degree projections, interactive virtual environments, and digital installations to offer deep immersion into cultural content. For instance, VR headsets transport visitors into historical reconstructions [2], while AR enhances real artworks by adding layers of supplementary information [45], enabling a multi-sensory interaction with the exhibits [37].

However, the use of immersive technologies in public spaces presents unique challenges and opportunities. These spaces include open-access areas such as public squares, parks, and building facades. In these environments, immersive digital art can capture attention unexpectedly, interrupting the habitual behaviours of passers-by and creating spontaneous artistic experiences. These immersive interventions, integrated into urban landscapes, offer dynamic artistic engagement where users are often surprised, altering how they engage with the artwork [28].

Yet, implementing these technologies in public spaces raises several practical challenges [3,30]. Users are not always equipped or prepared to engage with digital devices, and the infrastructure (such as VR or AR equipment) can be limiting, reducing the effectiveness of the immersive experiences. These challenges demand innovative design solutions to optimize the impact of immersion in unpredictable environments.

2.3   User Characteristics in Immersive Experiences

Previous research has already considered how parameters such as age, gender, and prior experience with immersive technology can affect immersion. Strikingly, the results found across the literature vary considerably and are often contradictory. For instance, several studies report significant gender-related effects [9,14,19,36,42], while others find no clear or consistent differences [26,27]. Regarding age, studies generally suggest no or only slightly negative correlations with presence [26,27]. Prior experience with immersive technology, by contrast, has been more consistently associated with enhanced user engagement and presence [10,36].

These findings highlight the need to further explore how user characteristics shape immersive experiences in real-world settings. While demographic variables are often reported, they are rarely analyzed in depth or used to explain inter-individual variations in presence, engagement, or social interaction.

Beyond demographic variables, immersive tendencies—defined as the individual predisposition to become cognitively and emotionally engaged in mediated environments—have also been investigated as potential predictors of presence and user engagement. The Immersive Tendencies Questionnaire (ITQ) [35,46] was developed specifically for this purpose and has been widely used in VR research. Although some studies suggest that immersive tendencies can influence dimensions such as presence, enjoyment, or attention, the strength and consistency of these effects remain limited, particularly in ecologically valid or public settings. These individual differences remain underexplored as potential moderators of immersive experience in real-world contexts.

2.4   Challenges and Opportunities of Immersive Installations

While immersive installations offer promising opportunities for cultural engagement and public interaction, they also present several technical, physiological, and environmental challenges. From a technological perspective, issues such as system latency, limited graphical fidelity, or unstable tracking can disrupt the sense of presence and break the immersive illusion [7]. On the physiological side, symptoms of cybersickness—triggered by mismatches between visual and vestibular inputs—can reduce the duration and quality of user engagement [37].

Moreover, immersive installations often require substantial resources, including high-performance hardware and energy consumption, raising critical questions about their environmental sustainability. These concerns are particularly relevant as such installations expand into public and cultural domains with growing visibility and impact.

Despite the growing popularity of immersive media in cultural spaces, most research has focused on controlled environments such as laboratories or VR studios. Comparatively little attention has been paid to open and semi-controlled public spaces, where interactions with immersive digital art are often spontaneous, multi-user, and shaped by the unpredictability of the setting. These contexts pose unique challenges in terms of design, user attention, social dynamics, and infrastructural constraints [30].

Addressing this gap, the present study compares four interactive digital art installations deployed in diverse public settings—ranging from enclosed exhibition spaces to open-access environments. Emphasis is placed on multi-user configurations and how variations in technical setup, social interaction, and physical context influence the immersive experience. Through a standardized comparative framework, this work contributes to a better understanding of the conditions under which immersive technologies foster engagement, presence, and meaningful interaction in public cultural environments, while also reflecting on sustainability and resource optimization.

3   Multi-User Interactive Digital Art Installations

This section presents the studied installations, their main characteristics and the environments in which they were exhibited. Table 1 summarizes and compares the characteristics. Videos of the installations can be found online for *The L∞p*[1], *Ariadne's Fibres*[2] and *The Eye of the Sun*[3].

3.1   Presentation of the Installations

Memory Box (MB) is an interactive, 6-degrees-of-freedom virtual reality experience for up to 8 simultaneous users. As part of the trans-media exhibition *L'Expérience Monroe* about Marilyn Monroe, *Memory Box* was exhibited during 6 months in the art gallery *Galérie Joseph* in Paris, France. The roughly 17 min long experience presents different scenes from Monroe's childhood and early career, as laid out in her autobiographical novel *My Story*.

During the experience, users find themselves in changing locations (e.g., an abstract cylindrical room, a battlefield during the Korean War, out on the ocean with the sun setting on the horizon) while watching subjects and objects from Monroe's memories appear and disappear. The story is recounted by Marilyn Monroe's spirit which is visually represented by a shape-shifting particle cloud

---

[1] https://vimeo.com/909495462 and https://vimeo.com/957587110.

[2] https://vimeo.com/1068742499 and https://vimeo.com/363742402.

[3] https://vimeo.com/955274163.

Table 1. Overview of the four considered installations and their main characteristics.

	Memory Box	The L∞p	Ariadne's Fibres	The Eye of the Sun
Video interface	VR headset	360-degree video projection on 2 m inner and 10 m outer cylindrical 4 m high screens and circular floor video projection	LCD video wall (4 m × 5 m) and floor video projection (4.8 m × 7.7 m)	Spherical video projection (1.6 m diameter)
Audio interface	VR headset speakers	8 central and 8 peripheral spatially distributed loudspeakers and 2 subwoofers	4 spatially-distributed loudspeakers integrated into the wall and 2 top loudspeakers	8 loudspeakers spatially distributed around the equator ring and 4 external ambiance loudspeakers
Interaction mode	6-DOF VR, hand tracking	person pose detection and tracking using 16 centrally distributed Kinect V2 cameras	person pose detection and tracking using 11 laterally distributed Kinect V2 cameras	motion and touch detection using 16 infrared cameras spatially distributed around the equator ring and 2 wide-angle infrared cameras
Experience duration	17.5 min	20 min	open ended	open ended
Experience includes a storyline	yes	yes	no	no
Number of simultaneous users	up to 8	up to 20	unrestricted (usually 1–5)	unrestricted (usually 2–10)
Exhibition space	art gallery	third place (cultural and shopping centre)	passageway in shopping mall	museum
Admission	admission fee (see Sect. 4.1)	free	free	included in museum admission
Participants included in the study	134	266	71	61

and acoustically embodied by specific sounds and the voice of French actress Stéphanie Sphyras (audio in French language with optional English subtitles). Apart from several original photos, the environments, characters and objects shown in *Memory Box* are figurative or stylized and often composed of particle clouds (Fig. 1, MB1). Users can interact with these particles using their hands of which they see a virtual representation inside the VR environment. In particular, users can attract or repel the cloud representing Marilyn's spirit by making a fist or performing a stop gesture, respectively.

On a technical level, the installation, as considered in this study, used eight HTC Vive Focus 3 headsets, each paired with a Dell Precision 5820 computer. The VR application was deployed using SteamVR and streamed to the headsets over WiFi for which a dedicated router and network were set up. Interaction within the VR environment relied on hand tracking, so no controllers were needed (Fig. 1, MB2). Each user followed their own storyline, which depended on their own interactions. However, stylized avatars were rendered when other VR users were close in the physical space.

The L∞p (LP) is a platform for creating, producing and disseminating new augmented experiences of performing and digital arts. It consists of a cylindrical structure (11 m in diameter, 4 m in height) which can be entered by up to 20 users simultaneously. It is equipped with 14 video projectors and five LED moving head wash lights projecting onto two 360-degree cylindrical screens (an outer 10-m-diameter cylinder and a central 2-m-diameter cylinder) and the floor

(Fig. 1, LP2). Moreover, 16 Kinect V2 cameras mounted onto the central cylinder enable the detection and tracking of users, while 16 loudspeakers, together with 2 subwoofers, positioned on the central cylinder and around the outer cylinder screen, provide spatialized audio. One Shuttle XPC nano mini-PC per Kinect camera is used for real-time streaming of the three-dimensional body pose data of the users while the main computation work (integration of the body pose data, interaction processing, graphics rendering, audio playback) is done by two Dell Precision 7920 computers.

During the period considered in this study, *The Loop* was exhibited in the cultural and shopping centre *Les Ateliers des Capucins* located in Brest, France. *Les Ateliers des Capucins* can be qualified as a typical *third place*, featuring several shops, cafés and restaurants as well as a cinema, theatre, library, museum and a leisure space where individuals, friends and family can meet or do indoor sport activities. Visitors of LP could participate in a 20-minute-long experience called *Spacetime Prospectives* about the concept of the arrow of time as it can be addressed by thermodynamics, special relativity, general relativity, and quantum physics. During the experience, multiple varying environments (e.g., abstract empty spaces that get populated by timelines or arrows of time, outer space with colliding planets, the Atlantic Ocean on which Columbus' ship sails towards the Americas; an infinite chess board, ...) were shown, following a fixed sequence, and narrated by several male and female voices. Visitors could not influence the progress or order of the environments but could interact with different elements in them (e.g., stimulate vibrations in the timelines, collide with moving planets, leave virtual footprints on the floor, or induce waves in the ocean). The experience was in French, free of charge and accessible, six days a week, from 11AM to 7PM, during two months.

Ariadne's Fibres (AF) is a permanent, digital artwork consisting of a video wall (5 m wide and 4 m high) composed of 4×2 4K LCD screens (Fig. 2 AF1), a floor video projection zone (7.7 m $\times$ 4.8 m) created with two 23,000-lumen-strong video projectors mounted 9 m above the floor (Fig. 2 AF2 and 3), 6 amplified ambient loudspeakers with 4 spatially distributed into the wall and 2 suspended on the ceiling over the floor. Eleven Kinect V2 cameras were distributed around the wall and connected to mini-PCs to enable real-time streaming of body poses. Two HP workstations (one Z4 and one Z8) process the user inputs (body pose and movement), compute interaction results, render the graphics and control the audio output. The artwork was commissioned by *Forum des images* and the City of Paris and is installed in the shopfront of *Forum des images* where it is freely accessible every day from 6AM to 12PM. *Forum des images* itself is located in the shopping mall *Forum des Halles* and specifically in a busy passageway (*rue du cinéma*) that connects (among other places) a large cinema to the entrance of the metro and local train system.

In its idle state, the visuals of *Ariadne's Fibres*, displayed on the video wall and projected onto the floor, are comprised of three main elements: a bright background of periodically changing colour, a real-time heat convection simulation, and a layer of slowly growing and moving drops that display videos related

Fig. 1. Photos of the installations *Memory Box* and *The L∞p*. MB1: Marilyn Monroe's spirit, represented as a particle cloud. MB2: Users of *Memory Box* wearing VR headsets and using their hands to interact in the virtual environment. Their gestures show that they were aware of the presence of other users. LP1: External view of *The L∞p* and visitors taking off their shoes before entering the structure. LP2: Users inside of LP moving around the central cylinder screen and causing a virtual grid to warp under their feet.

to the current program proposed at *Forum des images* (Fig. 2, AF1). When passers-by enter the interaction zone of *Ariadne's Fibres*, they are detected by the Kinect cameras and an associated avatar appears. This avatar resembles the user in shape and size and follows their movements and poses. However, instead of a solid body, the avatar is composed of anatomical fibrous systems (nervous, blood, lymphatic, or muscular systems) and sometimes shows bone structures. The appearance of the avatars as well as their dynamics (are the fibres stiff or supple) are partly governed by the local weather (live weather data streamed via openweathermap.org) and change with the seasons. By moving in front of the installation, users (or rather their avatars) can interact with the drops and even generate droplets which will spawn from the end of their nerve fibres. Moreover, their presence introduces a new heat source into the convection simulation, thereby stimulating turbulences (Fig. 2, AF2).

The Eye of the Sun (ES) is a motion- and touch-sensitive digital sculpture consisting of two hemispheres with a diameter of about 1.6 m which act as a spherical screen for two internal video projectors. Upon arrival, visitors find themselves face-to-face with a giant human-like eyeball (Fig. 2, ES1) which looks at them, periodically blinks, squints or changes its iris colour, and which follows visitors around as they move and try to walk around the eye. The result is a reversal of the established roles—it is now the artwork that curiously watches the human observer. When the visitor returns the curiosity and performs the correct gesture, the eye opens up to reveal its interior: an interactive simulation of the surface of the Sun, showcasing images of the solar corona captured at different far-UV wavelengths by NASA's SDO spacecraft [32].

The two hemispheres on which the images of the eye or the sun appear are connected by a 15 cm thick central disk that houses the two video projectors alongside the required optical equipment (lenses and mirrors), a network router, a sound card, and several power supplies and cables. Moreover, 16 infrared cameras, 8 loudspeakers and several ventilation fans are positioned around this technical equator. While the cameras are used to detect motion around the eye, the loudspeakers provide spatialized sound effects when the eye blinks, squints, moves or when certain interactions are performed. Finally, two more wide-angle infrared cameras are installed centrally on both sides of the equator disk allowing for hand detection through the semi-transparent hemispheres. This enables multi-touch interactions with the eye and especially the sun where users can trigger ripples in the solar surface (Fig. 2, ES3), cause coronal mass ejections or swipe between eleven coronal layers, corresponding to different wavelengths. The user detection, interaction, graphics and audio are controlled by a Dell Precision 7920 computer located a few meters away from the spherical sculpture and connected to it via two RJ45 cables for sensor, video, and audio signals.

For the exhibition considered in this study, *The Eye of the Sun* was installed at the *Museum of Arts and Crafts* in Paris and more precisely in the apse of the church *Saint-Martin-des-Champs* belonging to the exhibition spaces of the museum. The spherical sculpture was suspended on a 4.5 m tall aluminium structure, erected specifically for this occasion. Eight more loudspeakers as well as

Fig. 2. Photos of the installations *Ariadne's Fibres* and *The Eye of the Sun*. AF1: Users interacting with their avatars and the many video drops and droplets. AF2: Users interacting with their avatars and causing convection turbulences on the screens and on the floor. AF3: The video wall and floor projection of *Ariadne's Fibres* during technical maintenance. ES1: Young users interacting with the eye. ES2: The eye squinting after being touched. ES3: Users exploring the surface of the Sun and causing coronal perturbations with their touches.

two subwoofers were installed on and around the aluminium structure to provide the ambient soundscape and a standard 24-inch computer screen was attached to one of the aluminium pillars to represent a "thermometer", indicating the temperature and wavelength of the current coronal layer when in sun mode. The installation was included in the usual museum admission fee and was accessible for the general public during the event *Nuit Blanche 2024* and for the two weeks following the event.

4   Method

4.1   Participants and Experimental Design

We conducted a comparative field study to assess the subjective user experience, understood here as the individual experience of immersion, spatial presence, enjoyment, and comfort during interaction with each of the four interactive installations. Participants were recruited on site immediately after completing one of the experiences. Recruitment was carried out in naturalistic settings: *The Loop* (LP) and *Ariadne's Fibres* (AF) were hosted in public cultural and shopping centres, while *The Eye of the Sun* (ES) was part of a temporary exhibition in a museum and *Memory Box* (MB) was presented at an art gallery.

Participation was voluntary. In the case of MB, three groups of participants were identified: visitors who paid to access both the exhibition and the VR experience; visitors who paid only for the exhibition and were invited to try the VR experience free of charge in exchange for participation in the study; and invited guests with free access to both components. For all other installations, the experience was free of charge (excluding standard museum admission in the case of ES).

A total of 532 complete questionnaires were collected: 134 for MB, 266 for LP, 61 for ES, and 71 for *Ariadne's Fibres*. Only fully completed responses were included in the analysis. Table 2 presents a detailed breakdown of the number of participants per demographic group and installation.

Table 2. Number of responses to the questionnaire per demographic group and installation.

		MB	LP	AF	ES
Gender	Female	90 (67.2%)	171 (64.3%)	36 (50.7%)	34 (55.7%)
	Male	44 (32.8%)	94 (35.3%)	32 (45.1%)	25 (41.0%)
	Other	0 (0.0%)	1 (0.4%)	3 (4.2%)	2 (3.3%)
Age cohort	<20 years	9 (6.7%)	41 (15.4%)	19 (26.8%)	19 (31.1%)
	20–29 years	17 (12.7%)	74 (27.8%)	24 (33.8%)	21 (34.4%)
	30–39 years	21 (15.7%)	73 (27.4%)	8 (11.3%)	5 (8.2%)
	40–49 years	27 (20.1%)	33 (12.4%)	6 (8.5%)	4 (6.6%)
	50-59 years	36 (26.9%)	30 (11.3%)	8 (11.3%)	5 (8.2%)
	≥60 years	24 (17.9%)	15 (5.6%)	6 (8.5%)	7 (11.5%)
Prior experience with immersive technology	No prior experience	36 (26.9%)	45 (16.9%)	2 (2.8%)	11 (18.0%)
	Not very experienced	59 (44.0%)	113 (42.5%)	23 (32.4%)	26 (42.6%)
	Somewhat experienced	18 (13.4%)	78 (29.3%)	26 (36.6%)	12 (19.7%)
	Experienced	16 (11.9%)	24 (9.0%)	12 (16.9%)	7 (11.5%)
	Very experienced	5 (3.7%)	6 (2.3%)	8 (11.3%)	5 (8.2%)

4.2 Procedure and Condition Overview

Participants were approached by a member of the research team or a staff facilitator upon exiting the installation. They were briefly informed about the study's aim and procedure and assured that their participation was anonymous, voluntary, and could be withdrawn at any time without consequences. Digital informed consent was obtained at the beginning of the questionnaire. It should be noted that technical problems (e.g., frozen screens or software crashes) occurred during the experience in a few rare cases. Users affected by such events were not asked to participate in the study.

The questionnaire was made available in both French and English. It was administered via tablet or mobile device in a quiet area adjacent to the installation. Completion time averaged between 8 and 12 min.

4.3   Measures and Instruments

To evaluate the immersive experience and individual predispositions to immersion, we used two standardized and validated self-report questionnaires: the SP-IE (Spatial Presence for Immersive Environments) questionnaire and the Immersive Tendencies Questionnaire (ITQ), both available in French and English.

Spatial Presence for Immersive Environments (SP-IE). The SP-IE questionnaire [17,18] was developed to assess the user experience in immersive systems, with a particular focus on virtual environments and VR technologies. It builds on established presence questionnaires such as the ITC-Sense of Presence Inventory (ITC-SOPI [23]), the Presence Questionnaire (PQ [46]), and the Igroup Presence Questionnaire (IPQ [38]), while introducing updated factors tailored to contemporary immersive technologies.

The instrument consists of 20 items, rated on a 5-point Likert scale, and covers seven subscales: Spatial Presence (SP, 4 items), Affordance (AFF, 4 items), Enjoyment (ENJ, 3 items), Realism (REAL, 3 items), Attention (ATT, 2 items), Cybersickness (CYB, 2 items), and Social Presence (AVAT, 2 optional items used only when avatars are present).

In the present study, the SP-IE was used not only to measure spatial presence, but to provide a multidimensional evaluation of the immersive experience. In line with our broader research goal, this approach allowed us to investigate not only whether each installation was immersive, but also which experiential components—such as realism, affordance, or social presence—contributed most to users' perception of immersion.

To evaluate internal consistency, we calculated Cronbach's alpha for all subscales with three or more items (SP: $\alpha = .66$, AFF: $\alpha = .69$, ENJ: $\alpha = .74$, and REAL: $\alpha = .73$) and Pearson correlation coefficients for subscales with only two items (ATT: $r = .42, p = 0$, CYB: $r = .33, p = 0$, and AVAT: $r = .59, p = 0$). More details are provided in Supplementary Material. While the results can be considered comparable to those reported in [17], we found that the introduction of two modified subscales could improve reliability: *SP-mod*, excluding item 3 ("My sensory experiences..."), and *AFF-mod*, excluding item 11 ("I could easily examine the content of the environment"). These modified factors will be considered in the following analysis. For reference, the results obtained with the unmodified factors are presented in Supplementary Material.

Immersive Tendencies Questionnaire (ITQ). The ITQ [35], originally developed by Witmer and Singer [46] and adapted to French by Robillard et al. [35], measures individuals' predisposition toward immersive engagement. It includes 18 items, rated on a 7-point Likert scale, divided into four factors: Focus

(6 items), Involvement (5 items), Emotional Involvement (4 items), and Gaming Tendencies (3 items).

The overall internal consistency of the ITQ in our sample was satisfactory ($\alpha = .79$), consistent with prior reports for both the French ($\alpha = .78$) and English ($\alpha = .81$) versions. However, factor-specific reliability varied: Focus ($\alpha = .63$), Involvement ($\alpha = .45$), Emotional Involvement ($\alpha = .66$), and Gaming Tendencies ($\alpha = .60$). The relatively low alpha for the Involvement factor suggests potential item heterogeneity.

4.4 Data Analysis

The analysis of the collected data was guided by six initial hypotheses, formulated in light of prior research on immersive experiences in public and cultural settings.

First, we hypothesized that installations with higher technical immersivity would elicit stronger immersive experiences, as reflected by higher scores across key SP-IE dimensions. Specifically, we expected MB to score highest in SP mod, followed by LP, AF and ES. This hypothesis is grounded in the assumption that more immersive systems (e.g., VR headsets or interactive projections) elicit stronger feelings of "being there" through increased sensory richness and interactivity [37]. While spatial presence (SP mod) remains the central indicator, we also expected that other experiential factors, such as perceived realism (REAL), affordance (AFF mod), and social presence (AVAT, when applicable), would follow a similar trend. This multidimensional perspective reflects our broader objective of identifying which components of the user experience contribute most to the perception of immersion in public interactive installations (**H1**).

Second, we expected that more immersive systems would also result in higher levels of cybersickness. This is consistent with prior research showing that immersive systems involving strong visual motion or limited user control can increase sensory conflict and discomfort [14,42]. In particular, LaViola [22] emphasized that visually induced motion sickness in virtual environments often stems from a mismatch between visual, vestibular, and proprioceptive inputs—a phenomenon exacerbated in highly immersive systems (**H2**).

Third, we anticipated a slight decrease in presence and enjoyment among older participants. Although findings regarding age are mixed [26,27], some studies suggest that lower familiarity with interactive technologies and slower adaptation to novel environments may negatively influence immersion (**H3**).

Fourth, we assumed that participants with prior experience using immersive technologies would report higher affordance and lower cybersickness scores, in line with studies showing that technological familiarity can enhance the richness and interpretability of immersive content while simultaneously reducing susceptibility to simulator sickness [14,36] (**H4**).

Fifth, we did not expect significant gender effects on SP-IE outcomes, as the literature on this topic remains inconclusive and often contradictory, with some studies reporting effects [14,19,36], while others find no significant differences [26,27] (**H5**).

Sixth, we hypothesized that participants with higher immersive tendencies, as measured by the Immersive Tendencies Questionnaire (ITQ), would report stronger immersive experiences. This includes higher scores in SP-IE dimensions such as spatial presence, enjoyment, and attention. While some studies support the predictive value of immersive tendencies for presence and engagement [35, 46], these effects remain modest and context-dependent, especially in real-world or public settings (**H6**).

To test these hypotheses, mean scores were computed for all SP-IE and ITQ subscales for each participant. Normality of distributions was assessed using the Shapiro-Wilk test, which indicated that several subscale scores were not normally distributed. As a result, non-parametric statistical methods were applied throughout the analysis.

Group differences across the four installations were examined using Kruskal-Wallis tests for each of the seven SP-IE factors. The same test was used to compare participant subgroups based on age and prior experience with immersive technologies. The effect size η^2 of the Kruskal-Wallis tests was calculated as defined in [33].

To further explore pairwise differences, post-hoc Mann-Whitney U tests were conducted with Bonferroni correction of the p-values for multiple comparisons. Gender differences were also examined using Mann-Whitney U tests within each installation (installations were considered individually, so no p-value corrections were applied). The rank-biserial correlation r_{rb} was calculated as the effect size of the Mann-Whitney U tests.

All analyses were conducted using Python with the Pingouin statistics package (version 0.5.4) [44], and results were cross-validated using JASP (version

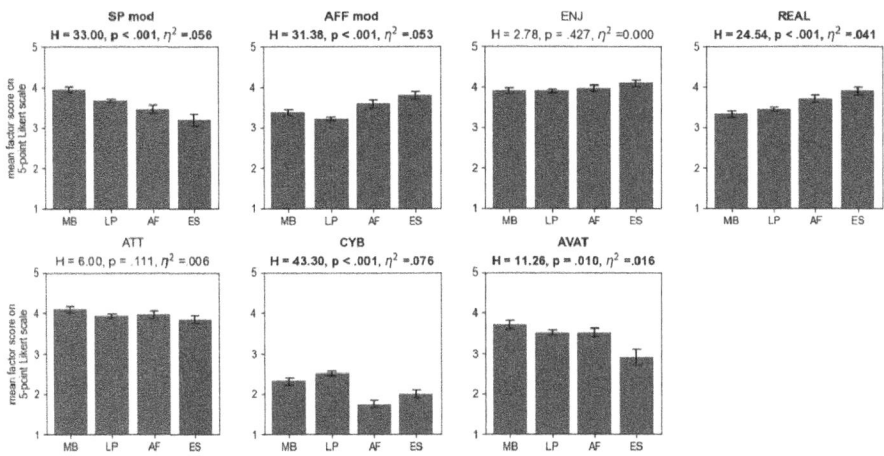

Fig. 3. The SP-IE factor scores for the different installations. The bar height indicates the group mean while the errorbars correspond to the standard error within each group. The results of a Kruskal-Wallis test are stated in the plot titles and factor with significant group differences are marked in bold.

0.18.3) [16]. A significance threshold of $p < .05$ was used for all statistical tests. Regarding the effect size, we followed the interpretation guidelines for η^2 provided in [33] (small effect: $\eta^2 < 0.06$, moderate effect: $0.06 \leq \eta^2 < 0.14$, large effect: $\eta^2 \geq 0.14$) and the recommendations by Cohen [6] for rank-biserial and Pearson correlations, where $|r| \approx 0.1$, 0.3, 0.5 are interpreted as small, moderate, or large effects, respectively.

5   Results

5.1   Technical Aspects and Immersivity of the Installation

H1 – Effect of Installation Type on Immersive Experience. To test H1, we compared the SP-IE factor scores across the four installations. As shown in Fig. 3, Kruskal-Wallis tests ($df = 3$ in all cases) revealed significant, although mostly small, differences for SP mod ($H = 33.00$, $p < .001$, $\eta^2 = .056$), AFF mod ($H = 31.38$, $p < .001$, $\eta^2 = .053$), REAL ($H = 24.54$, $p < .001$, $\eta^2 = .041$), CYB ($H = 43.30$, $p < .001$, $\eta^2 = .076$), and AVAT ($H = 11.26$, $p = .010$, $\eta^2 = .016$). Pairwise comparisons using Mann-Whitney U tests (Table 3) confirmed that MB scored highest for SP mod, followed by LP, AF, and ES. In particular, the tests revealed significant differences (small to moderate effect size) between MB and each of the three installations as well as between LP and ES. This supports the expected correlation between spatial presence and the technical immersivity level of the installation. A generally similar trend was observed for the subscale AVAT, however, only the difference between MB and ES (yielding the highest and lowest scores, respectively) was found to be statistically significant.

Importantly, the scores for perceived realism and affordance were higher in the technically less immersive installations AF and ES, with differences to MB and LP being statistically significant with small to moderate effect sizes in almost all cases. The possible implications of these results are further discussed in Sect. 6.

H2 – Cybersickness and Immersion Level. Consistent with H2, the analysis revealed significantly higher scores for cybersickness (CYB) in MB and LP (see Table 3 and Fig. 3), the installations with the highest degree of immersivity. This trend aligns with expectations from the literature on sensory conflict in VR systems and further validates the link between increased technical immersion and the likelihood of cybersickness symptoms.

5.2   User Characteristics

H3 – Effects of Age on Presence and Enjoyment. To investigate the role of age, Kruskal-Wallis tests were conducted for each SP-IE factor across age groups within each installation ($df = 5$ in all cases). A plot of the results is included in Supplementary Material. Significant age-related differences were observed in MB for SP mod ($H = 19.72$, $p = .001$, $\eta^2 = .110$) and AFF

Table 3. Pairwise comparison by means of Mann-Whitney U tests of the different installations for each of the seven SP-IE factors: Δ mean = difference between mean factor scores, U = result of Mann-Whitney U test, df = degrees of freedom, p_{bonf} = Bonferroni-corrected p-value, r_{rb} = rank-biserial correlation. Statistically significant differences are marked in bold.

		MB vs LP $df = 398$	MB vs AF $df = 203$	MB vs ES $df = 193$	LP vs AF $df = 335$	LP vs ES $df = 325$	AF vs ES $df = 130$
SP mod	Δ mean	**0.29**	**0.50**	**0.76**	0.20	**0.47**	0.26
	U	**21836.5**	**6356.0**	**5768.0**	10754.0	**10219.5**	2484.5
	p^{bonf}	**0.001**	**< 0.001**	**< 0.001**	0.421	**0.009**	0.863
	r_{rb}	**−0.225**	**−0.336**	**−0.411**	−0.139	**−0.260**	-0.147
AFF mod	Δ mean	0.16	−0.21	**−0.42**	**−0.37**	**−0.58**	−0.21
	U	19669.0	4098.5	**2768.5**	**7163.5**	**4747.0**	1711.5
	p^{bonf}	0.531	0.602	**0.002**	**0.010**	**< 0.001**	0.218
	r_{rb}	−0.104	0.138	**0.323**	**0.241**	**0.415**	0.210
ENJ	Δ mean	−0.0004	−0.07	−0.19	−0.07	−0.19	−0.13
	U	18111.0	4696.0	3650.0	9136.5	7025.0	1886.5
	p^{bonf}	1.000	1.000	1.000	1.000	0.596	1.000
	r_{rb}	−0.016	0.013	0.107	0.032	0.134	0.129
REAL	Δ mean	−0.12	**−0.36**	**−0.57**	−0.24	**−0.45**	−0.21
	U	16379.0	**3662.5**	**2458.5**	8045.5	**5488.0**	1756.0
	p^{bonf}	1.000	**0.038**	**< 0.001**	0.323	**< 0.001**	0.354
	r_{rb}	0.081	**0.230**	**0.398**	0.148	**0.324**	0.189
ATT	Δ mean	0.15	0.11	0.24	−0.04	0.09	0.13
	U	19858.5	5332.5	4873.0	9368.5	8691.5	2374.0
	p^{bonf}	0.343	0.878	0.169	1.000	1.000	1.000
	r_{rb}	−0.114	−0.121	−0.192	0.008	−0.071	−0.096
CYB	Δ mean	−0.20	**0.56**	0.31	**0.76**	**0.51**	−0.25
	U	16230.0	**6468.0**	4955.5	**13721.0**	**10671.0**	1811.5
	p^{bonf}	0.838	**< 0.001**	0.096	**< 0.001**	**< 0.001**	0.586
	r_{rb}	0.089	**−0.360**	−0.213	**−0.453**	**−0.315**	0.163
AVAT	Δ mean	0.19	0.19	**0.80**	−0.002	0.61	0.61
	U	19917.5	5433.0	**5202.0**	9569.0	9608.5	2514.5
	p^{bonf}	0.312	0.539	**0.012**	1.000	0.140	0.640
	r_{rb}	−0.118	−0.142	**−0.273**	−0.013	−0.184	−0.161

mod ($H = 16.70$, $p = .005$, $\eta^2 = .088$) and in ES for the AVAT factor ($H = 13.94$, $p < .016$, $\eta^2 = .163$). In MB, older participants reported lower spatial presence and affordance, partially supporting H3. However, no consistent effect of age was found in LP and AF, and enjoyment (ENJ) remained stable across age groups. Overall, these results suggest that age may influence certain immersive dimensions, but the effect is selective and context-dependent.

H4 – Prior Experience with Immersive Technologies. A series of Kruskal-Wallis tests ($df = 4$ in all cases) was also performed to evaluate the influence of the user's prior experience with immersive technology for each of the four installations. A plot of the results is again shown in Supplementary Material. Statistically significant group differences were found in MB for the factors AFF mod ($H = 10.85$, $p = .028$, $\eta^2 = .052$), CYB ($H = 11.41$, $p = .022$, $\eta^2 = .057$) and AVAT ($H = 12.14$, $p = .016$, $\eta^2 = .064$) and in ES for AVAT ($H = 11.99$, $p = .017$, $\eta^2 = .145$). For MB, a positive correlation between affordance and prior experience as well as a negative correlation with cybersickness were observed (albeit at a small effect size), thus generally supporting H4 and agreeing with previous works.

H5 – Gender Differences in SP-IE Factors. Participants were asked to indicate their gender with the options "female", "male", and "other". Due to the very small number of participants in the "other" category (6 out of 532), this group was not included in the statistical comparisons, as the sample size was insufficient to support meaningful analysis. To test H5, we compared responses between male and female participants using Mann-Whitney U tests across all SP-IE factors and for each installation. The results are presented in Table 4. Statistically significant small to moderate effects were observed in MB (CYB), LP (SP mod, ENJ, ATT, and CYB), and AF (CYB). Contrary to H5, these results suggest that gender may influence certain dimensions of the immersive experience—particularly cybersickness—even though the effect is not consistent across all installations or factors.

H6 – Relationship Between Immersive Tendencies and SP-IE Factors. To test H6, we computed Pearson correlation coefficients between each of the four ITQ factors (Focus, Involvement, Emotional Involvement, and Gaming Tendencies) and the seven SP-IE factors. A heatmap showing the individual results is included in Supplementary Material. Almost all correlations (except that between SP mod and GAMES and those between CYB and the ITQ factors) were statistically significant but only small to moderate ($|r| < .27, p < .05$), suggesting limited associations between reported experiences and immersive tendencies as assessed by the ITQ. H6 may therefore be considered not or only partially supported.

While this result indicates that participants with higher immersive predispositions tended to report slightly stronger spatial presence, attention, or enjoyment, the magnitude of these effects was small. This suggests that, although individual differences may play a role in shaping immersive experiences, contextual factor such as the nature of the installation and its level of technical immersivity likely have a stronger influence.

These findings are consistent with the view that immersion is not solely a trait-dependent phenomenon, but emerges primarily from the interaction between user dispositions and situational features of the environment.

Table 4. Comparison of **female and male populations** by means of Mann-Whitney U tests for each of the seven SP-IE factors and for each of the four installations. The degrees of freedom (df) for each installation are stated below the acronym. Δ mean = difference between female and male population scores (i.e. $\Delta > 0$ corresponds to a higher score in women and vice versa), U = result of Mann-Whitney U test, df = degrees of freedom, p = p-value, r_{rb} = rank-biserial correlation. Statistically significant differences are marked in bold.

Installation	Quantity	SP mod	AFF mod	ENJ	REAL	ATT	CYB	AVAT
MB	Δ mean	0.20	−0.19	−0.02	0.20	0.14	**0.34**	0.15
	$U(df = 132)$	2280.5	1791.0	1922.5	2262.0	2208.0	**2434.0**	2171.5
	p	0.152	0.368	0.785	0.179	0.268	**0.029**	0.357
	r_{rb}	−0.152	0.095	0.029	−0.142	−0.115	**−0.229**	−0.097
LP	Δ mean	**0.34**	0.22	**0.30**	0.24	**0.37**	**0.36**	−0.08
	$U(df = 263)$	**9799.5**	9031.0	**9576.0**	9162.0	**9871.5**	**9575.0**	7756.5
	p	**0.003**	0.094	**0.009**	0.058	**0.002**	**0.009**	0.635
	r_{rb}	**−0.219**	−0.124	**−0.191**	−0.140	**−0.228**	**−0.191**	0.035
AF	Δ mean	0.010	0.20	−0.02	−0.05	0.21	**−0.34**	0.11
	$U(df = 66)$	577.0	657.0	603.0	573.0	710.0	**357.0**	627.0
	p	0.995	0.317	0.740	0.975	0.094	**0.006**	0.525
	r_{rb}	−0.002	−0.141	−0.047	0.005	−0.233	**0.380**	−0.089
ES	Δ mean	0.04	0.06	0.10	0.04	−0.17	0.01	0.15
	$U(df = 57)$	434.0	430.0	482.5	423.0	387.5	412.0	439.0
	p	0.896	0.944	0.374	0.981	0.559	0.844	0.831
	r_{rb}	−0.021	−0.012	−0.135	0.005	0.088	0.031	−0.033

6   Discussion

A field study was conducted to compare four different multi-user interactive digital art installations, characterised by varying technical characteristics (in particular regarding the audio-visual hardware and immersivity levels) as well as different narrative contents, stimulus types, and interaction modes (Table 1). Moreover, the installations were exhibited in four distinct environments and visited by different audiences with slightly varying demographic backgrounds (Table 2).

In line with H1, the results show a clear correlation between the experienced spatial presence (SP mod) and the level of technical immersivity of the installation. The highest scores were reported for the VR experience MB, followed by the 360-degree projection room experience LP. Cybersickness was also strongest for these two installations, as expected in H2. Interestingly, the cybersickness scores did not strictly follow the immersivity level of the installations but instead were highest for users of LP, second highest for users of MB, third highest for users of ES and finally smallest for users of AF. However, only the differences between LP and ES, LP and AF, and MB and AF were significant.

A key finding of the study is that the perceived affordance (AFF mod) and realness (REAL) were found to be highest for the motion- and touch-sensitive sculpture ES with statistically significant, moderate to moderately large differences between ES and both MB and LP. Moreover, users of AF reported significantly higher scores than LP users for AFF mod and than MB users for REAL. Both ES and AF were designed as open-interaction installations without any explicit narration. In contrast, MB and LP featured a clear storyline which was apparent in the image sequences and narrated by one or multiple voices. Regarding interaction with virtual objects, users in MB could primarily attract or repel particle clouds which often only manifested after a short delay due to the programmed inertia of the particles. In LP, users could trigger different events through their position and movements within the 360-degree installation. However, the comparatively large number of simultaneous users (often 15–20) may have caused individual users to become confused about the correspondence between virtual events and their own physical actions. By comparison, interactions in both ES and AF may have provided users with a faster and clearer feedback on their actions. In ES, the virtual eye would follow users as they turned around the sculpture and touching the sphere would result in an immediate reaction under the users' hands (e.g., the eye would start squinting or there would be ripples in the solar corona radiating out from the position of the user's hand). Similarly, in AF, the avatars directly mirrored users' movements in terms of both the avatar's position on the screen wall and its pose. Therefore, it could be argued that ES and AF provided a simpler and more intuitive way of interacting. A dedicated follow-up study focusing on users' understanding of and appreciation for these interaction modes could further elucidate the importance of interaction design for affordance, perceived realness and the overall sensation of immersion.

Regarding the factor enjoyment (ENJ), it should be noted that comparable scores were reported for all four installations, and the Kruskal-Wallis test revealed no significant differences. Therefore, the results do not suggest a preference for a particular type of immersive technology, and no particular enjoyment-related bias should affect the other factors. A similar argument can be made for the factor attention (ATT).

When comparing the immersive art installations, it is also important to consider their specific characteristics in the context of public or semi-public exhibition environments. Unlike controlled laboratory settings, these spaces are inherently unpredictable: Users may encounter the installation unexpectedly, share the space with strangers, or divide their attention between the digital content and the surrounding physical environment. These conditions affect not only the depth of immersion but also the user's ability to engage with interactive features. For instance, the ambiguity in LP regarding who triggered a given visual effect may have been exacerbated by the presence of many simultaneous users. Similarly, in open setups like AF and ES, users could easily move in and out of the experience, creating a more fluid but also potentially more fragmented engagement. These findings underline the need to further investigate how immersion unfolds in real-world public contexts, where co-presence, shared agency, and environmental noise are not constraints to eliminate, but parameters to design for.

In addition to the comparison of the technical properties of the installations, this study also evaluated the influence of individual user characteristics on their immersive experience. Small gender-related differences were observed a few cases, in particular for users of LP where women reported significantly higher scores for spatial presence, enjoyment and attention. Cybersickness was also significantly higher in women in the technically more immersive installations LP and MB. Interestingly, the opposite result was observed for AF where male participants reported higher CYB scores (however, the overall CYB score was lowest in AF). Previous studies looking specifically at VR experiences also reported stronger cybersickness in women than in men [5,14,42] as well as a greater sense of presence [14] or enjoyment [19]. However, Felnhofer et al. [9] observed opposite results and other studies observed no significant differences [8,21,26,27,36]. Overall, the picture remains inconclusive.

Regarding age, a few statistically significant differences were observed for the VR installation MB. Here, older participants reported a lower affordance and the Kruskal-Wallis test indicated a significant difference for spatial presence, however, without any clear positive or negative correlation emerging (see Fig. 1 in Supplementary Material). The Kruskal-Wallis test also yielded a significant result for the AVAT factor for users of ES. However, this is explained by the very low score in the 30-39 years age cohort which most likely represents a statistical outlier. The absence of a clear age effect on immersion is mirrored in the results of previous studies [5,26,27]. A significant decrease of spatial presence with age was only reported by Kober et al. [21].

Considering the relationship between the SP-IE factor score and the prior experience level with immersive technology, a slightly positive correlation appears to be present in most cases, except for cybersickness which decreases with increasing experience (see Fig. 2 in Supplementary Material). However, statistically significant effects according to a Kruskal-Wallis test were only observed for the VR installation MB and the factors AFF mod, CYB and AVAT, and for the installation ES and AVAT. Positive correlations between prior experience with VR experiences or video games and presence are reported in the literature [8,10,36] as well as a negative correlation with simulator sickness [14]. Overall, it appears plausible that a greater prior experience with immersive technologies can facilitate or slightly enhance immersive experiences. Experienced users may understand and exploit the offered interaction possibilities more easily which can be crucial for a rich experience (especially for HMD-based VR installations). Moreover, users reporting a higher prior experience may simply have a personal predilection for such technologies and may therefore show greater appreciation for such installations and a higher motivation to engage with them. Dedicated follow-up studies could further evaluate this aspect.

Lastly, no large effect was observed for the self-reported immersive tendencies. A weakly positive correlation ($0.1 < r < 0.27$) was found between each of the four ITQ subscales and the SP-IE factors, except for CYB for which no significant correlations were observed (Fig. 6 in Supplementary Material). Further research is needed to understand if indeed individual tendencies play a subservient role for immersive experiences or if instead these results are a consequence of psychometric shortcomings of the ITQ (see analysis of Cronbach's alpha in Sect. 4.3).

7   Limitations

The diversity of the installations we considered, which differed in terms of their technical properties, content, narrative, user interaction modalities, exhibition interaction environment and audience, allowed us to investigate a wide spectrum of immersive, multi-user scenarios. However, as many variables were varied simultaneously between the four installations, it is difficult to ascertain which factors account for the observed differences in the user experience. Follow-up studies could focus on specific hardware aspects and consider a single exhibition environment to allow for more precise conclusions to be drawn.

Moreover, the results of the internal consistency analysis (i.e., Cronbach's alpha and Pearson's correlation coefficient) suggest that the psychometric properties of the SP-IE questionnaire and ITQ could be improved. In the case of the SP-IE questionnaire, this could involve adding items to the two-item factors of SP-IE (ATT, CYB and AVAT), for example. More generally, future studies should combine subjective user experience data (collected through questionnaires) with behavioural data (assessed, e.g., through the analysis of user trajectories, interaction time and interaction intensity). Such a multimodal approach would not only offer a more comprehensive view of the immersive process, but also allow capturing implicit or non-verbal dimensions of engagement that self-reports may overlook. Ultimately, this could help better characterize immersion in context and identify the mechanisms that facilitate or constrain it.

8   Conclusion and Perspectives

Demand for immersive experiences in the cultural and creative sectors is steadily increasing, whether for educational or entertainment purposes in museums or at live shows. This field study of four interactive multi-user art installations represents another step towards a better understanding of the strengths and challenges of different immersive technologies and their application in public, multi-user contexts.

While the results of this study confirm that high-immersivity setups, such as HMDs and 360-degree video projection spaces, can more easily elicit strong sensations of spatial presence, they also highlight the fact that immersion is a complex, multi-layered psychological phenomenon. In particular, an effective and intuitive interaction design, providing direct and clear feedback, appears to be one of several key factors for a rich and satisfying immersive user experience. Furthermore, while no large effect of individual user characteristics was observed in this study, prior experience with immersive technology may be a facilitating factor, especially for technically more complex installations.

Our study opens up several perspectives for future research. Firstly, different interaction modalities could be investigated in more detail by assessing not only the perceived affordance of an installation but also the user's comprehension of it. Scales like the *MeCue* questionnaire [29], which includes cognitive, emotional and sensory dimensions of user experiences, could also be considered for this purpose. Secondly, the impact of aspects such as the installation aesthetics (e.g., abstract *versus* photo-realistic style, anthropomorphic *versus* non-human avatars), installation narrative or the presence/absence of a clear storyline may be evaluated. In this context, an interesting question is how user interaction can be effectively incorporated into storytelling to produce non-linear narratives and how interaction with an artwork can or should depart from gameplay. Thirdly, future studies may explore different approaches to multi-user interaction in immersive art installations, particularly by comparing collaborative interaction and individual, independent interaction modalities. Finally, subjective user experience data could be combined with behavioural measurements, for example by quantifying interaction aspects such as duration, intensity, and frequency of specific movements, or through real-time emotion detection.

Acknowledgements. The authors would like to thank Michele Ziegler and Claude Farge (Forum des images), Alain Lelièvre and Romain Roget (Les Ateliers des Capucins), Bertrand Cousin (musée des Arts et Métiers), for supporting the on-site studies, and Fayçal Bouiddou, Zohra Benmira and Nayeli Hulot for their help in data collection.

Funding Information. This project work is part of Artcast4D (www.artcast4d.eu), which is funded by the European Union's Horizon Europe research and innovation program under the grant agreement No. 101061163.

References

1. An, J.: Assessment and application of digital museum visitors' emotional experience based on virtual reality technology and emotion recognition algorithm. PRESENCE: Virtual and Augmented Reality **33**, 255–268 (2024). https://doi.org/10.1162/pres_a_00425

2. Bonis, M.D., Nguyen, H., Bourdot, P.: A literature review of user studies in extended reality applications for archaeology. In: 2022 IEEE International Symposium on Mixed and Augmented Reality (ISMAR), pp. 92–101 (2022). https://doi.org/10.1109/ISMAR55827.2022.00023

3. Brignull, H., Rogers, Y.: Enticing people to interact with large public displays in public spaces. In: IFIP TC13 International Conference on Human-Computer Interaction (2003). https://api.semanticscholar.org/CorpusID:45271459

4. Cercle: Odyssey. https://odyssey.cercle.io/ (2025). Accessed 01 May 2025

5. Chang, E., Kim, H.T., Yoo, B.: Virtual reality sickness: a review of causes and measurements. Int. J. Hum.-Comput. Interac. **36**(17), 1658–1682 (2020). https://

doi.org/10.1080/10447318.2020.1778351, https://www.tandfonline.com/doi/full/
10.1080/10447318.2020.1778351

6. Cohen, J.: A power primer. Psychol. Bull. **112**(1), 155–9 (1992). https://doi.org/
10.1037//0033-2909.112.1.155

7. Cummings, J.J., Bailenson, J.N.: How immersive is enough? a meta-analysis of the
effect of immersive technology on user presence. Media Psychol. **19**(2), 272–309
(2016). https://doi.org/10.1080/15213269.2015.1015740

8. De Leo, G., Diggs, L.A., Radici, E., Mastaglio, T.W.: Measuring sense of presence
and user characteristics to predict effective training in an online simulated virtual
environment. Simulation in Healthcare: The Journal of the Society for Simulation
in Healthcare **9**(1), 1–6 (2014). https://doi.org/10.1097/SIH.0b013e3182a99dd9,
https://journals.lww.com/01266021-201402000-00001

9. Felnhofer, A., Kothgassner, O.D., Beutl, L., Hlavacs, H., Kryspin-Exner, I.: Is
Virtual Reality made for Men only? Exploring Gender Differences in the Sense of
Presence. In: Proceedings of the International Society on Presence Research, pp.
103–112, October 2012

10. Freeman, J., Avons, S.E., Pearson, D.E., IJsselsteijn, W.A.: Effects of sensory information and prior experience on direct subjective ratings of presence. Presence: Teleoperators and Virtual Environments **8**(1), 1–13 (1999). https://doi.org/10.1162/
105474699566017

11. Freitag, F., et al.: Immersivity: an interdisciplinary approach to spaces of immersion. Ambiances, December 2020. https://doi.org/10.4000/ambiances.3233, http://
journals.openedition.org/ambiances/3233

12. Goffman, E.: Behavior in Public Places: Notes on the Social Organization of Gath-
erings. Free Press, New York (1963)

13. Grassini, S., Laumann, K.: Questionnaire measures and physiological correlates
of presence: a systematic review. Front. Psychol. **11**, 349 (2020). https://doi.
org/10.3389/fpsyg.2020.00349, https://www.frontiersin.org/article/10.3389/fpsyg.
2020.00349/full

14. Grassini, S., Laumann, K., Luzi, A K.: Association of individual factors with simulator sickness and sense of presence in virtual reality mediated by head-mounted
displays (hmds). Multimodal Technol. Interact. **5**(3) (2021). https://doi.org/10.
3390/mti5030007, https://www.mdpi.com/2414-4088/5/3/7

15. Illsley, W.R., et al.: The edutainment scan: immersive media and its deployment
in museums. Museum Manage. Curatorship **40**(1), 18–35 (2025). https://doi.org/
10.1080/09647775.2024.2357066

16. JASP Team: JASP (Version 0.19.0)[Computer software] (2024). https://jasp-stats.
org/

17. Khenak, N.: Vers un modèle unifié de la présence spatiale et de ses facteurs : application à l'étude de la téléprésence en environnements immersifs. Theses, Université
Paris-Saclay, October 2020. https://theses.hal.science/tel-03098258

18. Khenak, N., Vézien, J.M., Bourdot, P.: The construction and validation of the
SP-IE questionnaire: an instrument for measuring spatial presence in immersive
environments. In: Bourdot, P., Interrante, V., Nedel, L., Magnenat-Thalmann,
N., Zachmann, G. (eds.) Virtual Reality and Augmented Reality, vol. 11883,
pp. 201–225. Springer, Cham (2019). https://doi.org/10.1007/978-3-030-31908-
3_13, http://link.springer.com/10.1007/978-3-030-31908-3_13, series Title: Lecture Notes in Computer Science

19. Kim, S.J., Laine, T.H., Suk, H.J.: Presence effects in virtual reality based on
user characteristics: Attention, enjoyment, and memory. Electronics **10**(9) (2021).

https://doi.org/10.3390/electronics10091051, https://www.mdpi.com/2079-9292/10/9/1051

20. Kim, Y., and, H.L.: Falling in love with virtual reality art: A new perspective on 3d immersive virtual reality for future sustaining art consumption. Int. J. Hum.–Comput. Interact. **38**(4), 371–382 (2022). https://doi.org/10.1080/10447318.2021.1944534, https://doi.org/10.1080/10447318.2021.1944534

21. Kober, S.E.: Effects of Age on the Subjective Presence Experience in Virtual Reality. In: Proceedings of the International Society for Presence Research 15th International Conference on Presence, pp. 149–157. Facultas, Vienna (2014). https://api.semanticscholar.org/CorpusID:53651666

22. LaViola, J.J., Jr.: A discussion of cybersickness in virtual environments. ACM SIGCHI Bull. **32**(1), 47–56 (2000). https://doi.org/10.1145/333329.333344

23. Lessiter, J., Freeman, J., Keogh, E., Davidoff, J.: A cross-media presence questionnaire: the ITC-sense of presence inventory. Presence: Teleoperators Virtual Environ. **10**(3), 282–297 (2001). https://doi.org/10.1162/105474601300343612

24. Li, B.: Le bal de paris. https://www.blancali.com/spectacle/le-bal-de-paris-de-blanca-li/ (2025). Accessed 01 May 2025

25. Liu, Q., Mi, G., Shmelova-Nesterenko, O.: Research on immersive scenario design in museum education. In: Zaphiris, P., Ioannou, A., Sottilare, R.A., Schwarz, J., Fui-Hoon Nah, F., Siau, K., Wei, J., Salvendy, G. (eds.) HCI International 2023 - Late Breaking Papers, pp. 167–175. Springer, Cham (2023)

26. Lorenz, M., Brade, J., Klimant, P., Heyde, C.E., Hammer, N.: Age and gender effects on presence, user experience and usability in virtual environments-first insights. PLoS ONE **18**(3), e0283565 (2023). https://doi.org/10.1371/journal.pone.0283565

27. Martingano, A.J., Duane, J.N., Brown, E., Persky, S.: Demographic differences in presence across seven studies. Virtual Reality **27**(3), 2297–2313 (2023). https://doi.org/10.1007/s10055-023-00805-z, https://link.springer.com/10.1007/s10055-023-00805-z

28. Michelis, D., Müller, J.: The audience funnel: observations of gesture based interaction with multiple large displays in a city center. Int. J. Hum.-Comput. Interact. **27**(6), 562–579 (2011). https://doi.org/10.1080/10447318.2011.555299, http://www.tandfonline.com/doi/abs/10.1080/10447318.2011.555299

29. Minge, M., Thüring, M., Wagner, I.: Developing and validating an English version of the mecue questionnaire for measuring user experience. Proc. Hum. Factors Ergonomics Soc. Annual Meeting **60**(1), 2063–2067 (2016), https://doi.org/10.1177/1541931213601468, https://doi.org/10.1177/1541931213601468

30. Müller, J., Alt, F., Michelis, D., Schmidt, A.: Requirements and design space for interactive public displays. In: Proceedings of the 18th ACM international conference on Multimedia, pp. 1285–1294. ACM, Firenze Italy, October 2010. https://doi.org/10.1145/1873951.1874203, https://dl.acm.org/doi/10.1145/1873951.1874203

31. O'Brien, H.L., Toms, E.G.: What is user engagement? a conceptual framework for defining user engagement with technology. J. Am. Soc. Inform. Sci. Technol. **59**(6), 938–955 (2008). https://doi.org/10.1002/asi.20801

32. Patel, A.: SDO | Solar Dynamics Observatory. https://sdo.gsfc.nasa.gov (2024). Accessed 11 Sept 2024

33. R: Documentation for package 'rstatix' version 0.7.2 —Kruskal-Wallis Effect Size. https://search.r-project.org/CRAN/refmans/rstatix/html/kruskal_effsize.html (2025). Accessed 08 July 2025

34. Robaina-Calderín, L., Martín-Santana, J.D., Muñoz-Leiva, F.: Immersive experiences as a resource for promoting museum tourism in the z and millennials generations. Journal of Destination Marketing & Management **29**, 100795 (2023). https://doi.org/10.1016/j.jdmm.2023.100795, https://www.sciencedirect.com/science/article/pii/S2212571X23000343

35. Robillard, G., Bouchard, S., Renaud, P., Cournoyer, L.: Validation canadienne-française de deux mesures importantes en réalité virtuelle : l'immersive tendencies questionnaire et le presence questionnaire. In: 25e congrès de la Société Québécoise pour la Recherche en Psychologie (SQRP). Trois-Rivières, Québec, Canada (Nov 2002)

36. Sagnier, C., Loup-Escande, E., Valléry, G.: Effects of gender and prior experience in immersive user experience with virtual reality. In: Ahram, T., Falcão, C. (eds.) Advances in Usability and User Experience, pp. 305–314. Springer International Publishing, Cham (2020)

37. Sanchez-Vives, M., Slater, M.: From presence to consciousness through virtual reality. Nature reviews. Neuroscience **6**, 332–9 (05 2005). https://doi.org/10.1038/nrn1651

38. Schubert, T., Friedmann, F., Regenbrecht, H.: The experience of presence: Factor analytic insights. Presence: Teleoper. Virtual Environ. **10**(3), 266–281 (2001). https://doi.org/10.1162/105474601300343603

39. Skarbez, R., Brooks, Jr., F.P., Whitton, M.C.: A survey of presence and related concepts. ACM Comput. Surv. **50**(6), November 2017. https://doi.org/10.1145/3134301

40. Slater, M.: Place illusion and plausibility can lead to realistic behaviour in immersive virtual environments. Philosophical Trans. Roy. Soc. B: Biol. Sci. **364**(1535), 3549–3557 (2009). https://doi.org/10.1098/rstb.2009.0138, https://royalsocietypublishing.org/

41. Slater, M., Wilbur, S.: A framework for immersive virtual environments five: Speculations on the role of presence in virtual environments. Presence: Teleoper. Virtual Environ. **6**(6), 603–616 (1997). https://doi.org/10.1162/pres.1997.6.6.603

42. Stanney, K.M., Hale, K.S., Nahmens, I., Kennedy, R.S.: What to expect from immersive virtual environment exposure: influences of gender, body mass index, and past experience. Hum. Factors **45**(3), 504–520 (2003). https://doi.org/10.1518/hfes.45.3.504.27254, https://doi.org/10.1518/hfes.45.3.504.27254, pMID: 14702999

43. teamLab: Borderless (2025). https://teamlab.art/e/tokyo/. Accessed 01 May 2025

44. Vallat, R.: Pingouin: statistics in python. J. Open Source Softw. **3**(31), 1026 (2018). https://doi.org/10.21105/joss.01026

45. Verhulst, I., Woods, A., Whittaker, L., Bennett, J., Dalton, P.: Do vr and ar versions of an immersive cultural experience engender different user experiences? Comput. Hum. Behav. **125**, 106951 (2021). https://doi.org/10.1016/j.chb.2021.106951, https://www.sciencedirect.com/science/article/pii/S0747563221002740

46. Witmer, B.G., Singer, M.J.: Measuring presence in virtual environments: a presence questionnaire. Presence: Teleoperators Virtual Environ. **7**(3), 225–240 (1998). https://doi.org/10.1162/105474698565686, https://direct.mit.edu/pvar/article/7/3/225-240/92643

47. Zhou, Y., Chen, J., Wang, M.: A meta-analytic review on incorporating virtual and augmented reality in museum learning. Educ. Res. Rev. **36**, 100454 (2022). https://doi.org/10.1016/j.edurev.2022.100454, https://www.sciencedirect.com/science/article/pii/S1747938X22000239

Point-of-Interest Based Portal Navigation Technique for Virtual Museum Visits

Michele De Bonis[1(✉)], Bruno Gomes[3], Huyen Nguyen[2], and Patrick Bourdot[1]

[1] Université Paris-Saclay, CNRS, LISN, VENISE Team, Paris, France
{michele.de-bonis,patrick.bourdot}@universite-paris-saclay.fr
[2] Université Paris-Saclay, CNRS, LISN, ARAI Team, Paris, France
huyen.nguyen@universite-paris-saclay.fr
[3] University of Porto, Faculty of Engineering, Porto, Portugal
up201906401@fe.up.pt

Abstract. Extended Reality (XR) offers a fascinating capability to transport individuals through time and space. However, are there ways to keep the users grounded in reality while exploring distant landscapes or unfamiliar places? We propose in this paper a Point of Interest portal-based navigation technique that takes full advantage of the available, often limited, physical space of the user while still facilitating natural walking in a virtual environment. This technique can be beneficial for the exploration of Points of Interest (PoIs), which is a recurrent situation in virtual museum visits. It ensures consistency between the physical workspace while a user moves from one PoI to the next, enabling applicability beyond Virtual Reality (VR) and into Mixed Reality (MR) scenarios. The connection of different PoIs in the virtual space is achieved with portals, which are strategically placed in the physical workspace. In order to evaluate the efficiency of this technique, in terms of time, presence and user subjective preference, we conducted an experiment with 19 participants who visited artefacts in various rooms of a fictitious virtual museum. The results indicated that the PoI-based portal technique delivers performance comparable to the most well-known navigation technique (teleportation), while maintaining a balance between immersion in the virtual environment and awareness of the physical space, and offering better spatial consistency. Therefore, it can be considered a viable solution for cross-reality interaction.

Keywords: Human-computer interaction (HCI) · HCI design and evaluation methods · User studies · Virtual Reality · Mixed Reality

1 Introduction

Extended Reality (XR) is increasingly emerging as an innovative and versatile technology across a wide range of fields, including industry [3], health [4], education [66], among others. In recent years, there has also been a notable surge of interest in the application of XR within the cultural heritage domain, particularly for enhancing the accessibility, engagement, and interpretive depth of historical and artistic content [10,21,26].

Virtual Reality (VR) interfaces, while offering high levels of immersion, inherently isolate users from their physical surroundings, often resulting in a sense of detachment

ⓒ The Author(s), under exclusive license to Springer Nature Switzerland AG 2026
D. Michael-Grigoriou et al. (Eds.): EuroXR 2025, LNCS 16101, pp. 292–316, 2026.
https://doi.org/10.1007/978-3-032-03805-0_16

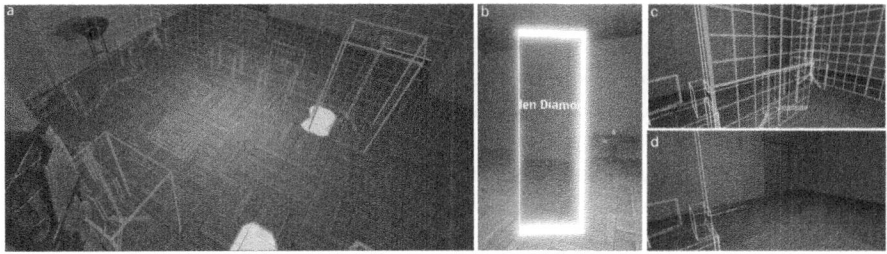

Fig. 1. Overall visualisation of our system: (**a**) Wireframe of the physical space manually reconstructed from the scans of the experiment room. The concentric squares indicate the portal activation area. (**b**) A portal with the name of the destination written on the threshold. To avoid showing distracting and irrelevant objects of the real world during the virtual experience, not all obstacles (**c**) in the physical space appear to the user, but only the nearest ones (**d**).

from the real world [63]. This dissociation can be problematic in contexts where spatial awareness and interaction with the physical environment remain important. Consequently, recent research has explored ways to help users remain aware of or even engaged with their physical context while immersed in virtual environments [54]. Although full immersion is often considered the hallmark of successful VR experiences [62], certain use cases, such as those involving safety, collaboration, or location-sensitive tasks, benefit from the integration of real-world cues or elements into the virtual experience [30, 34, 49].

Museology is an area that could particularly benefit from bridging virtual and physical environments [58]. In this context, XR technologies, which include VR and AR, can be employed to enhance both remote and on-site museum experiences, by providing narrative guidance, contextual information, and interactive exploration, all while maintaining a link to physical artefacts and exhibition space [48]. This hybrid approach supports accessibility, engagement, and educational outreach in cultural heritage [8, 38]. Because virtual reconstructions of sites or exhibitions often exceed the physical space available to users [6], effective navigation techniques are a functional necessity, especially those facilitating natural walking. In this work, we leverage Points of Interest (PoIs) as anchor nodes linking physical and virtual spaces, and employ a portal-based navigation method to support seamless transitions between them.

Among various navigation and travel techniques available both for VR and AR [33], the PoI portal technique [32] stands out as particularly appropriate for virtual visits. Its strength lies in its ability to support linear and sequential movement through content-rich environments. In many cultural heritage scenarios, such as guided museum visits or step-by-step walk-throughs of archaeological reconstructions, the user experience is inherently structured: visitors are expected to freely progress through curated PoIs in a specific room order [47]. The portal metaphor reinforces this structure by allowing users to visually and spatially "step into" the next part of the experience, making the transition both intuitive and narratively coherent. Furthermore, portals help to preserve immersion by avoiding abrupt perspective shifts or disorienting locomotion effects that are common in other navigation methods like teleportation or joystick-based movement. These methods can lead to issues such as breaking of presence [12] or Unintended Positional Drift, slowly moving users towards the physical boundaries of the workspace [15].

Beyond enhancing the visitor experience, this technique offers considerable benefits for professional use cases, particularly in fields such as archaeology. Professionals engaged in remote site exploration or digital reconstruction analysis can take advantage of an XR environment that maintains a contextual link to their physical workspace [24]. This connection allows users to interact with real-world tools, physical and digital documents [27], and collaborative surfaces without needing to remove the headset or interrupt their workflow, thereby fostering a more seamless and efficient working process.

The contribution of this paper is twofold: First, it proposes a novel adaptation of an existing concept by transforming it into a locomotion technique specifically designed to enhance guided visit experiences within virtual environments. Second, through the design, development, and thorough evaluation of this technique, the paper offers in-depth insights into the practical integration of physical obstacles within a virtual environment. These insights contribute to a better understanding of how to seamlessly blend physical and virtual elements to improve both user immersion and interaction, while maintaining the continuity of the user's real-world spatial awareness.

The paper is structured as follows. After some relevant related works presented in Sect. 2, we will detail our navigation technique in Sect. 3. We then present an experiment conducted to validate this technique in Sect. 4. Its results will be presented in Sect. 5 and a discussion in Sect. 6. The conclusion and future work in Sect. 7 will close this paper.

2   Related Work

Adapting physical space into a virtual environment requires effective navigation techniques. Building on this, we can then explore Mixed Reality (MR) strategies for blending physical and virtual spaces through PoI. This section reviews prior work on the definition of virtual museums, object substitution in MR, and locomotion methods, three key areas essential to defining the PoI-portal technique described next. While portals in VR are not novel, we found no existing approach that addresses all these aspects simultaneously.

2.1   Virtual Museums

The concept of virtual museum has been refined through the course of the last decades. In his article [7] in 2007, Antinucci gave some indications about what a virtual museum is not, such as "not the real museum transposed to the web", "not an archive of, database of, or electronic complement to the real museum", "not what is missing from the real museum." He also highlighted its value as a "communicative projection of the real museum". Virtual museums also emerged in the work of Carrozzino and Bergamasco [17], in which the ways of bringing virtual museum concepts into a real museum were explored in terms of interaction and immersion. However, they also warned us of the "Guggenheim effect": the emphasis on the container overshadows the core element or content, turning virtual museums into a distraction instead of a means to communicate information. A revised definition of virtual museum could be found in the work of Aiello *et al.* [5]. They considered it to be a digital entity that draws on the characteristics of a museum in order to complement, enhance, or augment the museum through personalisation, interactivity, user experience, and richness of content.

Another key aspect of virtual museums is the aggregation and linking of information, as explained by Schweibenz [59]: "In a real [museum], we used to build collections of objects. Now with virtual museums we can make collections of information, too." This idea represents, in essence, the nature of a virtual museum as the evolution of hypertext. It can be related to the concept previously expressed by Malraux [51], who fostered the idea of an Imaginary Museum that would bring together more works than even the greatest of museums could ever assemble within its walls. To summarise, virtual museum is not just a reconstructed 3D replica of a real museum. It offers more possibilities of interaction, personalisation, and provides different data about the way visitors move, interact and respond during a cultural visit. The solid artefacts can be enhanced through MR systems [57], user behaviour can be more effectively tracked [69], and users are no longer limited to passive observation but can interact more directly with the artefacts, including touching or even destroying them [5, 11].

Different attempts have been made to integrate these concepts into the overall experience of a museum visit. Silva and Teixeira [60] did a systematic review on the use of XR for museology. They found that there has been a growing trend in the adaptation of these technologies for interactive exhibitions or virtual assistants of guided tours, particularly in European countries like Italy and Greece. The goal is to increase visitor engagement, democratise access to culture, and to preserve cultural heritage. The authors concluded that even more institutions would adopt these technologies due to their clear benefits in attracting visitors and encouraging revisits, even though creating such experiences falls outside the expertise of museum curators and requires specific technical skills.

2.2 Space and Object Substitution

Another challenge in the implementation of an AR perspective for virtual museums is to bring and adapt intended museum experiences to the available physical space of remote visitors. This customisation would allow a personalised experience unthinkable in a traditional museum. Towards this goal, the most prominent issue is the fitting of the virtual content on the physical space or vice versa. One of the seminal works in this field is by Simeone *et al.* [61] in which the concept of Substitutional Reality was introduced. They considered that objects in the physical space are paired, with some degree of discrepancy, to their virtual counterparts. Moreover, in the work by Sra *et al.* [64], procedural virtual environments are generated based on real walkable areas. The work of Valentini *et al.* [68] is somewhat similar but with a different goal. By using RGB-D scans, virtual objects are placed in the reconstructed volume of the physical ones. Their aim was to increase the user's awareness of the real-world 3D structure. According to He *et al.* [36], the finding of the best disposition of virtual layouts to substitute real obstacles with content coherent to the current virtual environment is to be handled as an optimisation problem. However, in this work, as in the previous ones, there are several limitations due to the fixed layout of the real world and objects cannot be moved around.

These issues have been tackled in VRoamer [22] and TransforMR [42]. The former performs real-time 3D-pose-aware object substitution in a dungeon video-game-like scenario. However, the obstacles are procedurally generated from pre-authored virtual rooms while the user walks through unseen physical spaces. Moreover, sudden changes such as people or obstacles in the physical space are dynamically reflected into the virtual environment. On the other hand, while performing the same real-time 3D-pose-aware object substitution, TransforMR [42] relies on monocular RGB camera images fed through four neural networks in parallel. Similarly, based on neural networks, the work of Kniaz *et al.* [43] proposes an image-to-semantic voxel model translation framework. From a perceptual perspective, overlap between physical and virtual elements can introduce discrepancies that can be evaluated: to determine which characteristics of the physical space should be integrated into the XR experience [34], or to assess how participants respond in partially blended spaces [34,39].

2.3   Locomotion Techniques

In almost all VR applications using head-mounted displays or projection-based systems, the walkable physical space is usually smaller than the virtual environment, requiring alternative locomotion approaches [33]. Among the various existing locomotion techniques, we consider a technique that can help users to be fully aware the interactive physical space, both for user motion and obstacle avoidance. Additional issues arise when taking into account multiple-user scenarios and obstacles, as discussed in [20] who proposed an approach with an altered human joystick metaphor, or considering dynamic obstacles and irregularly shaped environments [19]. One method close to this objective involves reorienting users through turns or space modifications, such as Foldable Spaces [35]. However, it may be disorienting to the users with turns and spatial modifications. On the other hand, Redirected Walking aims to slightly change the visual perception of the user to influence their movement toward, or to steer them away from a certain direction [29]. However, depending on the implementations, it is limited to specifically constrained scenarios [45], or requires large open spaces, especially when avoiding collisions with actual objects used for tangible (passive haptics) interaction [65].

Freitag *et al.* [32] proposed portals to connect non-contiguous virtual spaces, to reorient the user when the space ends. Portals function as doorways in virtual environments, enabling users' seamless transition between locations by walking through frames like mirrors or gateways. Portals mitigate abrupt transitions between virtual locations. Husung and Langebehn [37] found portals to excel in presence, continuity, usability, and user preference compared to other transition techniques. In cultural heritage, portals have been used to switch between historical timelines, such as past and present site versions [23], allowing users to view reconstructed buildings as they appeared at their historical apogee [28]. In the work by Liu *et al.* [50], the placement of the portals is calculated and optimized to have the minimum number of redirections for a most fluid walking experience, while Misztal *et al.* [53] presented a method that uses portals to avoid tangling of HMD cables.

The portal metaphor is not novel, various visual representations have been explored [1], and in VR, portals have been used to access distant, non-contiguous locations and interact with remote objects [2, 44]. However, these implementations were not designed with physical space coherence in mind, their applicability in AR/MR contexts is not guaranteed. Moreover, their integration with Points of Interest (PoIs) to address navigation challenges in AR/MR remains underexplored; this is the focus of our investigation. In certain scenarios, it is more reasonable to focus only on some specific parts of the virtual environment that are more relevant to the current experience. For this purpose, Congdon et al. [25] proposed mapping the virtual space onto the physical workspace by arranging PoIs at available locations in this workspace.

To conclude, spatial and object substitution, when combined with an adequate locomotion technique, can provide the foundation for developing an optimal environment for virtual museums, facilitating remote visits and interactions while simultaneously accounting for the constraints of physical space, a factor that has not been thoroughly explored and tested in previous research on virtual museums.

3   PoI-Based Portal Technique for Navigation

Our aim is to create a MR environment where the elements that constitute a PoI are the links between the virtual environment and physical workspace. Virtual elements are strategically overlaid on real-word objects to maintain consistency with the visited virtual environment.

3.1   Rationale

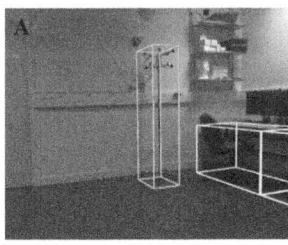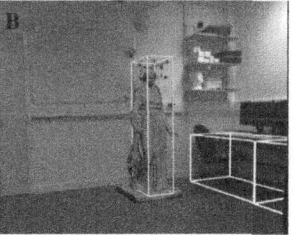

Fig. 2. A mapping Area can be positioned on an obstacle (i.e. coat hanger (**A**)) and then a PoI can be placed upon it (i.e. statue). This can be applied in AR (**B**) as well as in VR (**C**).

In the context of virtual guided visits to museums or cultural heritage sites, maintaining a connection to the physical space offers several advantages. It helps reduce disorientation and allows users to interact with real-world objects such as everyday tools without interrupting the XR experience. Moreover, during such visits, certain areas within a room or exhibition space tend to draw more attention, such as spots near particularly significant artifacts where the guide may pause to provide additional information. We refer to these areas as **Points of Interest** (PoIs). The designation of PoIs depends on the virtual environment's design.

These PoIs serve as the foundational anchors upon which the navigation system is built. To establish and maintain an intuitive connection between the physical space and the virtual environment, each PoI in the virtual environment is associated with a corresponding **Mapping Area** (MA) in the physical workspace.

Mapping Points are defined regions of the physical workspace, represented as wireframe boxes in Fig. 2, that may either correspond to real-world obstacles or to physical PoIs. These include areas suitable for MR interactions, such as spaces that allow for tangible interaction with real objects, enhanced by overlaid content of virtual visits. Each virtual PoI, representing meaningful content in the digital environment (e.g., artifacts, architectural elements, or segments of an archaeological site), is linked to a fixed MA in the physical space. This physical anchoring ensures that a user maintains spatial awareness and a coherent experience as they transition between virtual and real-world contexts. MAs can be manually positioned at strategic locations, typically aligned with structures or interactive elements of the physical space, and play a critical role in defining the orientation and layout of the virtual environment relative to the real one. Once established, the system sequentially rotates between the mapped PoIs to ensure users move across different physical areas when switching between them. In contrast to MAs, which are fixed and relatively arranged within the physical space, virtual PoIs are not constrained by spatial continuity. They may exist in separate or non-contiguous virtual environments. For this reason, a dedicated PoI-based navigation technique is required to enable seamless transitions and intuitive wayfinding between them. This approach ensures that the user can move fluidly from one point of interest to the next, even when those points exist across disparate virtual scenes.

Standard teleportation techniques are notably unsuitable in this context, as they disrupt the spatial consistency between virtual PoIs and their counterpart physical MAs. Each teleportation operation introduces an inconsistency between the virtual and physical spaces, leading to a misalignment between real and virtual spaces. When the virtual environment is anchored to the physical space, such inconsistency compromises the user's spatial orientation and the coherence of the experience. Furthermore, the inherent discrepancy between the size of the virtual environment and the limited physical workspace presents an additional challenge. To preserve the sensation of physical walking and spatial immersion during VR navigation, this mismatch must be carefully managed. Consequently, the navigation technique had to be designed with multiple constraints in mind: maintaining the spatial consistency between physical MAs and their virtual counterparts, and accommodating the expansive nature of virtual environments within the confines of the physical workspace.

In many VR applications, user workspaces are typically configured in obstacle-free areas, which is often considered the safest and most practical setup. In contrast, our objective is to enable XR experiences within everyday environments such as offices or homes that naturally contain physical obstacles. Rather than requiring a cleared space, our approach embraces these real-world elements as part of the interactive environment.

To support this vision, an XR navigation technique is essential to maintain spatial consistency between the physical and virtual realms. In a VR context, this technique helps prevent collisions by accounting for real-world obstacles, even though they are not visually present to the user. In AR scenarios, where physical objects remain visible, the technique plays a crucial role in integrating these elements into the navigation experience. This ensures continuity in spatial perception and avoids disruptive mismatches between what the user sees and what they physically encounter.

3.2 Design and Implementation

To address the challenges that arise when physical MAs and virtual PoIs are linked in a MR environment, we investigated a PoI portal-based locomotion technique. Portals in XR are a well-established technique that links two non-adjacent areas of space, enabling a user to move from one location to another simply by walking through a virtual doorway. It has been widely used in the case of reorientation (e.g., [32,50]). In our case, its main advantage would be the possibility of better exploiting the physical space surrounding the user.

In our system, the portals are the means of establishing a connection between the different PoIs. Both the portal and its corresponding target PoI must be positioned within the region of the virtual environment that overlaps with the physical workspace. To support natural walking, the portal is placed at the midpoint between its target PoI and the **Activation Zone**, a concentric square area that triggers all portals within a given room (Fig. 1.a). PoIs become subtly highlighted as users approach, enhancing visibility.

The orientation of each portal is based on the relative position of its destination PoI, prioritising spatial consistency in the virtual environment over alignment with the PoI's physical direction. This helps users better understand the virtual layout. When a portal is crossed, users are oriented toward the target PoI, for example, if the destination lies to the left of the current room, the user will turn left upon entering the new virtual room (Fig. 3). This spatial reorientation applies similarly for targets in all other directions. By constraining portal orientation to the virtual rather than the physical layout (e.g. [73]), spatial consistency between the real and virtual environments is preserved, helping to prevent user disorientation.

To activate a portal, the user must walk into the activation zone and remain still for 5 s. This activation threshold dynamically adjusts as the user steps onto or off the zone. If the user moves away, after 3 s, the countdown resets. The same timing applies when crossing portals in either direction. If ignored, portals automatically deactivate and disappear. This delay allows users to return to the previous room, if necessary.

Navigation through portals would be very effective to move from one PoI to another in a sequential order as each portal is placed between the two PoIs. There is also a mechanism to go back to the previous PoI by spawning another portal. Only the first and last PoIs connect to a single portal each; all others have two portals, one leading to the next PoI and one, when needed, back to the previous PoI. To differentiate between the portals leading to the previous PoI and the next one, they are clearly indicated with different colours and their names on a label (Fig. 1.b).

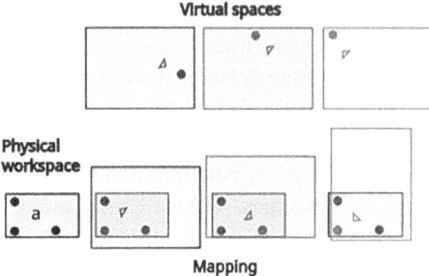

Fig. 3. A mapping of physical space to virtual environment, considering three MAs, shown in black, and three virtual PoIs, in colours. There is an activation zone at the centre of the physical space, indicated with an 'a'. The triangle (△) indicates the facing direction of the portal, pointing towards the PoI. The pivot of this alignment is the PoI.

The technique was conceived to be perfectly adaptable to a MR environment. To maintain the link with the physical space, the edges of the obstacles of the physical room become progressively visible, as the user approaches them (Fig. 1.d). The colour of the wireframe, would change in each virtual room, also when visible through a portal. The wireframe lines should be sufficient for the user to estimate the depth and distance to the real objects (cf. [9]).

The other important advantage of this technique would be to avoid disorientation and collision with obstacles, and improve the flow of the experience (as it would happen with Chaperone or Guardian system (cf. [40,52]).

4 User Study

To evaluate the performance of the proposed approach in Sect. 3.2, we compared the PoI-based navigation technique using portals to the most used locomotion technique in VR: controller-based teleportation, which serves as baseline. We aimed to prove that the performance of this technique, if not similar, would not be significantly lower than the teleportation, an already well-known method that does not need to be learned from scratch but does not allow for natural walking. Moreover, ease of use had also to be taken into account, so that even an inexperienced user could immediately understand how the technique works and navigate the scene. This comparison could not be done in MR because of the misalignment problem mentioned above (3.1). To be clear: controller-teleportation is only suitable for VR, while the PoI-Portal technique applies to both VR and MR.

For this reason, we designed a VR scenario for the user study to allow a meaningful comparison to the existing baseline of teleportation. The VR-based evaluation can equally give insights into the validity of this technique and justify its adaptation in a MR context. At the same time, we aimed to assess whether the portal navigation technique could improve spatial awareness during museum visits and information recall afterwards. To evaluate this, participants completed two quizzes in which, depending on the condition, a PoI was either omitted or provided as a reference for object alignment.

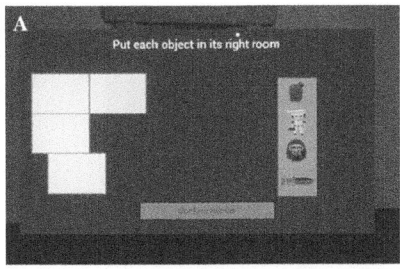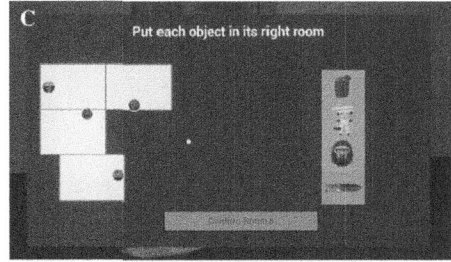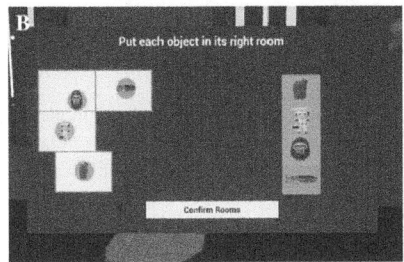

Fig. 4. The Quiz 1, shown to the participant after the visit, without reference (**A**) and with reference (**C**), and the results after the objects have been placed (**B** and **D**). Quiz 2 had the same interface, but the participants had to place the object in its exact spot, within the room.

4.1 Hypotheses

We aimed to assess the impact of the two locomotion techniques (portal and teleportation) on the overall visit experience. Additionally, we sought to evaluate participants' subjective preferences for each method. Our hypotheses were as follows:

- **H1**: The PoI portal-based navigation will provide results comparable to those of point-and-click laser-beam teleportation using controller in terms of user performance and usability.
- **H2**: The PoI portal technique will have a measurable impact on spatial awareness, either enhancing or diminishing it, compared to the conventional teleportation method.

We conducted a within-subject controlled experiment with two independent factors:

- TECHNIQUE with two variations: *Teleportation* and *Portals*;
- QUIZ with two variations: *Referenced* and *Not-Referenced* (Fig. 4).

4.2 Procedure and Tasks

The experiment lasted on the average 35 min for each participant. Each session started with the greetings, signing of the consent form, and filling a demographics questionnaire that also contains a question about the participant' previous experience in VR and

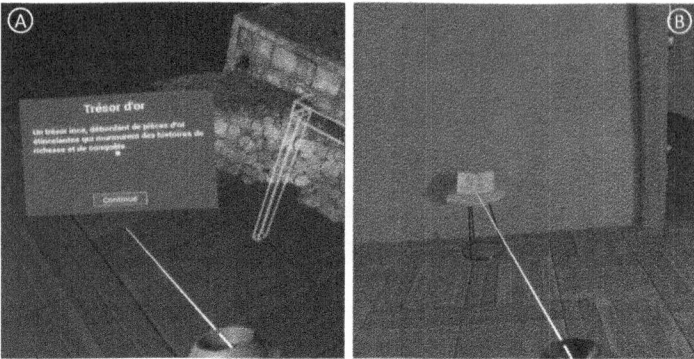

Fig. 5. A) During the visit, the user had to read a caption displayed near the PoI. Its content was shown only when the user was close enough to the PoI, otherwise only the title was readable. B) In the same room as the PoI, the user had to point and select another object, which was not necessarily semantically related to the PoI.

video games. In the instructional phase that followed, the participant was explained how to use the headset and the controllers for the teleportation as well as the portals.

During the evaluation phase, they had to visit a virtual museum whose setting consisted of four different rooms. Each room contained one PoI, represented by artifacts of a fictitious ancient civilisation. Near each PoI, there was a caption that the participant were instructed to check out and click on (Fig. 5), to confirm they had actually read it. Every room contained also another small, handheld object, such as a plate, a diary, or a violin, that the participant had to find as well. When the participant was close to the object, a ray would appear from the controller. When the object was pointed at, it would be highlighted.

At the end of the visit, the participant had to complete two recall tasks in the guise of quizzes (Fig. 4). In the first quiz, they had to place each object in its corresponding room, perceived during the visit. Once this quiz was finished, its solutions were shown to the participant regardless of whether they gave the correct answers or not. In the second one, they had to align each object in its exact placement within each room. For both of the quizzes, there were two different conditions: one displayed only the room layout (Fig. 4.A & B), while the other included PoIs for reference on the layout of the rooms (Fig. 4.C & D).

There were four L-shaped layouts in which the participants tested four different conditions. Each layout was randomly assigned to a condition at the beginning of the experiment. The museum layout was consistent across all conditions, featuring an L-shaped design (see Fig. 4). However, the Points of Interest (PoIs) and object placements within each room varied across four different sets, which were randomly assigned. Care was taken to ensure that no objects were repeated for any participant, and that each object was easily distinguishable to prevent confusion between conditions. Each participant completed a total of four virtual museum visits, one for each layout. There were four rooms to explore across these different layouts. Two layouts were used for repeated-measures of each TECHNIQUE: one with the quizzes including PoI reference and one without. The order of the setups varied for each participant. It could either start with two portal navigation setups followed by two teleportation setups or vice versa. There were 8 possible orders in total, to which participants were sequentially assigned (Table 1).

Table 1. Eight possible conditions of the experiment. Teleportation (T) or Portals (P), with (r) or without (x) PoI reference in the quizzes.

Tr-Tx-Pr-Px	Tr-Tx-Px-Pr
Tx-Tr-Pr-Px	Tx-Tr-Px-Pr
Pr-Px-Tr-Tx	Pr-Px-Tx-Tr
Px-Pr-Tr-Tx	Px-Pr-Tx-Tr

4.3 Participants

A total of 19 participants took part in the experiment, aged between 20 and 40 ($\mu = 33.3$, $\sigma = 4.5$). There were 12 men and 7 women, and 20% of the participants were left-handed. 45% of the participants played video-games every week or more. and 75% had used VR before.

4.4 Data Collection

We registered 76 trials from 2 TECHNIQUES $\times$ 2 QUIZZES $\times$ 19 participants. For each trial, we collected the following data:

– *Task Completion Time (TCT)*: The time elapsed between the start of the visit and the moment the last PoI was clicked on.
– *Travelled Distance*: The distance users walked in the real space and the corresponding distance walked in the virtual space, which varies because of teleportation.
– *Quiz answers*: The answer to the two quizzes. The first one required the participant to place a small icon of each object observed and highlighted during the visit into its correct room. The participant could get a maximum of four correct answers in this quiz. In the second quiz, the participant positioned the correct emplacement of each object within each room. The participant got a score from 0–100 which was assigned proportionally to the distance of the object from its right emplacement. Quiz 2 must necessarily follow Quiz 1 because presenting it earlier would reveal answers to Quiz 1.
– *Subjective questionnaires*: User engagement [55], Presence [72], and System Usability Scale (SUS) [46], on a 1 to 7 Likert scale.

At the end of the experiment, we also gathered some subjective feedback from the participants about their visit.

4.5   Equipment and Software

The following hardware was used for the development and execution of the experiment: a HP Z1 workstation, with NVIDIA RTX 3060 graphic card, Intel®Core™i9 13900, 32 Go RAM; and a Varjo XR-1 headset with HTC VIVE controllers. The available physical workspace had a size of 4×3.5 m^2. The experience was developed using Unreal Engine 5.3 with OpenXR plugins. The assets came from Epic Game Store and 3D models of objects from available online 3D content such as blendswap.com, turbosquid.com and Epic Games Store.

5   Results

5.1   Task Completion Time (TCT)

The average TCT needed to visit four PoIs and find four objects was repeatedly measured twice for each navigation technique. The QQ plots and Shapiro-Wilk test confirmed data normality. Since the TCT did not depend on the types of references used on the quizzes. We conducted a repeated-measures ANOVA with navigation technique (portal vs. teleportation) as a within-subject factor to assess its effect on task completion time. The result showed a significant difference in task completion time between teleportation and portal-based navigation, $F(1,36) = 18.78$, $p < 0.001$, $\eta^2 = 0.22$.

Tukey HSD revealed a significant difference between the first portal condition ($\mu = 230.61 \pm 101.49$ s) and first teleport condition ($\mu = 161.50 \pm 73.72$ s, p = 0.03) and second teleport condition ($\mu = 121.83 \pm 34.97$ s, p < 0.001), as shown in Fig. 6.

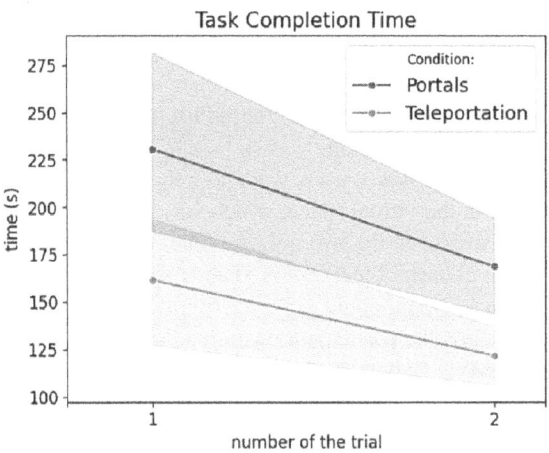

Fig. 6. Task completion time for each technique in the first and second trials for each technique. Shaded areas indicate CI. Error bars show 95% CI.

5.2   Travelled Distance

The *Virtual Distance* for both navigation methods did not reveal normality, as performed by QQ-plots and Shapiro-Wilk test. Different transformations such as log, square-root or cube-root could not normalise the data. Therefore, we conducted the Wilcoxon signed-rank test [71] on it. We found no significant difference between portals and teleportation technique ($Z = 84.0$, p = 0.97, effect size r = 0.01), with $\mu_P = 77.34 \pm 24.01$ m and $\mu_T = 76.80 \pm 24.09$ m (Fig. 7).

For *Real Distance*, the data was normalised with a log transformation (cf. [41] p.316).

We conducted a two-way repeated-measures ANOVA with navigation technique (portal vs. teleportation) and trial order (first vs. second) as within-subject factors on log-transformed real distance. The result showed a significant difference in real distance between teleportation and portal-based navigation, $F(1,36) = 118.15$, $p < 0.001$, $\eta^2 = 0.71$.

In fact, portals resulted in longer distances on average $\mu_P = 40.96 \pm 14.64$ m and $\mu_T = 14.04 \pm 5.88$ m. Tukey HSD test confirmed this difference (M = 26.92 ± 7.55 m, p < 0.01).

In addition, Fig. 8 offers an overview of the walkable space area, where participants collectively lingered for the most time during the experiment.

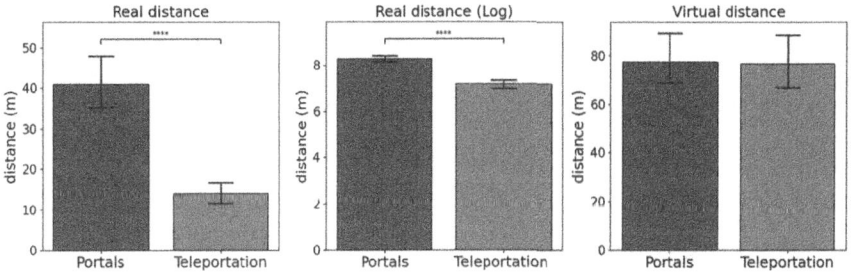

Fig. 7. Real and Virtual Distance travelled by participants with the two techniques. Error bars show 95% CI.

5.3   Spatial Awareness Quiz 1 and Quiz 2 Scores

The Quiz 1 and Quiz 2 scores were measured and analysed. Quiz 1 was about the positioning of each object in its right room and Quiz 2 the correct emplacement of the objects within the rooms. QQ-plots and Shapiro-Wilk tests did not reveal normality of the data and the transformations using log, square-root or cube-root could not normalise it. Consequently, we ran Wilcoxon rank-sum test on it and we got $Z = 60.0, p = 0.26$ for Quiz 1 and $Z = 233.0, p = 0.11$ for Quiz 2, showing that the two quiz conditions were not significantly different. The same procedure was executed for all the four possible combinations of two TECHNIQUES and two QUIZZES. However, the difference between groups were not statistically significant either.

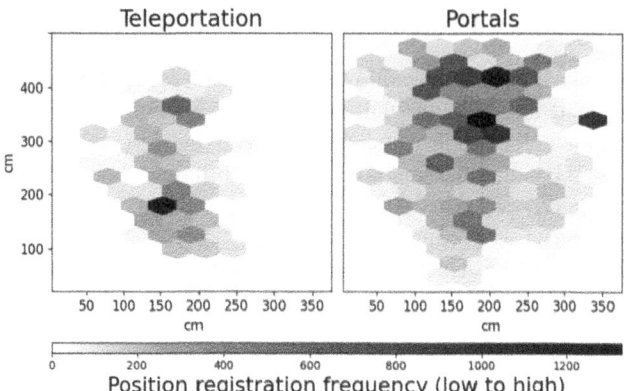

Fig. 8. Comparing the number of times participants walked over specific positions (indicated by their coordinates in the physical workspace), it shows that using portals, participants tended to explore a greater portion of the available physical space than in the teleportation condition.

Despite the results not confirming any significant difference, the lower score in Quiz 1 appeared when there were no reference points. In this case, portals performed worse than teleportation, with participants identifying one less correct room on average, as shown in Fig. 9. On the other hand, the best scores occurred in the conditions with references in the layout.

In Quiz 2, the performance was almost identical between teleportation and portals, with or without reference, even though the participants using portals had a slightly lower score compared to the teleportation technique. Notably, the presence or absence of references did not seem to impact the teleportation in either condition (Fig. 10).

5.4 Subjective Questionnaires

To compare the results of the three questionnaires (User engagement, Presence, and System Usability Scale) , their normality firstly was tested using Shapiro-Wilk test. The findings showed that the User engagement and Presence had a normal distribution, but the SUS questionnaire did not.

According to the ANOVA results, the means for User Engagement ($F(1,36) = 0.67, p = 0.42$) and Presence ($F(1,36) = 1.30, p = 0.26$) did not differ statistically significantly (Fig. 12.a and Fig. 11). Therefore, we did not have enough evidence to say that there was a difference between the two techniques regarding them.

For the System Usability Scale, Wilcoxon rank-sum test showed a significant difference between portals and teleportation technique, respectively 72 and 84 ($Z = 18.5, p = 0.002$). Both the conditions were above 68, which is considered the threshold for a system with an acceptable usability [46] (Fig. 12.b).

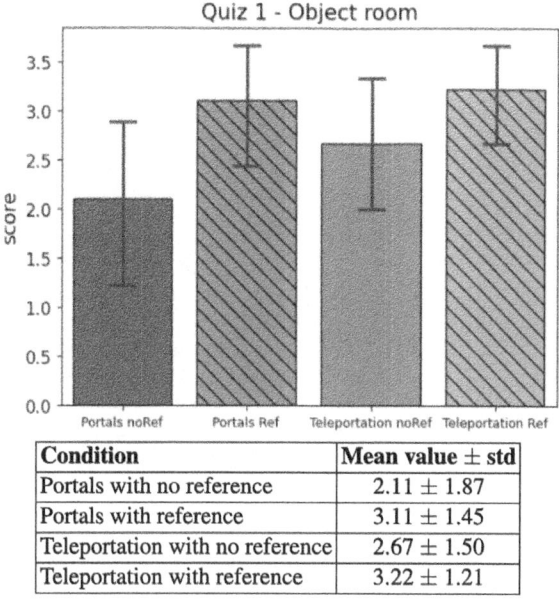

Condition	Mean value ± std
Portals with no reference	2.11 ± 1.87
Portals with reference	3.11 ± 1.45
Teleportation with no reference	2.67 ± 1.50
Teleportation with reference	3.22 ± 1.21

Fig. 9. Mean of right answers of Quiz 1. Error bars show 95% CI.

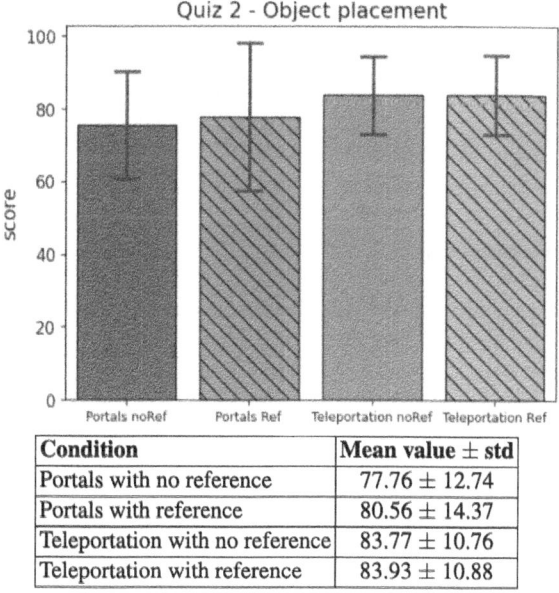

Condition	Mean value ± std
Portals with no reference	77.76 ± 12.74
Portals with reference	80.56 ± 14.37
Teleportation with no reference	83.77 ± 10.76
Teleportation with reference	83.93 ± 10.88

Fig. 10. Mean score from Quiz 2. Error bars show 95% CI.

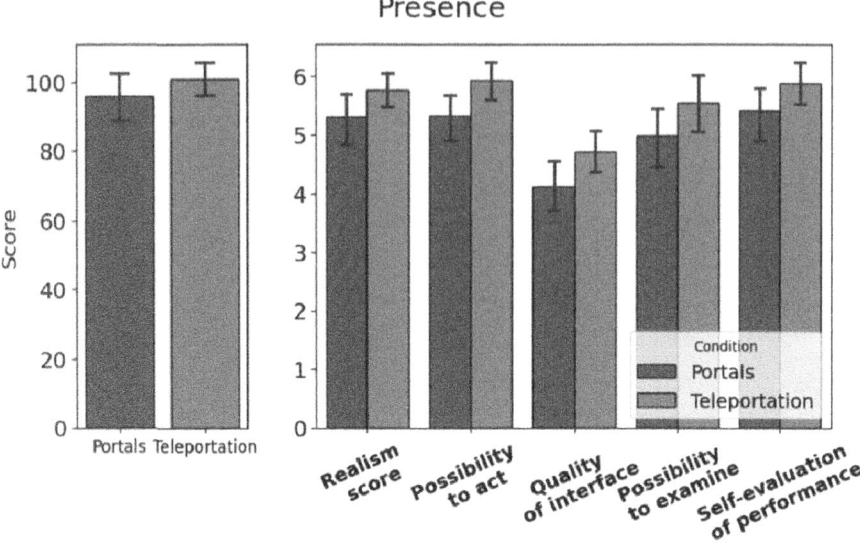

Fig. 11. Score of Presence questionnaire for portals and teleportation technique. Error bars show 95% CI.

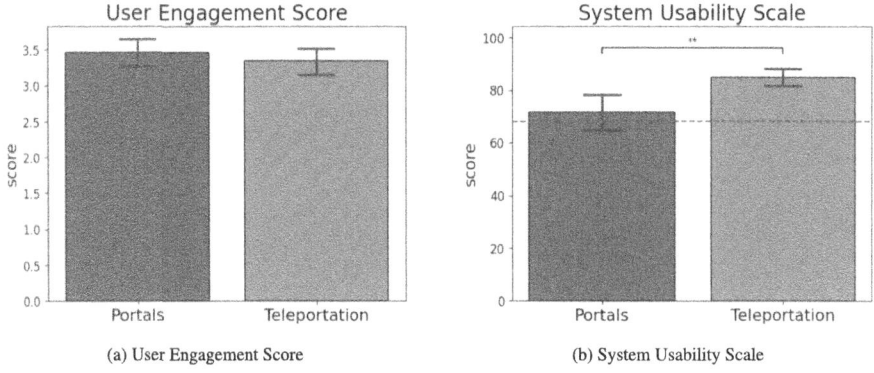

Fig. 12. Scores of the two questionnaires User Engagement and System Usability Scale for portals and teleportation technique. Error bars show 95% CI.

5.5 Participant Feedback

It was particularly insightful to collect feedback from the interviews with the participants after the experiment. They highlighted both the strengths and limitations of the portal technique. The main issues they raised revolved around three core themes:

– *Comfort with locomotion techniques:* Most participants expressed that they found greater comfort with controller-based teleportation, particularly those having more VR experience. However, some mentioned that the portal technique could be more comfortable, especially in scenarios where a tour guide activates the portals, relieving them of the burden of deciding where to go next.

- *Portal deactivation time:* The time required for the portals to disappear was seen as a nuisance by several participants. Although it was entirely possible to walk spontaneously to walk around the portals and continue moving, the participants rarely took advantage of this option.
- *Navigation limitations:* The portal technique limited navigation within each room to the walkable area. There would be inevitably places in the virtual environment which was outside of this area, whenever the virtual environment is bigger than the physical workspace. In certain instances, participants were unable to reach every corner in the virtual room due to these constraints. This limitation could be overcome simply by adding another POI in the room.

6   Discussion

The experiment result expectedly showed no substantial performance difference between portals and teleportation technique. Such equivalence would validate the use of portals in MR applications, especially considering that controller-based teleportation is not applicable. While a full MR evaluation remains necessary, prior research supports the use of VR-based studies as a valid first step for testing MR techniques [13,56] This initial evaluation was purposefully conducted in VR to isolate and validate the core PoI-Portal navigation technique under controlled conditions.

The hypothesis **H1** that portal-based technique would be equivalent to teleportation in terms of user performance and usability was only partially supported. The most considerable differences were in task completion time, real distance travelled, and score of SUS questionnaire. The reduced real walking distance performed with teleportation was expected, as walking was not required, but this could cause disorientation and be a detriment to the sense of immersion while limiting real workspace usage (cf. [14,18]).

Participants' familiarity with controller-based teleportation likely influenced task completion time (Fig. 6), along with portal activation-deactivation time delays. Trigger-based portal activation could improve performance, but using real walking avoids mixing interaction tasks (e.g., object manipulation) with locomotion ones. A closer analysis on the virtual distance travelled could have provided more insights into disorientation issue for the two techniques, but it was not the case in our experiment. Some participants remarked on more freedom of movement with teleportation than portals. This drawback is the trade-off for incorporating real-world imposed constraints into the virtual environment. Moreover, the SUS scores (Fig. 12b) favoured controller-based teleportation due to 75% of participants' prior experience, with 11% highly knowledgeable in VR. However, the SUS scores for portal-based technique remained acceptable and above usability thresholds. The PoI-Portal technique builds upon and extends the traditional use of portals, typically employed as thresholds separating spatially or temporally distinct virtual environments [23,28,31], whose application in Cultural Heritage XR remains relatively limited (cf. [28]). In contrast to techniques like World-in-Miniature, which prioritize global spatial awareness at the expense of immersion [16], the PoI-Portal approach offers a more balanced trade-off, enhancing immersion while still supporting spatial orientation. These findings are still aligned with prior comparisons of navigation methods, where portals consistently scored high in terms of presence, continuity, and user acceptance [37]. The hypothesis **H2** assessed spatial awareness and information recall during a virtual museum visit via two quizzes. Quiz 1 on recall of the objects' position within the rooms showed slight variations in the conditions with and without references, but no significant difference between techniques was found (Fig. 9). The result suggests that object-position recall is not linked to a memory association with the reference point. Quiz 2 on recall of exact position of objects within the rooms demonstrated comparable performances in spatial awareness between the two techniques (Fig. 10). Alternatively, our object memorization tests might be inadequate for assessing path recall, although this would contradict results from previous studies that showed better associative memory with real walking compared to virtual locomotion (e.g., [67]). Objects and PoIs differed across conditions, and participants appeared to struggle with the quizzes, as also indicated by high variance in their responses. Thus, the hypothesis **H2** remains open and may require alternative assessment methods. Some participants mentioned that the portal technique could be more comfortable, especially in scenarios where a tour guide activates the portals, thereby eliminating the cognitive burden of navigation decisions, which has elsewhere been solved with group locomotion [70]. Some observations emerged from the experience: For portal placement in small rooms, using a fixed distance was more effective in preventing users from nearing the physical space boundaries. To preserve the benefits of midpoint-based portal positioning for natural walking, an alternative approach could balance the current orientation strategy, which relies entirely on the virtual environment, with the spatial constraints of the real world. Additionally, participants rarely looked back and mostly followed the portal's sequential order, except when they forgot to search for another object in the room. Therefore, the portal deactivation time could be shortened, as participants seldom needed to immediately go back.

In conclusion, portals provided an effective alternative with a stronger physical component. Despite an initial adjustment period, participants adapted well, thus the portal technique can be regarded as a viable and effective navigation method for cross-reality applications.

7   Conclusion and Future Work

In this work, we evaluated the performance and user experience of Point-of-Interest (PoI) based locomotion technique using portals in comparison to more conventional VR techniques, notable controller-based teleportation, in the context of virtual museum visits. Our ultimate goal was to extend its application to MR scenarios where controller-based teleportation is not feasible. The PoI technique can prove valuable for those scenarios where maintaining spacial continuity is compelling, without interrupting the narrative flow. At the same time it could also mitigate disorientation, and accommodate both symmetrical and asymmetrical forms of remote collaboration. To conduct this comparison, we selected a virtual environment that included a wireframe representation of the surrounding real-world workspace. We conducted a within-subjects with repeated measures experiment involving 19 participants. The results revealed comparable performance between the two techniques on user experience in terms of presence and user engagement. However, the portal-based technique was slightly slower in terms of task completion time and received a marginally lower usability score.

For each visit in the experiment, we also assigned participants an object placement task in order to assess their spatial awareness and evaluate whether one condition led to more disorientation. The results from two quizzes showed similar outcomes across both conditions. Overall, it is reasonable to conclude that the portal-based technique effectively provided a satisfactory level of usability, despite some concerns. Therefore, it can be adopted as an alternative locomotion system, with performance on par with controller teleportation in all types of cross-reality systems. Having validated the portal technique against teleportation, despite increased completion times, we are now positioned to evaluate it in MR, where preserving spatial consistency between virtual and physical environments is essential. Its effect on spatial perception and immersion (potentially enhanced by the requirement for physical locomotion, unlike teleportation) remains to be examined.

For future work, we plan to further improve the technique, based on the users' feedback, from both a visual and usability perspective (e.g., virtual scene realism, occasional frame drops, improved portal activation needed). Additionally, we aim to evaluate how the perception of the physical environment influences users' experiences within virtual spaces, particularly in terms of presence and immersion. In this context, limitations encountered during the setup and execution of the experience can be addressed in two main areas. On one hand, precise alignment strategies are required to support meaningful interactions across both environments, enabling seamless transitions between virtual and physical elements. On the other hand, our current platform does not support automatic alignment. Future research may focus on dynamically adapting virtual elements based on the size and position of physical obstacles, in a way that remains coherent with the virtual environment. The proposed testing scenarios will focus on archaeology and museology, incorporating real-world, content-driven guided tours and expert-led tasks.

Acknowledgements. This work was supported by French government funding managed by the National Research Agency under the Investments for the Future program (PIA) with the grant ANR-21-ESRE-0030 (CONTINUUM project) and the grant ANR-23-CE33-0008-01 (MuseoXR project), and for the first author, by PhD grants from Région Ile-de-France and Noovae company.

References

1. Ablett, D., Cunningham, A., Lee, G.A., Thomas, B.H.: Portal rendering and creation interactions in virtual reality. In: 2022 IEEE International Symposium on Mixed and Augmented Reality (ISMAR), pp. 160–168 (2022). https://doi.org/10.1109/ISMAR55827.2022.00030
2. Ablett, D., Cunningham, A., Lee, G.A., Thomas, B.H.: Adaptive portals: enhancing virtual reality interaction spaces with real-time self-adjusting portals. In: 2024 IEEE International Symposium on Mixed and Augmented Reality (ISMAR), pp. 1010–1018 (2024). https://doi.org/10.1109/ISMAR62088.2024.00117

3. Adriana Cardenas-Robledo, L., Óscar Hernandez-Uribe, Reta, C., Antonio Cantoral-Ceballos, J.: Extended reality applications in industry 4.0. – a systematic literature review. Telematics Inform. **73** (2022). https://doi.org/10.1016/j.tele.2022.101863

4. Ahmad, H.F., Rafique, W., Rasool, R.U., Alhumam, A., Anwar, Z., Qadir, J.: Leveraging 6g, extended reality, and IoT big data analytics for healthcare: a review. Comput. Sci. Rev. **48** (2023). https://doi.org/10.1016/j.cosrev.2023.100558

5. Aiello, D., Fai, S., Santagati, C.: Virtual museums as a means for promotion and enhancement of cultural heritage. ISPRS - Int. Arch. Photogrammetry Remote Sens. Spatial Inf. Sci. **XLII-2/W15**, 33–40 (2019). https://doi.org/10.5194/isprs-archives-XLII-2-W15-33-2019

6. Albertini, N., Baldini, J., Pino, A.D., Lazzari, F., Legnaioli, S., Barone, V.: PROTEUS: an immersive tool for exploring the world of cultural heritage across space and time scales. Heritage Sci. **10**, 1–10 (2022). https://doi.org/10.1186/s40494-022-00708-3

7. Antinucci, F.: The virtual museum. Archeologia e Calcolatori **1**, 79–86 (2007). http://www.archcalc.cnr.it/journal/id.php?id=462, licensed under CC BY-NC-ND 4.0

8. Anwar, M.S., Yang, J., Frnda, J., Choi, A., Baghaei, N., Ali, M.: Metaverse and XR for cultural heritage education: applications, standards, architecture, and technological insights for enhanced immersive experience. Virtual Reality **29**, 1–29 (2025). https://doi.org/10.1007/s10055-025-01126-z

9. Bane, R., Höllerer, T.: Interactive tools for virtual x-ray vision in mobile augmented reality, pp. 231– 239 (2004). https://doi.org/10.1109/ISMAR.2004.36

10. Bekele, M.K., Pierdicca, R., Frontoni, E., Malinverni, E.S., Gain, J.: A survey of augmented, virtual, and mixed reality for cultural heritage. J. Comput. Cult. Heritage (JOCCH) **11**(2), 1–36 (2018)

11. Bergamasco, M., Avizzano, C., Di Pietro, G., Barbagli, F., Frisoli, A.: The museum of pure form: system architecture. In: Proceedings 10th IEEE International Workshop on Robot and Human Interactive Communication. ROMAN 2001 (Cat. No.01TH8591), pp. 112–117 (2001). https://doi.org/10.1109/ROMAN.2001.981887

12. Boletsis, C., Cedergren, J.E.: VR locomotion in the new era of virtual reality: an empirical comparison of prevalent techniques. Adv. Hum. Comput. Interact. **2019**(1), 7420781 (2019). https://doi.org/10.1155/2019/7420781, https://onlinelibrary.wiley.com/doi/abs/10.1155/2019/7420781

13. Bowman, D., et al.: Evaluating effectiveness in virtual environments with MR simulation (2011)

14. Bozgeyikli, E., Raij, A., Katkoori, S., Dubey, R.: Point & teleport locomotion technique for virtual reality. In: Proceedings of the 2016 Annual Symposium on Computer-Human Interaction in Play, pp. 205–216. CHI PLAY '16, Association for Computing Machinery, New York, NY, USA (2016). https://doi.org/10.1145/2967934.2968105

15. Brument, H., Bruder, G., Marchal, M., Olivier, A.H., Argelaguet, F.: Understanding, modeling and simulating unintended positional drift during repetitive steering navigation tasks in virtual reality. IEEE Trans. Visual Comput. Graphics **27**(11), 4300–4310 (2021). https://doi.org/10.1109/TVCG.2021.3106504

16. Caputo, A., Borin, F., Giachetti, A.: A comparison of navigation techniques in a virtual museum scenario . In: Rizvic, S., Rodriguez Echavarria, K. (eds.) Eurographics Workshop on Graphics and Cultural Heritage. The Eurographics Association (2019). https://doi.org/10.2312/gch.20191348

17. Carrozzino, M., Bergamasco, M.: Beyond virtual museums: experiencing immersive virtual reality in real museums. J. Cult. Herit. **11**(4), 452–458 (2010). https://doi.org/10.1016/j.culher.2010.04.001, https://www.sciencedirect.com/science/article/pii/S1296207410000543

18. Chance, S.S., Gaunet, F., Beall, A.C., Loomis, J.M.: Locomotion mode affects the updating of objects encountered during travel: the contribution of vestibular and proprioceptive inputs

to path integration. Presence: Teleoperators Virtual Environ. **7**(2), 168–178 (1998). https://doi.org/10.1162/105474698565659

19. Chen, H., Chen, S., Rosenberg, E.S.: Redirected walking in irregularly shaped physical environments with dynamic obstacles. In: 2018 IEEE Conference on Virtual Reality and 3D User Interfaces (VR), pp. 523–524 (2018). https://doi.org/10.1109/VR.2018.8446563

20. Chen, W., Ladeveze, N., Clavel, C., Bourdot, P.: Refined experiment of the altered human joystick for user cohabitation in multi-stereocopic immersive CVEs. In: IEEE Third VR International Workshop on Collaborative Virtual Environments (3DCVE@VR), pp. 1–8. IEEE Computer Society (2016). https://doi.org/10.1109/3DCVE.2016.7563558

21. Cheney, P.W., Hatch, D.: How virtual reality can be used in archaeology. In: 2020 Intermountain Engineering, Technology and Computing (IETC), pp. 1–6 (2020). https://doi.org/10.1109/IETC47856.2020.9249161

22. Cheng, L.P., Ofek, E., Holz, C., Wilson, A.D.: VRoamer: generating on-the-fly VR experiences while walking inside large, unknown real-world building environments. In: 2019 IEEE Conference on Virtual Reality and 3D User Interfaces (VR), pp. 359–366 (2019). https://doi.org/10.1109/VR.2019.8798074

23. Cisternino, D., et al.: Virtual portals for a smart fruition of historical and archaeological contexts. In: De Paolis, L.T., Bourdot, P. (eds.) AVR 2019. LNCS, vol. 11614, pp. 264–273. Springer, Cham (2019). https://doi.org/10.1007/978-3-030-25999-0_23

24. Cobb, P.J., Azizbekyan, H.: Experiments with mixed and augmented reality (MR/AR) for archaeological data collection and use during fieldwork: vision for the future. J. Comput. Appl. Archaeol. **7**, 370–387 (2024). https://doi.org/10.5334/jcaa.140

25. Congdon, B.J., Wang, T., Steed, A.: Merging environments for shared spaces in mixed reality. In: Proceedings of the 24th ACM Symposium on Virtual Reality Software and Technology. VRST '18, Association for Computing Machinery (2018). https://doi.org/10.1145/3281505.3281544

26. De Bonis, M., Nguyen, H., Bourdot, P.: A literature review of user studies in extended reality applications for archaeology. In: 2022 IEEE International Symposium on Mixed and Augmented Reality (ISMAR), pp. 92–101 (2022). https://doi.org/10.1109/ISMAR55827.2022.00023

27. De Bonis, M., Nguyen, H., Bourdot, P.: Context-based annotation visualisation in virtual reality: a use case in archaeological data exploration. In: Virtual Reality and Mixed Reality, pp. 95–119. Springer Nature Switzerland (2024)

28. De Luca, V., Barba, M., D'Errico, G., Nuzzo, B., De Paolis, L.: A user experience analysis for a mobile mixed reality application for cultural heritage. Virtual Reality **27**, 1–17 (2023). https://doi.org/10.1007/s10055-023-00840-w

29. Dong, Z., Xiao-Ming, F., Zhang, C., Kang, W., Liu, L.: Smooth assembled mappings for large-scale real walking. ACM Trans. Graph. **36**, 1–13 (2017). https://doi.org/10.1145/3130800.3130893

30. Duval, T., Nguyen, T.T.H., Fleury, C., Chauffaut, A., Dumont, G., Gouranton, V.: Embedding the features of the users' physical environments to improve the feeling of presence in collaborative virtual environments. In: CogInfoCom 2012 (3rd IEEE International Conference on Cognitive Infocommunications). Kosice, Slovakia (2012). https://inria.hal.science/hal-00745598

31. Efstratios, G., Michael, T., Stephanie, B., Athanasios, L., Paul, Z., George, P.: New cross/augmented reality experiences for the virtual museums of the future. In: Ioannides, M., et al. (eds.) Digital Heritage. Progress in Cultural Heritage: Documentation, Preservation, and Protection, pp. 518–527. Springer International Publishing, Cham (2018)

32. Freitag, S., Rausch, D., Kuhlen, T.W.: Reorientation in virtual environments using interactive portals. In: 2014 IEEE Symposium on 3D User Interfaces (3DUI), pp. 119–122 (2014). https://api.semanticscholar.org/CorpusID:23824566

33. Grasset, R., Mulloni, A., Billinghurst, M., Schmalstieg, D.: Navigation Techniques in Augmented and Mixed Reality: Crossing the Virtuality Continuum, pp. 379–407 (2011). https://doi.org/10.1007/978-1-4614-0064-6_18

34. Grønbæk, J.E.S., et al.: Partially blended realities: aligning dissimilar spaces for distributed mixed reality meetings. In: Proceedings of the 2023 CHI Conference on Human Factors in Computing Systems. CHI '23, Association for Computing Machinery, New York, NY, USA (2023). https://doi.org/10.1145/3544548.3581515

35. Han, J., Moere, A.V., Simeone, A.L.: Foldable spaces: an overt redirection approach for natural walking in virtual reality. In: 2022 IEEE Conference on Virtual Reality and 3D User Interfaces (VR), pp. 167–175 (2022). https://doi.org/10.1109/VR51125.2022.00035

36. He, Y., Liu, Y.T., Jin, Y.H., Zhang, S.H., Lai, Y.K., Hu, S.M.: Context-consistent generation of indoor virtual environments based on geometry constraints. IEEE Trans. Visual Comput. Graphics **28**(12), 3986–3999 (2022). https://doi.org/10.1109/TVCG.2021.3111729

37. Husung, M., Langbehn, E.: Of portals and orbs: an evaluation of scene transition techniques for virtual reality. In: Proceedings of Mensch Und Computer 2019, pp. 245–254. MuC '19, Association for Computing Machinery, New York, NY, USA (2019). https://doi.org/10.1145/3340764.3340779

38. Innocente, C., Ulrich, L., Moos, S., Vezzetti, E.: A framework study on the use of immersive XR technologies in the cultural heritage domain. J. Cult. Herit. **62**, 268–283 (2023). https://doi.org/10.1016/j.culher.2023.06.001

39. Irlitti, A., Latifoglu, M., Hoang, T., Syiem, B.V., Vetere, F.: Volumetric hybrid workspaces: interactions with objects in remote and co-located telepresence. In: Proceedings of the 2024 CHI Conference on Human Factors in Computing Systems. CHI '24, Association for Computing Machinery, New York, NY, USA (2024). https://doi.org/10.1145/3613904.3642814

40. Kanamori, K., Sakata, N., Tominaga, T., Hijikata, Y., Harada, K., Kiyokawa, K.: Obstacle avoidance method in real space for virtual reality immersion. In: 2018 IEEE International Symposium on Mixed and Augmented Reality (ISMAR), pp. 80–89 (2018). https://doi.org/10.1109/ISMAR.2018.00033

41. Robertson, J., Kaptein, M. (eds.): Modern Statistical Methods for HCI. HIS, Springer, Cham (2016). https://doi.org/10.1007/978-3-319-26633-6

42. Kari, M., et al.: TransforMR: pose-aware object substitution for composing alternate mixed realities. In: 2021 IEEE International Symposium on Mixed and Augmented Reality (ISMAR), pp. 69–79 (2021). https://doi.org/10.1109/ISMAR52148.2021.00021

43. Kniaz, V.V., Knyaz, V.A., Remondino, F., Bordodymov, A., Moshkantsev, P.: Image-to-voxel model translation for 3D scene reconstruction and segmentation. In: Vedaldi, A., Bischof, H., Brox, T., Frahm, J.-M. (eds.) ECCV 2020. LNCS, vol. 12352, pp. 105–124. Springer, Cham (2020). https://doi.org/10.1007/978-3-030-58571-6_7

44. Kunert, A., Kulik, A., Beck, S., Froehlich, B.: Photoportals: shared references in space and time. In: Proceedings of the 17th ACM Conference on Computer Supported Cooperative Work & Social Computing, pp. 1388–1399. CSCW '14, Association for Computing Machinery, New York, NY, USA (2014). https://doi.org/10.1145/2531602.2531727

45. Langbehn, E., et al.: Frozen factory: a playful virtual experience for multiple co-located redirected walking users. In: SIGGRAPH Asia 2020 XR. SA '20, Association for Computing Machinery, New York, NY, USA (2020). https://doi.org/10.1145/3415256.3421489

46. Lewis, J.R.: The system usability scale: past, present, and future. Int. J. Hum. Comput. Interact. **34**(7), 577–590 (2018). https://doi.org/10.1080/10447318.2018.1455307

47. Li, J., Nie, J.W., Ye, J.: Evaluation of virtual tour in an online museum: exhibition of architecture of the forbidden city. PLOS ONE **17**, 1–17 (2022). https://doi.org/10.1371/journal.pone.0261607

48. Lin, C., Xia, G., Nickpour, F., Chen, Y.: A review of emotional design in extended reality for the preservation of culture heritage. npj Heritage Sci. **13**, 1–22 (3 2025). https://doi.org/10.1038/s40494-025-01625-x
49. Lindlbauer, D., Wilson, A.D.: Remixed reality: manipulating space and time in augmented reality. In: Proceedings of the 2018 CHI Conference on Human Factors in Computing Systems, pp. 1–13. CHI '18, Association for Computing Machinery, New York, NY, USA (2018). https://doi.org/10.1145/3173574.3173703
50. Liu, X., Wang, L., Liu, Y., Wu, J.: Automatic portals layout for VR navigation. Virtual Reality **28**(1) (2024). https://doi.org/10.1007/s10055-023-00897-7
51. Malraux, A.: The Voices of Silence: Man and His Art. Princeton University Press, Princeton (1978), first part originally published in French as *Le Musée imaginaire*, Gallimard (1965)
52. Meta: Guardian system. https://developer.oculus.com/documentation/native/pc/dg-guardian-system/ (2024). https://developer.oculus.com/documentation/native/pc/dg-guardian-system/. Accessed 18 Sep 2024
53. Misztal, S., Carbonell, G., Ganther, N., Schild, J.: Portals with a twist: cable twist-free natural walking in room-scaled virtual reality. In: Proceedings of the 26th ACM Symposium on Virtual Reality Software and Technology. VRST '20, Association for Computing Machinery, New York, NY, USA (2020). https://doi.org/10.1145/3385956.3422109
54. O'Hagan, J., Khamis, M., McGill, M., Williamson, J.R.: Exploring attitudes towards increasing user awareness of reality from within virtual reality. In: Proceedings of the 2022 ACM International Conference on Interactive Media Experiences, pp. 151–160. IMX '22, Association for Computing Machinery, New York, NY, USA (2022). https://doi.org/10.1145/3505284.3529971
55. O'Brien, H.L., Cairns, P., Hall, M.: A practical approach to measuring user engagement with the refined user engagement scale (UES) and new UES short form. Int. J. Hum. Comput. Stud. **112**, 28–39 (2018)
56. Ragan, E., Wilkes, C., Bowman, D.A., Hollerer, T.: Simulation of augmented reality systems in purely virtual environments. In: 2009 IEEE Virtual Reality Conference, pp. 287–288 (2009). https://doi.org/10.1109/VR.2009.4811058
57. Ridel, B., Reuter, P., Laviole, J., Mellado, N., Couture, N., Granier, X.: The revealing flashlight: interactive spatial augmented reality for detail exploration of cultural heritage artifacts. J. Comput. Cult. Herit. **7**(2) (2014). https://doi.org/10.1145/2611376
58. Schott, E., et al.: UniteXR: joint exploration of a real-world museum and its digital twin. In: Proceedings of the 29th ACM Symposium on Virtual Reality Software and Technology. VRST '23, Association for Computing Machinery, New York, NY, USA (2023). https://doi.org/10.1145/3611659.3615708
59. Schweibenz, W.: The virtual museum: an overview of its origins, concepts, and terminology **4** (2019)
60. Silva, M., Teixeira, L.: Extended reality (XR) experiences in museums for cultural heritage: a systematic review. In: Lv, Z., Song, H. (eds.) Intelligent Technologies for Interactive Entertainment, pp. 58–79. Springer International Publishing, Cham (2022)
61. Simeone, A.L., Velloso, E., Gellersen, H.: Substitutional reality: using the physical environment to design virtual reality experiences. In: Proceedings of the 33rd Annual ACM Conference on Human Factors in Computing Systems, pp. 3307–3316. CHI '15, Association for Computing Machinery, New York, NY, USA (2015). https://doi.org/10.1145/2702123.2702389
62. Slater, M.: Immersion and the illusion of presence in virtual reality. Br. J. Psychol. **109**(3), 431–433 (2018)
63. Sra, M., Danry, V., Maes, P.: Situated VR: toward a congruent hybrid reality without experiential artifacts. IEEE Comput. Graphics Appl. **42**(3), 7–18 (2022). https://doi.org/10.1109/MCG.2022.3154358

64. Sra, M., Garrido-Jurado, S., Schmandt, C., Maes, P.: Procedurally generated virtual reality from 3D reconstructed physical space. In: Proceedings of the 22nd ACM Conference on Virtual Reality Software and Technology, pp. 191–200. VRST '16, Association for Computing Machinery (2016). https://doi.org/10.1145/2993369.2993372

65. Steinicke, F., Bruder, G., Kohli, L., Jerald, J., Hinrichs, K.: Taxonomy and implementation of redirection techniques for ubiquitous passive haptic feedback, pp. 217–223 (2008). https://doi.org/10.1109/CW.2008.53

66. Suh, A., Prophet, J.: The state of immersive technology research: a literature analysis. Comput. Hum. Behav. **86**, 77–90 (2018). https://doi.org/10.1016/j.chb.2018.04.019

67. Suma Rosenberg, E., Babu, S., Hodges, L.: Comparison of travel techniques in a complex, multi-level 3D environment. 3D User Interfaces **0**, null (2007). https://doi.org/10.1109/3DUI.2007.340788

68. Valentini, I., Ballestin, G., Bassano, C., Solari, F., Chessa, M.: Improving obstacle awareness to enhance interaction in virtual reality. In: 2020 IEEE Conference on Virtual Reality and 3D User Interfaces (VR), pp. 44–52 (2020). https://doi.org/10.1109/VR46266.2020.00022

69. Vasic, I., Quattrini, R., Pierdicca, R., Mancini, A., Vasic, B.: 3VR: vice versa virtual reality algorithm to track and map user experience. J. Comput. Cult. Herit. **17**(3) (2024). https://doi.org/10.1145/3656346

70. Weissker, T., Froehlich, B.: Group navigation for guided tours in distributed virtual environments. IEEE Trans. Visual Comput. Graphics **27**(5), 2524–2534 (2021). https://doi.org/10.1109/TVCG.2021.3067756

71. Wilcoxon, F.: Individual comparisons by ranking methods. In: Breakthroughs in Statistics: Methodology and Distribution, pp. 196–202. Springer (1992)

72. Witmer, B.G., Singer, M.J.: Measuring presence in virtual environments: a presence questionnaire. Presence **7**(3), 225–240 (1998)

73. Zhang, Y., Nguyen, H., Ladevèze, N., Fleury, C., Bourdot, P.: Virtual workspace positioning techniques during teleportation for co-located collaboration in virtual reality using HMDs. In: 2022 IEEE Conference on Virtual Reality and 3D User Interfaces (VR), pp. 674–682 (2022). https://doi.org/10.1109/VR51125.2022.00088

Lack of Eye Contact Detection Thresholds–A Two-Alternative Forced Choice Study

BreAzia Echols$^{(\boxtimes)}$ (ID) and Voicu Popescu (ID)

Purdue University, West Lafayette, IN 47906, USA
{echolsb,popescu}@purdue.edu

Abstract. The ability to establish and sustain eye contact is a prerequisite for effective communication. Unfortunately, eye contact is difficult to preserve in remote collaboration that relies on videoconferencing, mixed reality, or virtual reality technologies. Before proceeding with the design of remote collaboration systems that provide adequate eye contact, an important preliminary question is how good does eye contact have to be for a remote collaborator to not feel that their interlocutor is not making eye contact. This paper presents a two-alternative forced choice (2AFC) study with N = 139 participants that measured the lateral detection threshold for lack of eye contact. The findings suggest that a person sitting in front of a laptop has to have a fixation point within 1.5 cm (or 1.43°) of the laptop's video camera for their remote interlocutor to not perceive the lack of eye contact.

Keywords: Computing Methodologies · Computer Graphics · Graphics Systems and Interfaces · Mixed/Augmented Reality

1 Introduction

Advances in technology have made real-time remote collaboration ubiquitous. The appearance and voice of each user is acquired, transmitted, and rendered in real time, abstracting away geographic distances. Cameras have sufficient resolution, networks have sufficient bandwidth, and computers have sufficient processing power to enable effective real time collaboration across continents. Such remote collaboration is now used routinely in many domains, including education [7,21], healthcare [14,29], and social connectedness [4,10].

Remote collaboration solutions differ through how participants are acquired [8]. One option is to acquire participants in 3D, which has the advantages of allowing the viewer to perceive their remote collaborator with accurate depth cues, of integrating the remote participant seamlessly into the viewer's physical surroundings or into a collaborative virtual environment with fine grain depth compositing, and of allowing the viewer to change the viewpoint from where they see their remote collaborator [26]. The main challenge of the approach is that it is difficult to acquire a person in 3D in real time and with sufficient color and geometry resolution to allow for a realistic rendering at the remote sites [25]. Another option is to acquire the participants in 2D, with a

D. Michael-Grigoriou et al. (Eds.): EuroXR 2025, LNCS 16101, pp. 317–330, 2026.
https://doi.org/10.1007/978-3-032-03805-0_17

conventional video camera. The advantages are acquisition simplicity–most laptops, tablets, and phones do have a user-facing videocamera–and visualization realism. The challenges of remote collaboration based on 2D acquisition are the lack of depth cues, the difficulty of seamless integration into 3D physical or virtual environments, the limited range of viewpoints from where the 2D acquired participant can be seen, and the difficulty of supporting eye contact between a participant and their remote interlocutor.

Most remote collaboration is conducted through videoconferencing. Videoconferencing is the simplest form of 2D remote collaboration, where each participant sees a real time video of each of the remote participants. Videoconferencing ignores all challenges enumerated above. A participant does not see the remote participants in 3D, the remote participants are not integrated into the 3D physical space surrounding the local participant or in a collaborative 3D virtual environment, and participants do not make eye contact with one another. Whereas the shortcomings stemming from the lack of 3D data are palatable for many remote collaboration applications, the lack of eye contact is a fundamental limitation of videoconferencing that greatly reduces the effectiveness of remote collaboration [24]. Without eye contact, a participant is likely to find it harder to follow what their interlocutor says, the conversation turns to a series of monologues as opposed to a dialogue, and participants disengage [2].

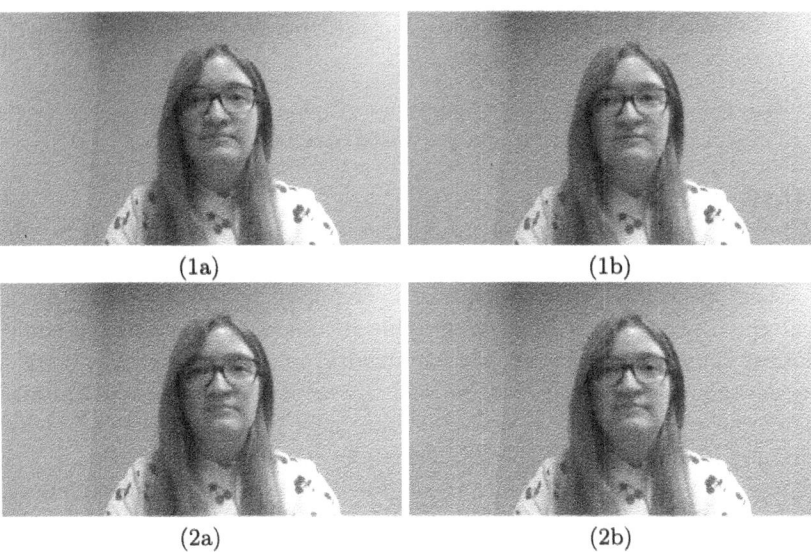

Fig. 1. Frames from pairs of videos like the ones shown to participants in our study. For the first pair (top), the offsets for *1a* and *1b* are 0 cm and 7 cm, respectively. For the second pair (bottom), the offsets for *2a* and *2b* are 1 cm and 0 cm, respectively.

Consider the scenario when participant A and participant B engage in videoconferencing, each using their laptop. If A looks on their laptop at the eyes of B, then A looks away from their laptop's webcam, and therefore A's video does not provide eye contact to B. For B to feel that A is looking at them, A would have to look at their webcam, which, of course, precludes A from seeing B. While there have been attempts to remedy the lack of eye contact in videoconferencing, prior work has not answered reliably the important first question of how good we are at detecting the lack of eye contact. In other words, what is the threshold above which eye contact in videoconferencing is detected by participants? Estimating this threshold would provide a target to any approach aimed at addressing the issue of eye contact in videoconferencing and in remote collaboration in general.

In this paper we present a study (N = 139) that measured the detection threshold for lack of eye contact in video conferencing. The study was approved by our institution's ethics board, i.e., the Institutional Review Board (IRB). The study follows a two alternative forced choice (2AFC) design, which is the golden standard for psycho-physical detection threshold studies. A participant is shown pairs of videos of a potential remote interlocutor, one at the time, and is asked which of the two videos had better eye contact. In one of the videos the interlocutor looks straight at their camera, and in the other the interlocutor looks away from their camera, by various offsets. Figure 1 shows frames from two pairs of videos. Whereas it is straightforward to choose *1a* over *1b* as the frame with better eye contact, choosing between *2a* and *2b* is harder.

2   Prior Work

2.1   The Lack of Eye Contact Problem

The problem of lack of "mutual gaze" in video conferencing has been noted for a long time [28]. The recent pandemic that disrupted all aspects of our lives and had us heavily rely on video conferencing triggered an intense research interest in video conference effectiveness and lack thereof [9]. Although eye contact is used sparingly in normal conversations, being able to establish eye contact when needed is essential for communication. For example, eye contact has been shown to influence problem solving and to facilitate conceptual understanding [18]. Full gaze awareness is the ability to know at what someone is looking, and is an important component when considering the necessities of utilizing videoconferencing platforms. Mutual gaze is the occurrence of two people making direct eye contact with each other. It is often difficult to achieve both full gaze awareness and mutual gaze in videoconferencing environments, due to the vertical discrepancy between the camera and the facial image that causes offset eye contact to be made [22].

2.2   Attempts to Address the Eye Contact Problem

Many solutions have been proposed to alleviate the problem of lack of eye contact in video conferencing, but none have found widespread use. Videoconferencing proceeds by and large without trying to address the problem. One solution is to rely on the user of the videoconferencing system to learn when their remote interlocutors are looking at them [12]. The user calibrates the various focus points and remembers which view direction the remote interlocutor assumes when they are looking at the user. The result is of course just the most indirect of eye contacts, and what is learned becomes obsolete when the videoconferencing participants–or the videoconferencing system itself–rearrange where each participant is displayed. Another simple solution is to rotate the plane on which the video is displayed to place the head of the viewer on the view direction axis of the person in the video [17]. The shortcoming is that the method lacks the benefit of the 3D geometry of the person's head, so the video becomes the video of a video projected on a slanted plane, and not the video of someone talking into the camera.

Neural networks rival humans in detecting eye contact [6], but neural network gaze manipulation is still primarily an offline process, unsuitable for real-time remote collaboration [11]. Neural networks have indeed achieved real time performance only by limiting the gaze redirection to the eyeballs, i.e., excluding the face [15]. However, real-time 3D gaze redirection continues to rely on modeling and re-rendering [13]. The work aimed at addressing the lack of eye contact is orthogonal to ours. Our focus is to measure the lack of eye contact detection thresholds, which informs any and all approaches for addressing the lack of eye contact.

Beyond videoconferencing, eye contact has long been, and continues to be, an important design concern in collaborative mixed reality [1,3]. Compared to videoconferencing, collaborative mixed reality has the advantage of greater flexibility in placing the visualization of the remote collaborator, as well as the benefit of a richer representation of the remote collaborator, which often includes 3D data. One study examined the effectiveness of a remote collaborative system where some participants are seated at a traditional computer, whereas another participant was in a mixed reality environment where the other collaborators were virtually placed around a table. One of the main benefits to the participant in the mixed reality environment was the ability to better perceive nonverbal cues, including natural gaze cues [3]. This highlights the importance of conveying eye contact correctly in collaborative XR systems, and our study gathers important preliminary data informing the design of such systems. Our work, conducted in the context of videoconferencing, does inform all remote collaboration approaches regarding eye contact requirements.

2.3   Lack of Eye Contact Detectability

Prior research on eye contact sensitivity is limited. One study examined four setups for video tele-consultation to find, unsurprisingly, that a 7° eye gaze angle yielded better perceived eye contact than a 14° angle [27]. Some studies relied on rendered stimuli based on virtual 3D head models, and others on video stimuli. A dense exploration of the gaze directions space was conducted with the help of a virtual 3D head, which was aimed away from the study participant with increasing angular offsets [20]; the study found that the cone of gaze directions from which a person feels looked at subtends 8.3° in the lateral direction. A subsequent study, also relying on a virtual 3D head, found that the region of perceived eye contact is symmetrical in all directions, except for a slight $0.5°$ asymmetry downwards, and that it is $6.8°$ wide [23].

Sensitivity to eye contact was measured with video stimuli in a study that used eight directions, i.e., every $45°$ [5], and fixation offsets between $0°$ and $5°$ in all directions except for downwards, which was between $0°$ and $15°$, with $1°$ increments. More than half of the participants perceived eye contact when the offset was approximately $1°$, except for the downward direction, where the offset was $7°$. This substantial asymmetry, which was not replicated by the later study of Van der Pol [23], prompted a second replication study that found that the sensitivity to eye contact is $1.2°$ horizontally and $1.7°$ vertically.

Another study was performed where the recorded subject focused their gaze on different offsets, and respondents were asked for a series of still-frame screenshots if the subject was looking directly into the camera. This study found that in order for respondents to achieve 75% accuracy, an offset of around $2.7°$ laterally was required. [19]

2.4 Anchoring Our Work Into Prior Work

Building on this prior work, our study contributes novel insights on eye contact sensitivity. First, prior work [5,19,20,23] employs an experimental design that relies on yes-no questions, e.g., "Do you feel looked at, yes or no?" or "Do you feel like the person is making eye contact, yes or no?". Such a design, sometimes called a pseudo 2AFC design, is more prone to bias than a true 2AFC design. For example, instead of answering the question whether the person in the video is making eye contact, participants might answer the question "Do you feel like the eye contact is good enough?", which depends on individual preference. On the other hand, in a true 2AFC design a participant will not choose the offset option over the no offset option just because they find it acceptable. In another example, a participant in a light detection study might truthfully answer "no" when presented with a dim light stimulus, although if that same stimulus were presented paired with a stimulus with no light at all, the participant might still be able to choose the dimmer stimulus reliably.

Similarly, in a pseudo 2AFC design, the order in which the videos are presented has a much larger impact, as the participant will likely end up rating later videos that they are presented with relative to the videos that they had already seen up until that point. In other words, in a pseudo 2AFC design, the participant's standards can change throughout the experiment due to the subjectivity of the question, whereas in a true 2AFC study such as ours, the user will always only be considering whether each offset video has more or less direct eye contact than the video it is paired with (where the video subject is looking directly at the camera). This leads to far less variance in each users' responses, resulting in more accurate results compared to prior works.

Our study employs a 2AFC design, which is the best design for threshold detection studies. Eye contact detection is a quick task that allows many repetitions per participant as needed to investigate a wide range of offsets, so a 2AFC design is possible and should be used, unlike, for example, in the case of gain detection threshold studies for redirected walking in virtual reality.

A second way in which our study is complementary to prior work is that we investigate lack of eye contact detection thresholds not in a laboratory setting, with stimuli recorded with a camera at the height of the user and with fixation points on the vertical plane [5,20,23], but rather in the realistic setting of a remote collaborator seated in front of their laptop, with the laptop screen angled as desired, and with fixation points around the laptop's webcam, which provides application validity.

3   Study

In order to fulfill the need for a detectability threshold at which individuals are able to notice a lack of eye contact, we performed an experiment to measure response rates in order to calculate such a threshold. Our study was approved by our IRB. The IRB protocol number will be included in the non-anonymous version of this paper.

3.1   Methods

Study Design. Our study follows a two-alternative forced choice (2AFC) design. As detailed in Sect. 2, the 2AFC design is the best known design for detection threshold measurement, as it less prone to bias compared to the yes-no question (i.e., "pseudo 2AFC") design employed in prior work [5,19,20,23].

We show participants pairs of short videos, each three seconds in duration. For each pair, in one video the person in the video is looking straight at the camera, and in the other video they are looking at a point that is offset with respect to the camera (Fig. 1). All video pairs have one video with no offset, and one with an offset in the 0 cm–10 cm range. The two videos of a pair are shown one at the time, in random order. After the participant has seen both videos of a pair, they are asked which video had better eye contact: the first or the second. The detection threshold is measured as the offset for which the average correct response rate is 75%, i.e., half way between chance (50%) and perfect (100%).

The focus of this study was limited to examining the detectability threshold of horizontal offsets. Part of the justification for this was to limit participant fatigue, as just the addition of examining vertical offsets would double the number of trials that each participant would be asked to undergo. Increased participant fatigue would likely lead to less accurate results and potentially a lower rate of users completing the entire study. An alternative method would be to divide the participants into subgroups which are each asked to undergo trials on only one direction, but this would incur further shortcomings, such as reduced number of participants per direction, and the possibility of each subgroup being imbalanced in terms of eye dominance or vision ability. Focusing on fewer directions also allows for greater granularity and range in the offsets presented to users, whereas prior studies presented far fewer videos to participants in the horizontal direction than our study, such as [5] which for the horizontal direction only operated on a range of $0°$ to $5°$, with a granularity of $1°$ between videos, whereas our study had approximately double the granularity and range, leading to far more accurate results.

Focusing on the detectability of the horizontal thresholds is also logical since, during video conferencing, users are more likely to have windows of other inter-locutors located on the left or right sides of their screens (meaning that their own gaze will be offset as they focus on the window of the other interlocutor). Furthermore, prior research has indicated that humans are more sensitive to detecting horizontal offsets than they are to detecting vertical offsets.

Participants. Our study had $N = 139$ participants from our university's community. Based on the demographics data we have collected, 37.4% of participants were female, 61.9% were male, and 0.72% checked the "prefer not to disclose" option. Furthermore, 84.2% of participants were in the 18–25 age range, 14.4% were in the 26–35 range, and 1.44% were in the over 35 range. Finally, 12.2% of participants indicated that they use videoconferencing daily, 48.2% use it at least once a week, 26.6% use it at least once a month, 12.2% use it at least once a year, and 0.72% had never used it. Participants were not screened for color vision deficiency, but the subject of the video has dark irises, so color vision deficiency should be less impactful than otherwise.

Stimuli. We recorded videos in a typical video conferencing setting, with the same person seated in front of their laptop. Each video was 3 s long and the person was asked to say the same line: "Hi, my name is <name>". The videos differed through the person's fixation point, i.e., the point where they looked when the video was recorded. We recorded 21 videos, one with a fixation point at the laptop's webcam, i.e., an offset of 0 cm, the next with a fixation point 0.5 cm to the right, the next with a fixation point of 1.0 cm to the right of the laptop's webcam, and so on, with the last video having a fixation point of 10.0 cm to the right of the laptop webcam (Fig. 2). The 21 videos were then mirrored left-right in software to create 21 left offset videos. Note that the 0 cm offset video was also mirrored to avoid lighting differences with the left offset images. The procedure created 42 videos that were shown to participants according to the following procedure.

Mirroring the videos from a single direction was done for consistency, as any minor asymmetries in the video subject's face, lighting, dominant eye, or environment could impact the viewer's perception of eye contact. These variables should be kept constant since we are only concerned with how the change in offset affect's the viewer's perception of eye contact, to reduce bias.

Also for consistency, the videos were all recorded by a single individual (an author of the study, to ensure accuracy of offset). There are many variables

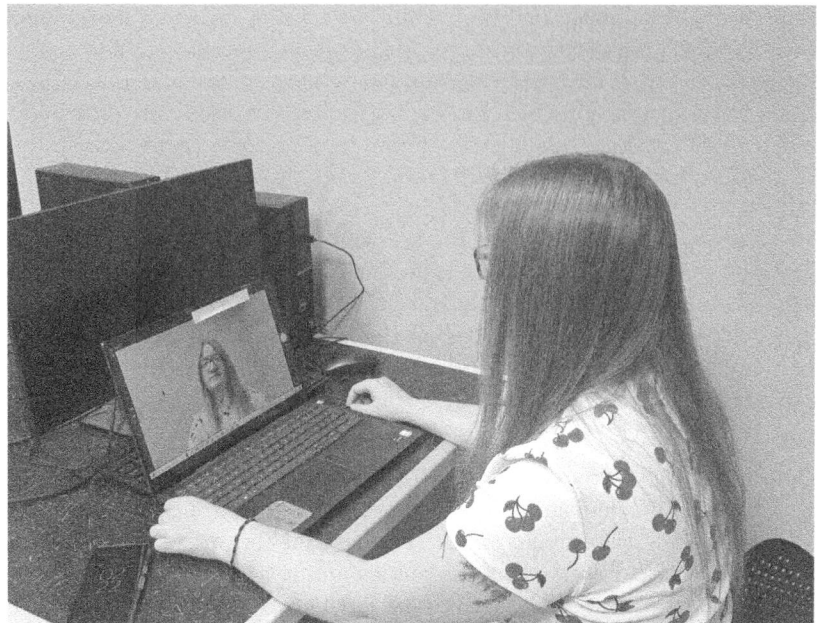

Fig. 2. Back lateral image of the setup used for the recording of the video stimuli.

of an individual's appearance (ethnicity, race, gender, age, glasses, etc.) which may affect a participant's ability to compare eye contact between two videos, and varying any of these attributes between videos would lead to inconsistencies in the users' selections, and attempting to cover enough variations of these attributes so as to not weaken the study would require an intractable number of participants to adjust for the variability between which variation they were presented with.

Since this variable could not be removed, it should be noted that the subject of the video wears glasses, as do 63.7% of individuals in the USA and over 4 billion people across the globe, meaning that it is meaningfully representative for the subject to have glasses.

Experimental Procedure. The study was run online, through Qualtrics. First a participant was prompted for demographics data and then the participant was shown pairs of videos and asked to choose the video with the better eye contact. The study took approximately 10–15 min per participant. Each participant was compensated with a cash gift card worth the equivalent of $5.

Each participant was presented with 42 pairs of videos, covering all possible left and right offsets. The left offset pairs were shown together, as were the right offset pairs. Compared to alternating left and right pairs, our approach of showing videos of the same type of offset in block translates to less variability between consecutive pairs. This in turn helps participants detect lack of eye contact, and it results in more conservative detection thresholds. Some participants saw the left-offset videos first, and some last, in counterbalanced fashion. For each type of offset, left or right, the 21 pairs covered all 21 offsets, from 0 cm to 10 cm, with 0.5 cm increment, with one of the two videos being the 0 cm video. The offsets were shown out of order, in counterbalanced fashion. After each pair, the participant was asked to identify the video with the better eye contact. The participant had to provide an answer to move on to the next pair.

Data Collection. In addition to the demographics data, we recorded for each participant and for each pair of videos shown to them whether the participant identified correctly the video with better eye contact. This amounts to 42 bits of data per participant. For the two video pairs, one left and one right, where both videos were the 0 cm offset video, the accuracy was defined as being 50%, since the two stimuli are perceptually indifferentiable, so the respondent is choosing at random between the two videos. This definition is consistent with 2AFC studies, where the point at which the stimuli can not be differentiated is defined to have an accuracy of 50%.

Data Analysis. We analyzed the data in three steps.

In a first step we computed the correct answer rate for each offset as a percentage. The correct answer rate for an offset is defined as the number participants who answered correctly for that offset over the total number of participants. This first step yields 21 data points for the left offsets, and 21 for the right offsets. Each 2D data point is defined by an offset and the correct answer rate at that offset.

In a second step we fit a sigmoid psychometric function to the 21 left offset data points, and one to the 21 right offset data points, using a least squares optimization. The sigmoid function, whose use is standard practice in 2AFC experiments, is given in Eq. 1.

$$S(x, \alpha, \beta, \gamma, \lambda) = 0.5 + (0.5 - \lambda) \left(\frac{1}{1 + e^{\gamma \frac{x - \alpha}{\beta}}} \right) \tag{1}$$

Here, x is the function's variable, i.e., the offset, and α, β, γ and λ are parameters set by the fitting process. We use γ to distinguish between the left and the right offset sigmoids. We choose the left offsets to be negative, i.e., from 0 cm to -10 cm, and the right offsets to be positive, i.e., from 0 cm to 10 cm. Therefore the left sigmoid decreases as the offset increases in algebraic sense from -10 cm to 0 cm, and $\gamma = 1$. The right sigmoid increases as the offset increases from 0 cm to 10 cm, and $\gamma = -1$. α, β and λ are set through the least squares optimization. α controls the lateral shift, β controls the lateral scale, and γ controls the maximum value, as data is unlikely to have a perfect response rate of 100%, even for large offsets.

In a third step, each of the two sigmoids was intersected with the y = 75% line to estimate the left offset and right offset detection thresholds.

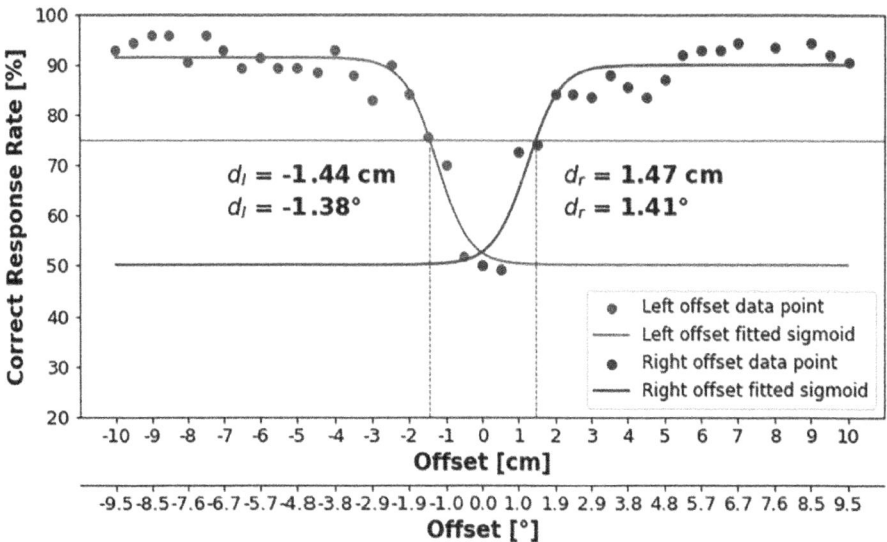

Fig. 3. Experimental data (dots), psychometric sigmoid functions fitted to the experimental data (curves), and detection thresholds (d_l, d_r), for both left (green) and right (blue) eye contact offsets. A data point (x, y) gives the correct response rate y at offset x. The detection thresholds are computed by intersecting each sigmoid with the $y = 75\%$ line. (Color figure online)

3.2   Results and Discussion

The experimental data is shown in Fig. 3. For small offsets, the correct response rate is close to chance behavior, i.e., 50%. For large offsets, participants identify the video with the better contact reliably, i.e., with correct response rates over 90%. Even for the largest offsets, the correct response rate is not 100%, which we explain as participants forgetting, or remembering incorrectly, which video had no eye contact offset.

The least squares optimization yields the following parameters (see Eq. 1) for the left offset sigmoid: $\lambda_l = 0.0863$, $\alpha_l = 1.25$, $\beta_l = 0.449$. The detection threshold d_l is 1.44 cm, or 1.38°. The fitting error is 0.0348, or 3.48%, which yields a detection threshold confidence interval of [1.441cm, 1.447cm] or [1.376°, 1.381°].

For the right offset sigmoid, the fitted parameter values are: $\lambda_r = 0.101$, $\alpha_r = 1.24$, $\beta_r = 0.458$. The detection threshold d_r is 1.47 cm, or 1.40°. The fitting error is 0.0447, or 4.47%, which yields a detection threshold confidence interval of [1.468 cm, 1.477 cm] or [1.401°, 1.411°].

These offset thresholds above which participants can reliably detect lack of eye contact are small. This is in line with some prior work, which also find detection thresholds in the 1° range [5], though it differs from other prior work which found a lateral detection threshold of 2.7° [19], for which we provide a potential explanation of difference in methodology (pseudo 2AFC for that study as opposed to true 2AFC for ours), as well as sample size ($N = 56$ for that study as opposed to $N = 139$ for ours). The small detection thresholds imply demanding targets for procedures aimed at remedying the lack of eye contact.

We have also estimated detection thresholds for the various sub-populations of our study. The results are shown in Table 1. The detection thresholds do not change much with gender or age. The only sub-population for which the thresholds are substantially different from those of the overall population is the sub-population of participants who use videoconferencing daily. For these participants the detection thresholds are much smaller, which is plausible since frequent users of videoconferencing technology might also have grown better at telling when their remote interlocutor is making eye contact, and when they are not. However, there are only 17 participants in this category, which is a relatively small number. Furthermore, the fitting error is also larger than for other categories, so additional experiments have to be conducted to confirm whether frequent users of videoconferencing technology do indeed have lower detection thresholds for lack of eye contact.

Table 1. Fitting error ε and detection threshold d in cm and in degrees, for both left (subscript l) and right (subscript r) offsets, for the various sub-populations of our study.

Sub-population	ε_l [%]	ε_r [%]	d_l [cm]	d_r [cm]	d_l [°]	d_r [°]
Female	4.12	5.75	−1.56	1.85	−1.49	1.77
Male	3.96	5.56	−1.34	1.42	−1.28	1.35
Age 18–25	3.47	4.52	−1.45	1.45	−1.38	1.39
Age >25	6.63	6.99	−1.39	1.55	−1.33	1.48
Daily	7.89	8.59	−0.83	0.53	−0.79	0.51
Weekly	3.27	5.80	−1.51	1.01	−1.44	0.96
Monthly	6.03	4.99	−1.64	1.86	−1.56	1.78
Yearly/Never	5.11	6.99	−1.30	1.41	−1.25	1.34

4   Conclusion, Limitations and Future Work

We have conducted a study for measuring lack of eye contact detection thresholds in a typical videoconferencing scenario with a remote participant seated in front of their laptop and being acquired by the laptop's videocamera. We have used a 2AFC design which is robust to bias in participant answers. We have collected data from a large number of participants (N = 139), which has resulted in a robust estimation of the detection thresholds, with small fitting errors. The results show that the user has to look within approximately 1.5 cm of their laptop videocamera for their collaborator to not detect the lack of eye contact. At 60 cm this translates to a stringent 1.5°. Our work informs the design of remote collaboration systems, whether based on videoconferencing or on other approaches, such as mixed or virtual reality, to make video sprites or avatars of remote collaborators convey eye contact adequately.

One limitation of our study is that most data points are for offsets that are well above the detection threshold. Indeed, for offsets with an absolute value of 3 or above, the detection rate is already quite large. A finer determination of the detection thresholds would require more data points in the 0 cm to 3 cm range. This is difficult to achieve with the current experimental apparatus, as it is difficult to record videos focusing on fixation points on a scale with 0.1 cm increments. Future work could look into implementing the fixation point as a dot moving on the laptop screen, which it can do with pixel or sub-pixel accuracy, providing a finer grain sampling of the offset range. As always, participant fatigue, which can manifest itself through mechanical answers, is a concern that competes with the potential benefits brought by more trials with finer offset differences.

Another limitation of our study is that we focused exclusively on left-right offsets, to minimize participant fatigue. Most laptops have their integrated webcam placed at the top of their screen, so users do not look above the camera when they look at the screen. Future studies could investigate detection thresholds for a downward offset, although, as prior work as shown, we are much better at detecting lateral offsets than downward offsets. This means that the lateral offset detection thresholds found in our study are a conservative estimate of the detection thresholds for downward offsets.

Finally, our study was performed using only a single actor in the presented video. While this was done for the sake of consistency between videos, this does lead to the limitation that this could impede generalizability, as certain physical characteristics (e.g. gender, race, eye color and size, facial structure, etc.) may influence a viewer's perception of eye contact. Ideally, more studies would be done in the future to verify that our measured thresholds are consistent across multiple demographics.

The lack of eye contact detection thresholds will be especially useful in informing the design of extended reality systems. Consider, for example, the scenario of remote lecture attendance, where the instructor wears an XR headset to see remote students rendered into the empty seats of a classroom [16]. Each remote student is seated in front of their laptop and is acquired by the laptop's webcam. The thresholds will inform on the quality of the eye contact perceived by the instructor and also on the amount the remote student video sprites have to be rotated to sustain eye contact, based on the classroom empty seat that accommodates each remote student.

It is plausible that our society's reliance on remote collaboration will only continue to increase. In order to satisfy this demand, and to make remote collaboration more effective, future work could propose and test computer screen designs that extend the display function with an acquisition function. A simple such display could integrate camera islands between the display pixels, and videoconferencing software could place each remote collaborator's video at one such camera island. This way, when collaborator A looks on screen at remote collaborator B, A will also direct their gaze towards the camera that acquires A for B, conveying to B that A is making eye contact with them. One challenge is that each participant will be acquired multiple times, once for each of their collaborators, which leads to a proliferation of video streams that have to be transmitted. As camera miniaturization continues to advance, the islands of "dead pixels" will continue to shrink, with the acquisition function not coming at the cost of a diminished display function.

Acknowledgements. The authors wish to thank Yuqi Zhou and Sarah Engle for their help, as well as our numerous user study participants without whom this study would not have been possible. This material is based upon work supported by the United States National Science Foundation under Awards No. 2318657, 2309564, and 2212200.

Disclosure of Interests. The authors have no competing interests to declare that are relevant to the content of this article.

References

1. Bai, H., Sasikumar, P., Yang, J., Billinghurst, M.: A user study on mixed reality remote collaboration with eye gaze and hand gesture sharing. In: Proceedings of the 2020 CHI Conference on Human Factors in Computing Systems, pp. 1–13. CHI '20, Association for Computing Machinery, New York, NY, USA (2020). https://doi.org/10.1145/3313831.3376550
2. Basch, J.M., Melchers, K.G., Kurz, A., Krieger, M., Miller, L.: It takes more than a good camera: which factors contribute to differences between face-to-face interviews and videoconference interviews regarding performance ratings and interviewee perceptions? J. Bus. Psychol. **36**, 921–940 (2021)
3. Billinghurst, M., Kato, H.: Collaborative mixed reality. In: Proceedings of the First International Symposium on Mixed Reality, pp. 261–284 (1999)
4. Bleakley, A., et al.: Bridging social distance during social distancing: exploring social talk and remote collegiality in video conferencing. Hum. Comput. Interact. **37**(5), 404–432 (2022)
5. Chen, M.: Leveraging the asymmetric sensitivity of eye contact for videoconference. In: Proceedings of the SIGCHI Conference on Human Factors in Computing Systems, pp. 49–56 (2002)
6. Chong, E., et al.: Detection of eye contact with deep neural networks is as accurate as human experts. Nat. Commun. **11**(1), 6386 (2020)
7. Correia, A.P., Liu, C., Xu, F.: Evaluating videoconferencing systems for the quality of the educational experience. Distance Educ. **41**(4), 429–452 (2020)
8. Druta, R., Druta, C., Negirla, P., Silea, I.: A review on methods and systems for remote collaboration. Appl. Sci. **11**(21), 10035 (2021)
9. Fauville, G., Luo, M., Queiroz, A., Lee, A., Bailenson, J., Hancock, J.: Videoconferencing usage dynamics and nonverbal mechanisms exacerbate zoom fatigue, particularly for women. Comput. Hum. Behav. Rep. **10**, 100271 (2023)

10. Gan, Y., Greiffenhagen, C., Reeves, S.: Connecting distributed families: camera work for three-party mobile video calls. In: Proceedings of the 2020 CHI Conference on Human Factors in Computing Systems, pp. 1–12 (2020)

11. Ganin, Y., Kononenko, D., Sungatullina, D., Lempitsky, V.: DeepWarp: photorealistic image Resynthesis for gaze manipulation. In: Leibe, B., Matas, J., Sebe, N., Welling, M. (eds.) ECCV 2016. LNCS, vol. 9906, pp. 311–326. Springer, Cham (2016). https://doi.org/10.1007/978-3-319-46475-6_20

12. Grayson, D.M., Monk, A.F.: Are you looking at me? Eye contact and desktop video conferencing. ACM Trans. Comput. Hum. Interact. (TOCHI) 10(3), 221–243 (2003)

13. Guo, Y., Zhang, J., Chen, Y., Cai, H., Huang, Z., Deng, B.: Real-time face view correction for front-facing cameras. Comput. Visual Media 7(4), 437–452 (2021). https://doi.org/10.1007/s41095-021-0215-y

14. Haleem, A., Javaid, M., Singh, R.P., Suman, R.: Telemedicine for healthcare: capabilities, features, barriers, and applications. Sens. Int. 2, 100117 (2021)

15. Hsu, C.F., Wang, Y.S., Lei, C.L., Chen, K.T.: Look at me! Correcting eye gaze in live video communication. ACM Trans. Multimedia Comput. Commun. Appl. (TOMM) 15(2), 1–21 (2019)

16. Huang, S., Popescu, V.: HyperXRC: hybrid in-person+ remote extended reality classroom-a design study. In: 2024 IEEE Conference Virtual Reality and 3D User Interfaces (VR), pp. 609–618. IEEE (2024)

17. Jaklič, A., Solina, F., Šajn, L.: User interface for a better eye contact in videoconferencing. Displays 46, 25–36 (2017)

18. Joiner, R., Scanlon, E., O'Shea, T., Smith, R.B., Blake, C.: Evidence from a series of experiments on videomediated collaboration: Does eye contact matter? In: Computer Support for Collaborative Learning, pp. 371–378. Routledge (2023)

19. Kushner, B.J.: Eccentric gaze as a possible cause of "zoom fatigue." J. Binocular Vision Ocular Motility 71(4), 175–180 (2021)

20. Macrae, C.N., Hood, B.M., Milne, A.B., Rowe, A.C., Mason, M.F.: Are you looking at me? Eye gaze and person perception. Psychol. Sci. 13(5), 460–464 (2002)

21. Martin, M.: Seeing is believing: the role of videoconferencing in distance learning. Br. J. Edu. Technol. 36(3), 397–405 (2005)

22. Monk, A.F., Gale, C.: A look is worth a thousand words: full gaze awareness in video-mediated conversation. Discourse Process. 33(3), 257–278 (2002). https://doi.org/10.1207/S15326950DP3303_4

23. van der Pol, D.: The effect of slant on the perception of eye-contact. Master's thesis, Eindhoven University of Technology (2009)

24. Riedl, R.: On the stress potential of videoconferencing: definition and root causes of zoom fatigue. Electron. Mark. 32(1), 153–177 (2022)

25. Rokhsaritalemi, S., Sadeghi-Niaraki, A., Choi, S.M.: A review on mixed reality: current trends, challenges and prospects. Appl. Sci. 10(2), 636 (2020)

26. Schäfer, A., Reis, G., Stricker, D.: A survey on synchronous augmented, virtual, and mixed reality remote collaboration systems. ACM Comput. Surv. 55(6), 1–27 (2022)

27. Tam, T., Cafazzo, J.A., Seto, E., Salenieks, M.E., Rossos, P.G.: Perception of eye contact in video teleconsultation. J. Telemed. Telecare 13(1), 35–39 (2007)

28. Vertegaal, R., van der Veer, G.C., Vons, H.: Effects of gaze on multiparty mediated communication (2000). https://api.semanticscholar.org/CorpusID:7393589

29. Viswanathan, R., Myers, M.F., Fanous, A.H.: Support groups and individual mental health care via video conferencing for frontline clinicians during the COVID-19 pandemic. Psychosomatics 61(5), 538–543 (2020)

Author Index

D. Michael-Grigoriou et al. (Eds.): EuroXR 2025, LNCS 16101, pp. 331–332, 2026.
https://doi.org/10.1007/978-3-032-03805-0

The manufacturer's authorised representative in the EU is Springer
Nature Customer Service Centre GmbH, Europaplatz 3, 69115 Heidelberg,
Germany. If you have any concerns regarding our products, please
contact ProductSafety@springernature.com

Printed and bound by CPI Group (UK) Ltd, Croydon, CR0 4YY

28/04/2026

02098524-0005